Dedicated with love to my family —

To Dirk,
thank you for being there to catch me when I was too weak to stand.

To Lexi,
thank you for being my ray of sunshine on many dark days.

And to Zach,
thank you for being my hero and teaching me the meaning of life.

Table of contents

Life Before

I have lived two lives. The first very typical and normal, much as I had pictured in my mind as I grew up—marriage, college, career and kids. This book is about the second life—the life that materialized on a day that started no differently than any other day and ended as no other had before. It contained a moment that changed our destiny—the moment we entered the world of pediatric cancer.

But let me tell you more about my first life. Our family was living the middle-class American dream. Married for twenty-three years, two kids and a cat, my husband Dirk and I felt we were blessed. We both had good jobs. Lexi, our soon to be eleven-year-old daughter, was getting ready to enter middle school. Zach, our son, was just a few days away from turning eight and was entering the third grade. Both kids did well in school and were generally well-behaved. Soccer games, guitar lessons, swim meets and basketball at the Y kept us busy in our free time. Zach had learned how to "push" Lexi's buttons, which created that irritating sibling rivalry we all hope to escape. But there was no denying the love they held in their hearts for each other.

Our lives were governed by the world as we chased the elusive dollar valued so highly by our culture. After working all week and managing the kids' activities, our priority focused on finding some friends with whom to share a drink or two. Taking the edge off the fast-paced lives we lived always included alcohol.

God was present in our lives, although typically just on Sundays. Soon after Lexi was born, we had decided we would give our children plenty of access to church by trying to attend every week. Dirk and I each had a relationship with God, but it was distant at best. My faith had been up and down throughout my life. It seemed to be strongest when I was not working outside the home and had time to read and pray on a consistent basis. No matter how hard I tried, the complications of too little time and too many responsibilities, particularly when my accounting career was involved, would inevitably eliminate the praying and reading time. God would disappear from my mind and become a fleeting thought through the week until Sunday rolled around again.

Don't get me wrong; we were good people. We were just on the fence when it came to Christianity. We wanted all the perks—a place in heaven, blessings and God's favor—but we truly did not understand what living for God meant. We were living *with* God but not living *for* God. Our lives were firmly planted on worldly goals, with little thought about the implications this type of living would have for our life after death. That seemed to be something faraway—a worry for another day when we were older.

We certainly never thought about pediatric cancer. Never dreamed it would become our destiny. If any thought of cancer were to cross our minds, it would be in relation to us or our parents, but never our kids—never Zach. Children did not get cancer. That only happened on those dramatic TV movies or to sickly kids in faraway cities. It never happened to anyone we knew, so why would we ever think it would come knocking at our door? But it did.

I now know pediatric cancer does not discriminate. It will appear out of nowhere and shatter your life faster than you can blink an eye. There are small clues, minor details that could tip you off—if you were expecting it to visit. Otherwise those details would just seem like a passing thought—a minor irritation to be checked into when things slow down. Things like Zach's increasing need to go to the bathroom with an intense urgency or Zach's hesitation to tie his shoes when he had been tying them for over two years. Never ever did I dream these were a few of the little clues dangling in front of our eyes, pointing toward the journey we would soon take.

The story you are about to read is not an easy one. It does not have a fairy tale ending. But I do promise: It is a story you will never forget, and it will touch your heart in many ways. Zach's life, although very short in time, was filled with lessons for all of us.

These lessons gave me a new life. Along with this new life came a new pair of eyes that now see past this world and all it holds. They are focused now on an eternal view that holds so much more than I allowed myself to ever see in my first life. Free now from the desire to have the "things" of this world, I have been changed from the inside out. Priorities of the past—wondering where the next party would be or trying to accumulate more stuff—have left my heart. Growing closer to God, helping others and sharing our faith have become the new priorities.

It is my hope that reading about our journey will help free you from some of the things that chain you to this world. I pray your heart will be softened as you see how God will shelter us through any trial in life as long as we allow Him to do that for us. Not only will He shelter us, He will carry us and draw us closer than we ever could imagine—if only we make that choice.

Thank you for allowing me to occupy your mind as you read this book. I pray it will inspire you in some way to live a better life—one that is closer to God.

Zach—competitive, determined and filled with joy. This photo was taken during his first triathlon competition in September 2004, ten months before diagnosis.

Photo taken by Action Sports International, www.asiphoto.com

CHAPTER ONE

Diagnosis

Will this traffic ever get better? I was racing across town to pick Zach up from the summer daycare program at his school. After much pleading and many persistent phone calls, I had managed to get him into the pediatric neurologist's office. Quite an accomplishment since the previous week the earliest appointment they could give me was a month away.

What was going on with Zach? Nearly three weeks had passed since he had quit using his left hand. It had become clumsy and uncooperative—his fingers would no longer extend. We had dismissed it as a sports-related injury until I noticed that during the previous week, the condition had worsened. It seemed his left arm was becoming more difficult to lift.

My concern intensified the night before as I held his bike seat and took a few awkward steps next to him, watching as he giggled nervously and tried to make his left leg and arm work the way they had in the past. My heart sank as I realized he could no longer ride his bike—a skill that had come to him so easily three years ago when he was four. A quiet panic set in later that evening as I watched his face and could see that as he giggled and smiled, the left side of his face was not performing in concert with the right half as it should.

I had attacked the internet searching for an answer. Why would a healthy normal seven-year-old suddenly lose the function of his left side? The urgent-care doctor we had seen ten days before felt it was a temporary condition caused perhaps by lying on his arm and pinching a nerve, something he called radial palsy.

The pediatrician we had seen a few days later was stumped. They both suggested we see a pediatric neurologist. I felt sure it had to do with a virus or something similar. Lyme disease, Rocky Mountain spotted fever and stroke came up as I searched online. I never thought to use the word paralysis in my search; perhaps if I had, a brain tumor would have entered my realm of thinking.

My worry increased as I continued driving in traffic that afternoon.

"C'mon, c'mon, light—change," I protested. Tedious and cumbersome best described the drive I had been making the last two years to Hall Printworks, my place of employment.

Tampa was a wonderful place to live, but left much to be desired in traffic flow. Unfortunately, the neurologist I had made the appointment with was near my office, but about an hour away from Zach's school and our home. My thoughts drifted to the schedule we were living.

I had felt a growing desire to simplify things and was hoping to find work closer to home soon. Leaving the kids at the aftercare program in the summer filled me with guilt. I felt like it shortchanged them of what summer break was really about.

Lord, we need to change our lives. Please guide us in the right direction.

My prayer time had been sorely lacking lately with our busy schedules. It had been easy to shove it to the background when I added fulltime work to my schedule. I promised myself to be more diligent with prayer as soon as things calmed down.

Relief washed over me as I parked the car next to the school. It was good just to lay my eyes on Zach. His beautiful hazel eyes seem to fill with relief as well when I entered the room. I had allowed Lexi, his ten-year-old sister, to spend the day with a girlfriend instead of at the school's program. I knew our day could be long if the neurologist needed to do some extra tests. Zach was angry because Lexi and her friends were going bowling, something he loved to do. Throwing his backpack over my shoulder, I hustled him into the car for the return trip across town. As I looked back at him curled up in the seat, my heart exploded with love and panic. What could be wrong? His eyes were shooting daggers in my back.

"Are you mad you have to go to the doctor, Buddy?" I asked.

"No...but it's not fair Lexi gets to go bowling with Allie and Michele and I don't!" he snapped.

"We have to find out what is going on with your hand, Honey," I replied, wishing I could be as worry-free as he was about this. "Maybe if we finish quickly with the doctor we can catch them for the last game, OK?"

"OK," he grumbled with a frown.

An empty waiting room greeted us as we walked into the neurologist's office, prompting me to wonder why it had been so difficult to fit us in when there were no other patients there. After filling out the exasperatingly large stack of forms our litigious society has created in order to visit a doctor, I gave the receptionist the $230 in cash they required just to see us. I settled back into the waiting room chair and Zach struggled as he climbed into my lap.

I pulled his left arm, which was dangling lifelessly at his side, up across his tummy and held it there. Hugging him tightly, I slowly rubbed my cheek on his soft dishwater blonde hair. My apprehension of what the doctor might tell us grew as we waited. Trying to calm myself, I mentally ran through my list of questions about Lyme disease and all the other strange things I had found on the internet the night before. Apprehension aside, it was good to know we would finally get an answer and hopefully a solution for Zach's condition.

Zach had been going crazy being limited by his uncooperative left arm. Now that his entire left side was hindered, it was imperative to determine the cause. Sports, games—playtime of any kind—were what Zach was all about. I had missed the methodic thumping sound of his basketball the last couple of weeks—but not nearly as much as he had missed producing the sound.

Finally they called us back to a room. More waiting.

Zach's mood improved as he inspected an extensive collection of baseball memorabilia that covered the walls and desk in the exam room. Carefully trying to figure out who had signed the various items, he scanned each one. To pass the time after he finished that diversion, I had him try to do various things, hoping to see improvement. He could not jump on one foot; he could not lift his left arm or move his left hand. He would burst out laughing at himself after each failed attempt to do something. He loved to be silly. In his unassuming mind, it was merely a game we were playing.

When the doctor came into the room, he had a very businesslike air of complete self-confidence. He did not waste any time starting his exam. He barked questions at Zach like a drill sergeant in the military and had little patience or tolerance for hesitation. With pleading eyes, Zach looked at me for help, but the doctor made him answer on his own. Nervous giggles punctuated Zach's answers. After the questions, he asked Zach to do many of the same things I had asked him to do while we waited. As he checked out Zach's reflexes, he could not help but crack a smile and chuckle when Zach exploded into a big belly laugh as his hammer caused spontaneous jerks from Zach's legs with each tap. Zach's smile and laugh always had come easily to him. With Lexi's help he had quickly learned to smile as a baby. Deep-down belly laughs could explode from him at a moment's notice if something struck his funny bone. His silly, easygoing nature had earned him many friends and captured many hearts.

Before I could even begin my barrage of questions about viruses, the doctor looked me in the eyes and his tone softened noticeably.

"Mrs. Tucker, I am sorry we did not allow you to come in sooner, but the diagnosis the urgent-care doctor gave you does not typically indicate an emergent need. I had a strange feeling about your call this morning. We should have seen Zach last week."

Feeling an increase in my heart rate, I smiled at him nervously. Why was he suddenly so serious?

"In the brain there is an area called the motor strip," he explained as he took out an anatomy book and opened it to a page with a picture of a brain. "This area controls the body's movements on the opposite side. I think there might be something creating pressure in Zach's brain that should not be there next to this motor strip on the right side."

It felt as if an electric charge went through my body. My heart fell to my feet as I looked from his finger pointing to the picture to his eyes that were filled with concern. My mind, teeming with questions just moments before, was suddenly blank. I went into "mommy shock," the kind where you know you have to stay calm for your kids, but you want to start crying and screaming, "Are you crazy? You think my perfectly healthy boy has something wrong with his brain?"

My hands began to tremble as I felt adrenaline pump through every inch of my body. The only word I could produce was "OK" as he stood and continued his conversation.

"I will have my nurse call St. Joseph's Hospital to admit Zach and schedule an MRI. That will give us a clear picture of what is really going on. OK? St. Joe's is just around the corner. They will take good care of you there. I will come over in the morning and we will go over the results."

I felt light-headed as I again answered, "OK." Zach had been sitting on my lap. Grabbing his hand, we both stood and followed the doctor into the hall. Our eyes met as I gave his hand a gentle squeeze and forced a smile on my face. I heard the doctor repeating the same instructions about St. Joseph's Hospital to the nurse, except this time his voice seemed to express more urgency as he said to schedule the MRI Stat. Stat—that means life or death. My heart felt like it was trying to burst out of my chest it was beating so hard.

Breathe, Sherry, breathe, I thought. *Paste a smile on your face; be strong. Zach needs you now. He is watching you to see how to react.* Trying to appear calm, I watched the nurse as she listened attentively to the doctor. A look of complete pity filled her eyes when she heard the words "MRI Stat." It was as if an unspoken message had been shared between them. It confirmed my fears—this was very serious.

She looked at me and asked if I knew how to get to St. Joe's. "I—I think it's just around the corner, right?" I stammered in a shaky voice.

It was apparent I had failed to mask my fear. The nurse gently grabbed my elbow and walked us out to the parking lot to physically show me which road to take. Thankfully the hospital was less than a block away and within sight.

Breathing had become a challenge to me as I could feel the very essence of our future fall into question. I had just learned Zach could have a brain tumor—*a brain tumor!*

Forcing myself to place one foot in front of the other, I helped Zach climb into the backseat. My thoughts turned to Dirk as I placed my body behind the steering wheel. I needed him to be with us. My hands continued to tremble as I fumbled for my cell phone. Tears were tumbling from Zach's eyes as he watched me. I felt the tears stinging my own eyes; I could not hold them back.

"Honey, I promise we will go bowling another day," I said through my tears.

"I'm not crying because of that, Mom," Zach replied. "I don't want to go to the hospital."

My heart broke. I wanted to climb back to him, hold him in my arms and dissolve in a puddle of tears. How could this be happening?

"I don't want to go either, Baby, but we need to figure this out. Are you scared?" I asked.

"Yes," he replied.

I was scared, too. Indescribable fear had gripped my innermost core. It was so oppressive I could hardly catch my breath or stop my body from trembling. My intuition was screaming that there was something terribly wrong.

"I have to call Dad to let him know where we are going."

It took an extreme amount of concentration to find his number in my phone. Breathing deep, I again tried to steady my voice as I waited for him to answer.

"This is Dirk," a greeting he always used when answering his cell phone.

"Hey, um…we…um, just saw the doctor and are headed to St. Joe's for an MRI," my voice began to falter as I uttered the words.

The tone of his voice filled with concern. "Oh really?"

"The doctor thinks…there might be something in Zach's head…that shouldn't be there. So he wants us…to go right now." The words came tumbling out between my sobs.

"OK, Sherry. I'll be right there. Just calm down; everything will be OK," he said reassuringly.

Turning the key in the ignition seemed to snap me back into reality. A sense of calm and strength surrounded me as I drew in some deep breaths. Working on autopilot, I somehow found a parking space and the correct entrance for admissions.

Zach had gained control of his emotions as well. We held hands tightly and shared small smiles as I gave the necessary information to the person at the admission desk. It was a strange feeling to have gained such frightening news just moments before and yet be expected to function as if everything were normal. Our reality had entered a new dimension, while everyone around us remained oblivious to our plight.

The hospital was foreign to us. Except for having the kids and a short stay with pneumonia, I had never spent any time in a hospital. Zach had only had an occasional earache or sore throat his entire life. We managed to find our way to the correct nurses' station and they settled us in a room. It was nearly 3 in the afternoon. Two hours had disappeared since Zach and I had arrived in the quiet waiting room a block away.

The hospital experience suddenly became an adventure once Zach discovered the bed moved when he pushed buttons and he found the remote control for the television. His eyes sparkled and a grin covered his face as he changed his position many different times. He was quite amused that he could make the bed contort into many different configurations.

Our brief escape from the reality looming in front of us evaporated when a nurse appeared at our door. She needed blood and to place an IV in his arm. Neither Zach nor I had expected this to be part of our day. She explained they needed to test his blood and during the MRI they would need the IV to inject contrast into his body to help make the images clearer.

The smile quickly disappeared from Zach's face as he grabbed my hand and we followed the nurse to the "procedure room." It had an ominous ring to it. I could sense fear in Zach's voice as he whispered, "Will it hurt, Mom?"

"Remember when you were going into Kindergarten and had to get four shots? You laughed as they were giving them to you! It should not be as bad as that," I said smiling, trying to bolster his courage.

Zach sat on my lap as the nurse carefully laid out all the tubing, tape and gauze she would be using. He whimpered in protest and pressed into me when he saw the needle. The nurse studied his arm, trying to locate a vein while rubbing an alcohol swab on his skin. When a vein did not readily appear, she enlisted the help of a more seasoned veteran. They went from arm to arm, tying the rubber tubing around his bicep, pushing on his skin, hoping to see a vein pop up. It was apparent his veins were going to be a challenge.

Zach became more nervous with each wipe but remained brave and still. We opened an *I Spy* book in an attempt to distract him. After three unsuccessful tries in his arm, they finally found a vein in his hand. Little did we know this would be the routine for many months to come.

Dirk soon arrived and sat with us while we waited for the MRI crew. We exchanged a few worried glances as he and Zach flipped the television channels from one sport to the next, finally settling on the Disney Channel. The nurses questioned whether Zach would be able to lie still for the twenty or thirty minutes required for the MRI scan. Because of his relaxed nature, I told them I felt sure he could. Even though he was athletic and strong, he had always been a mellow child. Zach seemed more confident when they assured him I could be in the room during the entire procedure.

Around 6 P.M. the technician came to take us to the MRI room. Before we could go, the nurse administrator entered the room with a look of concern. She informed us our insurance company was in the middle of a battle with St. Joe's Hospital and we would be considered self-pay for any procedures performed and for the night's stay. I was dumbstruck! I immediately called the customer service group at the insurance company to find out what was going on. The nurse was very apologetic and tried to reason with them that it was an emergent situation.

My mind kept hearing that word, emergent. It did not seem to fit with our family. Do they honestly think Zach really could have a tumor? It had to be a cruel joke—a mistake. No one in our immediate families had ever had a tumor.

Fighting to stay calm, we worked through the cost scenarios. An answer was our main priority; a couple of thousand dollars was an insignificant amount at this point. My heart broke as I saw tears dripping from Zach's face. Our confusion and concern over insurance issues had worried him. I assured him there were no problems with money. We signed all the necessary paperwork to get the MRI underway, but he would not be admitted. As long as we were not in the room for twenty-four hours, we would not be charged for an inpatient stay. I did not want to contemplate a reason we would need to stay longer.

The MRI was an experience in itself. I felt confident Zach would be able to lie still. What concerned me was how he would feel while enclosed in a tube. The technician was very kind and eager to make Zach comfortable. He gave us both earplugs and positioned me at the foot of the machine. With the magic of mirrors, Zach had only to look straight up to see me sitting at the end of the machine. True to their word, the entire process took about thirty minutes. Our eyes were locked on each other the entire time. My mind was racing during the process. I reasoned there would be no tumor. How could there be? It just wouldn't make sense. This had to be some type of virus or freaky brain thing—but not a tumor. A tumor had never entered my realm of thinking, so it could not be real.

The noises coming from the machine were extreme. They were loud and in every pitch and frequency imaginable. I made up songs to them as they thumped through their rhythms. "I want to go home" and "Please, God, no tumor" became the overriding themes of my songs. With every change in noise, Zach's eyes lit up with surprise and a smile would spread across his face. I kept giving him the thumbs-up sign for encouragement.

Zach had no problem staying still. The tech commented on what a great patient he was. Dirk, who had been waiting patiently outside the room, greeted us with a smile after we were done. It was approaching 8 P.M. as Zach climbed back into the hospital bed in our "temporary room." We decided Dirk would head home to rest and pick up some things for us. He planned to come back early so we both could meet with the doctor. Dirk smiled with confidence as he said he was sure the MRI would be clear. I smiled and shook my head in agreement.

As 9:30 P.M. approached, Dirk gave us both a hug and a kiss and we said good-bye. Zach and I relaxed together on the bed, searching for something to watch on television. I never knew when to expect my feet to rise or my head to sink as Zach continued to entertain himself with the adjustable bed. We were giggling and talking when I saw the doctor approaching. He appeared to be dressed for an evening out and irritated his attention had been diverted to us.

I laughed nervously and said, "I didn't expect to see you until the morning."

"I didn't expect to be here so late. Are you alone?" he responded with a concerned look around.

I knew he did not come to tell us the MRI was clear.

No, God no! This cannot be happening!

My mind raced, ready to explode with panic. Our confidence the MRI would be clear was not to be true. He asked Zach if he could talk to me for a few minutes. Zach was hesitant, but agreed if it would only be for a minute. I felt like I was walking to my execution in slow motion as I followed him out of the room to a nearby conference room. Somehow this all had to be a dream. *It was time to wake up!* I was screaming in my head.

He asked if Dirk could return to the hospital. When I told him he had been gone for at least forty minutes already, he asked me to call Dirk on my cell phone. My entire body began to tremble as I dialed the number. I placed the phone in the center of the table between the doctor and me and pressed the button to turn on the speaker option. The doctor's face was somber and firm as he stared at the ringing phone.

"Hello?" Dirk answered, surprised I was calling so soon.

"Dirk, the doctor has come back and wants to talk to us about the MRI. How far away are you?" I said quickly letting him know this was no casual phone call.

"I–I'm in Brandon, about fifteen minutes from our house."

Realizing this was too far for him to return in a reasonable amount of time, the doctor began to speak. "The MRI shows there is a brain tumor on the right side of Zach's brain. I cannot tell you what type of tumor it is or how it will have to be treated. I have arranged for you to be transported to All Children's Hospital tonight so that Zach can be scheduled for surgery tomorrow. They have fantastic neurosurgeons who will do a great job for you. I would send my own family there if I were faced with this situation."

The words just flowed out like it was an everyday conversation for him. Each word pounded my ears like a ten-inch nail. My head was spinning and my heart was pounding so hard I was sure he could see it from across the table. Dirk's voice came through the phone in a frantic manner. "What does this mean?… How long does he have to live?… Could he die now?"

The doctor repeated that he could not comment on those types of questions at that point. After surgery, they would be able to tell us more. Dirk continued to insist on something more concrete until the doctor threw up his hands in frustration and I intervened.

"Dirk, he cannot tell us any more right now. Go home and call me back so that you can pick some things up we will need. I will talk to you soon." It was like I had become a robot. I shut down my emotions so I could try to function and process this unreal situation. He had been blindsided while driving down the road. I was trying to calm him so he could get home safely for now.

The doctor asked me to look at the MRI scans with him. I blindly followed him, still trying to get my bearings. The world had taken on a dream-like state as I walked—I could not feel my feet hitting the floor, and everything seemed to be shrouded in a mist around me. We sat at a desk with a computer and he brought up the scan. There in front of my eyes I saw the cause of Zach's problems. The inside of my child's brain contained a golf-ball-sized tumor. The tumor was bright white against the gray and black brain matter surrounding it. It almost seemed to glow. The MRI was a series of scans—slices of Zach's brain either from the top to bottom of his head or side to side. We were looking at the view from the top. The tumor was bulging into the left half of his brain, creating pressure on the left side as well.

The doctor stood over my shoulder, pointing to the images with a pen as he spoke. He was saying things that were only halfway registering—things like the tumor was deep…a lot of circulation. I was not sure what to do. I looked up at him with tears welling in my eyes and asked in a whisper, "What do I tell Zach?" What do I tell my seven-year-old baby? This was impossible. This had to be a dream! My mind raced with a million thoughts, but my body felt like it was in slow motion.

He replied, "I will help you explain it to him as we prepare you to go to All Children's." As we walked back to the room, I tried to put a smile on my face. I am sure it looked as transparent as it felt. Zach turned from the television to face us as we entered.

"Hey, Baby," I said gently walking to the bed, "we get to go for a ride." I looked at the doctor for help.

"Zach, you remember the pictures we took earlier today of your head? They show there is something in there that should not be in there. We are going to send you to a hospital called All Children's and they are going to work on fixing things for you," he explained in a calm clear voice.

Zach just stared at him and then looked at me. The doctor patted him on the leg and went to speak with the nurses. I climbed into bed with Zach.

"Why are you shaking, Mom?"

"Oh, I am just cold and I need to snuggle with you." I pulled him close in my arms. That seemed to satisfy him and we turned to the television. It would be a couple of hours until the ambulance would arrive to transport us to All Children's. I began to try to relax my muscles so my nervous shaking would stop. He and I held hands and watched the television screen in the darkened room like nothing had happened. I wondered if he would sleep tonight. I was sure I would not. Even though my eyes were staring at the screen, the devastating state of panic I was feeling kept me from seeing anything. I knew I should be praying but, all I could manage was to think was *no, God, no.*

It was approaching midnight and Zach was finally getting drowsy. He was usually one to fall asleep easily and sleep soundly wherever he laid his head. I was thankful for that now. The less stress he had the better. Could he die right now? Why had the doctor not been clearer on what we should expect? Why didn't I ask more questions? I called Dirk to see if he was OK. He was not. He had made it home safely—a small miracle in itself—but he was an emotional wreck. Trying to speak to me was an effort through his sobs. Periodically, he would actually gag. I began shaking again as I spoke. I tried to use as calm a voice as possible. "They should be here soon to take us to All Children's. You will meet us there, right?"

"Yes. I am trying to figure this out, Sherry. I think God is punishing me. This can't be real," he said between sobs. "I have called our parents and the church. What do you need me to bring you?"

I quickly told him a few things to bring. A change of clothes and a toothbrush would get me by. I had no idea what we were facing as far as how long we would be at the hospital. My emotions began to overtake me as we spoke. I hadn't even cried at this point because I couldn't. Zach needed to know I could be strong for him. A few tears slid down my face as we finished our conversation.

The paramedics arrived and were ready to load us up now that Zach had fallen asleep. He would be sad he slept through the ride in the ambulance. I gathered our things and we were off. I followed the paramedics to the vehicle and climbed in the back with one of them and Zach.

I had never been in an ambulance before. As I buckled myself to the hard plastic seat, I took in the surroundings. There were many instruments and tools hanging securely all around, but they rattled and banged with every bump and turn. I sat on one side of Zach's stretcher and the paramedic on the other. She was young and soft-spoken. Her large brown eyes would shift from me to Zach. She seemed nervous about Zach sleeping. I felt like she was not sure if he would make it to the next location. I wasn't sure either. Silently, I watched the scenery go by out the slim windows in the side doors, thinking how many times I had traveled these roads, never dreaming I would be making this trip with Zach.

My gaze went to Zach. I stared at his sleeping face and my memories slid back to the countless mornings I would go in to wake him for school. He would always continue sleeping no matter how many kisses on his face or pats to his rear I gave him. Eventually I would turn him onto his back, grab his feet and pull him to my lap. Carefully, I would lift him to my arms and out of his bunk bed so I could carry him to the chair in the family room. I always kissed and admired his precious face as we walked. His sweet face looked just like I imagined an angel's would look—so beautiful and filled with peace until the lights hit his eyes. Then he would screw up his eyes and wrinkle his nose to protest the intrusion into his sleep. His face held that same peacefulness now. I felt like he was a lamb going to slaughter. The tears flowed down my face as I finally released some of my emotions.

Lord God, please let my baby live! I have always asked for both Lexi and Zach to be wrapped in Your love and protection. Lord, we need You now. I am not ready to lose my baby!

It was 1:30 A.M. little did I know, Dirk and I were about to begin the biggest nightmare of any parent's life.

Reflections

July 11, 2005—a day that would begin a new journey for our family. On this day all the future hopes and dreams we had once dared to imagine dissolved into a black abyss of unknowns. I was naïve enough to believe our family was somehow protected from the broken side of life. Tragedies swirled around us daily; yet, I only allowed them to enter my mind for the moment I read about one or another in the newspaper. Our lives had been normal. I had even prayed the prayer of Jabez—asking for God's favor, love and protection over and over when the kids were young! We had to be protected, right? My expectations of our future had contained only pleasant, happy scenarios.

I never expected to encounter this storm. Maybe hurricane would be a better description. Because of this complacency in my heart, I now realize I was taking so many things for granted! Dirk and I had bought into the worldly view of life. This worldly view had us chasing our tails as we both worked trying to buy our family happiness through material things and feeling the frustration of never achieving quite enough. The true implications of living a life centered around God did not quite fit our lifestyle. Had we known how hard our world was going to be rocked in the summer of 2005, we would have lived so differently. But isn't that true for anyone of us that has been thrown a major curve ball in our lives? If only we could start over...

Although this new journey took us kicking and screaming down a road we never wanted to see—much less travel—it also was the beginning of a journey into the center of our hearts. The Tour Guide we would be consulting and come to know in a much more intimate way had been waiting for us all of our lives. He knew we would be walking this path before we were even born. This journey would not only lead us through the world of pediatric cancer, it would lead us to challenge and understand God's purpose for our lives. Little did we know it would be a path filled with such unconditional love sent directly by God to soften our hearts and bring us closer to Him in a way we had never allowed ourselves to go.

The lesson to take from this is there are no "do-overs" in life. We all have one shot at this life on earth. We cannot afford to waste it. My relationship with God was in its infancy at best. He was my friend of convenience. I only called on Him when it fit my schedule or when I had an issue I wanted help solving. I had given Him little quality time. For this reason, I felt ill-prepared and confused when faced with this trial. My heart had not learned to surrender and have complete faith in our mighty Creator, no matter what the challenge. I know now it is the only answer. This life on earth is for learning...it is only the beginning...there is so much more waiting for us.

MARCH 2005—second grade and four months before diagnosis. Everyone thought Zach looked very mature in this photo.

Photo taken by Lifetouch National School Studios, Inc.

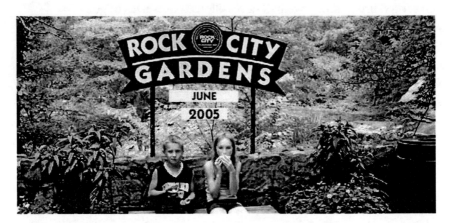

The moment on our vacation, two weeks before diagnosis, that it became clear to me something was wrong with Zach's left hand. He could not hold the bowl of ice cream in his hand. This photo also captures some left side paralysis in Zach's face that was not apparent to us at this time.

CHAPTER TWO

A Frightening New World

*I*had been to All Children's Hospital twice in my life, both times to visit friends' children, but never for my own. Entering the hospital holds a totally different feeling when you are going in for your own child. The urgency that was evident in the neurologist's voice that Zach needed brain surgery now seemed to eliminate any contemplation of where we would go. We would have to place our faith in this facility and its doctors. It turns out we were very lucky we lived so close. At the time, I did not realize All Children's was one of only two freestanding children's hospitals in the state of Florida and the only one on the Gulf Coast. The doctor's comment that he would send his own children to this facility helped bolster my confidence that Zach would receive good care.

As Zach continued to sleep, the paramedics took us to our room on the fourth floor. The nurse had to wake him to get his vitals and assess his current state. In his characteristic deep sleep, Zach barely opened his eyes and had very little interaction with her as she worked with him.

There was another patient in the room behind a curtain. I would quickly find out he and his mother were in the premium spot of the room because it was by the bathroom. There were two chairs for each patient bed. One reclined flat into what they humorously called a parent "bed"; the other stayed upright. Parents were encouraged to stay with their children all night. For this, I was grateful. Leaving Zach's side was not a consideration that had even entered my mind.

The nurse quietly hooked Zach up to an IV pump and taped a glowing red fingertip pulse oximeter around his finger. She handed me a stack of blankets and sheets, wrote her name on a dry-erase board and quickly left.

The reality sank in around me like the darkness in the room. *How can this be happening?* I listened to the beeping of Zach's heart and oxygen monitor. Not knowing Zach's current state, my anxiety was high with every noise. *Could he die tonight?* Was the paramedic justified in her obvious concern about whether or not he was breathing?

Every so often I heard an IV alarm screaming for assistance in the distance. The sound did not seem to elicit an immediate response as I thought it should. It was clear—my understanding of this frightening, foreign world of beeps, alarms and buzzers had a long way to go.

Relief overcame me when Dirk slipped into the room. It was almost 2 A.M. He and I huddled together in the dark, holding hands as we cried. We both were bewildered, not knowing if Zach was in imminent danger or not. He told me our parents were on their way. Living close to each other in Indiana, all four had decided to pack up and head to Florida together. In my mind, I pictured all of them, looking shell-shocked, barreling toward Florida in the dark of the night.

Whispers came flooding out of Dirk in a desperate manner. He was beside himself with guilt. Convinced God was punishing him for not being a better person, he felt responsible for Zach's tumor. While we were good about going to church on Sunday, that was as far as it went. We were not making God our priority, which was why Dirk was feeling so much guilt. We both knew we should have been doing better. Drinking alcohol had become an all too frequent habit for Dirk, and now his remorse was overwhelming him. He swore to me he would never drink again. He was desperate for none of this to be happening.

"Dirk, God does not punish like this; I just can't believe He would do that," I reasoned with him. "It doesn't make sense to me that He would pick an innocent child to punish."

"I don't know... All I know is I am not right with God and I need to be. I will do anything to make this better," Dirk replied through his tears.

Our conversation continued as we helplessly and desperately tried to make sense of the past twelve hours. Our minds were numb with shock and our nerves were frazzled. The pulse oximeter would occasionally scream out an alarm, indicating Zach's breathing or heart rate was too low for comfort. The nurse would appear, check his settings and quickly leave again. Fear and anxiety of all the unknowns we faced kept sleep from overtaking us. It was approaching 4 A.M. We wrapped the blankets the nurse had given me around our bodies and each of us took a chair. We tried our best to sleep, but neither of us could quiet the monsters now living in our minds.

Our attempt to rest ended an hour later when a physician's assistant with the neurosurgery group came into the room. Devon was a slight young man who appeared to be of Asian descent. He wore dark-rimmed glasses and had a warm, quick smile. His calm demeanor immediately put us at ease. He told us they had received only a few slides of the MRI scan from St. Joe's Hospital. Before the neurosurgeons could properly evaluate Zachary, they needed to see the entire scan. Dirk immediately volunteered to make the trip to St. Joe's to get the scan. The P.A. also told us it was not clear if they would perform surgery today or take a more comprehensive MRI of the head and spine first.

We asked if Zach was in imminent danger of dying—and to our relief, he said no. A tremendous weight lifted from our shoulders with this information. He explained they would be starting Zach on a steroid called Dexamethasone (Decadron) to help with the swelling in his brain and also on Zantac to help keep his stomach calm. Zach would not be allowed to eat, in case they wanted to proceed with the surgery.

Not eating would be a problem. The first words out of Zach's mouth every morning had always been "I'm hungry." Hot blueberry pancakes, scrambled eggs and toaster waffles were just a few of his favorites. Facing the day without food would be worse torture than the many pokes he had faced the day before.

With much difficulty, Devon woke an exhausted Zach and performed a standard neurological exam on him. He measured the strength in his arms, hands, legs and feet. He watched his facial expressions and how well his tongue worked. He peered deep into his eyes for evidence of swelling. When he finished, Zach dozed off again. Dirk left to pick up the scans. I listened as the hospital slowly groaned to life.

Traffic had been light in the early morning hours, making Dirk's round trip to St. Joe's less than an hour. The neurosurgeons would have time to review the complete scan before they made their rounds.

Zach woke and immediately stretched his hand toward me, wanting to feel my hand in his. What must he be thinking? He flipped on the television and was happy to know he was in control of the bed and television once again.

Rustling sounds came from behind the curtain as a technician entered the room with a wheelchair to whisk our roommate away for a test. Soon feeble cries and painful protests came from him as they lifted his small body from the bed to the chair. He had some issue with his brain and seizures from what I had overheard in discussions between his mother and a nurse. I was amazed as his mother rattled off his medications to the new nurse just coming on duty. Would this be my new life? Would we be living in the hospital indefinitely, having an uncommon knowledge of five-syllable medications? I shuddered to think this.

An entourage of doctors and residents wearing long white coats arrived at our door about 9 A.M. It was the neurosurgery group. It felt like we were in an episode of "ER." They all came in and gathered around Zach. It was evident who was in charge. Dr. Storrs was a middle-aged man with a full beard and wavy gray hair. He introduced himself and began his examination. Very similar to what he had done earlier that morning, Zach quietly complied with all the doctor's commands. All the other practitioners patiently stood by and watched in silence.

When he finished, Dr. Storrs sat on the corner of Zach's bed, looked him in the eye and patted his leg. He told us Zach would need a longer MRI study to give them a better surgical roadmap before they performed surgery. He explained they would make an incision on the right front quarter of Zach's head, from the top of his head to the top of his right ear. They would schedule the surgery for the next day, July 13th, which ironically, also happened to be Zach's eighth birthday.

Dirk and I followed the group out into the hall when they had finished. Anxiously, Dirk began to quietly ask Dr. Storrs questions similar to those he had asked the prior evening.

"Can you tell us what type of tumor this is, or the amount of time Zach has? We would like to have an idea of what we are facing."

Dr. Storrs paused with us in the hall as he began to explain. "We need to further study the tumor on the more comprehensive MRI to make sure there is no evidence of disease in the spine. Based on the current MRI, I would not want to speculate on the type of tumor or a prognosis at this point. But please remember each case is its own case and statistics of others cases do not matter. What matters in regard to Zach are his unique circumstances."

It was frustrating to not have anything more concrete. We desperately wanted to hear him say the tumor would be easy to remove and everything would be back to normal before we knew it. If we had been more experienced in the brain tumor world, perhaps we would have realized his conservative answers would have been reason for concern.

Feeling consumed by the unknowns surrounding the tumor, we did our best to paint on happy faces when we returned to Zach's room. On the inside, we were both screaming at the injustice of the situation. Reality slammed us in the face as we realized what seemed to be a horrific nightmare was really our life—not a dream. This reality intensified with each call we made to inform our employers and friends we were in the hospital with Zach.

It was clear from the anxious look in his eyes that Zach wanted one of us near at all times—preferably me. The hall outside his room became our telephone area as we took turns making our calls. We were very guarded on mentioning a brain tumor at this point since we had not been able to explain everything to Lexi, who had spent the night with her friend. I would waver from being abnormally strong—almost businesslike—when I told the story to some friends, to being wracked by sobs and tears as I told others. Even though I was repeating the story many times, my mind still could not quite accept it as true.

When things quieted down and all the calls were made, I asked Zach if he had any questions about what Dr. Storrs had told us. He shrugged his shoulders and looked at me through wide, innocent eyes and asked, "What does surgery and incision mean?"

Forgetting how unassuming and naïve a child's mind could be, I realized most of what had been discussed in front of Zach probably sounded like a foreign language to him. I quietly smiled and explained everything in the most simple terms I could. The entire time I was thanking God for Zach's innocence. His mind had not been filled with all the horrors I had accumulated in mine in regard to brain tumors and brain surgery. This would keep him from feeling as overwhelmed as we felt with each new piece of information we gained. Boredom and hunger were his biggest concerns.

We were in a waiting game all day. Graciously, the nurse was able to get permission to give Zach some Gatorade and Italian ice mid-morning to help with his insatiable hunger. One of the main side effects of the steroid he was now taking was a strong appetite, which was not helping the time pass any quicker.

To help combat the minutes dragging by and the loud grumbling coming from his stomach, we went exploring. We discovered a playroom filled with games, toys and a video game Zach loved. The IV pole was now our constant companion as I carefully guided Zach through the maze of halls to his new favorite destination. His left leg was dragging more noticeably today. Anxious questions kept buzzing through my mind as I watched his every move. Would he regain his mobility after the surgery? Would he would be the same "Zach" after surgery? It was a constant battle to push these thoughts away and keep my emotions in check.

He spent much of the morning in front of the video touch screen game with me or Dirk by his side. The touch screen made his motionless left hand a nonissue. He was thrilled to be able to soundly beat us at many of the games we played. Gratitude filled my heart that this great distraction was available for Zach.

Dirk left to retrieve Lexi and pick up more clothes now that we knew we would probably be residents of the hospital the rest of the week. It was time to share this frightening new reality with Lexi. We wanted to be the ones to tell her Zach had a brain tumor and would require surgery.

As Zach continued to play, I received a call from a lady, a member of our church, whose daughter was recovering from surgery to remove a brain tumor. She explained she was standing in my shoes just a month ago and everything had gone quite well for them. Their daughter was near Zach's age and the prognosis was excellent after the tumor was removed. She said that a week after surgery you wouldn't even know her daughter had had anything wrong. My heart soared! Could this be our case too?

Lord, I pray we can experience a successful surgery like this. If only Zach can have a simple outcome with no complications.

Her words helped sustain my hope that our lives would get back to normal soon, but the neurologist's description of the tumor lurked in my thoughts. Somehow "deep in the brain and a lot of circulation" did not correspond with simple surgery in my mind.

Zach's mood was getting more irritable as time passed. Devon came by mid-afternoon with some hair clippers and foam stickers that resembled gray lifesavers. "Are you ready for a new haircut, Zach?" he asked. Zach grabbed my hand and nodded his head yes. He was very apprehensive about anyone touching him after all the "pokes" he had experienced in the last twenty-four hours. Devon explained he would only shave small sections out of Zach's hair so he could stick the foam circles on his skin. These stickers would be tracked on the MRI so they would provide markers for the surgeons on where to make their incisions and to help them track the tumor location.

Lexi and Dirk arrived just as the nurses received word the MRI team was on its way. Lexi fell into my arms with a confused look in her eyes. The enormity of the changes our lives were about to take was just beginning to sink in for her—for all of us. Dirk had tried to explain the situation to her on the ride to the hospital. Zach really wanted to take Lexi to the playroom to show her how proficient he had become on the touch screen. But before we were able to leave the room, a technician with a wheelchair arrived to take Zach downstairs.

Zach would require anesthesia for this MRI because it would take two hours or longer. I marveled at how well all the staff we had encountered so far worked with children. Putting Zach at ease was the primary goal for all the staff members.

It was hard to leave his side when it came time for them to take him to the MRI. He put on a brave face, but I could see the fear in his eyes as we said good-bye and he entered the dark MRI room with the nurse and technician.

As we walked from the MRI area, my cell phone rang bringing news our parents had arrived! We waited in front of the hospital as they walked in from the parking lot. The tears began stinging my eyes as soon as I saw my mom and dad, Mike and Barbara, and Dirk's parents, Gib and Phyllis. Having them near brought relief to us, even though we knew they were as helpless to fix this situation as we were. I fell into their arms and hugged them with desperation. The strong façade I had been trying to keep up dissolved as my body shook with sobs. We all exchanged teary-eyed looks of bewilderment as we discussed what had happened up to this point. I felt like I was living someone else's life as we told them the story. This had to be a nightmare of some sort. *This can't be real,* I was pleading in my mind.

We knew Zach would not be out of the MRI for a couple of hours. The nurses had been urging us to get a room at the Ronald McDonald House, so Dirk, Lexi and I went to accomplish this task while our parents went to the cafeteria. They were exhausted and hungry after their sixteen-hour journey.

The Ronald McDonald House was located directly behind the hospital.

Originally built as a private residence, the large two-story home had been converted to provide accommodations for the immediate families of hospital patients. The neighborhood surrounding All Children's was not considered the safest area of town, which explained why we had to ring the doorbell to get inside. The well-worn carpets and furniture made it apparent that the house had held many families over the years. Most of the furniture was mismatched and out of style, but everything was clean and inviting.

A man who appeared to be in his late sixties greeted us as we sat at a large dining table. He started his routine interview to tell us all the rules and regulations of the house. My mind drifted. I stared at him, slightly nodding my head at his words, but I did not hear a thing. I could not focus on anything but Zach. Our lives were hanging perilously in an unknown, precarious world. This was never in my realm of possibilities of what the future would hold. Flashes and snippets of the events that had occurred over the last twenty-four hours kept replaying over and over in my thoughts. It was as if I had Ping- Pong balls of each step ricocheting madly in my brain— and they would not stop. Nothing made sense. This could not be real.

I was drawn back to reality when the man finished his obligatory interview. Dirk and I blindly signed the papers he slid in front of us that promised a room in exchange for a nominal fee and a few daily housekeeping chores.

The room was very tidy, but basic. It had a bed, dresser and a small cot to the side. (Lexi was disappointed there was no television.) There was also a small bathroom with a shower! I looked longingly at the shower, but knew there was not enough time now. In our short stay we had already discovered the facilities in the hospital were limited to public restrooms on each floor for parents to share with visitors. The bathrooms in each patient room were for patient use only. There was also one public shower available on each floor. Knowing what the hospital had to offer made this room feel like the Ritz Carlton.

We quickly headed back to grab some dinner. I had very little appetite, but forced myself to eat a sandwich as we joined our parents once again.

Guilt surrounded me as I thought about Zach's empty stomach.

The MRI was finished around 8:30 P.M. Zach was very groggy and grumpy when Dirk and I entered the recovery room. He was beyond hungry and had lost all patience with the situation. I was hopeful his mood would improve when he got back to his room and saw his new visitors, but it did not. He would not look at anyone or talk to anyone. All he wanted to do was go to the playroom with Lexi to show her the game he had mastered. His bad mood dove into despair when the nurse informed us the playroom was closed for the night. He buried his head in his pillow and sobbed loudly as we all exchanged helpless looks with each other.

When it was clear no one could console him, everyone left and I ordered him some dinner, knowing tomorrow would be another day with no food. He finally relented to eating when things quieted down. He and I played some Monopoly until he was sleepy. I pulled my chair as close to his bed as I could and spread the sheets out on my makeshift bed. I held Zach's hand through the safety sides on his bed as sleep finally crept into my mind.

I woke early, around 4:30 A.M. I tried to pray, but found I could not quiet my mind. All I could manage was, "Please God, don't let him die." I stared up at the ceiling and the tears started pouring out of my eyes as I realized Zach had been born at this time eight short years ago! How could this be happening? My beautiful baby boy was having brain surgery on the same exact day of his birth.

Memories of his birth replayed in my thoughts. His chest seemed so broad and strong even when he was first born. The all-consuming love I felt then had only grown with time. He was my baby and now he could forever be changed—he could die.

I knew I had to be strong for him today. Zach would not see my tears. The nurse came in to check his IV and saw me crying. She motioned me to the hall. Her face filled with concern as she asked if I had any questions. I looked at her and said, "I have to be strong for him, but I am so scared." I dropped my head on her shoulder and sobbed. She had no words to comfort me, only a gentle pat on the back and a tissue for my tears.

The quiet darkness of the early morning gave me time to calm my emotions. Soon after, Dirk and Lexi joined us as morning rounds began. Dr. Storrs was accompanied by another doctor this time, Dr. Tuite. They would be performing the surgery together. Blinded by my optimistic hope the surgery would simple and successful, I did not consider the glaring reality: Two neurosurgeons meant the procedure would be anything but simple.

They were pleased to report Zach's spine was clear of disease and there was only the one tumor that had shown on the initial MRI. They shared with us that the surgery could take anywhere from an hour to eight hours, depending on what they found. A pathologist would be standing by to evaluate a frozen section of the tumor and then they would decide their course of action. In this case, the longer the surgery, the better because that would mean they were able to get to the tumor and needed the time to delicately remove it.

They warned us Zach might be worse neurologically after surgery than he was currently—or he could be better. The conversation was again brief and to the point. They were obviously busy and anxious to continue their rounds. As I watched them stride off to their next patient, I wanted to run after them and demand more information. I wanted to see the MRI and have them show us their plan of action for the surgery. It was terrifying to have to place complete trust of Zachary's life in the hands of these two men who were essentially virtual strangers to us.

Although very hungry, Zach was in much better spirits than the previous evening. It was his birthday! A shy smile appeared on his face when all four grandparents came in singing "Happy Birthday." A steady parade of balloon bouquets and gifts started arriving early and continued throughout the morning. We were thankful his surgery was scheduled for 12:45 p.m., for this meant he would not have to suffer the entire day without food again. With me glued to his side, we took everyone to the playroom so he could show off his touch screen skills. His face beamed with joy as he easily beat anyone who sat next to him and played the games.

Nervous anticipation circulated through my body with each heartbeat as the morning slipped into midday. A surge of adrenaline shot through every raw nerve when we heard a page for Zach to return to his room.

Expecting a gurney to arrive for his trip to the surgical area, the silent stress we were all fighting disappeared as all the nurses on the floor came to his door with balloons. They sang "Happy Birthday" and handed him a $50 gift card to Toys R Us. The smile on Zach's face was priceless. His eyes sparkled and his face grew pink with all the attention. I was grateful for the much needed distraction from Zach's impending task lurking just around the corner.

Not long after, the gurney arrived. Dirk, Zach and I headed to the "holding room." This was where all patients and their parents were taken to meet the surgical team and sign consent forms. A sick, helpless feeling engulfed me as we walked through the swinging steel doors that contained the waiting area. There were many others in the room facing the same plight of surgery, but I doubted there were any there for brain surgery. The enormity of the next two to six hours of our lives pressed down on my entire body. Holding my hand in a tight squeeze, Zach quietly took in the room around us, particularly watching those wearing green surgical scrubs, knowing they would eventually become his guardians when he left us.

Dr. Storrs entered the room, looking much different in scrubs. Confidence and purpose surrounded him as he briefly explained the procedure again and handed us the consent form to sign. Expecting to see an involved, complex description of the surgery, I was surprised to see four simple words: craniotomy to remove mass. The words seemed too simple. Did they not realize Zach was having *brain surgery? This cannot be my life.* Why could it not be me waiting to go in for surgery? Why such an innocent little boy? Why Zach?

When the time finally came for the surgical nurses to wheel Zach away, Dirk and I tenderly kissed him and I held his hand tight. We walked with them until they pushed through the swinging doors labeled "Surgical Suite—Authorized Personnel Only." I called out, "Bye, Baby, we will see you real soon!"

Desperate panic consumed me as I realized that moment could be the last time I saw Zach alive. Dirk and I turned to face each other and embraced as our bodies shook with sobs.

Reflections

Overwhelmed and totally consumed with the unknowns, Dirk and I were functioning on pure adrenaline. Our lives had taken a perilous turn into a deep dark tunnel. We were desperately looking for a light to appear that would lead us back to the life we had been living. This new world did not fit with our expectations we had so completely taken for granted.

Little did I know God's journey deep into my heart had just started. I had given Him a small corner when I was a child and prayed for my salvation. At different times in my life, I had felt Him gently tugging at it, but the world had a bigger hold. Dirk and I were too "comfortable" with our current lifestyle to make God our priority.

In reflective moments after we had Lexi and Zach, fleeting thoughts of how it would feel to fully surrender to God would dance through my mind. I often wondered if we were missing the bigger picture or living a life that would guide our kids down a road to a fulfilling life. But it was scary to contemplate making such a change. What would our friends think if we suddenly became "churchy"? The enemy knew how to push just the right buttons in my mind and close down those thoughts quickly.

Now we were faced with a nightmare that would draw a line in the sand for us. Would I allow anger, hurt and bitterness to guide my heart away from God? Calling the church, asking for prayer as soon as he had found out about the tumor, had revealed Dirk would not allow this to come between God and him. His heart was broken wide open and he desperately was asking for God's help. I was still spinning, feeling confused about how and why we could be facing this giant monster. My mind did not have room for contemplation of God's plan at this point. I was living moment-to-moment, optimistically clinging to the hope God would realize an awful mistake had been made and the tumor would suddenly evaporate, giving Zach his life back and us a one-way ticket out of this frightening new world.

The lesson that came screaming out to us loud and clear was that we had taken so many things for granted in our lives. We were always in a hurry to get to the next milestone without truly appreciating all those every-day moments that now held so much meaning. Suddenly, waking up in our own bed, taking a shower or feeling confident in having a tomorrow was snatched away from us. We were quickly learning how misplaced our priorities in life had become.

Zach's opinion of the medicine he had to learn to take! Although he was good-natured about it here, it was quite a torturous ordeal as the number of medications increased in later treatments.

CHAPTER THREE

The Life-changing "C" Word

Numbly, we joined our parents and Lexi in the cafeteria for some lunch after leaving Zach in the care of the surgical team. Pangs of guilt swirled in my head as I pictured Zach lying in surgery surrounded by those green scrubs. I had to force the food down. We faced a long day ahead.

Nervous we would miss a call from the surgical nurse with an update, I soon announced I wanted to go to the family waiting area. A somber room lined with blue vinyl chairs, the family waiting area would have been better labeled the family worry area. Many tired, anxious eyes met ours as we arrived. An elderly female volunteer manned the desk. She asked our name as we entered so she could inform us when "our" call came.

They had taken Zach in at 1:30 P.M. An hour had passed when she motioned me to the phone. The nurse reported the incision had been made and everything was going well. As I sat back down, I quickly mumbled to my parents that the neurologist had told me the tumor was deep with a lot of circulation—even though I wasn't sure what it meant. I felt they deserved to know this small bit of information that held such huge implications and was the source for much of my anxiety.

Dear God, please be with these surgeons. Please let them remove this evil tumor and let this nightmare go away.

At 3:10 P.M., the phone rang again. My heart stopped when the elderly lady called out, "Tucker Family," and motioned me to the phone again. My hand trembled as I picked up the receiver. The nurse said they were closing and the doctor would be out soon to discuss the surgery. Hope for an end to the nightmare was gone in that instant. Gently returning the receiver to its cradle, I turned to see everyone's expectant faces looking at me. Tears sprung to my eyes as I blurted out, "They are closing already. It is too soon." It could only mean one thing: They were unable to remove the tumor. Remembering Dr. Storrs' words that a longer surgery indicated a better outcome, I feared the worst. It was clear: Our nightmare was long from being over.

Lexi had a frightened look on her face as she came to me and hugged me. Instantly understanding the implications of the call, my parents volunteered to take her for a walk so we could talk to the doctor alone. I could feel everyone's eyes looking at us with sympathy. They knew this was a room where tears only meant bad things.

Now what do we do? Zach cannot die; he has hardly begun to live. *Lord, why not me?*

My mind was working overtime and my body trembled uncontrollably once again. Each day was bringing more bad news. *I want off this ride now; please show me the way out!* I pleaded silently. Dirk put his arm around my shoulders as we waited. His parents sat nearby with pained, worried expressions on their faces.

Dr. Storrs, still dressed in his scrubs, came in a short time later. He sat next to Dirk and me. "We were able to remove approximately three-fourths of the tumor," he began. "The tumor had finger-like growths that have spread to the surrounding brain matter and were near a ventricle. We did not want to disturb these areas because that could cause brain damage. We will have to wait on the pathology report to determine the next course of treatment," he stated. "The pathology report could take anywhere from two days to a week to come back. Zach did fine in surgery, and they will come to take you back to him as he wakes up."

"How big was the part of the tumor you removed?" I asked quietly.

"I would estimate about this size," he answered as he held up his closed fist. "It should not be long before they come for you," he assured us as he stood to leave.

So that was it; we were not so lucky. The "next course of treatment"— that had an ominous tone. It would not be a simple surgical removal and back to normal scenario for us. I began to wonder what further treatment meant. Could this mean cancer? It couldn't be. How could a young, healthy child that had run triathlons and aced all his schoolwork get a cancerous brain tumor? Had I fed him something bad, was it when he smacked his head on the floor a few weeks ago, what could cause this evil, ugly thing to invade my Zach's brain?

My parents returned with Lexi soon after Dr. Storrs left. She climbed into my lap, concern covering her face, and asked if Zach would be OK. I relayed Dr. Storrs' words to my parents as I hugged Lexi. Tears were welling in my eyes as I told her, "Zach will be OK; we just have to get more information from the doctors." Her eyes reflected the uncertainty I was feeling. My mind struggled to grasp yet another blow to our new reality.

It was close to 4 P.M. when Dirk and I were allowed to go into the Pediatric Intensive Care Unit or PICU. My heart was pounding as we entered the room. This room had one central desk in the middle with beds separated by curtains all around like spokes on a wheel. There were a few rooms with walls and glass windows that I imagined were for the very guarded cases. Zach was in a spot with a wall on one side and curtain on the other.

It was such a relief to see his beautiful face and body again! His eyes were closed and slow to open when we arrived. The right front quarter of his head was shaved and a five- to six-inch incision had been made from his ear directly up to the top of his head. I had imagined he would have gauze wrapped all around his head like a mummy, but instead he had one piece of white bandage loosely positioned over the incision.

"Hey, baby boy," I said softly as I leaned close to his face and kissed him. His eyes flickered open and a small smile came to his face. "How are you, Honey?" I whispered.

"My head hurts," he said in a hoarse, quiet voice as he lifted his hand toward his incision.

My heart soared! All my worries melted away. I could tell by those three small words and the look in his beautiful hazel eyes it was still Zach! The tinkering that had gone on in his brain had not altered his personality in general. What an answered prayer we had received! As Zach slowly became more coherent, the nurse told us he was receiving morphine for pain, Decadron for swelling and Dilantin to help prevent seizures, a side effect common with brain surgery.

More tubes were coming out of Zach's body—a catheter, which he was quick to let us know he did not like, a PICC line IV, and the original IV. My poor baby was like a pin cushion. His perfect little body had been forever changed, but none of this mattered. He was still Zach!

Hunger was his main concern. Almost two days of no food had taken its toll on him. The nurse was hesitant to let him eat, but she did allow some Gatorade and later crackers. Elated that Zach seemed OK, Dirk went out to get Lexi. She was happy to see him. His spunk became apparent as he protested any form of affection she tried to give him. Any other time I would have scolded him, but now, I was just happy to see his personality come out just as before.

Dirk began a parade of visitors by sending in each grandparent for a quick visit one at a time since there was a limit of two visitors in PICU for each patient. The relief was evident on each of their faces as they laid their eyes on Zach and spoke to him. They saw for themselves he was still the same.

Many of our close friends had arrived while I was spending time with Zach in PICU. They came bearing birthday gifts which were promptly delivered by Dirk or Lexi. Excited and overwhelmed, Zach's biggest concern continued to be the removal of his catheter. Needing a distraction from his discomfort, I was grateful when the nurses allowed his buddy Dylan to come in for a visit. Concern and a hint of fear were visible in Dylan's eyes as he slowly approached the bed. He relaxed when he saw Zach's familiar smile. To help break the ice, I suggested they try out one of Zach's birthday gifts. Always loving to play board games, Zach asked to play The Game of Life with us. The irony struck my heart as I assembled the game board. Zach's very life had just hours before been so precariously fragile and still we had no idea how long a life he had before him. What better way to celebrate his survival of his surgery than to play a game called Life. It seemed we had entered our own crazy game. Why not play one where a happy ending was guaranteed!

Making it as much of a birthday party as we could, Dylan and I let Zach make up all the rules. Incredibly, Zach's cognitive skills seemed to be as sharp as ever. He had no trouble reading his game cards and would quickly add or subtract his salary and payments for the game. It was hard to believe that only a few hours before the doctors had been probing through his brain and removing most of a fist-sized tumor. Gratitude for the moment filled my heart. I was learning our life and happiness were now measured in moments and nothing more.

The 7 P.M. shift change required all parents to leave the PICU until 9 P.M. It broke my heart to leave Zach, especially when a look of panic filled his eyes. "Zach, I have to go for just a couple of hours. See the clock over there?" I asked pointing toward the nurses' station. "When it's 9 o'clock, they will let me back in. You can press the nurse call button if you need something. I don't want to go, but they need me to leave while they change nurses, Baby. Be brave, we can play more games when I get back," I said, trying at the same time to convince myself it was OK. Grasping the nurse call button firmly in his hand, he whispered for me to hurry back as I slowly walked away smiling at him over my shoulder.

Greeted by many familiar faces, I found the family waiting area had been overtaken by our friends. They all looked as bewildered as I felt. Everyone had nervous smiles painted on their faces. I reassured them Zach was doing well and his spirits were good. After giving many hugs and words of encouragement, our friends began to clear the room. As they left, many promised to return the next day.

Dylan's mother, Jenny, asked me to have some dinner with her in the cafeteria. Hoping to make the time away from Zach pass more quickly, I agreed. I found my body trembling again as I relayed all I knew of Zach's condition to her. Nerves and the uncomfortably cool temperature of the hospital seemed to be governing the tremors. If only I had known hospitals kept their climates comfortable for polar bears to help prevent the spread of germs, I would have asked Dirk to bring sweat pants and a jacket—not shorts and short-sleeved shirts! The food I selected held little appeal to me as I worked hard to keep my emotions in check during our conversation.

Realizing how ominous it sounded, I could contain my tears no longer as I explained that the doctor had indicated there would be further treatment for Zach. Jenny reached for my hand across the table as she dissolved in sobs along with me. Clinging to the sliver of hope that the pathology report would not indicate cancer, we both quickly wiped our tears away as we stood to leave. The fear and pity displayed in all of our friends' eyes that day had made it clear: The situation we faced was the ultimate worst nightmare for all of them. The problem was it was not a dream for us—we were living it.

By 8:30 P.M., I could not stand to wait any longer. Pleading through the intercom at the PICU door, the nurses took pity and agreed to let me rejoin Zach. He did not see me coming. Complete desperation filled his face as he frantically pressed the nurse call button over and over with his thumb. My heart melted on the spot. Why were they ignoring him? "Hey Baby, I'm back; it's OK. What's wrong? Do you need the nurse for something?" I asked, grabbing his hand with both of mine.

"You're late!" he hissed as relief filled his eyes. "I want this thing taken out of my wee-wee because I need to go to the bathroom!"

"Honey, you can just go, that is what it is there for," I explained. "Oh sweetie, I'm not late; remember I said at 9 o'clock. I'm sorry you were alone."

Soon the nurse we would have for the night came to check on us. I explained how uncomfortable Zach had been with the catheter and he agreed to check if it could be removed. Quickly getting approval, he returned and proceeded to pull it out. Zach cried out in pain. I was taken aback when the nurse gruffly told Zach to tough it out and that it would burn for awhile. Not quite the same attitude all of our nurses had displayed so far.

Little did I know this was the beginning of a very long night. An urgent need to go to the bathroom would overtake Zach every five or ten minutes. After straining a few minutes, he would produce a small dribble, just enough to make the bed wet, but not enough to get in the urinal. I was frantically using the paper towels to catch what was missing the urinal and tossing them over the side of his bed. A small mountain of crumpled towels soon formed on the floor. The nurse was clueless to the whole process. Frustrated after a few hours of this routine, I called to him asking if Zach should be peeing nonstop. He paused his conversation about his weekend plans, glanced over and shrugged, replying it sometimes happened when catheters were removed.

It was a miserable night for both of us. The PICU seemed to be colder than the fourth floor. I was freezing even when I wrapped the thin blanket they had given me tightly around my body. My bed consisted of a straight-back chair and tall stool. Sitting upright in the chair, I propped my legs on the stool as I attempted to sleep. As soon as I drifted off, Zach would call out in a panic to help him go to the bathroom. Between the nonstop urge to pee, vitals and cold, the most either of us slept at a stretch was twenty minutes. They came for Zach at 1 a.m. to have a CT scan to make sure there was no hemorrhaging in the tumor bed. To my relief, everything was clear.

Numb with fatigue, I was glad to see the room grow lighter as morning arrived. The new nurse, who arrived at 6:30 A.M., seemed much more experienced and sympathetic with children. She was willing to let me stay during the shift change after I explained how Zach had become so stressed the night before.

The clock seemed mired in molasses those last few hours before Lexi and Dirk came to relieve me. It had been three long days since I had stood in a hot shower. Mentally and physically exhausted, I headed to the Ronald

McDonald house as soon as they walked in the room. Whispering gratitude to the fast-food, red-haired clown, I could not walk fast enough to my waiting oasis.

My body ached and felt coated with a heavy layer of grimy stress and anxiety. The hot, steamy shower helped to get rid of the grime, but the fatigue remained. I dove into the bed, knowing I could not stay, but longing for a moment to bury my head in a pillow and have a good cry. The moment was lost with the ringing of the phone. Worried it might be Dirk, I quickly answered to find it was the youth pastor from our church. He stumbled over his words and asked what he could do to help. I wished I knew! I told him I did not know what he could do except to pray. My weariness, compounded by the continual disappointing news we were receiving, was causing me to wonder if God was even hearing our prayers. It certainly did not feel like He was.

Feeling an overwhelming desire to return to Zach, I hurried back to the PICU. My arrival was not soon enough for Zach. Dirk had tried his best to distract him, but he had been relentless in demanding to know what was taking me so long. The rest of the morning and early afternoon were filled with visits from friends and more birthday gifts. The pile of toys and games had grown taller than his bed.

It was mid-afternoon when the obligatory twenty-four hour stay in PICU after surgery had passed. We were released to go back to the fourth floor. Before we left, they had to pull the PICC line out of his arm. After the catheter experience, Zach was very leery of letting them do anything that had to do with pulling. Removing the tape around the line was bad enough, but when they pulled the line out, Zach wailed! It was the loudest, most heartbreaking cry I had ever heard leave his mouth. Because the line was threaded through his vein to an artery, they had to apply direct pressure for several minutes. Zach screamed out in pain over and over, telling them to stop. All I could do was lay my head on his chest and blink back my tears as I tried to comfort him.

At one point one of the nurses impatiently told him he would have to be quiet because he was scaring the other kids. I wanted to rip her head off.

Did she not understand what this child had just endured the last three days?

A bed finally opened up on the fourth floor around 4 P.M. and we were moved back to the same room we had left the day before. We were very happy to see improvement in Zach's left leg and arm movement. He could press his foot down again and was lifting his arm much better. He still could not straighten his fingers out, but his grip was stronger. I was amazed as I sat and watched him play that less than twenty-four hours ago he had had major brain surgery. Maybe the doctors would be wrong and there would not be any more treatment needed. We could deal with getting his hand working again. I just wanted to be able to leave this all behind and get back home to our life. It seemed so far away right now.

The recliner chair was like paradise to me as I stretched out to sleep that evening. Zach and I were both very tired after our previous night, and sleep came quickly. My mind still felt like it was going one hundred miles a minute as I drifted off. The overriding thought that kept ringing out was, *Is this really happening?*

Morning came early. Zach was scheduled for a 6:30 A.M. MRI. This would check his post-operative status and give the neurosurgeons a picture of how much of the tumor was left. Because it was an MRI of only the brain, there was no need for anesthesia and I was able to stay with Zach just as I had at St. Joe's. He was very drowsy and surprisingly slept through most of it. As the machine whirred to life with its loud clanks and peculiar bangs, I tried to focus my thoughts and pray, but instead my mind kept drifting from one thought to the next. The best I could do was *God, please let Zach be OK.* In my mind, I knew I should be praying, but my heart was confused. Why had God allowed this to happen to Zach? I was not feeling anger, but I was feeling hurt and confused.

To our relief, the surgeons were very pleased when we saw them later that morning on their rounds. They felt they had achieved a total gross resection, or in other words, had removed the entire tumor. Their satisfaction with the outcome buoyed our spirits that maybe there would be no further treatment needed after all. Maybe we would escape this nightmare and return to our life as it was before. Dr. Storrs felt we would hear about the pathology report soon—the report that would control our destiny. It felt as if my stomach turned inside out as I thought of that moment.

Deana, Curren and David Page came to spend the day with us. Curren was one of Zach's best buddies since early preschool. He had been one of the children we had visited at All Children's a year earlier when he broke his femur in a skateboard accident. Never would any of us have dreamed in a year's time we would all meet there again. (If only it had been for a broken bone again!) Zach's spirits were high as he skillfully challenged the boys to play against him on the touch screen game. Carefree belly laughs and animated conversations filled the room as often happens when young boys compete with each other.

After lunch, Dr. Tuite, dressed in scrubs, appeared at the playroom door. He motioned to Dirk and me to join him. My heart lurched and began to flail madly in my chest. I knew he must have news, and his downcast expression was not encouraging to me. The hall just outside the playroom door became our chamber of doom as he began explaining his news. "The pathology report has come back. Unfortunately, Zach's tumor is cancerous. This kind of tumor is normally found in older adults and is relatively rare in children. This tumor is aggressive; it is a grade four tumor with a very guarded prognosis. It will require more treatment that an oncologist can explain to you later. The oncologist is not available today, so we thought you should stay one more day and talk with her tomorrow before you are discharged."

As he was speaking I was picturing myself as a nail. With every sentence he uttered, I felt another blow from a gigantic hammer coming down on my head. I could not believe he was sharing such life-changing news with us in the middle of a hall with people walking all around. Dirk and I stared at him with dumbfounded expressions on our faces.

"But…there is still hope, right?" Dirk asked with desperation in his voice.

"There is always hope, and you will have to discuss the more specific treatments with the oncologist," Dr. Tuite replied stoically, not offering much reassurance.

"Does this tumor have a name?" I asked.

"Yes, it is a Glioblastoma Multiforme or GBM," he answered.

"A…what? Could you…will you write that down for me?" It sounded like a foreign language to me. I could not have repeated it even if he said it ten times. It was a mouthful of distasteful evil at this point.

Dr. Tuite looked around for some paper and grabbed a paper towel out of a nearby dispenser. He scribbled these two incredibly ugly words on the towel and handed it to me. I just stared at the words with disbelief.

God, what is going on here? We have not been bad people, I have always prayed for my children's health to be protected, what has happened? Where are You?

Unbelievably, neither Dirk nor I lost our composure. Shock overwhelmed our senses into quiet submission. Dr. Tuite apologized for the bad news and left us standing in the hall, forever changed and facing a monster we knew nothing about.

I turned to look at Dirk and told him I had to go to the bathroom to absorb this. I needed the world to stop for a moment—everything to just stop. I hurried around the corner to the haven of the bathroom. Staring at myself in the mirror, I kept repeating in my mind, *My baby has cancer. Zach has brain cancer.* It was clear: The world had gone mad.

After a few minutes and a few deep breaths, I stepped out to face our new reality. Our parents were huddled around Dirk, their eyes wide as they tried to comprehend what we had just learned. To show further proof what Dirk was saying was true, I showed them the words Dr. Tuite had written on the paper towel. Trembling, my dad copied them down. I looked at all of them and said, "Don't tell anyone about this yet. I need to think. I need to understand this better before people know more." Nodding in agreement, we hugged each other in utter bewilderment. I did not want everyone to find out that Zach had been given what felt like a death sentence. There was always hope and I was confident he would be OK. Somehow I would find a way to save him. There had to be a way. He was too bright of a ray to be taken away from us.

Painting smiles on our faces, we rejoined the kids in the playroom. It was extremely hard to function normally holding this hideous news inside. Later, after the Pages left, an occupational therapist stopped by to visit Zach and evaluate his arm and hand movement. She took him to a corner in the playroom we had ignored because it contained preschool toys.

Noticing a mirror low on the wall, Zach immediately made his way to it. He sat and gazed at his reflection. I had not realized he had not seen his reflection since we had arrived at the hospital. He had never mentioned wanting to.

We all watched in silence as he carefully studied his new appearance. He made no comment, but gave a little smile and shrug when I asked what he thought. The therapist went through some different exercises with him to test his left side weakness. She suggested we set up some therapy for his leg and arm after we left the hospital.

Lexi had spent the afternoon watching movies in Zach's bed by herself. It was clear she was exhausted and overwhelmed with our current living arrangements when I asked her to find her shoes. With tears welling in her eyes she said, "Everyone is always asking me to do something. I am tired, too, you know!" My heart melted for her as I pulled her to my lap and hugged her tight. She whispered her stomach hurt and she just wanted to go home. Gib and Phyllis volunteered to take her there so she could sleep in her own bed. This was so unfair to her; it was unfair to all of us. I had to remind myself this was all real, that Zach had cancer—a cancer that was really bad.

Reality of our future began to sink in as we started to teach Zach how to swallow a pill. Taking medicine had always been difficult for him because he would easily gag and throw up if he didn't like the taste. I knew this would be a challenge to master. The nurses were very good about showing us how to smash the pills, dissolve them and squirt them into his mouth with a syringe.

Zach fell asleep early, around 9 P.M. The intensity of the last five days had finally caught up with him. Dirk and I had some time to talk.

Zach's nurse was sitting at a desk outside his room, so we started asking her questions. The picture she painted was very bleak: long hospital stays, chemo that would make Zach very sick, needles and pokes. My head was spinning. Worry and grief over the dreams lost for Zach crushed our hearts. She reinforced my view of cancer as being nothing but suffering and misery. After watching Zach go through the pain in PICU with the PICC line, I was sick to think of his future. I wanted this to all go away—I wanted our life back.

Reeling from the devastation we were feeling, we decided it was time to update our siblings. Dirk left to call his two brothers while I contacted my two sisters. I knew my parents had been keeping them updated, but I needed to hear their voices. Kathy, my older sister who lived in Indiana near our parents, was getting ready to fly out for a weekend vacation in Minnesota. She immediately offered to change her flight to come down, but I told her to wait. I felt I might need her later. Michelle, my younger sister, made the same offer to fly in from her home in Vancouver and I told her the same.

Tears rolled down my cheeks as I struggled to steady my voice fighting the full-body tremors once again. I had found an empty hall near Zach's room and walked in large slow circles as I as spoke to each of them. My heartache poured through the phone to them as I shared my fears of all the sickness and needles Zach's future held. I did not share the severity of the tumor but just told them it was cancerous and we were facing further treatments. After hearing the nurse's description, I had come to hate those words.

Emotionally spent, I finally laid down to sleep in the recliner well after midnight. At least we would be going home tomorrow. How would we tell Zach and Lexi that he had cancer? I could hardly say the word, even to myself. I just could not make sense of any of it in my mind. Every time I thought we had reached the worse scenario, we were slapped with something even more devastating and unbelievable. It was like we were handed the black ball in life's lottery. We were being admitted to a club no one ever dreamed of joining.

Zach and I woke the next morning with smiles in anticipation of leaving the hospital. My parents came and began to load all the toys, bouquets and treasures Zach had received during our week-long stay. The nurse arrived with a large stack of papers including prescriptions for all the medications Zach would be taking at home. He would be continuing the Decadron (steroid) three times a day on a decreasing level, Dilantin two times a day and Zantac two times a day. The schedule seemed manageable, but their emphasis on the timing of the doses was a bit intimidating to me.

Dr. Grana from the Pediatric Oncology Practice came by mid-morning. Dirk and I followed her to a quiet office to find out how "further treatment" would be defined in her terms. Dr. Grana was a middle-aged, quiet-spoken woman with very kind eyes and a soft smile. She had a motherly quality about her that immediately put us at ease. Bracing for the worst, we sat around a small table as she began to explain our future. She admitted Glioblastoma Multiforme was not a tumor they saw very often in their practice.

She explained there were four levels of brain tumors with grade four being the most aggressive type and this was what Zach had. The best treatment protocol currently being used was radiation in conjunction with chemotherapy. The radiation could be started within the next week and the chemo would run concurrent with the radiation. A full six-week course of radiation was recommended with this type of tumor and then a four- to six-week break would be taken.

After that, the chemo would be given for another year in a cycle of five days on the chemo and twenty-eight days off. The chemo would be in a pill called Temador, which to my relief meant no needles or IV issues like I had envisioned. The side effects were normally minimal: no hair loss, a little nausea, but there was anti-nausea medicine for that. The radiation side effects would be more pronounced with hair loss, fatigue and some nausea. There would also probably be some loss of mental abilities, and cancer could develop later in life in the skull areas treated.

The words just tumbled out of her mouth effortlessly. Much less bleak than what we had heard the night before, they were music to my ears. She said further that Zach would have a good quality of life, should be able to attend school and spend limited time in the hospital if everything went as expected with the side effects.

Dirk then posed the question of survival and prognosis for GBM patients. Dr. Grana cautioned, just as Dr. Storrs had, that each case was extremely different, but overall she would expect a 40 percent chance Zach would survive five years without evidence of tumor and 60 percent chance of survival with evidence of tumor.

She indicated they had a patient who had a similar tumor seven years ago who was still alive. He had some issues with his cognitive abilities from the radiation, but overall was doing fairly well. We asked how often she had worked with children having GBMs. She responded there was a case maybe every two to three years in their clinic.

Finally we wanted to know if there were any other facilities that would provide any different or more advanced treatments. She replied that Sloan Kettering, Duke, St. Jude's and MD Anderson were the main programs in the eastern United States, but she assured us they were all on the same protocol and we would not receive any different treatments if we would choose to go to one of those institutions. She did offer to correspond with doctors at these locations to make sure nothing had changed.

She asked that we visit their office the next Friday after we had a follow-up with the Neurosurgery Group and we could get more information about the radiation at that time. There were two facilities in the area that could potentially treat children, but she would have to consult with a radiation oncologist to find out which would be available.

We were free to go! Dirk and I both felt we were walking on cloud nine when we left the office. Dr. Grana had filled us with such hope. We knew we could beat this thing. Zach was such a fighter. She had assured us he would not have to deal with the fragile body and needles I had so feared last night!

We were headed home around noon. I felt like a mole that had finally popped its head out from underground. It had been a week since I had spent any amount of time outside. Just to be in our own car and out of the hospital was so wonderful. Good-bye screaming IV alarms! Good-bye public bathrooms! Good-bye nurses and doctors! I sat with Zach in the back seat and let him lay on my lap. I had a smile on my face and a new appreciation of going home.

Our house was decorated with many welcome home signs, balloons and plants when we arrived. It all still seemed like a dream. I could not imagine what everyone was thinking. I was guessing they were as blown away by this past week as we were.

We made Zach a comfortable bed on the big chair in the family room. The smile on his face reflected all of our moods. Our never-ending week from hell was finally drawing to a close. We were home, and for now we could relax and try to find a way to get back to our normal routine if that was possible.

Reflections

To be suddenly faced with the possibility that we would outlive our son was earth-shattering and unacceptable to me. My mind would not entertain this thought, even though the reality had been clearly described to us. I did not understand that the moment the word cancer fell from Dr. Tuite's lips and entered our ears, our lives would never be the same again. Clinging to the hope I felt in Dr. Grana's words, I was sure that somehow we would find the successful treatment protocol that would solve the mystery of a Glioblastoma Multiforme tumor and we would get our Zach back. I just had to catch my breath first.

Leaving the hospital was a relief and scary all at the same time. Zach had cancer…they had not given us any resources or books to read that would explain the world of pediatric cancer. Similar to what we would have been told if he had had his tonsils removed, we were just given general instructions about keeping him quiet and cool until our follow-up visit. It seemed there should have been more…someone to direct us to two wonderful resources in Tampa we found later: The Children's Cancer Center and the Pediatric Cancer Foundation. Someone to call if we had questions or needed advice.

Instead, we were released to navigate our own way through the confusing and intimidating maze of information available on the internet. It seemed that if we were being forced to become members in this club, we should have been given some rules of membership.

This was our first exposure to the difficult challenges parents face when confronted with childhood cancer. What I have found is that while there are many wonderful treatment facilities, doctors, nurses and support organizations, there does not seem to be an organized coordinated system to supply emotionally overloaded parents with much-needed guidance.

It is a system that requires the parents to become completely versed and knowledgeable about their child's type of cancer immediately. Reliance on the initial treatment plan can be the biggest mistake a parent can make. Parents—like their child with cancer—have to become courageous and lose all fear in questioning the very doctors they have been taught to trust. If the parents find they are too overwhelmed, they must find a close trusted relative or friend to take on the role. It could be critical for their child's life.

My heart was still filled with confusion and questions for God. Just as I had told Dirk earlier, I still did not feel God had given Zach cancer, but I did cling to the belief that God could heal Zach in an instant if He chose to. What I did not understand was why the healing was not happening—*now*. Zach was so innocent; it was our job to protect him, and now it seemed that was going to be extremely hard to do. Because I had never taken the time to deepen my spirituality, I was feeling lost. All I could feel was the pain and panic of not being able to protect my child. God seemed so distant, like He had turned His back on us.

Little did I know that while God was grieving for Zach's suffering right along with us, He planned to use this crushing trial to completely transform my heart and our focus forever. Zach had been given to us so graciously by God eight years earlier, with a purpose I had never dared to imagine. There was still work to be done before I could start growing. I needed a moment to breathe…a moment to sort out my thoughts. Many seeds had been planted throughout my life…the Master Gardener had provided all the proper cultivation. Now it was up to me to decide if I would let them grow and pull me closer to the One who I needed now more than ever.

Lexi snuggled close to Zach after he arrived home from his first week-long stay at the hospital. I could not make myself believe he actually had cancer at this point.

CHAPTER FOUR

A Quest for understanding

R unning had become my favorite form of exercise after years of hating it. It helped me not only physically, but mentally as well. After being told Zach had a tumor, then a very bad tumor, and then the worst cancerous tumor possible, my state of mind was fragile to say the least. Quieting my mind continued to be a challenge even back in the peace of our own home.

Early the morning after we arrived home, I pulled on my running shoes. A week in the hospital, pent-up anxiety and an overworked mind were plenty of motivation for me. My faith had taken a beating, but it was not defeated. I felt God had turned His back to us many times these past five days.

As my feet hit the pavement, the fog began to lift. I realized He had been with us all along. We had had many answered prayers throughout the week: surgery was successful, Zach was mentally and emotionally the same, treatment seemed manageable, no needles, and Dr. Grana was awesome. My hope and attitude blossomed the longer I ran. Somehow, someway, we would beat this!

Fueled by this optimism, we all began to reenter the life we had left behind one short week ago. The first few days were a chance to catch our breath and sort through all the wonderful gifts friends were bringing by daily. We had hot meals every night, groceries coming and lots of calls asking what else needed to be done. It was a very humbling experience. I was used to being the helping hand, not the recipient.

Our parents set off on their return trip to Indiana with the understanding that no one was to know the type of tumor Zach had and the promise they would return the moment we felt we needed their help. Stacks of mail and phone calls to the office required my attention, but I found it was hard to concentrate on anything. After retelling the story many times, it became apparent how useful a website would be to share updates with family and friends. I added this to my growing mental list of things that needed to be done—Zach's cure being number one.

Dirk returned to work and found it to be very emotional. Facing the normal routine, knowing Zach had cancer, was extremely difficult for him. Thankfully, his coworkers surrounded him with understanding and support. I continued to be amazed with his dramatic transformation. Drinking a six-pack of beer or a number of vodka tonics in the evenings had become an almost daily routine for him over the last several years—a form of self-medicating, a stress relief he had developed. During the week of Zach's hospital stay, Dirk had dumped every ounce of alcohol we had in the house down the drain in a very emotional surrender of this habit to God. He was now finding his stress relief in the Bible and prayer. He had totally immersed himself in his faith. Grateful he was gaining strength in this way, I began to try to focus on prayer as well, although I was still finding it difficult to fully surrender as Dirk had.

Keeping Zach calm and cool, as the doctors had instructed, was a challenge. He was ready to get down to the business of being an eight-year-old boy. Arranging play dates and playing referee between him and Lexi consumed a great amount of my time. The steroids not only stimulated his appetite, but also fueled his mischief toward Lexi. Her sensitivity to the attention he was receiving was in overdrive, causing many outbursts of frustration directed toward him. Defusing the tension by bringing in playmates became the best strategy.

Zach's room became a gigantic tent made out of sheets and blankets—my attempt to provide a "cool hideout" where he and his friends could quietly play games. As I should have known, boys will be boys! Their nervous energy of being with each other created an overwhelming desire to race around the house, punching the many helium balloons Zach had received. I was frantic trying to slow them down, but inside my heart was singing to see so many smiles and hear the big belly laughs. Zach's eyes beamed with joy as the scary, painful memories of the prior week melted from his mind.

Zach loved playing. He loved physical activity. The unfairness of the situation overwhelmed me. *Why Zach? Why anyone?* I just could not make my mind understand how such a robust, happy boy could be so sick. Folding laundry, paying bills, watching television, I would catch myself repeating *Zach has cancer* in my head as I continued to try to make myself believe this was true.

Late at night when things were quiet, I found the courage to do some research. My parents had warned me the information was dire. Before my mom left, she grabbed my shoulders, looked me in the eyes and said very seriously, "Sherry, you have to remember to know when to say enough is enough with treatments they might want to try."

Those types of decisions could not occupy my thoughts at this point. Gaining as much knowledge as I could about GBMs and the treatments available was my goal. The doctors seemed to have their own lingo when talking about procedures and treatments. I wanted the assurance the protocol Dr. Grana explained was indeed the accepted—and best—practice.

Digging through the stack of information from the hospital, I found the paper towel Dr. Tuite had used to write Glioblastoma Multiforme. Staring at the words, all the events of the past week rushed through my mind again. These two words had changed our reality. My heart raced and my stomach churned as I clicked on the links the computer had generated. The facts were dismal and devastating. This truth soon became evident: GBMs were very difficult to treat. The body's natural protection called the blood brain barrier was good to keep infection out of the brain, but worked against treating brain tumors with chemotherapy. Surgery, radiation and chemo were the standard treatments, but only resulted in survival rates averaging fourteen months. Searching many message boards, cases of GBMs in children seemed to be nonexistent. The facts made it clear: We needed a miracle.

The treatment Dr. Grana had described was in line with what I found at most facilities: radiation in combination with Temador, the oral chemo. All the facilities Dr. Grana had mentioned on the East Coast—Duke, Sloan Kettering, St. Jude's—appeared to use similar protocols. The facts and figures about brain tumors began to spin faster and faster in my mind…leading cause of death from childhood cancer…most aggressive stage…guarded prognosis. Even though I was reading all the ugly words related to this tumor, I still could not make my mind comprehend this was really happening to Zach, to us.

I had received an e-mail from a friend of my father. The e-mail gave a link to a radiation center located in Bloomington, Indiana, which was very near our parents' homes. Skeptical that a facility in the Midwest would be able to offer superior radiation to the larger institutions on the East Coast or even Tampa, I at first dismissed this possibility. Now I started to read the information. Surprisingly, I realized they did have a unique form of radiation called proton beam radiation. The facilities in Boston, California and Bloomington were the only three in the United States that offered proton beam radiation. It was a new revelation to me that there were different types of radiation since Dr. Grana had just mentioned radiation in general. She had said there were different ways of delivering it—some more directed to the tumor than others—but nothing about different forms of radiation.

Finally finding a piece of good news, I became more and more excited as I read. The side effects were greatly lessened with this form of radiation because the beam could be stopped at specific points, limiting the damage to healthy tissue. Concern about the damaging effects from radiation—lower IQ, fatigue and nausea—had weighed heavily on me. This was an answer to my prayers!

My mind was swimming yet again as I lay down to sleep. Dirk had been very skeptical that anything in Bloomington, Indiana, would compare to what was available locally when I mentioned it to him earlier. He was concerned I was not placing enough faith in God versus relying too much on medical treatments. I explained I felt God had put tools here on earth for us to use and it was our job to be diligent to find the right tools.

His skepticism caused me to feel very alone in trying to find out more about this hideous disease that had invaded our lives. It was too overwhelming for Dirk to hear about the details of GBMs. He did not want to know all the technical facts and figures, fearing it would suck out all of the hope he was building in his heart through his faith. He wanted to rely on the doctors in Tampa. I was determined to find the right treatment for Zach. My research continued.

As the week progressed, the kids were getting stir-crazy and grumpy. And all the information I was learning about GBMs was really getting to me. We decided to rent some movies. As we left the rental store, my eyes were drawn across the parking lot to a pet store advertising puppies. The kids had always wanted to visit this store, and I had always found excuses not to. Today my perspective had changed. Their eyes sparkled with excitement as we pulled up in front of the store and they realized we were going in.

They could hardly contain their smiles as they looked at all the cute little fur balls running around in each pen. We went from one to the other, ohhing and ahhing at each puppy. We picked a cocker spaniel to take into a petting pen. Zach was so excited to play with the puppy. Lexi was a little nervous about its sharp little teeth. Zach would scoop him up with his right arm while he giggled and talked to him. My heart was breaking as I watched. Would Zach never know what it is like to have a dog for a pet? How was this all going to play out?

Lord God, please let him live; please grant us a miracle from this disease!

Blinking back tears as I watched them play, my resolve to find the right treatment grew. It was now my sole purpose in life to find a way to save our Zach.

Dirk and I had decided it was best to wait until the end of the week to tell the kids Zach's tumor was cancerous. Dr. Grana had warned us to tell them before our visit to their clinic because it would be full of kids with no hair and brochures and posters with information about cancer. At a loss for an easy way to tell them, I decided to divide and conquer, telling Lexi first. Seeing an opportunity during her bath time, I told her I needed to talk to her about Zach. "Honey, the tumor they took out of Zach's head turned out to be cancer." I held my breath waiting for her reaction.

"I knew that, Mom," Lexi replied nonchalantly.

I was flabbergasted. This was not the reaction I had anticipated at all. "How did you know?" I asked.

"Dad told me in the car the other day. He said he bet the tumor would be cancer when they did the test on it, so I just figured it was," she replied.

"Well, because it is cancer, Zach will have to continue to get some treatments to try and get rid of it. They will do some radiation and chemotherapy for about a year. The doctor told us Zach should be able to go to school and play; he just may get a little more tired and feel sick to his stomach sometimes," I told her.

"OK. Can you read to me now?" she asked.

What a relief! She was usually very dramatic when hard news came, but she handled this beautifully. I admired her calm acceptance of this news. I would have to find a good time to tell Zach. Hopefully he would be able to take the news this well also.

Hoping to be able to focus on more research, I arranged another play date for Zach and his buddies. Lexi went over to a friend's house. As I worked on the computer, the boys sat talking quietly to each other. All at once they were all doubled over in laughter! I sat back and relished the moment. How many times in the past had I taken something so simple for granted? It was the most uplifting beautiful sound to me now. Zach's buddies were so wonderful to him. A brain tumor did not cloud their fun in the moment or their innocence about life. They were being silly like they always had been.

When the boys left, I had an opportunity to talk alone with Zach about his tumor. We decided to watch a movie, so we settled into the big chair, which still was serving as his bed at night. I grabbed his left hand and started to work it around like the occupational therapist had demonstrated. "Zach, you know we are going to the doctor's office tomorrow to get you checked out, right?"

"Yeah," he mumbled.

"We are going to see two doctors. First the one that did the surgery on your tumor. They will tell us if you can go outside and do more things. Then we are going to another doctor called an oncologist. They help kids with cancer," I said.

"Is that what I have?" he asked.

"That is what the doctors are telling us about your tumor. So we will have to have some more treatments to work on getting rid of it," I continued. "They will have to do a thing called radiation and give you some pills. It might make you a little tired, but you should still be able to go to school if you feel like it."

"Will I have to go in the hospital again?" he asked

"No, we will just go to a place for the radiation everyday for about thirty minutes. It will take a little longer the first couple of times as they get it set up."

"OK. What's for dinner?" he finished.

He did not seem upset by this news. Giving his hand a squeeze, I felt a sense of relief that I could be upfront with him now. He did not seem frightened about it, just concerned about the details of how it would affect his day-to-day activity. Again my anxiety of sharing the "C" word seemed to be unfounded.

Zach was getting better about taking his medicine, but it was still a challenge. He was not swallowing any pills, only taking things in a lique-fied form. It was very difficult to get him to take any medicine after he went to sleep. I had to wake him every night about 12:30 A.M. for his scheduled dose. He would cry and yell at me as I tried to get him to sit up and take his "squirts." It was very stressful for both of us. Feeling like an unrelent-ing slave driver, I hated putting him through any more stress, considering what he had already been through. It was becoming clear things were not going to be as easy as Dr. Grana had led us to believe.

From my research I knew Zach would have to swallow the chemo pills whole. They were too toxic to dissolve and squirt in. Reeling my mind back in, I reminded myself to just focus on today. Worrying about Zach taking chemo pills would be something for another day.

The end of the week came and we had to get up early for the follow-up doctor visits. Dirk was driving separately so he could go on to work after we were finished. Zach was concerned about needing to stop to go to the bathroom and losing Dirk in traffic. His urgency to pee had been bothering him for about four months. Puzzled by this during his last school year, I was beginning to wonder if it had anything to do with the brain tumor. We eliminated his concern by having an empty water bottle available for him to use. (The convenience of being a boy!) Tension left his face when he realized there would be no need for a frantic stop along the way; he had his own port-a-potty!

The visit with Dr. Storrs, the neurosurgeon, went very well. He was pleased with the incision and how it was healing. He checked Zach's reflexes and was very pleased with the improvements he saw. His left arm was still very limited in movement, but he was able to lift it parallel with the ground once again. Zach was released to do whatever he felt up to physically, but we were to be careful about him getting overheated, which could lead to seizures. Zach was excited to hear this news. Playing games and watching movies at home had lost their appeal to him.

Next we went downstairs to the oncologist's office. I was not sure what to expect. Based on Dr. Grana's description, I pictured a waiting room full of bald, sickly patients. Thankfully, that is not what we found. The waiting room was pleasantly painted with flowering vines and there were a few kids, but none that seemed too sick and none that were bald. Feeling insecure with my understanding and knowing Dirk's resistance, I was not sure if I would mention my research on radiation to Dr. Grana. She had explained in the hospital that a "tumor board" would be discussing Zach's case with a radiation oncologist during the week. Dirk and I were both anxious to get the treatment plan underway, knowing the aggressive nature of Zach's tumor. We did not want to give this thing any chance to start growing again. The sooner it could be nailed with treatments, the better.

Dr. Grana greeted us warmly. She examined Zach and questioned us about how the week had gone. Zach was very nervous about what they were going to do him, so when she asked if he thought it would be OK to draw some blood so they could test it, of course, he said no! She told us that because their group had not been able to meet to discuss Zach's case that week, we would need to come back next Friday, so the blood test could be postponed until then.

Grateful for her understanding, we sent Zach and Lexi to the lobby to play some video games, leaving Dirk and me to question Dr. Grana further. Knowing there was not a plan in place, I decided it was worth a shot to bring up my research. When I mentioned proton beam radiation she agreed it was a good option to consider. Explaining there were four types of radiation available—photon (conventional), proton, conformal (photon more directed) and IMRT—she agreed that proton radiation was the best at protecting healthy tissue. My heart was soaring! I was not crazy for looking into these things after all. Dirk leaned over and with a smile whispered, "I guess you were right; I was wrong."

Dr. Grana went on to explain that with radiation, you get one shot at it. The body can only tolerate a certain dosage before it becomes lethal. In Zach's case, he would need the full dose, which is six weeks, five days a week or thirty treatments. Once that was done, it would be detrimental to expose him to any more. With proton beam radiation, however, only the area being treated—not his entire head—would receive the maximum level. He could receive radiation in other areas in the future if needed. She also agreed the side effects of future cancer in the bones, nausea and fatigue were greatly lessened with this form of radiation.

Dirk and I were very encouraged by her words. Maybe this would be the key to Zach's survival! Because now we fully understood that we basically had only one shot at radiation, we had to get the best form possible. I explained the facility was near our parents' homes and we would have a lot of support in the area. She was all for it and agreed to call the facility to see if she could expedite the process. I told her the intake nurse had e-mailed me that Zach would be a viable candidate, but the doctor, Dr. Thornton, would need to examine him and his records to make sure this was a feasible alternative.

Feeling we had made real progress, my optimism grew as we left. Zach and Lexi were excited with our newfound freedom to get out and have fun! Not wasting any time, I called Midwest Proton Radiation Institute (MPRI) while we were on our way to meet some friends for a movie. Explaining our situation to the intake nurse, she agreed Dr. Thornton would speak with Dr. Grana after reviewing Zach's MRI scan that I was sending them. I could hardly contain my excitement. This just had to be the answer. If this radiation could be directed so precisely, it must be much more effective. Radiation was obviously the key to controlling this tumor.

Thank You, God, for leading me to pursue this treatment!

We had a great afternoon of movies and bowling. Zach climbed into my lap as usual during the movie. Although he was getting a bit big to fit comfortably, having him in my arms felt like heaven. The stress of the week caught up with me as I fought to keep my eyes open during the movie. Crashing pins and bright lights solved this problem at the bowling alley. Zach loved bowling and did quite well using his natural athletic ability and strong determination to compensate for his limp left arm.

With a renewed sense of purpose, my goal was to have a treatment plan in place by the end of the next week. Based on the amount of time it was taking to research treatments and manage Zach's schedule, it was becoming clear to me that I would no longer be able to work full-time. We had enough savings to make it for at least six months without my income. Perhaps when we finished the radiation portion of Zach's treatment and things got into more of a routine, I could do some work from home, but it did not seem feasible to commute over an hour away from Zach for any type of work. Being available for him was now my top priority. Accepting the realities of this hideous tumor, spending time on anything other than Zach made no sense.

God, I pray we can beat these odds. Please let us be the ones to find a path to a more effective treatment plan.

That evening we continued to enjoy our freedom from home by attending a professional baseball game. Lexi had gratefully accepted an invitation to spend the weekend at the beach with some close friends. It was a relief to know she was getting a break. Our new routine had been very hard on her. While Zach's strength and courage had been amazing since his diagnosis, I could tell his confidence was shaken. Earlier in the day, a friend had asked him over to play. Normally he would have jumped at the chance, but Dirk and I had to do quite a bit of coaxing to get him to agree to an hour-long visit.

Since Lexi was with her friends, we had an extra ticket for the game and I offered to have one of his friends join us. His uncharacteristic answer melted my heart. "Sorry Mom, but I just want to go with you." He didn't want to hurt our feelings, but the thought of entertaining a friend seemed to overwhelm him.

As we drove to the game, we tried to get him to open up by asking if he had any questions about all that had happened to him. A shrug and shake of his head were all we got. Prompting him did not work either. It was like pulling teeth to get him to talk. We were left to wonder what thoughts were bouncing around in his head. We emphasized that if he ever had any questions we would try to answer them the best we could.

The three of us enjoyed the baseball game. I took Zach's medicine along and gave it to him as we sat and watched. He was getting better about taking it. His determination and willfulness to comply with all that was demanded of him made me ache inside. This was not how life was supposed to be. All of the innocence of being eight was being stripped from him by this disease. Why should an eight-year-old have to deal with such a harsh and bitter world so early? If only I could switch places with him—anything to take this away from him. With Zach's incision site in plain view, it was impossible to pretend we were a normal family out for a game. Everything changes when you are the family with the issues. This was never supposed to be us. How could life change so drastically and permanently?

We had a great time watching the Tampa team win. The change of scenery was good for all of us. Going to church together the next day held new meaning to Dirk and me. Cradling Zach in my arms as he dozed off, Dirk and I listened carefully to the message about how to witness your faith to others, something that had become very real to Dirk over the last couple of weeks. I thought of Dirk's dramatic change again—to that day he surrendered.

As tears formed in my eyes, I thought of our neighbor's description of finding Dirk wandering aimlessly and sobbing in our driveway after he had drained all the alcohol, crying out to God for forgiveness. And how from that point on his heart had changed. He was on fire for God and knew our answer laid in our faith. He was pouring himself into studying the Word and witnessing to as many people as he could. He felt Zach was a tool, a special messenger, sent from God as a wake-up call to all of us to connect or reconnect to God, since tomorrow holds no guarantees. How true we had found this to be!

After church we decided to get some of Zach's friends together and go bowling again. Zach did not get to have the birthday party he had planned, so we thought this would at least give him a little bit of what he missed. They all had a blast, eating pizza, bowling and playing air hockey. Zach's competitive nature was still going strong as he bowled. He was determined to beat all of his friends even though his left arm was no help. It was good to see him playing and enjoying the fun of friends. Being able to devote all of our attention to Zach the entire weekend without feeling the guilt of neglecting Lexi was a priceless gift. We all needed it.

Beginning to feel very guilty for neglecting my job for nearly three weeks, I had decided to try to stop by Hall Printworks to touch base when Monday rolled around. Zach would come with me and then we would go out to the beach and pick up Lexi. Being around a bunch of girls and riding in the car to my office was not Zach's idea of fun.

Lexi called before we started toward my work and asked us to come directly to the beach instead. Zach was hesitant, but Lexi talked him into it by promising that his buddy Jake was going to come too. We headed to the beach. Our visit to Hall Printworks could wait for another day.

The weather was beautiful—a bit warm, but a nice breeze. Zach went in the water with me soon after we arrived. Tanned and giggling, Lexi and her friends, Amanda and Alex, had become quite comfortable living as "beach bums." Amanda's younger sister, Ashley, was excited to have Zach there. Having known each other since they were toddlers, she was very concerned for and protective of Zach.

Zach became very shy and asked to stay in the condo for awhile when Jake arrived. It wasn't long until he decided I was not the best play partner so he joined Jake and Ashley in the pool. Staying very close to him as they played, I loved seeing him laugh and be silly with them. The awkwardness Zach had felt earlier melted away once his infectious belly laughs started and they saw he was the same silly Zach they knew and loved.

The afternoon breezes picked up and we went back down to the beach. Ashley, Jake and Zach started playing a game of who could look the silliest running from the water to our chairs. Zach was laughing so hard he could hardly catch his breath. I wanted to freeze that moment and live in it forever. It was complete childhood innocence in its most pure form. If only I had brought my video camera. As their game continued, I noticed two teenage boys jogging by. My gaze followed them down the beach. My heart ached as I wondered if Zach would see that age. I always had pictured Zach maturing into a very handsome boy, with a tan muscular body that moved effortlessly—someone the girls would be crazy over and the boys would love to have as a friend.

God, how can this not be? I pray we see this day, what a miracle we will rejoice in if Zach is able to experience his teenage years.

The allure of the beach was too great, making Lexi decide to stay another day. Zach and I had dinner with everyone and left before the meal was over because he was tired and it was time for his medicine. He crashed in the car as we drove home. The day had been priceless, but the reality of everything slapped me in the face the more I drove. I was no closer to having a treatment plan. Planting myself in front of the computer tomorrow was my number one priority. It had become clear after our conversation with the doctor about proton radiation that she was not necessarily going to volunteer information about other facilities. Digging deeper into the treatment protocols was going to be up to me. Dirk and I continued to share a sense of urgency to get something started to kill this ugly beast that was trying to overtake Zach.

My determination was very focused the next morning. My heart sank when I spoke with the administrator of MPRI. He informed me set-up alone would take close to a month because of all the detailed planning needed. Yikes! This seemed way too long to wait for radiation. Next, I called a friend of a friend who had recently lost his son to a brain tumor. He was so gracious to speak with me so close to his son's death. He reinforced Dr. Storrs' sentiment of not getting caught up in the odds. His son was given a summer to live and ended up surviving eleven years cancer-free after his initial treatment. To be given this amount of time would be absolutely glorious for Zach. They had worked with doctors at Duke University. I called Duke, and the doctor he recommended was on vacation. I was given an e-mail address to send a message to him.

I then e-mailed St. Jude's Children's Hospital, asking for their proposed treatment plan and their thoughts on proton beam radiation. Anxiety and tension filled my shoulders as my search continued. My mind was overwhelmed with statistics, protocols and words that were foreign to me.

Morning had faded into afternoon when I received a call from the program coordinator at St. Jude's. She said that Zach was a candidate for some clinical trials they had underway. I spoke with one of their doctors about the trial. It was a Phase 1 trial with a new drug called Terceva. His English was very broken, making the conversation difficult to follow and understand. He had just started the trial in March of 2005 and had four participants. They were trying to determine the appropriate dose for this drug with children. It had shown some "statistical significance" in use with adults. When I questioned him about proton beam radiation, he was quick to let me know it was not his choice for GBMs because he felt it was too focal. More confused than ever, I thanked him and told him I would get back to them. *Now what?* Just when I thought we had the answer with radiation, I was beginning to wonder if it really was the way to go.

The weight of this decision was pressing down on me. This was the most important decision we had to make so far in our lives. How do you know what is best to save the life of your child? My ear was hurting from being on the phone so much. What if the St. Jude doctor was correct about the proton beam? Because we had been told a GBM spreads through brain matter like fingers, it would make sense that a focused beam might miss some of the cancer.

My stomach was in knots. Lexi had come home from the beach and Zach had a friend in to play. Trying to clear my head and loosen my very tense neck muscles, I walked out into the oppressive Florida heat. My friend Jenny was walking by. She is a television news reporter and I remembered she had visited St. Jude's, so I questioned her about her trip. She had nothing but praise for them. It was all so confusing.

When Dirk came home and we sat down to eat dinner together, I started bombarding him with all the information I had gathered. Overwhelmed with the dizzying array of options I had shared, we both had unsettled stomachs but no resolution about what to do.

Surprisingly, my information gathering was not over. Dr. Thornton with MPRI called near 8 p.m. Impressed by his obvious dedication, I listened as he began to explain his review of Zach's MRI scans and why he felt Zach would be a perfect candidate for proton beam radiation. His calm deliberate explanation of the process put me at ease. Confident he could help Zach, he also praised Dr. Grana and the neurosurgeons on a job well done with Zach's surgery. He said it was clear the surgeons had carefully selected a path that would cause the least damage and had done a wonderful job removing the tumor.

When I asked about the set-up time and the hesitation of the doctor from St. Jude's in regard to focal radiation, he informed me that usually there was a three- to six-month wait for patients to receive their treatments. But he added that they just happened to have a spot open up for a pediatric case and could start on Zach as soon as he had an initial evaluation. He explained that since the proton beam was not available in many locations, many oncologists were not aware of the procedures and coverage of the beam. He felt this form of radiation was perfect for this type of tumor. It would take a few weeks to set up, but we would still fall into the six- to eight-week post-surgery window recommended for radiation therapy.

A sense of peace filled my body as my heart told me this was the path God wanted us to take. There were too many things falling into place for it not to be. To reassure myself, I called a doctor in Indiana who was a friend of my parents to find out her opinion of MPRI and Dr. Thornton. She confirmed my thoughts and agreed it seemed clear that with everything working out in our favor the way they had, this was from God and meant to be. She added that she had heard nothing but positive things about the facility and Dr. Thornton.

Finally a plan was in place! Relief flooded over Dirk and me as we both agreed a trip to Indiana for treatment made sense in many ways. We could work out the details tomorrow. One big detail I had put off too long was my job. We decided Dirk would stay with the kids the next day and I would go in to tie up some loose ends. The weight from my shoulders was gone as I lay down to sleep.

Carefully, I laid out all Zach's medicine and a time schedule to follow for Dirk the next morning. I had been diligent in documenting the size of each dose and the time it was taken for future reference.

The hour-long commute that had become so routine and burdensome was now very different to me in this new reality we were living. My mind got lost in endless thoughts of the past two weeks and how many times I would be relaying the story over the next few hours. I did not want to become emotional, but I did not know how I could escape the emotions. They were too close to the surface, too raw. Realizing this would probably be my last trip in as an employee, I knew it would be hard to say good-bye to my coworkers, many of whom had become close friends. It certainly was not how I expected this job to end.

Hoping to slip into my office quickly and unnoticed, I arrived early and was relieved to be greeted with silence. I had started this job a couple of years prior, when Dirk and I decided the kids were old enough for me to reenter the work force. The Halls had been very flexible with me, letting me start on a part-time basis. As with most accounting positions, the work soon made it a full-time position. We had developed a great relationship that had grown into a wonderful friendship as well. They had generously been paying my salary for the last three weeks even though I had obviously not been able to perform any of my duties.

PB, the company president, arrived soon after me and came to my office. After filling her in on Zach's current status, she told me to keep my door closed so I would not be interrupted in my work. I was greatly relieved to do that so I could focus and review the current status of their financial picture.

Before I dove into the numbers, I phoned MPRI to make an appointment for Zach's evaluation. They had an opening for Friday. After a few calls to Dirk, Zach and I were scheduled to fly to Indiana one way. We were hoping to stay and get the treatments started right away.

I had maintained my emotions fairly well as long as I stayed focused on the numbers. As the afternoon progressed, I met with all three owners, Bob, PB and George, to bring them up to date on their financial standing. We discussed my trip to Indiana and I warned them I could be gone as long as three months. They still were toying with the idea of my working from home and then coming back full-time after Zach and I returned.

Not wanting to mislead them, I told them I did not feel I would be able to be so far away from home with Zach's illness, and to emphasize the point I blurted out, "Most of the information is saying patients with this type of tumor have about fourteen months." The number seemed to bounce off the walls as the ugly truth sank into their minds. I had not been brave enough to share this statistic with anyone up to this point. The look on their faces let me know they understood it was very unlikely I would be coming back.

After I had gathered all my personal things in a box, I walked through the shop and said good-bye to everyone. I received many sympathetic hugs and noticed looks of concern on their faces as tears slipped from my eyes. Many said they just didn't know what to say. What can anyone say? Words seemed very cheap and empty in this type of situation. Relieved to have this detail behind me, I was anxious to get back home and lay my eyes on Zach. This was the longest I had been away from him since the day he was diagnosed.

Emotionally drained as I made the long trek home, the enormity and uncertainty of what we were facing came crashing down around me. *Lord, if You are trying to get our attention, You have it! I just ask for a miracle; this world needs Zachary; we need Zachary. Please make this all go away!*

Tears spilled down my cheeks as the overwhelming sense of fear and loss of control consumed me. I would have to face this challenge one step at a time, one day at a time. *Be thankful for every day, every moment, Sherry,* I told myself. One day at a time. I could not let my thoughts wander too far ahead because that was when all the negative questions would start chipping away at my hope.

My mind shifted into overdrive as I realized all that had to be accomplished before we left for Indiana. Dirk had let the kids know Zach and I would be going to Indiana. Concerned I would not be with her for the start of her sixth-grade year or her birthday sleepover, Lexi had become upset. There were no easy explanations to give her. Life was not going to be easy for any of us. The unfairness of everything welled up in me. I wanted to scream and break something, but I pushed the emotions away. I knew the best thing for everyone was to appear calm and collected. I had convinced myself we would all get through this.

The rest of my time was spent frantically trying to tie up loose ends around the house. I reshuffled our budget to account for my loss of income. The numbers indicated we would be fine at least until the end of the year. Having equity in our house, I knew we could refinance if we needed funds for the radiation treatments. Our parents had assured us they would be willing to help if we needed it.

With school scheduled to start in two weeks, we needed to get Zach's schoolwork coordinated. Zach was excited to find out his two good friends, Curren and Connor, were in his class. Mrs. Sapp, his teacher, and all the administrative staff were extremely supportive. It was difficult for me to keep my emotions controlled as I recounted the last three weeks of our lives and the plan for Indiana. We left with an armload of textbooks and assurance they would do whatever we needed to keep Zach on schedule.

Then it was on to the toy store. In an effort to cheer Lexi's spirits, we had told her she could pick out her birthday present early. She and I were able to talk more about her feelings. I told her it was important to share her concerns with us so we could help her. She said she was afraid to cry because she knew Zach was really sick and she should not be feeling sorry for herself. Hugging her, I told her to cry whenever she felt like it and reminded her nothing was her fault. It all was unfair to everyone.

That evening, while Zach stayed with Allie, his favorite babysitter, Dirk and I took Lexi to orientation night at the middle school. Thankfully, I could meet her teachers and fill them in on what she was facing at home before I left. Middle school intrigued Lexi and scared me. She was a leader and knew right from wrong. I knew she would be OK, but I remembered how big a change middle school was for me. It troubled me to know I would not be there to support her when she started this new adventure. Supportive and anxious to help, Lexi's teachers assured us they would cooperate fully as we explained Zach's treatment plan. Lexi was relieved to see many familiar friends would be in her homeroom.

Time kept slipping away and before I knew it I was packing in the early morning hours. How to pack for an unknown amount of time was very difficult. Knowing Dirk and Lexi would be coming up to see us in a couple of weeks if we stayed, I managed not to take my entire closet. Trying to simplify as much as possible, I had made a bill-paying schedule for Dirk to follow while we were gone. Burdening him on top of his job was the last thing I wanted to do, so I tried to take as much as I could with me. We finally closed the last suitcase. As my head hit the pillow, I felt the weariness of the week deep in my bones. Although relieved we had accomplished the goal of getting Zach's treatment plan rolling, fear began to creep into my mind. What would be waiting for us in Indiana? Would they agree to treat him? Was this the answer to Zach being healed? I had to stop my racing mind and get some sleep. More tears rolled silently down my face as I tried to quiet my thoughts and build my faith that everything would be OK.

Reflections

In a matter of three short weeks, our priorities, our dreams, our lives had been shattered. Suddenly, the precious moments laughter, hugs and love brought were no longer ignored or taken for granted. We were walking in a wilderness so thick we dared not to look further ahead than the present day. Maneuvering the complicated maze cancer had brought into our lives proved frustrating and difficult. The only consistent truth we could find was that no matter what we were facing, drawing closer to God was giving us strength and hope with each new day.

The panic that had consumed my mind during the initial week in the hospital had evolved into a quest for knowledge and understanding. Training my mind to accept the path we were now walking was a constant battle, but I was finding, through Dirk's encouragement to pray, a peace I so desperately needed.

Wanting God to show up in a big way, I was focusing my prayer on a miracle—the kind that causes doctors to throw their hands up in the air and shrug their shoulders—a complete healing for Zach. But God's timing is perfect, and as I would learn over and over, His schedule did not necessarily correspond to mine. He was working miracles for us. They were all around us every day in the hearts and minds of our families, friends and even strangers that heard of our brave Zachary. Lives were being changed, priorities examined, appreciation of a basic normal day was not being forgotten any longer.

The lesson learned: Life is about vision. Are your eyes looking for God each and every day? Nothing happens by chance. There is purpose to every joy and sorrow we experience. It is up to us to find the purpose God has placed within each experience and allow our hearts to grow new dreams when old ones are shattered. Will we open our eyes and seek out His miracles that surround us?

God is grooming us for eternity with all the life experiences we face. It is our choice how we face these moments—with love and growth or defiance and anger. It is His desire to see our character mature and grow no matter what the circumstance.

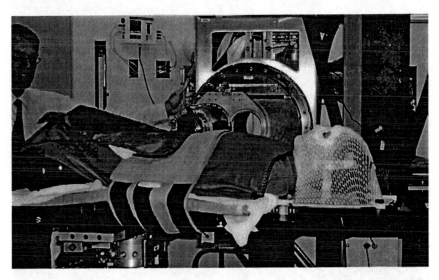

AUGUST 2005—Zach covered with his favorite blanket on his first day of proton radiation treatment. I felt completely helpless for him. He did not move or complain during any of the thirty-three treatments he received.

At my parents' home in September 2005 – Zach and Lexi playing with the bike from the physical therapy center while my dad watches. Zach loved to chase Lexi and try to bump her with the handle on the front of the bike!

A happy time in Indiana – celebrating Dirk's birthday soon after Zach's radiation treatments had started. Lexi made the cake for Dirk.

CHAPTER FIVE

Looking
for Faith

A nticipation mixed with fear created a large knot in my stomach as we made our way to the airport. Zach's sweaty palms let me know he was nervous as well. Fighting the morning rush hour traffic was a challenge for Dirk's patience and did not help our mental state. After saying a tearful good-bye to Dirk, Zach and I were able to relax once we had made our way to our gate.

"Hey Buddy, what do you think about going to Indiana? Are you excited?" I asked.

"Yeah," he replied.

"Do you have any questions about our trip? You know why we are going, right?"

"I think I do. Will I have to go to a hospital or have another MRI?" he questioned.

"No, no. We are just going to get you checked out to see if they can do the radiation at a place called MPRI. We will be staying with Grammy and Papaw and seeing Grandma, Grandpa and all your aunts, uncles and cousins. Won't it be good to see everyone?" I continued.

"Yeah," he said with a smile. He and Lexi always loved going to Indiana. Most of our extended family lived in Spencer, where Dirk and I grew up.

"Do you have any more questions?" I asked.

"No," he replied as he snuggled his head on my shoulder and relaxed. His lack of questions worried me. What if I was not telling him enough? If only I could read his mind. I didn't want to give him more information than he could handle or tell him something that would take any of his optimistic hope away. Hope was all we had at this point, and we knew it was a key ingredient to Zach's survival.

We arrived at Indianapolis ahead of schedule and went to the baggage claim area. I had expected to see my parents waiting for us there. But since we were early, I figured they would arrive after we got our luggage. Our luggage came but they did not show up. Alarmed because they had never been late to pick us up, I tried their cell phones. Both went to voice mail. Zach was looking around and asking me where they were. Hoping they had missed us upstairs, I had them paged. No response. Fear of a car accident began to consume my thoughts. I tried their cell phones again. Voice mail again.

Smiling nervously, I looked at Zach only to find his questioning eyes looking back at me. Pictures of them lying bloody in a ditch flashed through my mind as tears began to fill my eyes. Panic set in after I called my sister to confirm that they had left on time to pick us up.

I hugged Zach and explained I was confused why Grammy and Papaw were not there to pick us up. I went back and had them paged again. No response. Where could they be?

God, I am trying to be strong with Zach, but I don't think I can handle any more. I need my parents. Please let them be safe.

Concerned we would be late for our appointment, and with my mind beginning to spin, I contemplated renting a car. Just as I got ready to approach the rental desk, I heard Zach exclaim, "There he is! Hi, Papaw!"

I spun around and saw my dad walking quickly toward us. Relief engulfed me like a warm blanket. I ran up to him and hugged him. Sobbing on his shoulder, I told him I thought they had been in an accident. Crushed they had worried us, he explained they had been waiting upstairs and realized the arrival board had to be wrong. It had said our flight was unloading when we were actually downstairs getting our luggage. They had not heard the pages and had left their cell phones in the car. What a way to start our trip to Indiana!

We all calmed down and headed south to Bloomington. The experience made me realize that even though things might seem very bad in the present, they could be much worse at a moment's notice. Trying to accommodate Zach's unending appetite, we stopped for lunch and watched him devour a large plate of chicken legs and macaroni and cheese. The six pounds he had gained since starting steroids was beginning to show in his cheeks and belly. Knowing his appetite would not always be strong, I did not mind seeing him bulk up while he could.

When we arrived at the MPRI facility with my parents, I thought about how ironic it was that a place I had passed thousands of times without knowing its purpose was suddenly the central focus of our lives. The facility was located on the campus of Indiana University, my alma mater. I had earned my Bachelor of Science in Business degree from IU in 1987. At that time, there was only a cyclotron research facility nestled back in the rolling hills across from the football stadium.

I found out later from Dr. Thornton that when the Clinton administration cut funding for atomic research in the late 90s, the cyclotron lost its usefulness. But the president of the university, Miles Brandt, knew a similar cyclotron in Boston had been used for proton beam radiation. In order to utilize the cyclotron, he went to Boston and recruited Dr. Thornton, with the promise of building him a proton beam radiation facility to his specifications. I hoped his foresight would lead to a cure for Zach.

The receptionist directed us to the seating area. The part of the building that housed the radiation center was new. It was nicely decorated and had a children's play area next to the main lobby. Exploring the children's room, we discovered the place was so new there were no toys or other playthings on the many shelves in the room.

We had been there about thirty minutes when I noticed a man walking quickly toward us. I recognized his voice immediately when he introduced himself as Dr. Thornton. He had very kind eyes and a big smile as he spoke to Zach. Bored with the lack of entertainment, Zach was less than enthusiastic in his response to the doctor. Apologizing for the wait, he explained his intake nurse and another staff member had both had babies within the last week, causing the office to be shorthanded. He would be performing Zach's initial checkup himself.

My parents, Zach and I followed him down a long hallway. The wall to our right was covered in varying shades of brown and tan rough sandstone. Leading us into an exam room, he began to explain the history of MPRI and how he had arrived in Bloomington, Indiana. Since he had grown up in the East, he worked at Boston General after graduating from medical school. Patients with tumors near or around the sinus or eye were his specialty. But because of his frustration with the imprecise nature of conventional radiation, and the fact that it often did more harm than good—causing blindness, mental impairment or even death—he received training with proton radiation and was eventually recruited to Bloomington.

He continued to explain that the advantage of using a proton beam over conventional radiation was that the proton beam could be programmed to stop at a specific point. Holding up a clear plastic brick with a transparent, inch-thick gold beam that ran halfway through the brick, he explained it was a visual of a captured proton beam. Explaining further, he said that in conventional radiation, the bulk of the radiation is deposited when it first enters the head near the skull. But with proton beam, the largest deposit is made where the beam ends, which should be in the tumor site.

His passion and ability to speak in a manner we could easily understand solidified my confidence in using the MPRI facility for Zach's treatment. Agitated with the amount of time the appointment was taking, Zach began to sigh and fidget, hoping we would soon end our conversation. Trying to pacify him a little longer, I fished through my bag and found an electronic game for him to play.

Our education continued as Dr. Thornton pulled up Zach's MRI scans on two computers and explained each slide to us, comparing the pre- and post-surgery scans. Viewing the scans with his guidance was priceless to me. It was what I had wanted to see before Zach had his surgery. Using his notes from a lecture he had given about a similar case, he pulled up a slide on his computer to show us how the radiation would treat the entire right side of Zach's frontal lobe. The technology would also allow them to intensify the treatment around the tumor bed and any other areas of concern.

Noticing Zach was busy with his game, I asked Dr. Thornton for his guess of Zach's prognosis. Noting the difficult nature of the tumor and that he had never been able to cure an adult, he indicated thirty-six months was a possibility. Not a cure, but at least it was more than the fourteen months I had found in my research on the internet.

Realizing Zach had hit his limit, Dr. Thornton began his examination. He performed the same tests we had seen in Florida, but he also looked deep into Zach's eyes with a light-magnifying scope, explaining that he could tell if there was swelling in Zach's brain by looking at the sharpness of a lens in his eye.

After he completed his exam, he took us down the hall to see the rest of the facility. Entering a room with a CT scan machine, we noticed on the shelves behind the machine many molds of different body parts that had been made with a hard white plastic mesh. Showing us one made for the head, he explained Zach would have a similar mold made of his face that would hold his head stationary during treatment. Horrified at the thought of this, I tried to lighten the mood. "Wow, Zach, it looks kind of like a hockey goalie mask, doesn't it? You will get your very own. What do you think about that?"

Smiling uneasily, he shrugged his shoulders and looked down, obviously feeling uncomfortable with the prospect of what was to come.

As the doctor and I continued to talk, Zach began tugging on my hand—he was ready to leave. Wrapping things up, we were told to come back in one week to make his mask and then Zach could start his treatment on August 24th, almost a month away. Knowing the aggressive nature of

Zach's tumor, I tried to get a closer date, but was told the team needed time to do the appropriate planning and programming for his specific treatment. It would test my patience, but I knew this still was within the six- to eight-week window suggested for radiation to begin after surgery.

A sense of peace settled over me after the appointment. We headed to a miniature golf course—Zach's reward for enduring the marathon appointment—and had an especially good time. Laughing like a maniac at anything and everything, his silliness filled my heart with joy. Partially steroid induced, his laughter seemed much more spontaneous and his eyes seemed to twinkle brighter than ever since his diagnosis. His unrestrained excitement was contagious. Appreciation of these simple moments had taken on a whole new meaning in the last two weeks.

Later that evening after Zach was in bed, I sat down with my mom to talk. Feeling helpless to do anything for Zach or for me, it was killing her to watch Zach suffer, but she was also concerned for me. I was her child and she wanted to help me but didn't know what to do. The helpless feeling was magnified in my heart every time I looked into Zach's eyes. Why couldn't it have been me? I just wanted to have it all come into me and give Zach his life back. He had so much to do and see. He was just beginning his journey. Feeling tears well in my eyes, I looked at Mom and just shrugged my shoulders, not knowing how to respond.

As I woke the next morning, I was thankful the night medicines were ending. Zach had become so angry when I woke him to take his medicine. Still semi-sleeping as I tried to sit him up, he looked at me with so much anger in his eyes and shook his finger very forcefully in my face while saying, "No, no, no!" After about ten or fifteen minutes of coaxing, I had been able to squirt the medication into his mouth and the torture ended. It was wearing on my emotions to do this to Zach. I wanted to be only a source of love and comfort to him. It felt wrong to have to administer medicines and be firm with him, but I knew it was only beginning. I would have to dig deep to find the resolve to stay on schedule. Zach was counting on me.

Zach was still sleeping when I noticed his left hand moving freely as it had before the tumor. Smiling in hopes this meant he would soon regain the use of his hand, I remembered how he had not even tried to use it during miniature golf the day before. I kept trying to remind him to use both hands, but he just became frustrated with it and used only his right hand.

Anxious to hit the running trail to clear my head, I slipped on my running clothes after Zach had his breakfast. He protested my plan as he realized I would be away from his side. Using food as a lure, Grammy promised to take him to the grocery store for some snacks while I ran and then pick me up on their way home. She dropped me off at McCormick's Creek State Park, which was only a mile from her house, at a trail she frequently walked.

Growing up in Spencer, I had many fond memories of McCormick's Creek Park. The park was founded in 1916 by the State of Indiana. Filled with ravines and forest, it is located on the east bank of the White River. Centered around a mile-long canyon as much as one hundred feet deep in parts, the creek winds its way through the canyon, and along the way contains some beautiful waterfalls. Entering the park gate and driving the roads under the forest canopy, I had always felt a great sense of peace. Being in nature brought a sense of calm to my mind.

As I ran the first lap, my thoughts were scattered and filled with fear for Zach and our family. The unfamiliarity of the trail made it seem difficult. My feet felt like lead weights and I could barely put one leg in front of the other as I faced a large hill.

After the first lap, I felt my mind clearing and my energy rise. Attacking the hills instead of dreading them, my thoughts turned more positive. Realizing it was my choice which thoughts to embrace, it became clear how much each day with our loved ones was such a gift that should be enjoyed to the fullest extent possible. The trail seemed to symbolize the path we were about to travel. The hills represented all the challenges that we would face. Some were big and some small. Some long and some short, but each hill had a summit and a downside. The downsides represented the good times to me, when everything was going right. As I ran down I threw my arms out wide and ran as fast as I could. The breeze in my face and speed felt exhilarating and a little out of control. I realized through it all my faith in God was the key—believing in what was unseen and unknown with all of my heart.

Ahead of me, I saw a man who looked to be in his eighties. His legs were bowed with age and he struggled to walk the trail with a cane. Stopping to watch me as I approached, he smiled and said, "I wish I could do that!" Returning the smile, I laughed. He inspired me even more. His determination was a clear message to never give up no matter how slow or hard the battle. Push forward, keep going.

As I approached the end of the second lap, I felt I could run a marathon. With no sign of Zach and my mom waiting for me, I went for a third lap. Determination grew with each step. I decided if Zach could deal with the physical challenges, the least I could do was be his advocate and make sure he had the best treatments available. Laughter and joy would fill as many days as the treatment would allow. There would be bumps in the road, but our end goal would not change: to find a cure for Zach.

As I came to the end of the third lap, I felt renewed and ready for what lay ahead. Although it had not been an audible conversation, it was clear to me God had been speaking to my heart as I had allowed my mind to open to Him. Hands on my hips, sweat pouring down my body, I saw Mom's shiny white Cadillac pull into view. Zach was grinning from ear to ear as he explained all the good snacks they had found in town. Life was good, at least for the moment. This moment, this day was what mattered. Worry about the future had left me.

We faced an open week before getting back to the reality of treatments. Everyone was anxious to entertain Zach in a variety of ways. Content to hang around my parents' house, he shied away from being around crowds or doing unfamiliar things. He was still adjusting to his new reality. It had been less than two months since our previous visit to Indiana. On that trip, Zach discovered a love for playing croquet on a course in my parents' yard. After challenging everyone to play, he would compete against himself if there were no more opponents. I remembered watching him through the window then, smiling to myself at his intensity as he played the course over and over. Having a brain tumor had not changed his competitive spirit.

Now he just played with his right hand and quickly became as good as he had been with both hands.

I stayed up journaling or reading after Zach fell asleep most nights. It was my time to reflect on how life had taken a sudden turn on us. Neither my family nor Dirk's family had ever experienced anything that even came close to this. It still did not seem real—I was not sure it ever would. I now knew cancer could come out of the dark and rip your heart right out of your chest. It was real—it was not just something you heard sad stories about, sympathize and go on. When it strikes, you had no choice but to strike back.

In my reading I had found a great story to share with Dirk so he could understand my need to make sure we were getting the best treatment for Zach. It was a story of a man caught in a flood. He climbs to his roof and prays to God for help. As he sits praying, believing God would miraculously save him, a man in a boat comes by and asks him to climb aboard. The man says, "No, my Lord will save me." He continues to pray and soon a helicopter comes by and drops a rope ladder to him. Again the man says, "No, my Lord will save me." Eventually the flood waters rise and the man is washed away and drowns. When he finds himself standing in heaven, he asks God, "Why didn't you save me when I asked?" God replies, "I sent a boat and a helicopter. What more could I do?" Dirk loved this story when I shared it with him. It gave us the confidence to keep pushing forward and know God's help could come in many ways.

Wanting to make sure there were no barriers to Zach receiving the proton treatment, I discussed the cost and insurance issues of the treatment with MPRI's chief financial officer. Based on an earlier conversation with our insurance company, I was not sure if the treatment would be covered. Assuring me treatment would not be delayed due to a financial issue, I was told the cost of the entire thirty treatments would be $110,000 if the insurance refused payment—an amount I felt we could manage by refinancing the house if needed.

Next on my agenda was calling Dr. Grana to relay the information I had gotten from Dr. Thornton. When I reached her, she seemed a bit distracted and rushed. As I explained the schedule to her, she agreed she would manage the chemotherapy aspect of Zach's treatment. Concerned about feeding Zach food that would help his body battle the disease, I asked about Zach's diet. She assured me it would be fine to let him eat whatever he felt like eating. And she indicated the chemo would start after he received his first radiation treatment, causing her to emphasize that Zach would have to learn to swallow pills. When Zach and I returned to Florida the next week, we would visit her office for further instructions.

Being able to give Zach my complete attention while we were with my parents was a precious gift to both him and me. Leaving the heat and humidity of Florida behind, we were able to enjoy many hours together outside. One activity that held many memories for me was catching lightning bugs. Scurrying and giggling from one flashing light to the next, Zach and I filled a glass jar with the glowing wonders.

One evening, there was a bunny hopping through the neighbor's yard. I watched as Zach slowly crept up behind it. Getting within two or three steps from it, he looked back at me with his finger to his lips telling me to be quiet. Soon it hopped a few feet farther and Zach followed. These things that were so normal a month ago had become magical to me. I wanted to capture everything in my head, never to let it escape. Snapping photos to freeze the magic, I wanted to document as much as I could. These images were priceless.

As the week slowly crept by, we continued to entertain Zach with bowling, croquet and a new pastime he discovered, playing the claw machine. He had played these machines before on occasion, but now whenever he saw one he studied the stuffed animals carefully to determine if there were any easy targets. It sometimes took a couple of tries, but more times than not, he would snag his target with a proud grin on his face. He managed to clean out my supply of quarters within a few days!

As much as I was enjoying my time with Zach, my heart was aching for Dirk and Lexi. Thanks to the help of many friends, Dirk had managed to juggle his hectic work schedule and Lexi's care in the last few days of summer break. Now the real test had arrived, getting her off to her first day of middle school. Calling to check on their progress before she left for school, I discovered how excited Lexi was as we discussed her morning. I reviewed with her my mental checklist of things she should have done—brush teeth, breakfast, made her bed. She had done them all. Feeling her nervous anticipation of starting a new adventure, I told her I was very proud of her and reminded her to call me when she came home that afternoon. Frustration overwhelmed me as I hung up the phone. My heart was torn that I could not be there to give her a hug before she left.

Later that morning, Zach and I met a high school friend of mine, Becky, and her son Sash. During our June visit, we had joined her family in a five-kilometer run. Showing his competitive spirit, Zach had amazed Becky at the end of the run with his determination to be the first one in their group to cross the finish line. That was Zach—always doing his best and letting his competitive drive fuel his energy.

Her eyes reflected the bewilderment my mind felt as I explained how quickly our life had changed since our last visit.

After lunch we took the boys to the local YMCA. It was a relatively new facility for Spencer and had many nice amenities. Hoping to get Zach in the pool with me, I wanted to see how well he could move his left arm in the water. I was concerned with it becoming stiff and weak from lack of use. Zach was hesitant to swim, so we watched as he and Sash played ping-pong. Laughter filled the room as they tried to volley the ball to each other.

Basketball was Zach's next request. He loved shooting hoops and had developed a great shot. My heart broke as I watched him struggle with his shot now. Working hard to make his left hand cooperate, he laughed at himself as his shot missed the entire backboard. Not to be deterred, he started shooting one-handed. Giggling, dribbling and running with Sash, he stumbled—and my heart stopped.

"Zach, slow down. Remember Dr. Storrs told you not to get overheated," I yelled.

Tossing me the ball, he answered, "Mom, pass me the ball for a layup."

As he ran toward the basket, he lost his balance and fell hard. Unable to break his fall because of his weak left arm, he fell headfirst to the floor with a loud thump.

Panic filled my body as I ran to his side. "Zach, are you OK?"

Rubbing his head as I pulled him to a sitting position, he giggled at himself.

"I think we need to find something else to do for awhile," I said, relieved he seemed to be OK.

After resting for a moment, Zach was ready for more. We headed upstairs to the indoor track. Sash loved running around the track and timing himself against a big digital clock on the wall. After Sash did it, of course Zach had to try. Testing his abilities, he wanted to prove he was as good as he was before his surgery. I warned him it was too far for him to run, but he insisted he could do it. Tears of frustration welled in his eyes as he came around the track and realized he could not run like he did before his surgery. His anger bubbled out of him as he pushed me away when I tried to comfort him.

Trying to get out of the competition mode, he finally agreed to a swim with me. He stuck close to me in the beginning, but soon found he could swim underwater quite well. Relieved to see his frustration fade away into laughter once again, we left the Y on a positive note.

As our visit ended, Becky handed me a book called *Believing God* by Beth Moore. Dedicating her life to God soon after we had graduated from high school, Becky's faith was much more evident than mine. Always a bit intimidated by the growth of her faith, I could see her total devotion to God had really impacted her life in a good way. I knew I needed to become more diligent in my faith, but could I? More and more I was realizing it needed to be a much bigger part of my life.

I woke early without my alarm the next day and watched Zach again as he slept. So innocent, like an angel. His body was changing. His strong appetite and decline in physical activity was showing in his belly. He always was more solid in stature than Lexi, but he was muscular and lean, solid from the constant activity he so enjoyed. I lay close to him and prayed for a miracle. Putting my head near the top of his head and breathing deeply,

I savored "his smell" and the softness of his newly cut hair. If only we could reverse time, freeze it and go back to before this all happened. Why did life have to be so complicated? A few tears slid down my cheek as I listened to his slow deep breaths.

My mind drifted to Florida when I called to check on Lexi. Dirk had left early for work so she was alone. Sounding tired, she agreed to call back when she was headed out for the bus. Forced to grow up fast, I could tell she was nervous, but she was being strong because she knew she had no choice. Thankfully, her first day had gone well. What a relief to know she was at least happy with school. One less worry to think about.

I noticed as the day progressed that Zach was stumbling and developing a slight limp. My mom noticed it as well. The fear began to rise in my core again as memories of our visit to the neurologist flooded my mind. Surely the tumor had not grown back already. Maybe we had just overdone things yesterday, I reasoned. Dirk was worried too when I shared what I saw with him that evening. Time could not go fast enough for me. I was anxious to see Dr. Thornton again and have a CT scan to see what was going on.

The weekend loomed as I lay down with Zach that evening. He was sleeping soundly as I gently placed my hand on his head over his incision site.

Lord, it's me again. God, I am coming to You asking for a miracle for this sweet angel, Zach. I just ask for this tumor, this cancer to leave his body. He is so young, with so much ahead of him. I know You have the power, Lord; we need a miracle. Thank You for all the blessings we have received. Lord, please make this tumor go away.

The tears streamed down my face as I stared at the ceiling. Closing my eyes I imagined how Zach would look at his fifth grade celebration, finishing middle school and high school. I could see his handsome face with his beaming smile as he strode across a stage to receive his diploma. I continued to visualize him going off to college and being married. What a day that would be to see him waiting at the altar for the love of his life! Cancer had completely changed my perspective on life. It had stormed into to our life when we were not looking and ripped it apart, turned it upside down and left us feeling vulnerable and confused. Thank goodness we had our faith and it seemed to be growing. I was not sure what a person could grab onto if they did not believe in God.

The weekend was challenging. Zach's limping became more pronounced. He fell again as we played croquet. Life was beginning to spin out of control once more. I felt helpless because I knew the treatments were still almost twenty days away. If we could just start now! Anything to fight this monster invading our lives. Maybe the limping was just a result of swelling. We had been decreasing the steroids slowly; maybe bumping them back up would be the answer. Monday could not come soon enough for me.

Sunday morning arrived and I took Zach to church with me. He did not want to go with the kids to junior church so we sat together. The sermon was on faith—a message I needed to hear desperately. The pastor shared Matthew 14:27—31:

But Jesus immediately said to them: "Take courage! It is I. Don't be afraid."

"Lord if it's you," Peter replied, "tell me to come to you on the water."

"Come," he said.

Then Peter got down out of the boat and walked on the water and came toward Jesus. But when he saw the wind, he was afraid and, beginning to sink, cried out, "Lord, save me!"

Immediately Jesus reached out his hand and caught him. "You of little faith," he said, "why did you doubt?"

I could identify with Peter. I had heard and read this passage many times, but it really sunk in as I heard the words again. "You of little faith." I felt God telling me to wake up and realize I must rely on my faith if I was going to make this journey. My job was to be strong for Zach and to be strong in my faith.

The running trail was calling my name when I woke on Monday. Worry and fear consumed my thoughts. The first lap was difficult as I battled my negative thoughts and uncertainty about what the day held. I remembered the sermon about faith as the power of the Bible became real to me for the first time. As I ran the second lap, I held my hand up high, like Peter, reaching for God to take hold and pull me up. As I ran, I cried and pleaded with God for strength.

God, I need You now. I am so scared and want to have faith, but it is hard. I am holding my hand out for You. Please be with me today.

Peace entered my heart once again. Ready to face the day, my heart melted as I was greeted by Zach with his smiling face when I returned. He was ready for his big plate of scrambled eggs.

MPRI was very busy when my parents, Zach and I arrived for our 1 p.m. appointment. Concern spread over Dr. Thornton's face when he saw Zach limping. He agreed we should increase the steroids again. We walked back to the CT scan room where a group of people were waiting to explain everything to Zach. They prepared the plastic mesh mask to mold over his face. As the technicians worked with Zach, we waited just outside the door. I could hear him belly laughing at all their silly jokes. He captured all their hearts in that short first visit as they saw what a crazy, silly boy he could be.

As we waited, the administrator informed me it did not appear that Blue Cross was going to cover the treatment. Although it concerned me, my thoughts could not leave Zach and finding out why his condition was worsening. Insurance was not my priority.

Before long, they called me back in the room when the mask was made. Relieved—but not surprised—I was glad to find that once again Zach had complied fully when they had him lie still on the CT table as the softened plastic mesh was placed over his head and attached to the table as it hardened. After a few adjustments they were ready for the first CT scan. The scan took less than five minutes—so much easier than an MRI. They needed to do one more, this one with contrast, using a dye they placed in an IV to enhance the images in the scan.

Zach was very hesitant to have a poke. The nurse who normally placed the IV was out on maternity leave. Another nurse tried a couple of times, but with Zach's challenging veins, the nurse decided we would have to come back the next day and have the anesthesia team place the IV. Dr. Thornton could not see any swelling on the initial CT scan. "What if the tumor has grown back?" I asked, hoping he would assure me that was not possible.

"Unfortunately, little can be done if we see rapid regrowth at this stage," he replied with obvious concern in his eyes.

We left disheartened and with no more answers than when we came.

Sleep did not come easily for me that night. I woke at 2 a.m. and could not shake the feeling of losing Zach. Playing everything over and over in my head, I began to question waiting for the proton radiation. Pulling Zach close, I prayed again with all my soul asking for God to take my hand and to protect this beautiful child in my arms. I fell asleep breathing in the smell of Zach's hair.

A new day had come—Lexi's eleventh birthday! It was our first birthday apart. Hoping we could have flown home today and surprised her, the IV problem at MRPI yesterday had prevented that. But we would be home tomorrow and I could put my arms around her and Dirk once again. It had only been a week and a half, but I missed them terribly. Even though we were surrounded by family and lots of love, it wasn't the same as being home. I called Lexi early and sang Happy Birthday to her. She sounded wonderful. I was so proud of how strong she had become.

A friend had sent me a link to a wonderful website that was set up for situations like ours called Caringbridge. Established to allow families to share news about loved ones who were sick, it was exactly what we needed to keep everyone informed of Zach's status. Posting the first entry was my attempt to share the reason why we were not discussing the type of tumor Zach had.

August 9, 2005
I know many of you have been wondering what specific type of tumor Zach had. It is human nature for us to try to understand a situation as much as we can by researching and studying information. Dirk and I

decided when we were told the diagnosis, we would not share it with any-
one except the doctors involved. They are truly the only people that need
to know for the purpose of applying the correct treatment. We as humans
try to equate a diagnosis with an outcome by accumulating data about
the disease. The thing we have to remember is the data is never consis-
tent from case to case. It is never the same result for any two people.

Each case will have its own result. That is why we are not sharing
the specifics. If we shared this information, our fear is people would come
to conclusions based on other cases and project these conclusions (good
or bad) on to Zach. We truly believe God has a specific plan for all of us
and must have faith that His plan for Zach will be a cure for this disease.
It does not matter what anyone else with this disease has had happen to
them. We leave those outcomes to the doctors to use for their research and
treatment plans....

Arriving at MPRI, Zach was nervous about his poke. We made the now familiar walk to the CT scan room. I sat next to Zach as the anesthesiologist prepared the IV materials. Zach started to get very panicked as she sprayed a numbing spray on his hand. I grabbed his face in my hands and looked deep into his eyes as I said, "Calm down; it will be all right." She had it in on the first try. After that, everything went very smoothly. Zach was able to lie still with the mask on as they administered the contrast and took the CT scan.

My parents and I hovered just outside the room where Dr. Thornton was reading the scan. He asked to go over the results with me. My dad and I stepped into the room as Zach and my mom went out to the lobby to play. The CT scan was very unclear compared to the MRI scan. Dr. Thornton was obviously concerned. It appeared the tumor site did have swelling. It was filling with liquid again, a cyst-like formation. The tumor did not seem to have changed, but the swelling was not good. He said it was very important to monitor Zach closely and watch for worsening of his symptoms. Too much swelling could result in a seizure, convulsions or worse.

He suggested I keep Zach close at hand and quiet. No school when we went back to Florida. He made a copy of the scan for me to take to Dr. Grana.

"Can't we start the treatment any sooner?" I pleaded as we walked down the hall to leave.

"Two weeks is the fastest we can prepare the programming for Zach's treatment. There are too many calculations that need to be checked and rechecked before we can start," he replied.

"Is that going to be too long? Should I just have the Tampa group line up conventional radiation as soon as we get back?" I asked. I was starting to panic. I felt my hope slipping away; maybe I had made a big mistake coming here for treatment.

"As I said yesterday, if Zach is experiencing regrowth at this rapid a pace, there is no form of radiation that will be able to do much good for him. This tumor is very aggressive, and while we don't normally see regrowth this fast, it is possible," he replied in a low tone.

I could feel my emotions slipping out of my control. I took a deep breath as tears started to form. "What can we do while we wait? Should we start the chemo early? I talked to a doctor at St. Jude's who was working with a Phase 1 drug called Terceva that had some good results on regrowth. Should I check into that?"

"I would not go to that level yet. You could check with Dr. Grana on starting the chemo. I do not see why you shouldn't. Just stick to the course we have mapped out. Sometimes you will see a cyst form after surgery and it will swell then stabilize. That could be what we are seeing here. Show her the CT scan and she can let the neurosurgeons decide if they need to do anything with the changes. Call me with any updates. I think things will work out," he finished.

I smiled weakly and waved as he walked away. I felt like we were being sent home to die. My world was turning to a dark shade of blacks and grays as my hope fell into a pit of despair.

Zach and my parents played some games when we returned to their house. I went outside and called Dirk. No answer. I left him a voice mail. I tried to be strong, but started crying as I said things didn't look so good. He soon called back and I went over everything with him. I broke down as I explained the seriousness of it all. I hated getting emotional when there was nothing he could do. I knew it was tearing him up as he listened helplessly. I warned him Zach would be struggling with his walking when we arrived tomorrow. I worried how I would make it through both airports with him and our carry-on bags.

Zach insisted on bowling with the Dirk's family to celebrate our last night in Indiana. I was hesitant because he was having more trouble with his balance, but decided he may not be able to bowl later if he continued to get worse. Frustration filled everyone as Zach unsuccessfully struggled to make his body cooperate.

That night as we lay in bed, I talked to him about the news from the day. "Zach, Dr. Thornton told me you are having some swelling again where your tumor was taken out. That is why your left side is not working so well. Honey, we need to pray for this tumor to go away, and I want you to picture it as a little ball in your head that is shrinking and shrinking and finally disappears. Will you do that for me?"

"Yeah, Mom," he said as he turned to go to sleep. My night was filled desperate thoughts as I felt my hope dissolving away under the weight of Dr. Thornton's words. I kept picturing us trying to get through the long walks at the airport, the stares of curious onlookers. What if he could not make it? I couldn't carry him and our luggage. Maybe I should ask for a wheelchair, but would that create negative thoughts in Zach's mind?

God, where are You? I am desperate for Your hand to guide us through this confusing time. I can't do this alone. We need a miracle, Lord! Please make this cyst quit swelling—just make it all go away! Give Zach back his life; he is such a sweet soul that You have given us to look after. This world needs his bright light, Lord—we need him.

It felt as if Satan was all around sending negative thoughts into my head. I was weak and having a hard time finding the positive outlook I had just a few short days ago. I placed my hand on Zach's head again and mustered all the strength I could as I told the tumor it had no power over us and it would not win. My pillow was damp from tears as I finally gave in to a restless sleep. As I drifted off, I visualized Zach getting better, trying to stay positive and keep my faith alive. I kept repeating that God was in control. We were doing the right thing. We would defeat this disease. Zach was strong and determined. Miracles do happen!

Reflections

The uncertainty of our future had a tight grip on my mind. The initial separation of our family had torn my heart and clarified the challenges we would be facing as Zach's treatment progressed. Again and again, I was finding my strength as I opened my heart to God. Speaking my fears out to God allowed me to release anxiety and clear my mind. Trying to understand why our family had been thrown into this deep dark pit was being replaced with trying to understand how to climb out—back into the light, using our faith as our ladder.

Encouragement leading to confidence was coming to me in many directions. Being surrounded by family was an uplifting support. Seeing Zach's unending determination and courage humbled my fears. If he could face the intimidating treatments that lay ahead without complaint, I could quiet my fears and create an environment of smiles and fun for him. Finding hope in messages from God's Word spoke to my heart and created a thirst to know more. Feeling love from friends both far and near helped to hold all of us up when the days began to feel heavy.

So, as my family stood facing the biggest mountain we had ever faced in our lives, I was learning to cling to my hope that having God as our leader, we would find a way up to the top. The love He was showering over us would be our lifeline and the messages He was sending us would be our guide map. We just had to have faith and believe.

climbing the Mountain

Thankfully all my negative thoughts about the airport did not come true. Zach made it without the need of a wheelchair and soon we were settled in our seats flying back to Florida. He put his head in my lap and covered himself in a new soft blanket he had received from Becky's church. She had told me their entire congregation had prayed over the blanket for Zach to get better.

Please, God, hear their prayers!

With Zach sleeping, I had two hours to fill before we landed. Grabbing the book Becky had given me, I started reading, hoping to find some inspiration. With the title of *Believing God*, I hoped it would help chase the worries from my thoughts.

There was a note from Becky written on the inside of the cover:

Sherry,
Always remember that Zach is the Lord's. He is a loving heavenly Father,
worthy of our trust, even when we do not understand...

I knew these words were true. Children were only ours as a gift from God. My faith was not strong enough to accept that God might ask me to give up Zach. I was not finished with my work. I had so much more nurturing and teaching to do!

From the introduction, it was clear this book did not land in my hands by chance. God's peace began entering my mind as I read. The words on the page in front of me were speaking to my heart. Believing *in* God was not enough, I had to *believe God!* I had to have faith and know God had a plan for me, for Zach, for our family. Occasionally I would stop and just close my eyes and breathe, whispering a prayer of thanks, knowing that God had heard my prayers. My hope was growing with each chapter I read. As we landed in Tampa, I felt as if my life had been transformed. The sun was shining. We were home!

Dirk was waiting for us at the gate. Eager to feel his hug once again, I fell into his arms. Zach was beaming from ear to ear. Dirk's eyes immediately reflected his concern when he saw Zach limping through the airport. Seeing the worry consume his heart, I was anxious to share the peace and hope that I had just found, but the bustling airport was not the right place.

Stopping on our way home to pick up some presents for Lexi, we were ready to have a celebration for our eleven-year-old sweetie when she came home! Later, I greeted her at the bus stop with a big hug. Even though it had only been a week and a half, she seemed older—more mature—to me. Oh, how I hoped I would be meeting Zach at this bus stop in three years, when he was in middle school.

Being together once again made our celebration extra special. Fearing Zach would fall, I did not let him stray far from me all evening. As bedtime approached, Dirk and I decided Zach would sleep with us until his balance improved. The risk of a fall was too great at this point. Zach fell asleep quickly. Laying our hands softly on his head, we prayed over him, hoping the strength of our love and faith would somehow transfer from our hearts to his tumor and make it all disappear. How we longed for our old lives to return.

Waking in my own bed was a luxury I had never appreciated so much until now. Happy to be able to gently wake Lexi with a hug, instead of waking her with a cell phone call, I helped her get ready for school—much to her relief. The past two weeks had been a very hard and abrupt transition in her young life. Cancer was unrelenting in its reach.

After Lexi was off to school, Zach and I prepared for a visit to his class. I had spoken with his teacher and explained our plans had changed. We originally thought Zach would attend school for the time we were home, but with the balance issues and possible increase in brain swelling, I did not want to let him out of my sight. She and I decided it would be good to at least let Zach visit his class during their recess break period.

Apprehensive when we arrived, the reality of the kids, stairs and building overcame Zach. We slowly made our way to his classroom, which required the now-difficult task of climbing two flights of stairs. On the way, he peered over the wall to the playground area. Stopping as he saw many of his friends playing soccer, his eyes lit up with excitement as he watched. My heart ached for him. What must he be thinking? His eyes were filled with desire to be in the middle of the game. He loved soccer or any game involving a ball, and he was good at all of them. Now his competitive drive and determination that had always been evident when he played sports would have to help him to face what lay ahead.

Entering an empty classroom, we weaved around the desks in search of Zach's name. Zach found it and anxiously looked at who was sitting next to him. A smile spread across his face when he saw it was his friend Curren. The door opened and all of his classmates poured into the room. Their eyes and faces were filled with excited anticipation when they saw us there. Expecting our visit, they all greeted Zach warmly. He was overwhelmed and embarrassed by the attention. Mrs. Sapp directed them to quietly find some games to play while she and I talked.

Quietly, I updated Mrs. Sapp on Zach's status and she gave me direction on her lesson plans for the next two months. Occasionally, I paused to watch Zach as he and his friends tested their math skills with flash cards. In that moment, he was normal again, an eight-year-old boy at school, just as it should be. I sensed he regretted leaving as he beamed a broad smile to everyone when we said good-bye. The trip had given him a visual of what he was missing, of what he loved. According to the plan, our next visit wasn't going to be until mid-October. That seemed very far away.

Zach spent the afternoon anxiously waiting for the school bus to bring his friends home. Insisting on hanging out with them, he made me leave after I positioned him on a bed at our neighbor's house so he could watch his buddies play video games. Again searching for the normal routine he had before cancer entered the picture, his young mind seemed to be clear of the worry and fear that kept consuming mine.

Lexi arrived home a couple of hours later, happy to be greeted with a hug instead of an empty house. After discussing her day, I realized it was time for Zach's medicine. Fatigue seemed to be hitting him hard. I had to hold his right hand and put my arm around him to help him walk across the street to our house. Dire thoughts of what could be causing his deterioration swirled in my mind, causing me to be overly attentive to his needs. Seeing how tired he was, I began to feed him his dinner, which resulted in an unexpected meltdown from Lexi. Shocked, I quickly realized that she had reached her breaking point and this had put her over the edge.

"I can't believe you are feeding him! He is not a baby, Mom," she protested loudly. "You have been spending all your time with him. You have a daughter, too, you know!" She stormed out of the room in tears.

Dirk walked in to hear her door slamming. We exchanged puzzled glances. Leaving Zach with his food, Dirk and I went into Lexi's room to find her attempting to wipe her tears away.

"Lexi, Honey, I didn't mean to upset you. Zach was really tired and I was just trying to make it easier for him," I said.

"I'm OK; that's OK. I shouldn't have yelled. Zach is sick; you go be with him," she sighed.

"Lexi, this is tough for all of us. It's OK for you to feel mad; we all do. You have to tell us when you're feeling bad before you get so frustrated you feel like yelling. OK?" Dirk asked.

"OK. I'm sorry," Lexi replied. Still trying to find our way in this new life we faced, we were discovering it much harder than we ever imagined, certainly not the life we had envisioned just a few short weeks ago.

Our visit to the oncology office the next day brought a surprise. Instead of Dr. Grana, we were greeted by Dr. Aung, a young, pretty Asian woman with a quick smile that lit up her face. Zach looked at her cautiously, knowing he was due for a blood draw. Handing her the CT scan from Dr. Thornton, I explained his concern with the swelling cyst and asked her to share the scan with the neurosurgeons to determine if anything should be done before our return to Indiana. She stuffed it in Zach's medical file and asked how his radiation was going.

Alarmed, I wondered if she had even looked at his chart or spoken with Dr. Grana. Quickly explaining our story, I told her Dr. Thornton and I had discussed starting the chemo before the radiation. She agreed and emphasized we needed to get the radiation started as soon as we could, and she ordered another MRI to be performed before we left for Indiana. Fighting the urge to scream, I wondered if she didn't realize we understood the urgency and would do anything to start treatment now. Thinking it couldn't be much worse, I began to wonder if our world had slipped into hell when we weren't looking.

Zach reached out to me when the nurse returned to take the blood sample. Placing him on my lap, I explained Zach did not have very cooperative veins. Panic gripped him as she unveiled the gleaming needle from its package. After tediously searching both arms, she settled on a small vein in his hand. Hugging him tight, holding his face to my cheek as she made her first try, I realized how naïve I had been to think Zach would not be facing many needles in his treatment. His heart pounded madly as he felt the familiar rub of the alcohol swab and protested. "No, no, no," he wailed.

Thankfully, the blood started flowing through the collection tube after the first poke.

After learning his blood results were acceptable, we left with a handful of prescriptions to be filled at a pharmacy thirty minutes away in their Tampa clinic. The chemo schedule required Zach to take two 100 mg. capsules once a day for five days. Zach and I had been practicing with mini M&M's, but these pills were much larger. Along with these, he also had three other pills to swallow that would help prevent pneumonia, thrush, and nausea—all wonderful side effects of the chemo.

Dr. Aung wanted Zach to have a physical therapy evaluation before we returned to Indiana to address his left side deficiencies. Thankful we were at least starting *something,* we discovered that the physical therapy office was in the same building. The therapist was nice enough to take us back to the therapy room to show Zach what to expect. The room was filled with balls, treadmills, stairs and various toys. Seeing these fun things brought a smile to Zach's face and a twinkle to his eyes. Finally a treatment that didn't involve pokes!

We made it home just as Lexi was arriving on the bus. It had been a long day for all of us. As we settled ourselves in front of the TV, Zach looked at me and said, "I'm dying. I'm dead." He fell on the couch with his tongue hanging out. I was caught off guard. He had said this before, always in a joking manner and with a giggle. I had been smiling at him and telling him he was silly up to this point, but now I wondered if this was his way of trying to open up or ask questions.

"Zach, are you worried about dying, because you keep saying that?" I asked.

He looked at me with a serious face and then smiled and brushed off my question.

"Honey, if you're worried about this, just tell me and we can talk about it, OK?" I prodded.

"OK, Mom," he answered, turning back to the TV.

I wished I knew what to tell him. If only I could say, "You are not dying," with confidence that it was true. In desperate need of bolstering my own hope, I noted I would have to make time to read and pray more often.

Lining up peanut M&M's as chasers and yogurt to make his pills slide down, Zach was able to swallow his pills after a couple of tries. Making a game of it, he laughed and poked his finger in his mouth as if he were gagging and I snapped some photos. Although, he didn't like it, his ever-present determination came through as he faced this newest challenge.

As an additional motivator, I pulled a jar out of the cabinet and Zach dropped in a marble for each pill, five for pokes and five for procedures like MRIs. It was a game I decided would challenge Zach to endure all the pokes and pills by rewarding him with his favorite prize—money. Each marble represented a quarter to be redeemed when the jar was full. A smile spread across his face as he released a handful of marbles noisily into the glass jar.

When Saturday rolled around, I woke with dread of the day we faced. I felt like I had lead weights in my legs as we gathered our things for the championship swim meet. I hated that it was hot. I hated we would be surrounded by inquiring eyes. I hated that Zach would not be swimming. I hated he had to be so brave. I hated cancer.

Watching Zach's age group swim their events brought tears to my eyes. I saw many of the boys he had swum against just a month and a half ago. His swimming had reached a new level this season. In each meet we attended in June, he was steadily improving his time, placing first or second in all of his events. How could Zach have cancer? What could have caused him to have this? So strong and healthy, so smart and athletic. It just didn't make sense. Aching to scream, "THIS IS SO UNFAIR," I knew it would do no good. We were trapped in this new reality, and the walls seemed to be closing in as we waited for treatments—as we waited to see how this would all play out. If only I had a crystal ball.

Celebrating Lexi's birthday with a sleepover that evening, it was such a relief to have made it through the day. Before lying down, I updated the website by summarizing our feelings:

August 12, 2005
…Dirk and I are finding it very hard to wait for the treatment to begin. Please pray for our faith to stay strong and for Zach not to have any further symptoms. He has done very well with the chemo pills. He has had two doses and no problems with feeling sick. Pray the chemo is effective and really begins to work on any remaining tumor. One section of the book Believing God *I keep reading to renew my faith is as follows:*

"…We may well accept faith challenges as a fact of life and not be

shocked or feel picked on when they come. God brings them to build our faith, prove us genuine, and affords Himself endless excuses to reward us. He delights in nothing more than our choice to believe Him over what we see and feel."

I hope this is helpful to some of you as you read this. I know I will be rereading it many times this upcoming week.

The website had become a source of inspiration for me. Receiving messages daily from friends and family, it was uplifting to know how many people were spreading Zach's story and praying for us.

The church we attended was nothing like the traditional ones we had attended in Indiana. With no stained glass windows or steeples, the sanctuary more resembled a theatrical auditorium. After the service the next day, the pastor asked if he and the elders could pray over Zach. Able to hold over two thousand people, the sanctuary seemed even bigger now that it was empty and quiet. A group of six men stood waiting near the front as we walked in. Feeling a bit uncomfortable and not knowing what to expect, I did not want to scare Zach, but I wanted these prayers to be heard. After the introductions were made, Pastor Greg asked Dirk and me what was troubling us most. "Anxiety over the unknown and maintaining our faith," we answered. The pastor opened his well-worn Bible to Philippians 4:4—7: "Rejoice in the Lord always. I will say it again: Rejoice! Let your gentleness be evident to all. The Lord is near. Do not be anxious about anything, but in everything, by prayer and petition, with thanksgiving, present your requests to God. And the peace of God, which transcends all understanding, will guard your hearts and your minds in Christ Jesus."

Gathering around each other, Zach stood facing me and I put my arms around him. All of the elders placed their hands on us as Pastor Greg laid his hand on Zach's head. He began to pray for our peace and for Zach's healing. As he did this, all of the elders audibly added their affirmations. Overwhelmed to hear so many different voices all at once, I opened my eyes and found Zach staring up at me with questioning eyes. A big smile started spreading across his face and a big belly laugh exploded from him. He quickly buried his face in my stomach as he tried to control his emotions. Smiling, I hugged him close. When the prayers were finished, Pastor Greg knelt down with Zach and asked him if he believed Jesus could heal him. Zach answered yes. Peace filled my heart as we left the church.

Dear God, please hear our prayers. We know You are the answer. We believe You have a plan for Zach and our family that will bring glory to Your name. Lord, thank You for this church for all the wonderful friends and family You have placed in our lives.

It seemed I was in constant conversation with God these days—quite a change from my prior life a few months ago. How had I let myself slip so far from the most important relationship in my life? Hoping Zach did not get sick just as a wake-up call for all of us, I was still amazed to see how it had caused many of our friends and family members to rekindle their prayer lives as well.

Except for a bit of nausea when he first woke up, Zach weathered the five-day course of chemo relatively well. Chasing away his boredom became my biggest challenge. Schoolwork did not interest him, but miniature golf did! With a heat index of 110°, we compromised by going bowling.

I worried about his balance, but decided if he felt up to it, we should at least try. When I expressed my concern, he quickly put me in my place by wagging his finger in my face with a scolding, "Negativity, negativity!" Telling him he was my hero because he was being so brave with everything, I was amazed at his resilience and positive attitude. Not letting a thing like cancer cause him to curl up and hide from life, he continued to face each day with optimism and the energy to keep living life to its fullest.

Bowling was a blast. I held my breath as I watched him pick up the lightest ball we could find and sling it down the alley using only his right hand. Skipping with a limp up to the end of the alley as he released the ball, he rolled three spares on the first three frames! My heart melted each time he turned around, both of us beaming with pride at his accomplishment. He was so beautiful. He actually seemed to be glowing from his joy.

Time had become precious. Time had become our worst enemy. Savoring every moment was our desire, but watching Zach's abilities deteriorate made the days seem too long.

The new day brought another appointment at the oncology practice. Relieved he only had to endure a finger poke, Zach had made it clear it was still a poke, which would be good for five marbles. Always Mr. Accountable when money was involved!

My heart sank as I helped him dress and realized he could no longer direct his left foot into his shorts without my assistance. August 24th—the date for the radiation treatments to start—could not come fast enough for me.

As they tested the blood, we saw another oncologist, Dr. Ayala. She was very nice, but I was getting concerned that we were seeing too many different doctors and no one was specifically in charge of Zach. Explaining our plan once again, we discussed the MRI and moved it to Friday so everyone would have time to review it before our flight to Indiana the following Tuesday. (I had learned earlier that if there was too much swelling present, our two-hour flight could turn into a sixteen-hour drive.)

Concern filled my mind when I asked Dr. Ayala if she had seen the CT scan I had brought from Indiana and she appeared to not know what I was talking about. Wondering if the neurosurgeons had received a copy, I quickly realized I would have to take the lead in Zach's care. I could not depend on the doctors to prompt me; instead I would have to prompt and manage them.

Another day arrived, another appointment to keep. Fighting his morning nausea, I held off giving him his medicine until we reached the clinic for his physical therapy evaluation. As we drove, he dozed. Tears welled in my eyes as the drudgery of Zach's new schedule hit me. No longer able to run or play, he faced appointment after appointment, procedure after procedure—with no end in sight.

My mind drifted back to a soccer game last season when I watched him charge down the field and score a goal. He turned to locate Curren, and both with arms held high, ran to each other and jumped high in the air, bumping chests in congratulations. It was magical. He loved to run! He loved to score! How I longed for those days to return. Having these memories, I could not imagine how Zach was able to keep from complaining about all he had lost. But maybe the memories were the reason he could keep from complaining—maybe they were the very motivation that kept him going so he could get back to them.

The physical therapy evaluation went well. Zach seemed nervous as we entered the room. Kathy, the therapist, was petite, young and full of smiles. Zach would look at me when she asked him questions for reassurance. Eager to please her, he tried his hardest to do everything she asked of him. Explaining our Indiana trip, she was kind enough to show me ways to stretch Zach's arm and leg to make sure he kept his full range of motion while we were there.

We visited the pharmacy once again to fill the chemo prescription that would be required during the radiation. Instead of taking 200 mg., Zach would have to take only 75 mg. I was floored when the pharmacist told me that meant Zach would be taking six pills! Apparently the drug manufacturer only made pills in 5, 20 and 100 mg. sizes. Unbelievable! I wanted to march into the office of the executive who chose to manufacture only these three sizes. My heart broke for Zach. This dose would last for about forty-two days, which equated to more than 250 pills to be swallowed. I left the office very disgusted with the situation.

Dirk was in a great mood when he got home. He had been having his hair cut and was sharing our story with our stylist when the customer next to him shared a story about her nephew. She said he had a GBM and was treated with radiation and chemo seven years ago. He was still alive! This was great to hear. Seven years seemed like an eternity in our new reality. If we could have seven more years with Zach, if we could have two more years, if we could just get his treatments started …

With the MRI looming over us the next day, it was hard not to be filled with worry. I had told Dirk at the beginning of the week I thought it would be clear—that I *believed* it would be clear. All week, I hoped to see improvement in Zach's coordination and movements. Now that it was the day before the MRI, I knew my optimism was not going to be proven true. Relieved the symptoms had not grown dramatically worse—but sad they had remained—I prayed we would be at least given the opportunity to start the proton radiation.

Settling Zach in the back seat of the truck the next day, we were off on our journey for the third day in a row, heading back to the Tampa clinic where they had a mobile MRI unit. Another IV stick. I was thankful the nurse hit the vein on the first try. The mobile unit was housed in a modified recreational vehicle. Maneuvering the stairs up to the entrance was a challenge for Zach. He could barely lift his left leg. Diego, the technician, greeted us with a smile, but I could see the concern in his eyes. Zach quietly settled in under some blankets after Diego settled him on the table. He knew this routine all too well.

As the familiar beep, clanks and ticks started, my thoughts went back to the first MRI at St. Joe's. I had been so sure it would be clear. If only it had been, these last five weeks would not be our nightmare. How could life change so fast? I now realized what a sheltered life I had lived up to this point. Bad things like this had never happened to anyone I even remotely knew. Growing to hate the familiar noises I was hearing as the MRI proceeded, my eyes rested on Zach's face. I wondered what he was thinking. If only he would open up and talk to me. Trying to give him opportunities to ask questions or talk seemed to always result in silence.

The look on Diego's face was not promising. He asked if Zach had received any radiation yet. I sighed as I explained the proton radiation schedule once again. Zach and I slowly made our way to the car with the fresh MRI scan in hand. Helping him climb in the back and get settled, the ride home was filled with fear for me. A scripture from Isaiah 41:10 that had been e-mailed to me during the week wound through my mind: "So do not fear, for I am with you; do not be dismayed, for I am your God. I will strengthen you and help you; I will uphold you with my righteous right hand."

This comforted me, but it was so hard to push the growing fear out of my mind. Anxious to view the scan when I arrived home, I watched my hand tremble as I placed the disk in the computer drive. Tears rolled down my cheeks as I looked from one ugly slide to the next. The cyst appeared bigger and was surrounded by white. Dr. Thornton had told me tumor cells displayed as white on these slides. Even worse, there was also white at the location of the original tumor. This must be regrowth of the original tumor. There was nothing good to report as I slowly lifted the phone to call Dirk. Answering quickly since he had been waiting on my call, he heard me sobbing as I tried to explain what I saw to him. *This sucks!* We haven't even been given a shot at beating this thing and it was overtaking Zach's brain.

Lord God, what is going on? I feel like You are not hearing my prayers. Lord, I am begging for more time. Zach is too young to leave us. I want to have more time to teach him and love him. Lord, I know he belongs to You, but You gave me a heart full of love and I need to give it to him. You know my heart and how broken it would be if I lost Zach. Please let us get to Indiana and start these treatments. I was so sure this was the path You laid out for us. Was I wrong? Lord give me strength.

Unable to concentrate on work, Dirk came home soon after I called. I left to overnight the MRI scan to Dr. Thornton. Pounding the steering wheel as I drove, I screamed my frustration out to the empty car. Our baby was so sick and we could do nothing but watch. There was no doubt in my mind our world had changed to hell while we weren't looking. How could hell be any worse to any parent? My thoughts were jumbled and my head was spinning.

The evening was filled with horrible negative thoughts racing through my head. I tried to sleep, but I could not escape the ugliness of the MRI scans. Giving up on sleep at 4 a.m., I gently snuggled close to Zach. Praying again for strength, for healing, for peace, the worries would not leave me. I slipped out of bed to pour my fears into my journal. Zach came shuffling out at 7:30 looking for me. Not ready to face the realities of the day, we climbed back in bed and I finally dozed off. Awakened a few hours later by the phone ringing, I steeled my emotions and answered with a cheerful hello.

"Mrs. Tucker, this is Dr. Grana. I need to speak with you about Zachary's

MRI results. They do not look good. He has developed a large cyst and there is evidence of regrowth at the original tumor site," she informed me.

"Yes. I looked at them last night and saw that. I expected your call. What do we need to do?" I asked.

"I have scheduled Zachary for a short-stay admission on Monday. He needs to have surgery to drain the cyst. He needs to have the radiation start as soon as possible, but this cyst will cause him continuing weakness if we do not drain it. I don't want him to start radiation and have to stop because of complications from the cyst. I have talked to Dr. Thornton and he is willing to delay treatment for a week so we can take care of this cyst," she continued.

I felt the same frustration I'd experienced in my conversation with Dr. Aung. Of course we knew the radiation needed to be started. It is not like we told them to hold off while we came home for a visit. I wanted nothing more than to have the proton beam zapping the cancer cells—*right now!* I wondered if any of the doctors had looked at the CT scan I gave them from Dr. Thornton. It seemed like we would have had this conversation last week if they had.

If only I could crawl in their heads and suck the information they had into my head, I would not have to be so dependent on others to know how to treat Zach.

I was numb with the reality of the aggressive nature of this tumor. I had read all the words in my research, but somehow I thought we would get a break. Zach was only an eight-year-old kid. How could something so powerful overtake his system? After asking me to explain the phone call, Zach was ready to find some playmates. We walked hand in hand across the street to find them all out in a garage playing video games. It wasn't long until the kids tired of the games in the garage and drifted inside to find something more entertaining. My neighbor Theresa and I sat together as I shared with her the devastating news we had received. The familiar feel of salty tears flowed down my cheeks as I shared my fears with her.

Tears began to spill down her cheeks as she listened. "I don't understand why this is happening. Zach is such a good boy. He is always so happy and smiling," she said, quietly dabbing her face.

"It isn't fair is it? It makes no sense to me. I would switch places in a second if I could," I whispered back.

The cry was cleansing to me as I headed back to our house. The sledgehammer was pounding us again, but we would keep going. We must. We owed it to Zach to be strong. He certainly had displayed courage and strength beyond his eight years in all he had faced.

As the day wore on, Dirk and I began calling our parents and friends to tell them of the new plan. They were obviously concerned. A couple of Zach's friends wanted to come for a visit. They had not seen him since the surgery and were worried about him. Zach was shy when they first arrived, not knowing what to say. But he soon cracked a smile and began to be his silly self. I could tell his buddies were relieved to see him be his old self, and they joined in the giggling.

We ended the evening with a quiet dinner and a movie. I sent a message out on the website describing our change in plans. I was trying to keep the site as positive as I could while still being realistic. I found it a perfect opportunity to share some strength we were gaining from God's grace.

August 20, 2005

Nothing brightens my day more (except for Lexi and Zach's smiles) than reading the entries in the guestbook. Thanks to everyone for sending all the messages our way. I was asked if it was OK to pass the website address out to anyone and the answer is yes! I feel like the more people we have praying and sending positive thoughts to us, the better off we are. Prayer is a powerful thing!

We have had a change in plans. Our oncologist called this morning and was concerned with a cyst-like bubble that has developed. This sometimes happens after surgery. This is what is causing the swelling and left side weakness for Zach. They have scheduled Zach for a surgery at All Children's on Monday. We are to be at the hospital between 6 and 7 A.M. This is supposed to be a pretty routine procedure where they put a shunt-like device in to help drain the cyst. They will leave it in so if any other development occurs, it will be able to drain as well.

There are a couple of passages in the Believing God *book I have read over again today that I would like to share. They have helped me to deal with our change in plans.*

"Remember, faith is never a denial of reality. It is a belief in a greater reality. In other words, the truth may be that you are presently surrounded by terrifying or terribly discouraging circumstances. The reason you don't have to buckle to fear and discouragement is the presence of God in the middle of your circumstances.

"If you pray that God will move a mountain and He doesn't, or you have the faith to tell a mountain to move and it won't, assume Christ wants you to climb it instead ..."

Well, I kind of feel like we are on Mt. Everest! Dirk and I know our family is facing a tough road ahead, but with faith and the power of prayer, we can endure. Please pray hard this coming week that we can make some progress on our mountain!

I had gained a lot of strength as I thought about these words. We would endure and we would get through this. Sleep came, but did not last long for me. I woke at 2 A.M. with my thoughts racing.

How will this end, Lord—happy or sad?

Getting everyone to the hospital by 7 A.M. on Monday was quite a challenge, but we managed to arrive on time. Lexi had decided to skip school and join us rather than face another morning alone. Much to his dismay, Zach was NPO again—no food or water until after the procedure. Complaining his head hurt when he laughed, I was thankful and relieved we were getting this procedure done—today.

Waiting to be taken to the surgery holding room was agony. Unrelenting hunger turned Zach very grumpy. He announced very loudly to whoever could hear him that he was going to sue the hospital for not letting him eat when we were told for the third time "just a little longer." When they finally came to wheel us to the holding area, he grabbed my hand and squeezed hard.

Dr. Storrs came in with his scrubs on and greeted us warmly. He explained the procedure. They would place an Ommaya reservoir under Zach's scalp. The reservoir consisted of a little bubble with a straw that extended to the cyst area. They would leave it under his scalp in case the cyst needed to be drained in the future. We signed the consent forms and Zach was off once again to surgery.

Dirk, Lexi and I went to the family waiting area and settled in for word to come. After an hour passed, I began to feel butterflies in my stomach. It seemed like a long time for a "standard procedure." An hour and a half had passed when Dr. Storrs finally entered the room. Everything went well. He was able to drain the cyst completely and wash it out. Pending a clear CT scan in the morning to make sure no bleeding occurred, he gave us approval for a Sunday flight, but said it could be sooner if everything looked good in the morning. What a relief! My heart was doing flip-flops, knowing we could get the treatment started soon.

Thank You, God, for answering our prayers. You are an awesome God! Please forgive me for my doubts during this scary time. I know You are in control and we must trust You.

My faith was gaining strength again. I had been focusing on reading and meditating for thirty minutes each morning through the last week and it had helped.

Waking from anesthesia proved once again to be difficult for Zach, but after a corn dog and French fries were positioned in front of him, the world was good once again.

Before long, evening arrived, leading Lexi to become an emotional basket case as she knew she and Dirk had to leave. She was tired, scared and frustrated with the whole situation. The drive to and from the hospital made her nauseous. It was too much for an eleven-year-old to handle. She was so fragile. Feeling helpless as I gave her a big hug and kiss, I worried about Dirk too. He was frazzled by the stress of his work on top of dealing with the emotions of Zach's cancer. If only life would stop while we tried to figure this out.

Zach and I were happy to have a room to ourselves this visit. He had bounced back quickly and had his happy disposition again. Complaining that it hurt his head when he laughed, I tried to be careful not to be funny. The only evidence of the procedure were some fresh stitches on his original scar and a noticeable bump about half an inch long and two inches in diameter directly behind his scar. His hair covered most of it.

The next day we received good news: The scans looked good and we could go home. Further, we were cleared to fly the next day, meaning treatments could start on time! Zach and I were very glad to hear this news. We ordered him a big breakfast and decided to get a little more sleep after he finished eating.

The ring of my cell phone pulled me out of a sleepy haze. We had managed to squeeze in an hour of rest before reality came flying back at us.

As I tried to shake the sleep from my head, I heard the social worker from MPRI saying she and the accounts receivable clerk had calculated the cost of Zach's treatments to be $139,000. She said that if they discounted them to the rate of insurance reimbursement, the cost would be $54,593.

At this point she had my full and complete attention. She finished her conversation with a pleasant, "So how would you like to take care of paying for this?"

I was floored. My mouth hung open as I tried to digest what she had just rattled off to me. My heart started pounding as I tried to find the words to speak. Asking her why they were not submitting this to insurance first, she said it did not appear insurance would pay, so they needed to receive the payment up-front.

Twice I asked her if she was telling me we had to pay before they would treat Zach. Her response was that was what "they" wanted to do. Feeling the world crumbling around me, I wondered if we had waited a month for a procedure that was not going to happen. Knowing I could raise the money through an equity line on our house—but not overnight— I asked to speak to her manager. She said he would call me.

My head was spinning. How could this day start out so positive and bright to only nosedive to this pit? The more I thought about the conversation, the more anger started to build in me. They could not do this to us now. Not after I specifically questioned them about financial issues and was told it would not hold up treatment. Thankfully she called back to apologize and said they decided they could not require payment this late in the process without trying to bill the insurance first. They would just require us to sign a guarantee to agree to payment if insurance did not pay within thirty days of treatment. Just when I thought things were hard enough with the medical issues, the financial challenge of the treatments started raising its ugly head.

Dr. Aung came by to clear Zach for travel and informed us his Temador dose had been increased to 95 mg., meaning it was now up to seven pills. I could not believe we could not just increase it to 100 mg. and only have one pill, but she insisted the toxicity would be too high. We were finally released at 5 P.M.

Our two-week wait for treatment was finally coming to an end. The mountain we climbed felt extremely steep, but I felt we were approaching the peak and hoping one of those wonderful, carefree downhill periods was waiting for us in Indiana. Our prayer warriors had come through—treatments would be starting on time. We had made it!

Reflections

Someone once wrote, "Worry is an old man with a bent head, carrying a load of feathers he thinks is lead." Our load of feathers had felt like a ten-ton truck as we waited for the radiation treatments. Worry, anxiety and fear seemed to surround us each day as setbacks grew and the ugly realities of cancer appeared before our eyes. Our faith, prayers and church family had helped lighten this load, just as Matthew 11:28—29 so beautifully tells us: "Come to me, all you who are weary and burdened, and I will give you rest. Take my yoke upon you and learn from me, for I am gentle and humble in heart, and you will find rest for your souls."

My heart had been opened to spiritual depths I had never reached before through the book *Believing God*. It was as if God had placed the book in my hands and spoke directly to my heart. Learning to lean on Him and not rely on my own understanding of the world was the only way I could face the deterioration of Zach's physical condition with hope.

I was learning fear is the absence of faith. Choosing faith over fear every day when I opened my eyes was a new way of living. Surrendering my fears to God, living each day for the joy of that day and being inspired by the courageous optimism Zach brought to each day had become my routine. My heart was changing from the inside out.

Only one more radiation treatment left! After the tech removed his mask, Zach always looked up to see if I was waiting for him. His patience and courage always amazed me.

OCTOBER 2005, one week before completing his radiation treatments – Hair gone, body growing daily from steroids, Zach is ready to "save" some more claw machine friends. What a priceless smile!

CHAPTER SEVEN

Golden Days
of Radiation

*I*t seemed my head had just hit the pillow when it was time to get ready for our flight to Indiana. Relief flooded over me, knowing we were starting the treatments on schedule, as I prodded Zach and Lexi gently awake. Our plan was to have Dirk and Lexi spend two weeks with us, then they would head back to Florida for two weeks and return for two more weeks. Hopefully Lexi would maintain enough face time with her teachers and classmates to stay connected and not fall behind on this schedule. Dirk would work via e-mail, fax and phone.

The drive through Tampa traffic was typical, stressful and congested. Our friend Debbie had volunteered to take us to the airport. The van was filled to its limit with our bodies and luggage. As I stepped out of the van at the airport, I saw that Lexi was in distress. I grabbed her hand and led her to the nearest trash can where she deposited the contents of her nervous stomach. Travel was not her favorite activity. So much for a smooth start!

We all settled down once we checked in and were waiting for our flight. The dreaded pill time came as we waited. I pulled the bulging Ziploc bag of Zach's medications from our carry-on. I felt the stares from those around us. What must they think? I used to be one of them, naïve and carefree to cancer. Zach worked so hard to get the medicine down. It crushed me every time he struggled because I had to keep pushing him until he succeeded. It was torture for both of us. This was a job no parent or child should endure. Thankfully, his determination and the trusty marble jar kept him going.

Two hours later we were in Indiana once again.

Thank You, God, that we could fly and not have to make the sixteen-hour drive. Thank You for letting these treatments start on time. Forgive me for my doubts.

My dad was waiting with a smile at baggage claim. We had decided to always meet in baggage claim to avoid the miscommunication we had experienced on the last trip. We headed directly to MPRI. I was anxious for Lexi and Dirk to meet the wonderful staff there. Zach started grumbling as soon as we pulled into the parking lot; his stomach was telling him a long wait could not be tolerated this time. As if summoned by his thoughts, my mom glided into the parking lot like an angel in her gleaming white car. She had a loaded picnic basket full of Zach and Lexi's favorite foods. They swarmed around as she quickly set out a picnic in the parking lot.

Once their tummies were full, the smiles started appearing again. Entering the waiting room, we settled into a game of Crazy Eights. When Zach's name was called, we all walked back to the treatment room with him. The staff was moving with purpose as they readied Zach for a "dry run" treatment. They wanted to determine if the mask would irritate his fresh incision area, as well as gauge his reaction to the table.

Zach was the focus of attention as we walked into the cold room. In the center of the room stood the long black treatment table where he would lay. It was attached to a large robotic arm similar to the kind used on car assembly lines. Behind it was a large machine that contained a circular plastic protrusion similar to the end of an x-ray machine found at a dentist's office. The proton beam came through to the patient at this point. This complex nest of wires, metal and plastic was the technology we so hoped would give

Zach back his life by obliterating the tumor cells remaining in his brain.

Zach held my hand as the technicians positioned him on the table they had softened with pads. He giggled nervously as they questioned him about how everything felt. They slowly lowered the white mesh mask over his face and attached it to the table. Once the mask was in place, they gingerly mapped out an area of the mask to cut away in order to protect the fresh incision. Zach didn't move a muscle the entire time. My heart swelled with pride at his courage.

Since the beam was stationary, they had to move him into position with it. They asked us to step back as they moved the table up, down, and side-to-side. His hand slipped from mine, and a helpless feeling engulfed me. He looked so small and vulnerable compared to the machine. I had to fight an overwhelming urge to snatch him up and run away.

Getting him positioned correctly would consume the bulk of each thirty- to forty- minute treatment time, even though the actual time of beam exposure would be about five minutes. Zach was scheduled to receive two treatments each day. First the beam would enter the right side of his head, then they would rotate the table and it would enter the top of his head.

Soon the testing was done and the mask came off to reveal a smiling face. Zach had mesh pattern indentations on his forehead and cheeks. The chief technician smiled and told him he now officially had what they called "waffle face." He grinned and his eyes sparkled. Tomorrow would be the real thing. Noting the concern deep in the technicians' eyes, I could tell they were as anxious as us to get the treatments started.

Zach and Lexi left with my parents, as Dr. Thornton took Dirk and me into an exam room to sign consent forms. Explaining Zach would have to have MRIs for the rest of his life, he indicated the frequency would be governed by the disease but would start with every two months after radiation was complete. He would also need to see an endocrinologist within the first year after treatment and plan on an annual visit. This was to assure his growth hormones functioned as they should as he matured.

Talk of Zach's future! My heart did cartwheels to finally hear a doctor speak this way. It filled me with such hope that Zach could possibly live years—not just months. The doctor had clearly said thirty-six months at our first visit, but I was grateful for Dr. Thornton's optimism—even if the possibility of a long life for Zach was slim from a medical standpoint. In my heart, I believed God had the ability to heal Zach at any time. Praying this would happen, we hoped we would see Dr. Thornton's words become a reality.

The deterioration of Zach's left side coordination was painfully apparent later at my parents' house. He no longer could play croquet without me hovering at his side to assist him with his balance. Seeing how alarmed my mom was with his loss of balance, I realized I had been in denial that he was getting worse. Climbing the stairs in the house also displayed a profound difference. Taking only one step at a time, his left foot dragged on each step as he swung it around to put it on the next step to join his right foot.

Dear Lord, I thank You we have made it back to Indiana for this treatment. I pray this is part of Your plan to establish a new radiation protocol for GBM tumors. Lord, please work through this treatment to heal Zachary. Completely heal him, Lord, so he can run and play like he so much loves to do.

The next morning we were greeted with a beautiful Indiana fall day. There was no humidity and the air felt cool as we ate our breakfast on the outdoor deck. Dirk, Zach and I left Lexi to work on her homework as we headed back to MPRI. Our drive was a short twenty minutes from door-to-door.

Appearing a little nervous, Zach did not feel like talking about what he was about to experience—as usual. Standing to the side, Dirk and I watched as the staff carefully positioned Zach for treatment. Needing the room cleared, they led us to an area at the entrance of the treatment room that contained three computers and a TV monitor. Directing our eyes to the monitor, we saw Zach's face covered by the mask filling the monitor's screen.

Joining us as we watched, Dr. Thornton explained that with each treatment the staff would position Zach and take a preliminary x-ray to determine if he was in the correct position by comparing it with the original plan diagram. When the correct position was found, Dr. Thornton would review it and approve the treatment to begin.

After about twenty-five minutes of adjusting, they staff requested approval. When the doctor approved everything, a bell similar to the sound an elevator makes when it arrives at a new floor started ringing and everyone scurried out of the treatment room, leaving Zach completely alone. A physicist sat at one computer and called for the beam strength he needed. Two technicians sat at the other computers and double-checked all the settings as they waited for the beam to gain strength. When the physicist indicated the beam was at full strength, one of the technicians pressed her computer to activate the treatment. During this time a message flashed above the treatment room doors: "Beam On," for less than a minute. As soon as it stopped, everyone went back in to reposition Zach for the treatment that would go through the top of his head.

Dirk and I stood in awe as we watched our child receive a treatment that would be frightening to an adult, let alone an eight-year-old boy. What a hero! Amazingly, Zach did not move or make a sound as they continued with their work. After a total of fifty minutes, the first treatment was finished. As we entered the treatment room, showering Zach with praise, the technician unclipped the mask from the table and Zach instantly raised his head to look for us. A large grin spread on his face when our eyes met. Telling Zach he was a better patient than most adults, Dr. Thornton patted him on the back. Zach, our boy of few words, just grinned as we headed down the long hall to the exit.

Our next stop was the Bloomington Hospital for a blood draw. Dr. Thornton had explained the Dilantin Zach was taking to prevent seizures needed to be at a specific level in his blood to be effective. Black and purple, Zach's hands were terribly bruised from the recent hospital visit, limiting possible access points. I took two tries to find a vein. I hoped the Dilantin levels would be acceptable so we could go back to finger pokes soon.

Now that treatments had started, it was time to start the chemo again. The doctors had suggested giving him the chemo right before bedtime since he was not supposed to eat anything an hour before and for three hours afterward. He would have to take eleven doses of medicine as he prepared to go to bed!

We managed to get the steroid squirt and all the pills that had to be swallowed down him. The only thing left was the Dilantin, which thank-fully was chewable. But that bothered him because the pills had a mint fla-vor and they stuck to his teeth. I suggested we use his toothbrush to help get the residue out of his teeth after he chewed the pills. His anger spilled out as I handed him the pills in the bathroom. Looking at me as tears formed in his eyes, he said in a very loud voice, "I don't like this!"

Feeling the sting of tears begin, I said, "I don't like this either. I am sorry, Zach. If I could take all these pills for you, I would. This is not very fun, is it?"

He took a deep breath, turned to the sink and quickly chewed the pills, trying hard not to gag. I held my breath, hoping everything did not come back up. A smile came back on Zach's face later, as he listened to the many marbles he earned clink into the glass jar.

I anticipated some side effects from the radiation and chemo, so getting up the next morning was already making me anxious. What a happy sur-prise when the first words from his mouth were, "I'm hungry." Eagerly bounding down the stairs, I prepared his latest favorite breakfast item—scrambled eggs. My paranoia from reading about all the side effects of the chemo and radiation seemed to be unwarranted for now as I watched him hungrily shovel the eggs into his mouth.

Dirk and I both felt such a sense of relief that the treatments had finally started and many of our uncertainties about the procedures had been answered. We spent the weekend trying to find physical things Zach could enjoy. Dr. Thornton had ruled out bowling due to the weight of the ball. Zach found a way around this by reminding us the bowling alley had metal ramps he could use. Anxious to encourage him to get out and be active, we agreed to try. His disappointment was apparent when it became clear the ramps were not easy to aim. With all of us feeling frustrated at the end of the game, it was obvious bowling would be a thing of the past until Dr. Thornton gave his approval for the real thing again.

As the weekend flew by, we were completely surprised by my two sisters. Kathy had invited us and my parents to her house for lunch on Sunday. When we arrived, Michelle and her youngest son Nolan appeared around the corner. She had flown all night from Seattle to squeeze in a visit before her older children, Caylee and Jayden, started school. Zach's face immediately brightened when he saw Nolan. Overwhelmed with emotion, I was amazed with the support we were feeling from family and friends. There were no words to appropriately express our gratitude.

We faced a full week of treatments when we woke on Monday. At the same time, the Gulf Coast of Mississippi and Louisiana was facing an unwelcome visitor named Hurricane Katrina. Having experienced many close calls with hurricanes in Florida, I knew a category-five storm meant many families would be devastated in the next twenty-four hours. My heart ached for them, knowing how it felt to open your eyes one morning with expectations of how your life would proceed only to close them hours later knowing that life would never be the same, knowing how the brokenness of this world can sneak up behind you and slam you to the ground before you knew what was happening.

As the week progressed, I was feeling overwhelmed with managing Zach's treatments, pills and schoolwork, as well as trying to keep Lexi on track with her work. I did not expect Dirk to help since he was trying to keep up with a full-time job. The emotions of the situation worked on me mentally. Finding time to run in the park was a requirement for me to stay upbeat. The website was also an outlet for me. I tried to journal every day and find something positive to report.

September 1, 2005
We all had a good day today. Zach's treatment was early and for the first time there was a slight technical difficulty. Not a big deal except that Zach had to lie in the treatment room about ten extra minutes. He was very brave during his blood draw. We will find out the results tomorrow. He has been and remains so upbeat about the treatments. He said today "only twenty-five more to go!" What a boy. We thank God for the patience he has with this procedure. There is another little guy getting treatments that has to be put under anesthesia everyday. He is miserable because he is so hungry. My heart breaks for him and his parents.

God was working in so many ways through the process. We were all being held, guided and comforted just as we needed in our own special way. Michelle had shared how she and her husband Kevin had been drifting in their faith. When they saw how God was surrounding us with His love, their faith was renewed. Many others as well had shared this same sentiment as they followed our story on the website.

Thankful to have my faith and feel it growing, I shuddered to think how desperate it would have felt to not have God in my life. All my hope and confidence was coming from my heart knowing God was watching over all of us. It was uplifting to know we were able to use this horrible situation to glorify God to others and that God was using us. I was beginning to realize this was what life was truly all about.

Zach handled the first full week of treatments like a pro. He did not display any negative side effects from the chemo or the radiation. This convinced me even more conclusively that proton radiation was superior to conventional. Not only were we able to protect Zach's mental abilities, he did not have to experience the nausea and fatigue that went along with conventional radiation.

We went shopping after the final treatment on Friday for warm clothes. Katrina had devastated the South and had deposited a lot of rain on us. This cooled the evenings considerably for our thin Florida blood. Dirk and I were excited to be able to take the kids to our high school for a football game that evening. Loving the excitement of live football, Zach had a grin on his face the entire game. Although, I felt many curious stares as I helped Zach maneuver the bleacher steps, he did not seem to notice.

After church on Sunday, Dirk, Zach and I went to see a soccer game at Indiana University. The walk to the soccer stadium was long, but Zach managed to make it the entire way. All the bright colors on the field and in the stands were especially vibrant on the warm fall day. Since his left hand did not want to cooperate, he clapped his right hand on my left hand when the IU fight song played. It amazed me how Zach would not let the loss of something as simple as clapping his hands get him down. He would just find another way of doing it. Watching Zach study the game, I noticed him looking at the young ball retrievers positioned around the field. They looked like they were his age and from a local soccer team. It seemed he was imagining in his mind himself down on the field, chasing down balls and tossing them back in. Someday...

Waves of sadness overcame me every time we attended a sporting event. It reminded me of all that Zach had lost—hopefully temporarily—to this beast called cancer. Watching the players, I wondered if I would ever see Zach at that age or see him playing sports again. Hating that I even had these thoughts, I was determined not to let negative thoughts drown my hope of Zach beating this disease.

On our way home, we stopped and picked up pictures I had dropped off for developing. As I began going through the photos, I was shocked to see how many had captured the left side paralysis of Zach's face and arm on the vacation we had taken two weeks before his diagnosis. Obviously, we did not see it in our daily interactions with Zach at the time, but with the camera catching expressions in the blink of an eye, it was clearly there. It made me wonder if it would have made any difference if we had found the tumor sooner. I also wondered what other symptoms could have given us clues.

My mind raced as I lay down to sleep that night. *How can this be our reality?* It is not the reality I had ever pictured for us. On the many mornings before school when I carried Zach from his bed when he was healthy and admired his beautiful sleeping face, I had always dreamed of when he would be able to carry me! That dream seemed to be slipping through my fingers. With his determination and courage, if there was any way, I knew he would overcome the many obstacles he faced. I wanted him to be able to experience more life here on earth as a growing healthy boy and later a man. Wasn't that how it was supposed to be?

Dear Lord, I don't want Zach to suffer or be burdened with illness for the rest of his days. I want him to run and play like he was able to before. He enjoyed it so much; it was such a part of him. Please help me to help him to be the best he can be. Help me to place You first in our lives. Help us to face these challenges with determination and strength. Help us to face each one, large or small, one at a time and overcome them with Your peace and guidance in our hearts.

Glad to get back to treatments after the long Labor Day weekend, it was a relief to know we were actively fighting the cancer cells with each dose of chemo and radiation. Zach was feeling well and not showing any signs of nausea or fatigue. It was quite the opposite. His appetite was strong, his mood was generally good and he was always looking for something to do. Being very accommodating, we were happy to allow any visitor to walk back and watch our brave Zachary endure another dose of radiation. The staff at MPRI was wonderful. Each visitor was amazed, and it reminded me how blessed we were to have such a patient, mature boy. Never complaining about the treatments, Zach would always greet the staff with a smile. It was so sweet to hear him respond consistently, time after time, "good" when they asked him how he was feeling.

We located a children's physical therapy group in Bloomington and went for an initial visit after treatment eight was complete. We met with a physical therapist who immediately put us at ease. He could see the way Zach was swinging his leg around would eventually damage his back and knee and suggested a brace for his left leg to keep his foot from dragging. The brace would hold Zach's foot parallel to the ground, which would enable him to walk in symmetry again.

The best part of the visit was when they strapped Zach onto a large three-wheel bike and let him ride it around the clinic. Eyes sparkling with excitement, Zach had the biggest smile on his face! Freedom at last. He could move quickly again under his own power. The staff told Zach we could have the bike every weekend. Dirk and I were elated Zach would have an outlet for some of his energy.

Feeling frazzled as we worked our way through the second week of treatments, I continued to struggle to manage my time between Lexi and her schoolwork and Zach and his treatments. There was very little time for Dirk and me to spend together, but we managed to squeeze in as many runs in the park as possible since running helped both of us maintain our sanity.

With Dirk and Lexi leaving for Florida soon, Dirk and I made a point to have an actual date. Nervous to be too far away from Zach, I made sure I had my cell phone with us. We were just relaxing over a quiet dinner when my phone rang. I was alarmed to see it was the oncologist's office in Florida. Zach's blood test results indicated his platelet count was low. The doctor requested another blood test to determine if the counts were correct. With our moods spoiled and tension filling our bodies, we headed back to my parents' house.

Not knowing what function platelets played in the body or what happened if they did not get to an acceptable level, I researched the internet and found platelets were the part of blood that was needed for clotting. Zach was not excited to hear he had to endure more pokes the next morning. It was hard enough to face pokes once a week. But much to everyone's relief, he did not have to take the seven chemo pills before bed for awhile. We were told to wait for more test results before resuming the chemo.

Unfortunately, the blood test results were no better the next day, and much to Zach's dismay another test was needed the following Monday. Relieved he would have a break from swallowing pills over the weekend, I could not help but worry about his missing three straight days of chemo. Having a busy day of radiation, as well as physical and occupational therapy, Zach's reward was watching the red gleaming three-wheeled bike get loaded in our truck for the weekend.

A beautiful day greeted us the next morning. Taking Zach and Lexi to the park, we let Zach ride the bike. He was full of spunk as he chased Lexi down the roads. She ran, giggling all the way as Zach furiously pumped his legs to catch her. I savored the sight. The air was fresh and the trees gently waved their leaves at us as we brushed past. Soon these leaves would be falling. There was already a hint on some of the bushes and trees of the color that would be bursting out in a few weeks.

We headed to Bloomington for dinner and more fun after we finished at the park. Dirk and Zach went to play putt-putt golf while Lexi and I shopped at the mall. Forgetting the challenges our family was facing, it was nice to just be together. We went into a pet store to watch the puppies play and browsed in fun accessory shops. When the "boys" finished and rejoined Lexi and me, Zach decided he was feeling lucky and wanted to try the claw machine again. His feeling was right on target. The machine was overflowing and both he and Lexi grabbed a ton of stuffed animals. Zach's excitement was obvious as he snatched four animals in one claw! It was a great end to a perfect day.

My eyes did not want to open when the alarm softly rang in the dark at 4:30 A.M. Dirk and Lexi had an early morning flight. It was extremely foggy as the three of us made our way to the airport in Indianapolis. Tolerating the ride fairly well, Lexi stuck her head out the window occasionally to help alleviate waves of nausea as they hit her. Telling her she reminded me of the puppies we had watched the day before, I hugged her tightly at the curb when we arrived. They were heading back to a reality I would not see for five more weeks. I hated to see them go.

The drive back to my parents' house was difficult. It was always when I was alone that I found it hard to block the reality of Zach's prognosis from my thoughts. "Good Riddance," a song by Green Day, that I had heard a million times before came on the radio. It held new meaning to me as I listened to the words explain how we can't ask why life brings us challenges, but that if we live the best we can, we can hope that we have the time of our life.

The words caused my tears to fall as I thought about what life would be if Zach did not make it. *Did he have the time of his life? Did I do everything as his mom to make sure of that?* It was too overwhelming.

Quickly changing my thoughts, I remembered a quote I had just read by Corrie ten Boom: "Worry does not empty tomorrow of its sorrow, it empties today of its strength." Clinging to that, I decided my motto would be to focus on faith, not fear.

The week was very quiet without Lexi and Dirk around. Continuing to face each treatment with smiles and no complaints, Zach's biggest concerns were the pills and pokes. Learning his platelets had rebounded in a big way, we resumed the chemo. Dirk and Lexi had a tough time getting settled on Sunday night, but soon adjusted to their schedules as the week progressed.

My focus became Zach. Giving him my full attention was glorious. Already having a close relationship before his diagnosis, I could feel it was growing even closer. Being dependent on me to help him with so many things he could do before, he also considered me his main playmate now.

This meant many card games, board games, croquet and, of course, many visits to the claw machine. Anxious to comply with his requests, I wanted to make his days as happy as possible.

As the first week went by, one of the few side effects of the radiation became evident. Zach's hair was falling out. His hair had started growing back around the incision site, but it did not last. More and more of his hair was showing up on his pillow and in the shower.

By mid-week Zach called out as he sat watching television, "Mom, Grammy, watch this."

As we watched, he quickly rubbed his head and his hair fell like snowflakes to the floor. Surprisingly, it was not a big concern to him. Giggling at himself, he considered it more like entertainment. By that evening he had rubbed all the loose hair out and the entire right side of his head, from top to bottom, was bare. There was a very distinct line where the treatment pattern started and stopped, and the only remaining hairs were where his sideburn should be and a small tuft at his hairline in the front. The back, top and left side hair remained intact, but was growing much darker.

Noticing that he was walking much better, everyone agreed it seemed the radiation and physical and occupational therapies were helping. I did not feel I had to hover quite so closely. Not seeing much movement in his arm and none in his hand, we kept working on his stretches. Playing "games" at physical therapy was fun for Zach. Meeting all kinds of challenges using beach balls, sponge Frisbees and sponge ramps, Zach liked winning tickets for prizes and McDonald coupons.

The end of the week brought treatment sixteen—almost halfway done! Going to the IU football game on Saturday afternoon with my parents was our entertainment for the weekend. To start the fun off right, we had to swing by the claw machine. On a mission to accumulate at least one hundred stuffed animals, he had well over seventy already. It was crazy how many quarters we pumped into these machines, a small price to pay to keep Zach smiling. So much had been taken away from him; it was the least we could do.

The weather was beautiful when we arrived at the game. Visiting a pregame party that had a football toss contest for kids to play, Zach asked to play. Afraid he could not do it, I was hesitant. His determination floored me again. Marching up to the line, he was able to throw the ball through the tire once and came very close the next two tries. Amazed at his perseverance, I loved the smile he maintained even when he did not "win." Zach had become our teacher, showing us how vital optimism was in the healing process.

Using my hand to clap for the fight song once again, Zach loved watching the game. Our time in Indiana seemed almost magical, being away from the realities of life. Feeling sure we were on the right track with the proton radiation, everything was working out so well.

Starting the fourth week of treatment, Zach's mood continued to be happy. Sometimes he was downright silly. He had started a game with me where he would walk up and bury his head in my tummy then make an oinking sound like a pig, bursting out in laughter every time he did it. I could not believe this child who was facing so much adversity could be so playful and loving. God was certainly covering him with His grace.

While our playful times continued, the treatment schedule came to a screeching halt. A severe thunderstorm one Monday evening caused the power to go out in Bloomington. MPRI called early Tuesday to report the beam was down and there would be no treatments that day. I was alarmed on Wednesday when they called again to cancel treatment, explaining that a part had failed and they were working frantically to fix it.

Swirling with negative thoughts, I remembered Dr. Thornton had explained how radiation worked in a cumulative manner. Cancer cells took longer to repair than healthy cells, so by having the radiation daily, the cancer cells were getting destroyed because they had no time to repair themselves between treatments. Were we loosing that advantage by missing two days in a row? The technician from MPRI said they would treat some cases on Saturday and Zach would be one of them. That meant we could go in on Thursday, Friday and Saturday to catch up.

It seemed everything was crumbling on Thursday. Zach became very upset when his many claw machine attempts ended in only two surprises. He screamed and pounded on the car door as we drove away. Never hearing him express his anger in such an extreme manner, I quietly listened, understanding it was more than just frustration with the claw machine he was releasing.

His radiation treatment was scheduled for 5:30 P.M. that afternoon and we received a call around 4 P.M. to let us know the electricity was out. No treatment for the third day in a row. My fears building, I wondered why this was happening. When I talked to Dirk, he was like a ticking time bomb. The two weeks of trying to be dad and mom, as well as work a full-time job had taken its toll. Life was suddenly very dark and scary again.

Walking outside to try to get a better frame of mind, I heard the song of a nearby wind chime. Suddenly I felt a sense of peace wash over me. The wind chime belonged to my grandma or "Mom" as we called her. She had passed away a few years ago. Mom had always shared her faith with me. I knew she was in heaven sending me a message.

Lord, please help me remember it is Your plan and Your schedule. I want to control things so much, but it is not up to me. I surrender to You, Lord.

I spoke with Dr. Thornton later that evening and he assured me we could get Zach treated two times on Friday and two times on Saturday to get back on schedule. It smacked me in the face: This must of have been God's plan all along. Maybe that is what Zach needed at this point in his treatment. My journal entry that night summed up my feelings for the day.

September 22. 2005

Remember when I talked about many twists and turns in our journey? Well, we are on a roller coaster this week. We were supposed to go for a treatment at 5:30 today, but I received a call at 4 and the electricity in Bloomington had gone out! The plan now is we will go over for two treatments tomorrow and two on Saturday to get back on track. Dr. Thornton assured me that this was a good solution.

The good news is all of Zach's counts were in the normal range. We are always very thankful for that. The physical therapist was very impressed with Zach's strength in his movements today. Zach feels really good, which is a blessing in itself.

Today I had to remind myself many times that God has His plan and we do not control it! We are focusing on living with faith and not fear, and that helps to get through these crazy curves we face. Please keep your prayers coming and remember Dirk and Lexi as they try to get every-thing done to come back up north. They are both working so hard right now. I wish I were there to help them.

After a few anxious hours the next morning as I waited for a call, the treatments were scheduled. Before we left for physical therapy, Zach grabbed me in a big bear hug. Tears sprung into my eyes when I realized he was hugging me with *both* arms—something I had not felt for almost three months! It was the best hug I had ever received.

After his first treatment of the day, Zach and I headed to the mall to find some new shoes to fit over the leg brace that had finally arrived. Later, the MPRI waiting room was packed when we arrived for the second treat-ment. It was approaching 8:30 p.m. when Zach was taken back for his treat-ment.

Finding it was hard to sleep after we finally settled into bed that night, I was excited to be back on track and to be picking Lexi and Dirk up at the airport the next day. We had made it through the two weeks. Zach was doing great—improving as treatments progressed. Only two and a half weeks left!

We were happy to find they were running on schedule when we arrived for Zach's first treatment on Saturday. My parents had accompanied us so I could leave to pick up Dirk and Lexi before the treatment was finished. It felt very strange to walk out of the clinic without Zach. It would be the first time he would not see me standing at the foot of the treatment table when they removed the mask and he lifted his head.

Facing another drive alone, my excitement to see Dirk and Lexi helped make the time go by without being overtaken with negative thoughts about the future. Seeing Lexi standing on the curb, I jumped out of the car and ran to her and Dirk. Zach called us twice during our drive home to find out how far away we were. Excited to have his football-watching buddy back, he wanted Dirk to know the games were on!

I had warned Dirk and Lexi that Zach's appearance had changed substantially since their last visit. Continuing to gain weight, his face was very round and he was totally bald on his right side. None of that mattered. They were ecstatic to see Zach was regaining the use of his left side. Showing off how well he could move, he took a Nerf football outside to play catch with Dirk. I was thrilled to see him almost run as he caught pass after pass and to watch him throw perfect spirals to Dirk.

My parents had gone above and beyond all expectations to be accommodating during our stay. They had planned to spend the weekend out of town to give us some family time. The time they were spending with Zach was priceless. Grabbing Zach in a big hug and kissing his very round cheeks over and over had become my mom's favorite thing to do. It made Zach giggle and protest, but he really loved it.

Beginning the fifth week of treatment, Zach enjoyed having Dirk and Lexi for an audience at physical and occupational therapy. He was getting very good at all the tasks they required him to perform. Later, Zach surprised us all at the Tuckers when he started to really run on his own. He surprised himself too because he just kept going as we watched, smiling at his progress.

Treatments went smoothly all week. As the weekend neared, we were all treated to a ride in a limo with Dirk's brother Darin and his fiancée Carol who wanted to share some free limo time they had received when they purchased their wedding bands. Knowing the kids would be thrilled with the ride, they had even requested that one of our stops be at the claw machine for more toys!

The weekend went by quickly and before we knew it Zach was starting the final full week of treatments. Wrapping up our visits to physical and occupational therapy, we were happy to see a flicker of movement in a few of Zach's fingers—for the first time in three months.

We began the transition back to the doctors in Florida. I hated leaving

Dr. Thornton. We had grown accustomed to his amazing intelligence and passion for his work. With all of Zach's progress, he decided it was time to start weaning him off the steroids. That was a relief since it would be good to give his body a break from the many side effects they had caused.

So many exciting things were happening as we neared the end of treatment. Zach was receiving many fun things in the mail. Our friends in Florida were planning many fun surprises for our return and my Aunt Diane was writing a special story for him on the website titled "The Claw Machine Warrior." It was all so fun for Zach and amazing to see this journey affect so many.

All too soon it was time for Dirk and Lexi to leave again. Managing to get all of Lexi's homework completed created a few tense moments between us, but as usual she complied with all that was asked of her. This experience had been so hard on her, pulling her in many directions. I looked forward to getting back home and giving her a more stable environment again. They had the same early morning flight as before. Zach and I would follow the next week on Thursday. Knowing we would soon be home with them, it was not such a difficult good-bye. I could not wait to be a family again in our own home.

It was a big day of celebration for Zach as many of my aunts, uncles and cousins came to visit. They brought him a special surprise—a signed hat and jersey from his favorite NFL quarterback, Peyton Manning of the Indianapolis Colts. He beamed with pride as he slipped the hat on his head and held the jersey.

There were only two treatments remaining for Zach. I watched him sleep when I woke on Monday. He giggled in his sleep again. I wondered what his dreams were about now. Did he dream of life before this new reality? Did he dream of what could be? Whatever they were, I was glad they made him laugh.

As Zach and I climbed into bed that night, I was floored as he asked, "Mom, what are they doing to me during the treatments?"

Wondering why it had taken him this long to ask this question, I answered, "Well, they are sending radiation into the spot where you had the tumor. This radiation is going in to kill any cancer cells that might still be in there." He seemed satisfied with this answer and soon fell asleep. Once again, his simple acceptance without questions or complaints of the treatments he endured amazed me.

The final day of treatment was anticlimactic. The staff at MPRI wanted to have a special party for Zach, but the gift they were getting him would not be ready until Wednesday. So we went in as usual and left as usual without much fanfare. In an attempt to express our gratitude to the staff for the wonderful way they had handled Zach, we bought a shadow box and arranged some thank-you notes and mementos for them. I hoped this would allow other patients to see how grateful we were and how wonderful they all had been to us.

Returning on Wednesday for the party, Zach proudly walked down the hall, knowing he had accomplished a major task. They presented him with a signed football from the IU football coach, Coach Hep. Receiving his mask and many other fun little mementos, it was bittersweet to be leaving all the new friends we had made that had been such a big part of our lives for the last two months.

I made my final entry from Indiana that evening on Caringbridge.

October 12, 2005

This will be my last entry from Indiana for now. We will return in December for Christmas and Uncle Darin and Carol's wedding. We have made many special memories while we have stayed in Indiana. What a wonderful opportunity it has been for both kids to spend time with their extended family and enjoy the Indiana fall season!! It has been a blessing for all of us. I feel like I have been so pampered and loved as well. Dirk and I are truly blessed with the families we have.

Zach also received a very special package yesterday. It had a Vermont Teddy Bear in it. It was from Westra Construction (Dirk's employer) and had a card saying "Way to go, Zach!" They timed it to be delivered on his last day of treatment. The bear's jersey says "U did it!" on the front and "Zach #1" on the back. Zach has had a blast playing with the mini-football and "tackling" me at every opportunity! Thanks to the Westra Crew for being so thoughtful.

Well, we have a very early morning. We will be leaving Spencer at 5:30 A.M. to head back to the warm sunny weather. We will miss all our Indiana friends, but we are looking so forward to seeing all our Florida friends. Get ready, Sunshine State—Zach Attack is coming back!!!!

My parents helped me pack the many items we had accumulated while in Indiana. It seemed an eternity since we had arrived with a very sick little boy. Happy to be going back with a much stronger, not so little boy, physically, Zach was quite different. Although he was fourteen pounds heavier and bald on the right side, he was running again! God had answered so many prayers during the last seven weeks. After a tearful good-bye with my parents, Zach and I headed through the airport on our own. I smiled as I thought about the surprises waiting for Zach in Florida. Thankful to be finished with this phase of the treatment—it had been a wonderful time— I thought of the golden fall we would always remember.

Reflections

Our time in Indiana was magical, filled with blessings from God and many lessons from Zach. By leading us to MPRI, God had provided Zach with a protective haven filled with the special love of many—family members, friends and the staff at his treatment facilities. In this environment, he had grown strong and shown us that living with hope and optimism made challenges much easier to overcome. His unending smiles and willingness to do whatever was asked of him was amazing and exceeded our highest expectations. He taught us how to live in the moment and find joy when circumstances were difficult. It was clear God was using his life in a very special way to reach many hearts and remind each one of us how powerful faith could be.

Dirk, Lexi, Zach and I faced the unthinkable challenge of finding a way to live apart while fighting this monster called cancer. Forced to continue "living" Dirk and Lexi faced work and school with amazing strength and perseverance. It had not been easy, and the stress was overwhelming at times, but the help of many friends had gotten them through. It gave me the time to pour unending love on Zach—an immeasurable gift I will always treasure. My relationship with Zach grew to a level every mother longs to have with her child—one of complete trust and understanding.

Sharing my growing faith through the website had changed my heart. My purpose was selfish: a place to pour out my heart about all we were facing. But seeing how the love that was coming from God through my words could touch many, the purpose seemed to be deeper than I ever imagined. Never expecting the words I wrote to be used for His purpose, I did not feel qualified or worthy when I was told God was speaking through me.

Centering our lives on God, loving each other as if it could be our last day, and taking nothing for granted were our new priorities. God's love had taken over our hearts completely and filled us all with a sense of optimistic hope. We felt we were on the right track with the treatment plan and life would soon be settling back into a more normal routine. Getting through the radiation treatments was a giant step for all of us. Little did we know that we were only beginning to understand the journey that was ahead.

The power of encouragement was the lesson we learned through this part of the journey. We were constantly overwhelmed with the support and love we received all around us. Guestbook entries on the website expressing love, concern, inspiration and support appeared many times a day and lifted us up just when we needed it. Gifts, cards and letters sent to Zach brought smiles to his face and excitement to his day when they arrived in the mail or on the doorstep. We were truly surrounded by many "angels on earth."

Zach with is "U did it!" bear after completing his final radiation treatment. He was feeling so strong and happy at this point. He thought it was fun to pretend he was a running back with this football and try to knock me down.

Welcome home celebration in Florida! Twenty pounds heavier than when he left, Zach and his buddies get ready to play with his surprise claw machine in our garage. Zach is wearing his signed Peyton Manning jersey.

Left to right: Grant Brus, Kyle Norris, Zach, Kyler Williams, Spencer Brus, Zack Keller.

Zach's first official day of third grade. His smile shows his excitement over being at school again. He made sure to wear his hat, but did not like that I made him wear his leg brace.

CHAPTER EIGHT

Ugliness of cancer

The flight home was so different. On the last flight, I had felt my hope dwindling from fear. But on this flight I felt triumphant. Zach had persevered and conquered the radiation and chemo regimen! He amazed me with his strength and optimism. God's love and protection seemed to be surrounding us. I was anxious to get back to our friends, our house, our life. Zach would be on "rest" from treatment for six to eight weeks. Anticipating this to be one of those downhill times—filled with good days and getting Zach settled into a school routine—I thought I might even figure out a way to get back to work by working from home.

Dirk and Lexi greeted us with excited smiles. They could hardly wait to see Zach's expression when he found his first surprise: a ride home in another limo. He appeared quite confused when we walked out to the curb where he saw Lexi climb into the big, black shining car. I laughed and hugged him tight as I explained that our friends had arranged for him to have a fancy ride home. He loved it!

Overwhelmed with joy as we drove through Tampa to our home, Lexi and Zach played around with balloons Debbie had left in the car. She and my friend Karen had arranged for the limo as well as all of the festivities that awaited us at our house. Zach had slipped on his autographed "Peyton Manning" Colts jersey at the airport to show it off to Dirk. Little did he know he would have a much larger audience when we arrived at our home!

I felt like we were on a version of *Extreme Home Makeover* as we turned onto our shady, tree-lined street. Lexi and Zach stood up so their heads were sticking out of the moon roof of the limo as they waved and smiled to a sea of faces. There were at least one hundred friends waving and cheering! Tears of happiness sprang into my eyes as I watched Zach climb from the car with a big smile on his face. Becoming shy as Debbie filmed his reaction, he managed to mumble, "It's fine," when she asked what he thought of all the excitement.

As soon as we were through our initial hugs and greetings, it was time for Zach's second surprise—his very own claw machine. Dirk raised the garage door to reveal the machine. Zach's smile grew wide and his eyes sparkled as he took in the sight. Soon there was a large line of kids waiting their turn to play.

When I slipped into the house after things calmed down, it almost seemed foreign to me. It had only been eight weeks, but things looked bigger here, smaller there, a different shade than I remembered. Funny how your mind changes memories ever so slightly, I smiled as I walked through and touched all the familiar things I had missed.

Our family was together again. Lexi could not stop spontaneously coming up and hugging me all through the evening. Paying for all of the activity earlier with an aching thigh muscle, Zach had a long bath and massage to help him to relax. Sleeping in his own bed again—the first time since July 10th—Zach and I cuddled close for quite awhile as we both adjusted to the fact we would not be sleeping in the same bed anymore.

I slowly traced his face with my fingertip, around his beautiful eyes, over his full pink lips, to his perfect little nose. Both he and Lexi loved for me to do this as they drifted off to sleep. As I did, I would always marvel at their soft, smooth skin and how utterly blessed Dirk and I were to have these two precious children. Now that our lives had taken this drastic turn down a road we never expected to travel, these feelings intensified. I so desperately wanted to be tracing Zach's face when he was a fifth grader, an eighth grader, and a senior in high school.

Dear Lord, thank You for these two precious gifts You have given us. Lord, I pray it is Your will to have Zach defeat this cancer in his body, to be the greatest testimony for You the rest of his days. He is such a special soul and we need him here with us. Thank You for the many blessings we have experienced today, and for all of the wonderful friends You have put in our lives.

After Zach's breathing became deep and steady, I slipped out of his room and gladly climbed into my own bed. Dirk had already drifted off to sleep. I felt the fatigue in my bones come to the surface as my eyes became heavy. It was so good to be home!

When Monday arrived, happiness filled me as I helped Lexi leave for school. After she was off, my focus settled on Zach since it was going to be his first official day of school! Feeling a bit nauseous, he did not eat much for breakfast. It seemed the few remaining pills were getting harder and harder for him to get down, but he managed to get through it as he always did. Excited and nervous, he wanted so much to be normal again. I chuckled to myself remembering his response when I ask him in Indiana how he wanted to get back into the swing of school. "You can just drop me off at car line, Mom," he had responded nonchalantly. What a kid!

As we gathered his books and backpack, I was surprised when he went to his room to retrieve a hat. This was the first time he had been concerned about covering his head since they shaved it for his original surgery. He chose a Tampa Bay Lightning hat and we were off. Though Zach grumbled about it, I had put his leg brace on him. He worried it would hinder him on the playground, so we made a deal to remove it at lunch. I just wanted to protect his body and not have any additional damage occur because of his left side deficiencies.

Lithia Springs Elementary was located just two miles from our home. It opened in 1992 and housed kindergarten through fifth-grade students. Zach knew the school well even before he was a student there. He always accompanied me when I dropped off and picked up Lexi. Plus he sat in my lap and chewed on his beloved blankie as I read stories to her kindergarten class. When it came time for him to start kindergarten three years later, he felt like he owned the place.

Following my routine to take the kids' picture on their first day of school each year, I quickly snapped a shot as he stood by the car when we arrived at the school. What a sweet smile he had, and his eyes reflected the excitement he was feeling. Being equally excited, his classmates welcomed him with applause as we entered the room and shouted greetings of "Zach, you're here!"

After settling him at his desk, I suddenly realized I had to leave him. It was such a strange feeling to walk out of that room without him by my side. He had been with me nonstop for the last four months. Now I had to loosen my protective hold and let him be more independent again. Easing the transition, I knew I would rejoin him in a couple of hours for lunch and then we would have to leave for a clinic visit.

Grateful when the two hours had passed, I sat outside near the lunch area, my eyes glued to his classroom door on the second floor, about halfway down the long building. I watched as the door opened and saw his Lightning hat above the low wall. Then I saw his eyes peeking over the wall to see if I was there. My heart beat a little faster and a warm smile spread across my face as his hat came bouncing down the wall in line with all his classmates. He appeared around the corner as his class filed past to the lunchroom door. And there was his ever-present smile.

Of course, he wanted to play with the "guys" after lunch on the play-ground. He lived for recess and P.E. during his first three years at Lithia. His teachers had often told me about the many times he had come in from recess or P.E. covered in dirt and a few scraps on his knees. Sweat would be dripping from his hair, but he was completely filled with joy over the game he had just completed. Today, he had that in mind as we removed his brace and put his regular shoe on his foot.

Watching him try to join in the pick-up soccer game that had started on the playground was bittersweet. He quickly realized he could not make his body move like he was used to. The extra weight and left side weakness betrayed what he had pictured in his mind. Tears stung my eyes as I watched. I could not believe how completely unfair life had become. To my amazement, Zach did not let any of this bother him. He just smiled and tried again as they played. Lost in the moment, he was glad to be back to what he knew—to what he should have been doing the last three months.

I had purposely scheduled his appointment after lunch so he could experience most of his school day. We headed off to the clinic after the whistle blew to end recess. Little did I know this was a big mistake. My training of how to be a cancer mom was about to begin. The problem was there was no teacher. I had to figure this new assignment out on my own.

After the nurse did a quick finger poke, Dr. Ayala came in the room to check Zach over. Confusion filled my mind as she started talking about a variety of chemo medicines other than Temador. She asked if we had consulted with Duke about treatment. My head was spinning. Had the plan changed while we were in Indiana—without my knowledge? The plan—the one I thought we had decided on—had sounded so simple and easy: Do the radiation, come home, take a rest, and then start a ten-month routine of Temador five days on, twenty-eight days off and with few quality of life issues. This was what had been in my head the last four months. This is what we were supposed to do. And life would settle into a routine.

After I explained my confusion to her, she indicated there had been changes in the protocol for GBMs and there were some other chemo drugs that showed promise. In addition, there were other drugs that could be taken with the chemo that would help prevent the blood flow to the tumor.

Why was I hearing all this for the first time now? Had I totally dropped the ball by not looking for other treatments? This was the second time Duke had been mentioned. Was this a sign I needed to contact them?

Because this information was confusing and completely unexpected, I became very skeptical of everything she said. To top everything off, Zach's platelets had dropped to 15, well below the acceptable level of 40. He would need an infusion of platelets, but the doctor said it was too late in the day to receive one at the clinic. We would need to be admitted to All Children's for his infusion. Lesson number one: Never schedule a blood draw appointment in the afternoon, unless you wanted to end up at the hospital for an infusion.

Everything had become really complicated—really fast. Discovering there was no clear treatment plan in place, when I thought it had already been determined, disturbed me greatly.

We had to get across Tampa—and it was almost rush hour—to pick Lexi up from our house and then get to All Children's. Having Lexi stay home would have been simpler, but I feared she was too emotionally fragile at this point to be left alone again.

We arrived at All Children's just before 6:30 P.M.—just in time for shift change. Lesson number two: Try to beat the shift change because it will add at least an hour to any procedure. Dirk came to the hospital on his way home from work and dined with us on carryout from All Children's cafeteria. The infusion finally started at 11 P.M. and Zach was a trooper through it all. With a large smile covering his face and lying in his hospital bed, he talked to Grammy and Papaw on the phone. I snapped a picture of him. Not the picture I expected to be in line right after the one I had taken earlier of his first day of school. I was beginning to see that our lives would never be back to a predictable routine. That was something in our past and long gone.

The week started out rough, and did not improve. Research consumed my days once again, and concern over Zach's growing nausea and intolerance to taking his pills filled my nights. Many times he gagged and threw up at even the thought of swallowing another scoop of yogurt filled with some form of pill or capsule.

We visited the clinic a few days later and found he needed more platelets. I was confused and frustrated. It didn't help that the doctor assumed someone had told me about this new routine as a possible side effect of the medication. I felt like an outsider to this new "cancer club" and realized we were completely on our own to learn the rules of this new reality by trial and error.

Zach was not feeling the greatest but wanted to join his class for Fun

Friday, a day of playing games and extra recess. After dropping him off, I went back to my research. E-mailing Duke and Dr. Thornton for advice only resulted in more confusion. The doctor at Duke felt more than Temador was needed, but Dr. Thornton was not convinced of this. As I walked up to the school to get Zach, I was an emotional wreck. Seeing all the statistics again made the optimism we had brought back from Indiana hard to hang onto. Wearing sunglasses, I tried to avoid talking to anyone for fear I would lose it and allow my fears to spill out for everyone to see. Keeping up a brave front was emotionally draining to me, but it was necessary to protect Zach. I did not want him to lose his optimism because of my fears.

Seeing Zach's sad face after school, I knew he was not feeling much better. Worry about the evening filled my heart. Our friend, Craigg Page, had arranged an amazing night for our whole family. Because he worked for Kraft Foods, he was able to schedule the Kraft Wienermobile to come and pick us up to take us to a Lightning hockey game. Craigg had even arranged for Zach to be the Lightning's special guest. Zach was excited, but I could tell it would be a challenge for him.

Laughing as we rode to the game in the large hot-dog-shaped vehicle, we noticed several cars pull up alongside us and people taking pictures with their camera phones as they smiled or waved to us. Zach was treated like a celebrity. His queasy tummy issues melted away as he received an autographed jersey, saw his name on the JumboTron and watched the players warm up from the sideline of the hockey rink. Exhausted, but happy, we all carried away many great memories because of Craigg's efforts.

Throughout the weekend, Zach struggled to eat and keep his medicine down. I wasn't getting any answers from the doctors regarding why he was feeling so bad and felt was like everyone was brushing off my concerns and not hearing me. His Dilantin levels were my biggest concern. Letting the levels get too low could provoke a seizure. It broke my heart to watch him need two or three tries each time he had to take another bothersome pill.

The weekend also brought Hurricane Wilma to Florida. Although school was closed on Monday, the clinic remained open despite the advice to stay off the roads. Lexi, Zach and I ventured out to brave the winds and rain only to spend the entire day at the clinic for another platelet infusion. The downward spiral Zach had experienced since returning from Indiana was so confusing and unexpected to me. This was supposed to be the rest time! It seemed rest was defined as "the time the treatments work a number on the patient's body" in the cancer world.

Later in the week, the physical and occupational therapists were impressed with Zach's improvements from his last visit in August. Not wanting to pull him out of school too often, I was hesitant to schedule more than one visit per week for these treatments. It became a moot point when I was told our insurance would not cover any further physical or occupational therapies this calendar year. Zach was doing so well on his own, we decided I could work with him at home, and we would decide after January if we wanted to find another facility that would be covered.

As the week progressed, Zach continued to feel worse each day. It had become next to impossible for him to swallow the pills on the first try. My heart broke when he looked at me between dry heaves and said, "Sorry, Mom." Feeling like I had been kicked in the stomach, I realized maybe I was pushing too hard. I called the doctor's office to see if we could skip all the pills except for the Dilantin. Agreeing it would be OK, they explained that going off steroids sometimes gives patients flu-like symptoms. I just wanted him to feel better and be able to eat again. Gone were the days of his eating half of a medium pizza. His food intake had dropped to a few bites at each meal.

Feeling lost, I again thought maybe the cancer world we had entered was really hell. Maybe we were walking in hell now and all these kids who become so sick were angels sent to teach us lessons.

Lord, I know You have a plan and I trust Your will. I ask for strength to be patient and know I will not always understand why Zach has to struggle so much.

Waking early on Thursday for a follow-up MRI and blood draw, Zach struggled. He looked pale. I knew he would need some type of infusion. Rushing to the bathroom as soon as we arrived at the clinic, Zach lost what little contents he had in his stomach. And he shook with chills. Unprepared to see Zach suffer so intensely, I felt anger welling up inside me. I struggled to understand. *Why Zach? Why cancer? Why, why, why?*

Finding that he needed both platelets and red cells made the walk to the mobile MRI unit seem like one hundred miles. With Zach too weak to protest, the nurse managed to get a small smile from him after placing his IV line for the MRI contrast. Grateful he could rest during the scan, I found myself once again watching him sleep as the machine captured pictures of his brain. Leaving with my copy of the scan, we headed to the clinic in St. Petersburg for his infusions.

I begged him to eat when we arrived and he managed to force down a couple of crackers before chewing up his Dilantin pills. The rest of our day was spent sitting in overstuffed recliners as first the platelets and then the red cells poured into his weakened body.

By 7 P.M. we were finally home. Lexi was a nervous wreck even though I had called her to tell her what was happening. Having slept most of the day, Zach perked up a little after I fed him a cup of Jell-O and chased Lexi around the house. It was good to see him smile a little again.

After putting the kids to bed, Dirk and I nervously sat in front of the computer and viewed the MRI scan. Dr. Thornton had warned us not to expect major changes right away, telling us that the true effects of radiation would not show up for at least four to six months. My heartbeat quickened as I opened the file. As we compared that day's MRI with the previous one, relief washed over both of us when we saw that things looked the same or smaller. Fearing we would see more white tumor or new spots, we were thankful that our untrained eyes only saw hope.

My hope for a better day quickly turned to despair as Zach continued to boycott food and struggled to take his Dilantin the next day. The lively, boisterous Zach that had come home from Indiana was nowhere to be found. Feeling progressively worse as the day faded to night, he was a mess when it was time for his medication. Immediately throwing up after the first try, he couldn't even put another pill near his mouth without having dry heaves. I tried everything—pleading, demanding and begging. He was trembling and telling me how sorry he was as he stood over the toilet with dry heaves.

There was no doubt in my mind now: We *were* in hell. Beginning to panic as I imagined Zach going into a seizure from lack of Dilantin, I called the after-hours number for the clinic. I felt deceived and mislead. When Dr. Grana returned my call, I wanted to scream into the phone, "Is this the good quality of life you were telling us about?" Deciding to let Zach rest for the night, she asked that we try to get the pills down in the morning. And if that didn't work, we would go to All Children's and receive them through an IV.

My mind raced throughout the restless night watching Zach as he tried to sleep. "What if he has a seizure?... He has got to be starving... How can I get him to eat?... What did Dr. Thornton tell me to do if he has a seizure?" On and on my thoughts circled until I was in tears. I called Dr. Grana back at 7 A.M. She felt we should come in and promised a quick stay. Grabbing a few things to entertain us while they gave him an IV, I woke Dirk and Lexi to let them know we were leaving.

Once we got there, we had to stop many times to rest as Zach and I slowly made the long walk to the admit office. Already bewildered by his condition, my frustration grew when we were told there were no rooms available. I suddenly had a glimpse of the panic Joseph and Mary must have felt! Thank goodness there were no stables nearby.

After an hour of waiting in the admit office, I noticed a very pronounced tremor in Zach's left hand. I had seen it sporadically the last few days and was scared it was an indication he might have a seizure any minute. I announced my fears to the clerk, and we amazingly had a room within thirty minutes.

Equally concerned with the tremor, Dr. Grana reviewed the recent MRI scan and ordered a consult with the neurosurgery group. Overall, she was pleased with what she saw, but was concerned fluid buildup was causing his nausea. Clearing any brain issues, the neurosurgery group's review indicated Zach's symptoms were probably from gastro-intestinal issues. My sense of urgency for Zach to receive a dose of Dilantin seemed unnoticed as we waited three and a half hours for an IV to be started. Looking much better after he received his medicine, he still refused to eat.

Although the thought of the foldout recliner was not too exciting to me, in his weakened state it was clear Zach needed more rest and would need to stay in the hospital overnight.

Joining us later, Dirk and Lexi brought us overnight bags. Carving pumpkins had filled their afternoon—just the kind of thing that should happen on October 29th. How had our lives come to this point? Where was God? My faith was faltering as frustrations with the unknown kept eating away at my thoughts.

Because of four days of nothing substantial to eat, Zach's body seemed to be in total revolt. Throughout the torturous night he woke me for a drink several times, only to throw it back up in a few minutes, which caused his tremors to intensify. Trying to comfort him, I laid myself gently on his arm until he relaxed. Thankfully, he was receiving hydration and his medicine through the IV.

The challenges continued the next day. After a quick exam, Dr. Storrs, the neurosurgeon, concluded that going off the steroids had to have been the main culprit causing Zach's current condition. Asking what was next for Zach's treatment, I explained my dilemma of trying to decide if we needed to go to Duke. Advising against it, he explained that trying new protocols sometimes brought unneeded troubles.

Much to my surprise, he told me that after looking at the most recent MRI, he felt the cyst was larger than after he had drained it and that there appeared to be more enhancement in the tumor. Spinning in confusion after he left, I felt like I was getting a different answer from every doctor who walked through the door—and none of them could give me a good reason for Zach's condition. I wanted to scream. All I wanted was a straight and definitive answer!

When they told me Zach might have a GI infection and that his Dilantin level was dangerously low, it was clear our "overnight" stay was not going to end soon. My state of mind was spiraling downward into a dark place as the triumphant hope built up in Indiana evaporated. Our future suddenly looked bleak, filled with many hospital stays and constant doctor visits.

Looking in the mirror, I found a stranger looking back—someone with hollow eyes and worry wrinkles all over her face. Watching Zach made my heart break. His little body had been through so much—and he was only eight years old! I thought about Dirk and Lexi, knowing we were all so lost. None of us wanted to walk this path. Life continued on around us. It was flying by and we were in slow motion, waiting to jump back in, yet knew that wouldn't happen. We would always be the family with cancer. We were all struggling to understand how to live our lives in this hell.

I struggled to even come up with a prayer. I felt that God was not hearing me anyhow. How could He be, with Zach suffering so much? I could not believe how quickly our outlook had changed. It was only fifteen days ago that we so triumphantly arrived home, ready to conquer the world.

Lord, please give us strength to get through this trial. We pray Zach's suffering will be brief and ultimately be used to reach others to know You. Lord, help us to keep our faith strong because I am feeling weak.

Another day passed, another doctor visited us in the hospital. He scheduled Zach for an upper GI scope to check for germs and irritation as an explanation for his continued refusal of food. I was relieved that it finally seemed someone was doing something proactive to help. The scope indicated Zach's stomach and lower esophagus were irritated and inflamed and causing some pain, but not enough to explain all of his symptoms. At least it was something tangible.

Frustration and depression haunted me as it seemed no one was focusing on Zach completely. We appeared to be a fleeting thought on many doctors' minds, but a passion to none. Adding to my frustration, it seemed the chemo plan had changed once again as Dr. Grana explained that in addition to the Temador Zach would take two additional drugs that were shown to slow the ability of tumors to grow the blood vessels needed to keep them alive. Of course, both had multitudes of side effects that would have to be considered, especially since his stomach seemed to be so sensitive. Through all of this, I continued to watch helplessly as Zach's amazing determination seemed to be slowly slipping away.

I lost track of what was happening outside of the dark hospital room, Dirk visited and reminded us that to the rest of the world, it was Halloween. Thoughts of Lexi preparing to trick or treat without us and Zach missing the event totally saddened me. Although normally sleeping, Zach was awake for Dirk's visit, but he did not want the lights on nor did he want us to talk about food.

Later, a bit of hope entered my heart when the hospital's neurologist agreed with me that we needed to find an alternative or eliminate Dilantin from Zach's regimen. He said that besides being a challenge to manage, a common side effect of Dilantin was suppressing bone marrow function, which was the last thing Zach needed while taking chemo.

That evening, Zach's ninth Halloween quietly passed as we held hands and watched television. His opportunity to trick or treat in the halls of the hospital was limited by his low white blood cell counts—not that he really wanted to anyway.

As we entered day four of our "brief visit," I was tempted to step out in the hall and scream at the top of my lungs, "SOMEONE PLEASE HELP MY CHILD!" But who would I yell it to? No one seemed to have any definite answers, and Zach continued to tremor, throw up and not eat. Never feeling so helpless in my life, I realized things were not much better at our house. Being overcome by the anxiety of our absence, Lexi had thrown up three times during the night. She was going to school, but sounded small and scared when I talked to her. We all were so fragile mentally. Ironically, Zach seemed to be the strongest with all he faced. Even though he felt completely lousy, he was not "losing it" like the rest of us were. I tried to pray again.

Lord, I am at rock bottom. I am reaching out my hand to You to pull me up. My faith is weak. I feel lost.

Attempting to improve our outlook, I took Zach on a wheelchair ride around the hospital. Wearing his required mask, he directed me to the cafeteria. With much hope, we slowly scanned all the selections they offered, looking for something he wanted to eat. Milk was the only thing that appealed to him. As we walked back to the room, I could feel my anger and frustration pushing to the surface. Why did the nurses or doctors at the clinic not take me more seriously when I was asking about Zach's upset stomach? Surely he was not the first patient to experience something like this. Did anyone care? Or were we just another chart to get through?

The maddening cycle of no answers, no eating and no end in sight to our visit continued. Trying to encourage Zach to get his muscles moving, I felt my heart sink as I watched his left foot drag once again while he walked to the playroom. All the progress we had made on his left side seemed to be going out the window. In the playroom, Zach played pool using only his right hand instead of a cue, reminding me of our vacation to Georgia right before his diagnosis when he used the same technique. *Was that another life?* Who would have ever guessed five months later we would be here?

As the fifth day of our stay passed, Zach's lack of nutrition became the focus of everyone's concern. Determination to find something he would eat consumed me when we were told he would have a feeding tube inserted through his nose to his stomach if he did not start eating. I ordered eggs, toast, ice cream, pudding and Italian ice for his breakfast. He took a couple of bites of Italian ice and turned away from the rest. My heart sank.

When I felt I was at my lowest point, help arrived. Wearing her wonderful, bright smile, my friend Debbie came bouncing in the door. Like a breath of fresh air, she perked Zach up by playing a new game with him and brought me a God-sent gift—a book called *The Case for Faith* by Lee Strobel. Unfortunately, she had no more luck coaxing Zach to eat than I did. His involuntary hunger strike continued.

After Debbie left, Zach slept and I began to read. My eyes were opened to how weak I had become in relying on God. My heart had hardened to the hope I once held. I felt it softening once again as I read words about staying strong in faith.

Lord, I am ashamed of my weakness and doubts. Please forgive me for losing my faith this week. I am praying for You to fill me with the Holy Spirit. Give us all strength. I pray for wisdom in making decisions for Zach's care. I am scared of the feeding tube. Please guide us to know Your will.

Waking Zach before Dirk and Lexi arrived for an evening visit, I wanted to give him time to get over the tremors that had been consistently appearing each time he woke up. The tremors almost made it seem that his body was rebelling at the assault of waking. I did not want them to witness his struggle.

During the visit, it was evident Lexi was still battling her own extreme anxiety and Dirk was filled with stress. Leaving with heavy hearts as the clock neared 9 p.m., we were separated for yet another night. I never knew what a toll cancer could have on every member of a family. Now it would be seared into my memory forever.

Desperate to stop Zach's constant throwing up the next morning, I begged the nurses for help. They tried a dose of Benadryl, and relief filled me when he drifted off to sleep. All sanity seemed to be slipping away from me. I questioned why a nutritionist had never shown up with suggestions about how to get Zach to eat only to be told she had come by and left a report in Zach's chart.

As my baby lay starving, I felt that all everyone wanted to do was to jam a feeding tube down his throat without determining why he was so sick. Anger raged inside me. He had lost eight pounds since we arrived. I felt Zach's case had been terribly mismanaged by all the doctors. No one seemed to be communicating or trying to solve his issues.

Each phone call or doctor visit ended with me in tears as I lost all control of my emotions. Zach looked at me with worried eyes. I tried to explain to him that I was sad and concerned he felt so bad.

It was then I felt sure we needed a different solution than was being offered by these doctors. Hearing yet another version of the chemo plan earlier in the day, I felt everyone was reactive—instead of proactive—and only guessing what to do next. As I explained my feeling to Dirk later, he agreed we needed to find one doctor who would take complete charge of Zach's case.

Day seven arrived and my emotional tirades the day before had apparently scared all the doctors away. No one came in to check on us the entire morning except the nurses taking vitals. I wondered if they had put a sticker on our chart saying, "Watch out for the crazy lady."

Feeling defeated, I had agreed to the feeding tube after Zach showed no signs of improvement. I made a last-ditch effort to get him to eat before the nurses came in with the tube, but he would have nothing to do with it. Hoping to prepare him for what was about to happen, I explained how the tube would go in his nose to his tummy to feed him until he could eat again.

Entering the room with a long thin plastic tube, two nurses positioned themselves—one holding the tube, the other Zach's arms as he sat on my lap. Working quickly, the nurse inserted the tube into Zach's right nostril and proceeded to push it farther and farther in. In a panic, Zach called out, "Stop, stop, I can't." It felt as if my heart broke into a million pieces as his pleading eyes met mine.

Over in less than a minute, it seemed to last forever. His eyes were blank and sad now. It was a terrible violation of his body. Unfortunately, they were not finished positioning the tube. They had to take us to x-ray and push it farther down through his stomach to the upper intestine. Bypassing his stomach would limit the possibility of throwing up all the formula as it was pumped in later.

Zach had been such a rock through everything, full of optimism and smiles. Now that was gone. Holding his hand, I had tears streaming down my face as Zach pleaded again with them, "Stop, please stop," when they began to further position the tube in the x-ray room. Wanting to yank him from the table and run away, my pulverized heart felt like it was now being ripped out of my body. His empty, defeated eyes made me feel that I had betrayed him by allowing this awful procedure. Not realizing how extreme the procedure would be for him, I could barely talk to Dirk about it through my tears later.

Waking for the first time with the tube in place, Zach was very uncomfortable and nauseous. Trying to calm his tremors and keep the tube in place as he gagged, I sat close to him encouraging him softly to try and relax. He would not speak or try to eat. He was despondent. Arriving with the formula, the nurse showed me how to hook the tube up to a pump. Encouraged he was finally getting some nutrition, I no longer asked him to try to eat. We were all exhausted, sad and broken.

The night was rough. Knocking his knuckles against the bed rail when he needed me, it seemed I heard the knocking all night long. Facing another bout of uncontrolled vomiting as I attempted to hold the tube in place, I finally asked the nurse for some more Benadryl, which allowed him to finally drift off to sleep.

Later that morning as Dr. Aung examined Zach, I asked what she would do if Zach were her child. Without hesitation she indicated she would go to Duke for a treatment plan. As our conversation continued, she looked me in the eye and whispered, "I cannot cure Zach, but I will try to give him as much time as possible."

Her remark cut me to the bone. I felt she had no hope for Zach. Even though the prognosis for a GBM did not allow for much hope, hope was always there. To eliminate that was inexcusable to me. If only we had been given this advice during our first consultation, we would have gone to Duke in July.

Receiving a two-hour pass to leave the hospital for some fresh air, Zach and I played with a Nintendo machine and watched a movie as we waited for Dirk and Lexi to arrive. He still was not speaking and was instead scribbling notes to me when he needed to tell me something. He wrote:

It hurts my throaght to talk. It hurts my throaght and stomach no matter what. Where is dad? I can't drink or it hurts but I want to. I don't like watching you drink because I want to drink but I can't.

When Dirk and Lexi arrived, we headed out for a drive. After being holed up in the hospital for eight days, the world seemed much brighter as we drove through the streets of St. Petersburg. Stopping at a park near Tampa Bay, we found a parking space along a grassy area with benches. Since Zach was so weak and frail, Dirk and I each held one of his arms as we helped him out of the car. Very slowly, we walked his pale and unsteady body to a bench. His appearance, for the first time since diagnosis, truly encompassed what I had always pictured for a cancer patient.

Lord, I must have faith. It has been so hard for me to focus on this. My anger and bitterness at our lack of control has surfaced. You are in control. I surrender this to You, Lord. Please forgive my harsh thoughts. I pray for Your healing arms to embrace Zach and help him to feel better quickly. Tomorrow always holds renewed hope and promise. Thank You for that, Lord.

He threw up a little when he tried to drink water the next morning, but at least he was trying to drink. It was difficult for him to walk the short distance to the bathroom to have a bowel movement—his first one in a week. I walked behind him with both of his arms over my hands to keep him steady and standing. He slowly seemed to be making small improvements although his eyes still did not have the sparkle I was so used to seeing, and there were no smiles to be found.

Finishing *The Case for Faith* book, I was sure God had put the book in my hands. With my faith teetering on the edge, reading it had pulled me back to where I needed to be. My heart had softened again as I realized God had never left us at all. I shared this with my sister Michelle when she called, "We just have to understand some things we are not meant to understand. We must continue to have faith no matter what we face. There is a greater good that will come of everything. What this situation with Zach holds I am not sure. I am just thankful my faith has been renewed once again."

After nine long days, the day arrived when we were finally released. I felt like we were being released from prison and wanted to burst through the doors with my arms held high. Zach was still extremely weak and not speaking, but I knew getting him back home was the best way to find his smiles once again. Finally able to update the website again I made this entry:

November 7, 2005
The Tuckers are finally all under one roof again tonight! What a relief to get home. Zach and I had enough of the hospital for a long time. Sorry it has been so long since I have been able to journal to all of you. Thanks to Dirk for keeping you all informed.

We have experienced quite a bit the last nine days. When Zach and I left the Saturday before last, we thought we would be going in for a couple of hours for some meds through an IV. We never dreamed we would be there for nine days! After about day three, I was ready to strangle a lot of people because we were not getting many answers and Zach was suffering so much. I am happy to say he is getting better—slowly. He was really hit hard by this. We still are not sure why his nausea and vomiting became so bad.

We all have experienced the full range of emotions from this experience. A lot of frustration because there are no black-and-white answers to our questions. Anger and bitterness from watching Zach suffer so miserably through the week. Hope each day things would improve and despair when they didn't.

Having the feeding tube inserted was mentally and physically very hard for Zach. It was one of the most difficult things I have ever experienced as a parent. Ultimately, it was what had to be done in order for Zach's body to start healing. We are still in the process of determining how long it will need to be used. Each day Zach handles it better. The doctor felt maybe a couple of weeks would do it. He still is not eating by mouth. We pray that he will start to get an appetite again because the sooner he starts eating, the sooner the tube goes away.

We have all lost our smiles through this experience, but they are starting to reappear as we see Zach gain strength and feel better. He has had a hard time smiling with the tape on his face, but every now and then a nice big one breaks through. I have seen many more since we are back home now. It makes my heart sing when I see one!

This past week has been a test to me. I am sure you can imagine some of my conversations with God. Through it all, I have found this experience has strengthened my faith. My dear friend Debbie brought me a book last week called The Case for Faith by Lee Strobel. It has been clear to me God has been putting these different books in my hands as I have needed them. This book helped me to find some answers to questions I was having and reinforced our "faith, not fear" belief. It helped to remind me we cannot always understand why we are faced with challenges, but that there is a reason and it is for a greater good. One quote from the book that I found appropriate is "a faith that's challenged by *adversity or tough questions or contemplation is often a stronger faith in the end." I have found this to be true.*

One other thing that has come from this experience I would like to share is no matter how much we would like to be—we are not in control. This is another reason why holding on to our faith is so important. We do not know what tomorrow holds. I had thought after getting through the radiation and chemo in Indiana we would be home-free for the "rest period." Boy, was I wrong! I have caught myself trying to look too far down the road with my plans and losing sight of the fact that my plans are not the determining factor.

Cancer had reared its ugly head and revealed how unrelenting and unforgiving it could be to a little boy. Our eyes had been opened to just how hard a fight we faced, but we were now ready to face any mountains or giants in front of us because we knew God would be with us every step of the way.

Reflections

I had always believed *in* God, but facing this mountain, I was having trouble *believing* God and His promises. My faith was pushed to the limit as I watched Zach suffer like never before. Anger grew in my heart because of my lack of ability to control or fix the circumstances. I could not understand why my innocent child had to endure the unrelenting grasp this disease had on his life. Had God conveniently forgot about us? Had we done something terribly wrong that God's wrath was hitting us full force? Questioning my faith were the darkest days of this journey I was on. I wondered if my prayers were being heard. Doubt and anger bombarded my mind.

God did show up by sending me just the right message when I needed it most. I realized God *was* listening because He was speaking to me through the book and our friends, dissolving my doubt and anger. I found the questioning that resulted from my doubt actually made my faith grow stronger. It drew me closer to God. As I drew closer to Him, the more peace grew in my heart.

The overriding lesson I learned was we will always face challenges in our lives. Some may be small; some may be very large. These challenges will always present us with the opportunity to be faced with doubt and feel anger. What we have to do is remember to cling to those promises of hope that God gives us—*no matter what!* To always believe and be filled with hope because God has perfect timing that we will only understand when we reach heaven. To remember this world is filled with sin because God loved us so much He chose to give us free will. This sin makes the world a broken, unjust place to be, filled with disease and heartache, but God seems to be able to take the suffering that results and turn it into good if we make the choice to let Him work in our hearts.

OCTOBER 2005—Zach, Craigg Page and the Kraft Wienermobile drivers before we leave for the Tampa Bay Lightning game. The ride to the game was a blast!

This is the photo we used on our 2005 Christmas card. It was our tradition to send out cards with photos of Lexi and Zach.

CHAPTER NINE

A New Normal

I woke to Lexi shaking me. "Mom, Zach's alarm is going off," she whispered. Being in my own bed after our long hospital stay had put me into a deep sleep. Springing from the bed, I hurried to Zach's room to find the formula pump methodically beeping and blinking its red light, demanding attention. The cord had become kinked as Zach slept. Reprogramming the settings, I watched as it began to pump the formula into Zach's body once again. It was strange to think Zach was getting nutrition as he lay sleeping in his bed.

As the night turned into day, Zach faced a new adjustment to his world—navigating everywhere he went with a tube hanging out his nose and pushing an IV pole with the pump attached. That limited his motivation to move anywhere, except the bathroom. He was still very weak anyway and napped most of the day. Thankfully, all but one of his medications were now being administered through the tube. There was still one antacid he had to swallow once a day. It was nice to be able to continue his hiatus from the grueling challenge of swallowing tons of pills every day. I dreaded starting the next round of chemo, knowing it would require the pill-taking process once again.

Zach took these changes to his life in stride just as he had everything else that had been thrown at him. I was continually amazed at his ability to simply accept things. Never questioning why, he very seldom complained or voiced frustration over these inconveniences—he just found a way to incorporate them into his life.

Working on finding a specialist for Zach's care, I called Duke and set up an appointment for twelve days later, November 22nd. Since that was the week of Thanksgiving, travel by air would be too expensive and we would make the ten-hour trip by car.

As soon as the appointment was set, I felt a sense of peace. Now we could focus on getting Zach strong again. He had missed numerous days of school, so I investigated the homebound program the school system offered. I knew he would not want to attend school with the feeding tube, and even after the tube was removed I figured he would be too weak to stay all day. Removing him from his classmates did not seem fair; I hoped he could still visit his classroom periodically.

He still battled even the thought of swallowing the one pill he had a day, and the actual process usually ended with him throwing up. I struggled to understand his suffering by remembering God had a plan for Zach; it was just hard not knowing what that plan was. Learning to accept the challenges, I fought to find the patience to know it would all become known to me when God decided it should be known.

A few days later, Zach and I made the long journey to the clinic to have his blood tested. Expecting a long day of infusions, we packed a bag full of snacks and games to take with us. Finding fun in the strangest ways, he covered my eyes as his blood was drawn into the testing machine—one that made a slurping noise—in front of us. Watching as the readings appeared on a screen, he was excited to see if he could beat the acceptable levels. His optimism and light-heartedness were contagious, always making me laugh. We were both ecstatic and surprised when all his counts returned in the acceptable range.

After a week of tube feedings, Zach was gaining weight and flashing his beautiful smile once again and even asking to go to the grocery store. He would not let anything bring him down for long. Still unable to walk long distances, he was disappointed we couldn't find a grocery cart with a bench attached to allow him to sit as we shopped. The only viable option sat in the corner, a wheelchair with a food basket attached. Without hesitation, Zach climbed in and smiled. It was all a game to him—a new experience to try.

As we walked through the store looking for anything that appealed to Zach, my thoughts drifted. *What do people think when they see us now?* I could not believe we were living this life, walking through the grocery store, Zach in a wheelchair with half his hair missing and a feeding tube hanging out of his nose. This was not supposed to happen to us. We were just a normal family—double income, two kids and a cat. *How can this be our reality?* We should be going to soccer practice or basketball games like all of Zach's buddies and their families.

Sunday arrived and we all journeyed to church. Glad to be going, Zach curled up next to me and rested his head in my lap as we listened to the worship music. Letting the words speak to my heart like never before, I had an overwhelming sense of calm come over me that Zach was going through all of these challenges to mold him for greater things in life. I had a sense he would live a full and complete life and make a tremendous difference in the world.

Lord, thank You for giving me this feeling in my heart. I pray that this is Your will and Zach can be a great tool for You and Your kingdom.

Later that evening I told Dirk about my feelings and he was uplifted by hearing it. As Zach and I cuddled in his bed before he drifted off to sleep, I shared the same thing with him. He looked at me with sparkling eyes and asked, "What is the greater thing, Mom?" I hugged him tight and told him I wasn't sure, but I knew it would be wonderful whatever it was.

Anticipation and apprehension mixed in our minds as the day finally arrived for Zach to get the tube removed. After eleven days of constant nutrition, Zach's body and spirit had recovered from the assault of his unexpected ten-day fast. Happy to see Zach had gained weight and that his strength was building, Dr. Aung was amazed at his sparkling eyes and huge smile as she examined him. Stepping back a few times to take it in, she shook her head as she asked if he was always this happy. If only she had known him before he had become a cancer patient. Or if she had seen how upbeat he was during the radiation treatments, then she would have known this was his normal way of acting. It was very unlike what she had seen in the hospital.

When the time came to pull the tube out, Zach's eyes grew very large and filled with worry. Remembering his heartbreaking protests when the tube went in, I feared the worst as well. "OK, Zach, this will only take a few seconds," the nurse promised. "I will count to three and you blow out a big breath as I pull the tube out. Ready, one, two, three!"

Zach grabbed my hand tight and blew out a breath. The tube slid right out and he coughed a couple of times before the biggest, brightest smile appeared. It was gone! His eyes twinkled as the nurse bragged about how well he had done.

It felt as if we were floating to the car we were so lighthearted and happy the tube was gone. As we drove home, Zach asked to go to school for P.E. Amazed by his never-ending optimism, I laughed and said, "I think we better take it easy the rest of today, but if you feel like it, you can go to school tomorrow." Good-bye homebound for now. Zach was ready to be with his friends again.

His classmates gave him a standing ovation when we walked into the classroom the next morning. Zach's face turned pink as he melted into his seat. He did not like being the center of attention—he only wanted to be normal again.

Leaving him instructions to call if he needed me, I spent the morning battling insurance issues related to the radiation, physical and occupational therapy treatments. Facing inconsistent processing for the same procedures, I was soon overwhelmed with frustration as I spent more time on hold than I did talking to a real person. Armed with an accounting background, I could not believe the time it was taking to monitor the bills and follow up on payments. It was obvious: The system needed a lot of work.

Watching Zach devour his pizza when I arrived for lunch was gratifying and scary at the same time. Knowing how little he had eaten over the past month, I was nervous his stomach would reject such a large amount of food all at once. Thankfully, everything settled in his tummy fine and he was able to enjoy the rest of his day. Although he was exhausted that evening, he studied for two tests, determined to remain on track with the class. His ability to solve math problems quickly and memorize his science definitions made it clear that the proton radiation had not affected his healthy brain cells and nor diminished his cognitive abilities.

Although Zach's stomach issues were steadily improving, he still fought some nausea and found that taking long, hot bubble baths helped settle things down. During one bath, as he was listening to a football game on the television the announcer began talking about the death of a colleague's brother to a brain tumor. I sat frozen as I watched Zach, wondering what he was thinking about hearing this. Looking at me with wide innocent eyes, he asked the question I had been dreading, but knew I'd eventually hear: "What if I die, Mom?"

In a panic, my mind raced with a million thoughts. *How do I answer this question that I had been fighting not to think about?* Surprising myself, I smiled calmly as words seemed to just flow out of my mouth. "Zach, we are all going to die sometime. Are you worried about it?"

"What would you do?" he continued.

"Honey, I don't know. I would miss you terribly, but I know I would see you again in heaven where everything is perfect," I answered.

"But, how would I find you?" he asked.

"You know, I am not sure how it works. But I know it will be easy to find each other because God is so smart. He makes it that way. Everything is happy and good there and you don't have any problems. I hope everyone we know will be there with us."

"What about hell; Mom, what is it like?"

"You know the book I was reading in the hospital? It tried to explain what some people thought hell would be like. They said it would be a sad place where no one ever quite got what they were wanting. They thought the people there would be able to see the people in heaven, but would not be able to get to them. The people in heaven would not see the people in hell though," I explained.

Satisfied, he leaned back to relax more in the warm bubbles. Thankful he had finally asked a difficult question, I was relieved we had the opportunity to talk about it in a calm manner. It was hard to know how to much to talk to him about these difficult subjects, but now that we'd had this conversation, I felt like it would be easier to talk about it again if we needed to.

Lord, thank You for giving me the words and calmness to explain this to Zach. I pray for a complete cure for Zach so he can spend more time here to bring more people to You. I pray I am able to do this too, Lord.

Feeling like the doctor at Duke held our future in his hands, we were relieved when the day to leave finally arrived. Pumped full of caffeine, Dirk was prepared to drive through the night so we could arrive in time for our 11 a.m. appointment the next day. Wanting to avoid the marathon car ride, Lexi had opted to stay with friends. Determined to stay awake and keep Dirk company, I climbed in the passenger seat and buckled in as dusk settled around us.

Dozing in the back seat, covered with blankets and surrounded by pillows, Zach would open his eyes momentarily during bathroom and rest breaks and reach for my hand. The traffic was light as we drove back roads through the state of Florida, Georgia and then South Carolina.

Staring at the road ahead, I replayed the last five months over and over in my mind, trying to make sense of it. My eyes grew heavy and I found myself drifting off when my neck started to ache from drooping sideways. Always concerned Dirk was fighting the same fatigue, I would quickly glance over only to see he was still intently focused on the road. A few days earlier he had shared how difficult it was to maintain his faith in light of all the unknowns we were facing. Hoping to eliminate some of those unknowns with this trip, he had become a man on a mission.

Arriving in Durham at 7 A.M., Dirk was finally showing signs of fatigue. Chatting about anything I could think of to help his eyes stay open, I felt the cold fall air seeping into the car as we drove. Although we arrived well before check-in time, our hotel graciously gave us keys to our room. Cold, tired, yet grateful to have arrived, we all buried ourselves in the blankets on the hotel beds for a nap before the appointment.

It was clear from the moment we arrived that their specialty was brain tumors. We surveyed a lobby filled with information about MRI scans, radiation and other challenges children face when battling a brain tumor.

Greeting us warmly, the clinical social worker led Dirk and me to a small conference room as Zach was taken to a playroom to play cards with their child-life specialist. Asking us to tell our story from the beginning, the social worker listened intently as we walked back through our Georgia vacation, the horrid week in July, radiation and the stomach mess we had just experienced. Sympathetic and understanding, she put into words many of our feelings. Affirming we were living every parent's worst nightmare, she helped us realize we were grieving the many losses we had experienced with this illness as we tried to find a "new normal." Our old life was gone forever, and now we had to learn to live an entirely new way.

The emotion-filled conversation lasted for more than an hour. Zach was happily winning at Uno when we were ready to leave. We had a bag full of information and were confident we had made a good decision in coming. Making the long, cold walk to the Children's Hospital, we had a quick lunch before finding our way to the bright airy lobby filled with color and artwork. Each of the facility's four floors was open to the lobby and a glass-sided elevator swished quickly up and down to each floor. Taking the elevator to the fourth floor, we signed in at the oncology desk.

The nurse practitioner who met with us had us repeat our story as she took notes. She examined Zach—full of smiles and laughter—making the same requests he had heard many times before.

When the doctor arrived, he sat down with us and began to explain his plan. He had obviously devised the plan before we had arrived and knew exactly what he wanted to do. Direct and to the point, he explained that in 85 percent of the cases Temador alone had not worked for GBM tumors. Because of this, he wanted to put Zach on a schedule of two different chemo drugs that would be administered through a port, and alternate them with the Temador. The side effects of these drugs were nausea, diarrhea and some hair loss.

In addition to these treatments, he wanted Zach to start taking Thalidomide and Tamoxifen as "helper drugs." Both of these drugs were thought to help hinder the blood flow to the tumor, thus helping to kill it. They would be given in increasing dosages until they reached the maximum allowed level or until Zach could not tolerate them any longer.

Spreading out a diagram he had made to show the timing and dosage of each medication, he explained the side effects of the Tamoxifen and Thalidomide, which again included nausea and also constipation. The Thalidomide was known to cause nerve damage to the fingers and toes as well. My head spinning, I was overwhelmed with what I was hearing. It seemed the plan was to poison Zach with all these medicines until he could no longer tolerate them and hope that somewhere along the way we killed the tumor too.

Explaining how difficult it had been for Zach to take pills, especially with his sensitive stomach lately, I asked for advice on how to help him get all the pills down. He said that applesauce was the best way—not yogurt. He explained that yogurt changed the acidity of the stomach, causing the Temador to be less effective. That worried me because I had used yogurt the entire time we were in Indiana.

Realizing Zach did not have a port, he wanted to start the first round of Temador immediately and schedule Zach to have a port placement so he could receive the IV chemo drugs three weeks later. That would be when we were supposed to be in Indiana for Christmas. The doctor decided Zach could have the port placed after we returned from Indiana and start the IV chemo then. He did not feel an extra week's delay would be detrimental.

As the doctor finished, I noticed Zach patting his tummy and making a sad face. "Are you not feeling well, Buddy?" I asked. He shook his head no. I understood—my stomach was in knots too.

Asking if we had any more questions, the doctor quickly examined Zach and was gone. I was disappointed we did not have a chance to speak to him privately about his experience with children Zach's age and GBMs.

Because he was treating others like Zach, I wanted to know his guess at prognosis. When I asked Zach what he thought about everything he had just heard, he said it made his tummy hurt. I agreed.

Had I made a big mistake coming here? It seemed our fears of lots of needles, pills and sickness were coming true. What if all this medicine did no good? The blood-brain barrier that I had read about made me skeptical of chemotherapy being the answer. Knowing I had to trust the doctor, I reminded myself that his life's work was dealing with these tumors.

After Dirk and Zach fell asleep later that night, I tossed and turned. I went into the bathroom so I could read an article the doctor had given us about the effectiveness of the drugs he was proposing. Very technical in nature and difficult to read, there were some statistical differences using the approach he was proposing, but only in an adult population that had experienced recurrence of tumor. There was no mention of how children responded.

Lord, are we following Your plan by coming here? Is this Your will?

Reasoning through what choices we faced—either we attack the tumor head-on or it will attack Zach—I decided the doctor was being proactive, which was what I was looking for after the frustration in Tampa with Zach's stomach issues. The odds of Temador alone working was only 15 percent, which was unacceptable. Remembering my same unfounded fears when Zach started the Temador, I decided I had to have faith and realize this was the best place to be to receive the most advanced treatment.

Quietly climbing back in bed, Dirk stirred and mumbled, "I am glad we came to Duke. They really seem to know what they are doing." Finding strength in his confidence, I resolved to set my fears aside and stay positive.

On the way back to Florida, I sat in the backseat with Zach to entertain him. Our trip home seemed twice as long as we found the roads jammed with Thanksgiving holiday traffic. The stop-and-go traffic did nothing to help Zach's weakening appetite. Knowing the medicine schedule was troubling him, I asked what he thought of our visit to Duke. "It seems like a lot of medicine to take, Mom," he answered. I hoped we were not beginning another downward spiral.

Glad to finally be released from the confines of our car, we arrived home at 8 p.m., just thirty-six hours after we had left. Lexi and her friends had made a special bear dressed in a hockey uniform for Zach while we were away. She presented it to him with an excited smile.

The anticipation of swallowing more pills weighed heavily on Zach. Not able to calm down with a bath, he shook like a leaf the entire time he was in the tub. I tried to create a very relaxed environment by playing ocean sounds that he liked and staying very calm myself. But when I gave him the smallest of the three pills, he immediately threw up. He looked so pitiful as he apologized that my world collapsed around me. Not able to inflict any more pressure on him, I told him we would start the pills tomorrow.

Desperate to find a quiet spot to myself, I left him lying in my bed and went in Lexi's darkened room and fell to the floor. Releasing my emotions, my tears rolled into the carpet. How were we going to do this?

Lord, why is this so hard? We are trying to follow the path we think You want for Zach, but it seems like we keep running into barriers. Please give me strength to do this Lord. Zach is so innocent and this is all so unfair. I don't understand why he is suffering so much.

My body was wracked with sobs as I lay in the dark on the floor. Lexi appeared behind me and I quickly tried to wipe away my tears and gather my emotions. "Mom, what's wrong?" she asked.

"Oh Honey, I am just sad Zach feels so bad. He could not take his pills and everything seems so hard right now," I explained. Her eyes filled with tears and she hugged me tight. I again wondered how this could be our life. This "new normal" really stunk and threatened to destroy us if we let it defeat us.

At 5 A.M. I awoke to Zach gently nudging my shoulder asking, "Mom, would you lay with me?" He had a frightened look in his eyes and his left arm was trembling. We walked back to his room and climbed in his bed. He didn't seem to want to talk but was shaking and felt sick just like in the hospital. Holding his left arm to still the constant movement, I began asking him questions.

"Are you scared of pills and throwing up, Honey?"

"Yes."

"Are you scared of food or eating?"

"No," he said, shaking his head.

"Zach, I want you to think about the pills like this: The little white ones are for your tummy to make it feel better. The other two are like Power Ranger pills. They are supposed to go in and fight the bad cells the radiation has already beaten up. Some other pills you will take later are going to help the Power Ranger pills. They are like the weapons that will make them fight even better. Does that make sense?"

He shook his head yes and relaxed enough to be able to go back to sleep.

I slipped out of his room and went back to tell Dirk what was going on. Just as frustrated with Zach's suffering as I was, Dirk, too, was at a loss to know what to do to help Zach through this extremely difficult trial.

We joined our neighbors to celebrate Thanksgiving the next day, hoping to take our minds off the pressure we were all feeling. It turned out to be a good plan. Zach loosened up and actually ate some macaroni and cheese. Some of his spunkiness returned as he teased Lexi and made funny faces when we gathered all the kids for a group picture. It was good to see him relax again.

Staying true to our family tradition, I had Dirk retrieve our Christmas tree and decorations from our attic after Thanksgiving dinner. Lexi's eyes sparkled with excitement when she saw all of the ornaments and decorative nutcrackers we had collected through the years. She got busy arranging them as I put the tree together and strung the lights. Dirk and Zach watched football and had no interest in the Christmas decorating.

As the tree slowly grew, my thoughts became filled with next Christmas. Would Zach be here with us? Blinking back the tears, I tried to block these thoughts from my mind, but could not imagine living without him here.

Anticipating his chemo pills, Zach refused dinner later that evening. As the dreaded hour approached, I once again tried to create an atmosphere to calm his anxiety. Determined to have success, I quietly encouraged Zach to keep trying as he battled his gag reflex each time he tried to swallow a pill. He took only a small sip of water and I held my breath as he quickly curled up on my bed and relaxed to try to keep the pill from coming back up. Leaving the ocean sounds softly playing, I allowed thirty minutes to pass to make sure the pill had time to be absorbed before we started the process once again for the second pill and then the third pill. An hour later, the process was complete. One day down, four to go.

Miserable, Zach came to get me early the next morning because he had thrown up and was still shaking and nauseous. I gave him another anti-nausea pill, but because he could not stomach the smell of applesauce, this time I wrapped the pill in a fruit rollup and dipped it in water. It worked! The water made the pill super slippery. Together, we moved to the big chair and he was able to fall asleep again.

This round of chemo was so unlike the first experience. Wracked by unending nausea and anxiety, Zach could do little more than watch television and shuffle to the bathroom throughout the day. All of us were disappointed that we had to miss an opportunity to watch the Lightning play from a suite provided by Brad Richards, a player who had dedicated the suite to children with cancer.

Repeating the pill-taking ordeal again the following night, I was completely puzzled why the Temador was making him feel so bad this time. It seemed his battle had become one in his mind, and I didn't know how to help him fight it.

My eyes flew open the next morning at 5:30. I realized Zach had hardly been drinking any water with his chemo pills in our attempt to keep them down. In a panic, I remembered that the prescription label clearly stated the importance of drinking at least eight ounces of water with each dose.

What had I done? What if his stomach was being eaten by the chemo and that was what caused all the nausea and vomiting? I ran to his room to check on him. My heart fell to the floor with what I saw. Zach was propped up against his pillows with a terrified look on his face, and he was trembling terribly.

"Honey, are you OK?" I whispered as I climbed into bed with him to calm his shaking. He turned his head back and forth and pointed to his tummy.

"Oh Baby, I just realized I was supposed to have you drink more water with your pills, and I'm afraid this might be what's making your tummy hurt. I'm going to call the doctor and see if he can tell me what to do. Are you OK for a few minutes?" He shook his head yes.

Trembling, I found my cell phone, ran to the office and quickly dug through all the pamphlets that were in the Duke bag, frantically looking for the doctor's card. Stepping outside, I felt the cool morning air surround me as I dialed the number and left my number on his pager.

Lord, please let Zach's stomach be OK. Let the doctor be in and call me back!

Amazingly, within a few minutes he returned my call. The words quickly spilled out of my mouth about all the problems Zach was having with the pill-taking and that he had limited water with each of the last two doses. "Have I totally eaten up his stomach?' I questioned.

"No, no. The water just aids in digestion," he replied. Relief washed over me as I listened to the rest of his explanation. Thanking him for being so prompt in returning my call, he said he was glad I had called.

Hurrying back into Zach's room, I scooped him up and we moved out to the big chair, trying to find comfort. Unfortunately, comfort never came. He was completely miserable. It was heart-wrenching to watch him suffer so much. I could not help wondering *why, why, why* all over again. Trying his hardest to feel better, he camped out in a long shower. But he could not find an escape from the unrelenting nausea. There were no smiles on his beautiful face all day.

I felt like we were stuck in some kind of nightmare, and an ugly pattern appeared each day. Zach would struggle all day as we demanded then pleaded for him to eat; evening would come and the pill-taking process would arrive. As I wrapped the pills to give him, Zach's eyes would fill with fear and dread. Without complaint, he would carefully dip it in the water and try with all his might to swallow it with a small sip of water. I hated this ride; I hated this life; I wanted to take it all away from Zach. Most of all, I wanted to throw all the pills down the toilet.

By the fourth evening, my determination faltered. As I gently woke Zach from a nap after his second shower of the day, I saw how pale and drawn his face was. I could see the dread in his eyes as I handed him his first pill. Throwing up as soon as he tried to take it, he whispered, "Sorry, Mom," and lay back on his bed, curling up into a ball. That was it—I was done! I softly rubbed his leg and said "Just relax, Baby. I'll come back in a little bit and check on you." We would try again tomorrow, but for now his torture would end.

Thoughts raced in my head. *Am I doing the right thing? What will Dirk think?* Sitting with Dirk, I told him I did not want to give the pills to Zach. A panic spread on his face as he stood up and walked toward the bathroom, beginning to gag. I had expected him to be concerned, but not to this level.

"So...you just want to give up after only trying three days?" he slowly asked.

"No, no," I quickly responded. "I just want to give him a break tonight. I don't know if it is wrong or right—I just know I can't make that poor little baby take another pill right now. I won't even tell him about it; I'll just let him sleep and we'll try again tomorrow. I'm not ready to give up by any means. I just think he needs a break for his mental well-being."

Dirk was relieved that he had misunderstood me—that I didn't mean I wanted to quit the chemo treatments all together. Panicked to think we had only begun to fight, he did not want to give up too soon. Later that night, he felt a strong sense of peace flood into his body as he prayed in the shower. He reassured me he agreed with giving Zach a break. Searching for spiritual support, he had decided to go to a men's prayer group that met in the morning before church, hoping to find strength.

Lord, I need strength; we all do. This is such a hard test to watch Zach suffer so much. Please help us to know what we are supposed to do. Lord, we just want Zach to be better, to be able to do all the things he loves and not have to do all these ugly treatments and take all of these pills. Please hear our prayers. Give us guidance, peace and wisdom as we face a new day.

The sound of a ringing bell woke me at 3:30 the next morning. We had hung a small bell from Zach's top bunk; it was his way of summoning me when he needed help and could not come find me. Ironically, Zach had given me the bell a few years earlier for me to use to call everyone for dinner. I stayed with him the rest of the night, holding his trembling body in an effort to comfort him.

The next evening, Lexi could no longer contain her frustration with our torturous routine. Bursting into tears when I told her it was too late for me to read to her before bed, she exclaimed, "It's just not fair, Mom!"

"I know, Lexi; none of this is fair… Do you want to talk about it?"

"I can't help it Zach is sick. Why should that cause me not to be able to have you read to me? Do you know how hard it is to lay here and listen to Zach get sick and see him feel so bad? It is just not fair," she repeated.

I hugged her as we lay together in her bed. It wasn't fair. I knew that, but who said life was fair? How do I explain this to an eleven-year-old who should be burden-free? This world that surrounded me felt like it was closing in fast—and there was no escape. There were no easy answers and no trap doors to find my way out.

I woke the next morning thinking, *only two days left to complete this round of chemo.* Cringing as I tiptoed to Zach's room to check on him, I could not shake the picture in my head of how I had found him the last couple of days—scared and trembling in his bed. My heart soared when I peeked in and found him sleeping soundly. Finally, a good night of rest for him.

He had a much better day than he'd had for awhile, managing to play games on the computer and nibble on food throughout the day. We watched as his pills went down without much trouble that evening. It was as if a heavy cloud of anxiety had been lifted from our house. Our moods were greatly impacted by how Zach was feeling.

The next day was a bit rougher for Zach. This short round of chemo had been such a roller coaster ride. I never knew what to expect when I opened my eyes each morning. That morning, he did not feel like eating and only wanted me to lie with him in front of the television. Deciding a little exercise might help, I had him climb on our treadmill and walk for two minutes—much as he had done during his physical therapy in Indiana. The change in his left side was noticeable as the familiar limp reappeared. All the inactivity of the last month had really set back his progress.

Getting the last pills down later that evening, we were all relieved to know it would be a couple of months before we had to do this again. I hoped the chemo he received through the port would be easier on him.

Lord, thank You for giving me the strength today. You are an awesome God. Please fill me with Your Holy Spirit so I can continue to focus my faith on You. Thank You for Your blessings and helping us through this tough round of chemo.

Zach steadily improved each day after the chemo was finished— enough that we were able to stop by his class to pick up his work and say hello to his friends. Digging deep into his determination, he asked to go to school for awhile later that week. Once again joining him for lunch and recess, I realized he was still too weak to play with his friends. Fighting back tears as we watched his friends run around, I felt the frustration of the situation come crashing down on my shoulders again. *Why did this happen to Zach? He was such a good boy and so strong and healthy. What must he be thinking?* I just could not make sense of any of it.

Having finished the chemo, the "old Zach" reemerged over the weekend—much to our delight. He spent most of Saturday outside doing his best to keep up with his friends. Dirk and I were again amazed at his determination to ignore the challenges cancer had placed in his path and be normal. Gone was all the extra weight he had gained while on steroids. In fact, he looked much like himself before diagnosis except for the missing hair and pale skin.

Needing a rest from all of his play, Dirk and Zach planted themselves in front of the television the next day, totally engrossed in football. Dirk had introduced Zach to a football pool at his office the previous year. They had played it together then, but when this season started, Zach wanted to pick his own teams. This had been a great form of entertainment for him the entire time we were in Indiana. He and Dirk had studied and strategized about the games each week.

Zach knew the teams well and had been very good at making his picks.

He had been ecstatic when he finally won a week. Amazed at his abilities to compete against many veteran players, I was thankful for the enjoyment both Dirk and Zach received from sharing this passion. It was a great diversion, especially on days when Zach did not feel like moving around.

Excited to see Zach feeling much better the next week, Dirk and I wanted to hold off on any new medications until after Christmas, which was only three weeks away. We felt it would be nice to give Zach a break and let him continue to feel good the rest of this month.

Unfortunately, the doctor at Duke did not think that was a good idea. He felt we should start the additional medicines as soon as possible for the best result. After a blood check at the clinic, my heart sank as the doctor there began to explain all the side effects we should expect with the medications—nausea, constipation and drowsiness. *Why did this have to be so hard?*

Later that evening Dirk got upset when I told him of the plan.

"I can't believe we have to do this to him just when he is feeling good again," he said in a frustrated tone.

"I know. I really would like to wait until after Christmas, but the doctor really feels strongly about starting them now," I explained.

"Does he know how hard it has been for Zach to take the chemo pills?"

"Well, I told him what a rough time Zach had, but I could e-mail him again and explain our thoughts. I just don't want to not be aggressive enough and let the tumor get a better chance at growing."

"This just really sucks!" Dirk replied as he left to take a shower.

I agreed. It did suck. Staring at the computer and wondering how to explain our fears in a way that made sense, I began to wonder if maybe we were letting our fears rule our heads too much. Both of these drugs were supposed to decrease the tumor's ability to create circulation around itself. Without circulation, the growth would be inhibited. What was the right answer? If only we had a crystal ball and could see how this was going to go.

Talking with other parents who had been through this ordeal would be so helpful. At Duke, I had received a pamphlet about a network for parents of children with brain tumors. Hoping to receive support from someone who had lived through this, I left a brief message about our situation at the number on the pamphlet.

Dirk came back after his shower and asked if I had sent the e-mail. "No, I am not sure if I should. Will it just sound like we are whining and scared?" I asked.

"Don't send it. Maybe we should just do it. That is why we went to Duke—to get someone who was an expert with brain tumors to tell us what to do. I guess we should listen and just pray that Zach can handle it," Dirk replied.

"I agree. I called the parent network to see if we can talk to someone that could tell us how it went with their child. I think it would be nice to get someone's perspective that has been through this," I said.

A few days later, tension filled Zach's body when I told him we had some new pills to take. The first night he took them, the gagging and throwing up resumed. One of the pills was quite large and he could not get it down. Determined to stick with it, I kept reassuring Zach he could do it. We had been given three smaller pills that could replace the one big pill and I decided we'd try that. It was a solution, but made the pill-taking a very long process. The next evening, I told Zach we were not going to worry about the pills and just take them out by the television. Hoping that by changing the environment Zach would not get so anxious about it, I was surprised to see it actually worked! The pills went down with out any gagging and no throwing up.

Ever since Zach's diagnosis, I had watched our savings account rapidly decline due to my loss of income and mounting medical bills. I reluctantly opened an assistance fund to allow friends to help us financially. Immediately, many friends began organizing fundraisers to help us. The first was a community garage sale.

Waking before sunrise, I was shocked when Zach appeared from his room asking to join Lexi and me at the event. Thinking the Thalidomide would make him too sleepy, I had underestimated his determination not to be left out. The day turned into a celebration as Dirk and I were overwhelmed with the generosity everyone displayed. Amazed to hear they had managed to raise $2,220, I was humbled by how hard everyone had worked for us.

Things were going well once again. I was learning our "new normal" was anything but normal. Each day had to be enjoyed for what it was in itself. No longer could we take for granted the things we once expected. Going to school, playing with friends, feeling well enough to eat were now luxuries to Zach. This new normal was filled with challenges, but Zach was teaching us how to be a hero as he faced them all with courage. No matter how bad he felt, Zach continued to try. He never questioned why or complained about the task. Without his knowing it, he was teaching us about determination, perseverance and faith—more than he would ever know.

Reflections

Feeling battered and tossed about, the journey we had endured in five short months had taken us far away from the plans we had prepared in our minds. Although, confusion and frustration had overtaken us at many points, it was clear to our hearts that God was walking with us, continuing to stretch our boundaries of learning more about our character as we went. As we had found out, cancer was a big reminder that the plans we had painted in our heads of our future were not what God had planned for us. The challenge was how to find the patience to wait on God's plans for our lives to play out.

God's written Word gives us instructions on how to find patience as found in 1 Peter 5:8—11 from *The Message:* "Keep a cool head. Stay alert. The Devil is poised to pounce, and would like nothing better than to catch you napping. Keep your guard up. You're not the only ones plunged into these hard times. It's the same with Christians all over the world. So keep a firm grip on the faith. The suffering won't last forever. It won't be long before this generous God who has great plans for us in Christ—eternal and glorious plans they are!—will have you put together and on your feet for good. He gets the last word; yes, he does."

It is not easy and answers are not always readily apparent, but if we humble ourselves and take the time to ask God for his guidance, our decisions will not be made in haste and end in regret. God will show us the way in His timing and in His way. Patience is a gift of the Spirit given to us from God. It is up to us to take the time to use it in our lives.

God wants us to be patient, but when we ask God to give us patience, we may receive something we had not bargained for—a way to learn patience. The point is we are faced with challenges and frustrations, big and small, throughout our time here on earth. We have to decide. Are we going to humble ourselves and take the time to patiently wait for God to show us the way, or will we try to fix everything in a knee-jerk reaction? Contemplation, prayer and reading the Bible all help to find the path God has planned for us. He never said this life would be easy, but He is patiently waiting on us to find all the blessings He has in store for us.

Opening presents in Florida on our "Christmas morning." Zach was not feeling the greatest (see the bucket near his feet), but was excited to open his gifts. He was wearing his new soft scarf and trying his best to tear the paper with only one hand.

CHAPTER TEN

Happy Holidays?

We were in the full swing of Christmas now. Zach was feeling better with each day. Anticipating sleepy days and more nausea, I was thankful the side effects of the new pills were not materializing. Because we were on an increasing dosage schedule, I knew these symptoms could be in our future. The doctor's words of "we'll see how much he can tolerate" kept floating through my mind. For now, we were happy to see Zach energetic and smiling.

I managed to find the perfect presents for everyone during the two-hour blocks of time I spent away from Zach while he was in school. My goal was to find as many sports-oriented games and toys as I could for Zach—ones that could be operated with one hand and also required physical activity so we could tie some physical therapy into playtime. Surprisingly, I was able to find quite a few fun games for him. As the stack of presents under the tree grew, Zach's desire to "open just one" grew too. What a blessing—he was feeling good again for Christmas!

Trying to schedule Zach's surgery for the port placement was a challenge. After a couple of cancellations, Zach and I went to visit the general surgeon for a pre-op examination. The doctor, a woman about my age, looked over Zach's chart then glanced at him over her reading glasses. "Everything looks in order here. We will place the port on January 4th and leave it accessed so the chemo can be administered directly after surgery. Do you understand the procedure?" she asked me.

"Yes, the child-life specialist showed Zach what the port looked like at the oncologist's office last week," I replied. "Is it OK to administer the chemo right after surgery?" I asked, wondering if that might be a lot of trauma for Zach's body to endure all at once.

"Yes, that is a common practice since the port will have to be accessed during surgery to make sure it is working properly. There is no need to de-access only to re-access the next day. It should be fine," she added. With that she gave the nurse some admit information and disappeared out the door.

Although relieved to have everything scheduled just as we had planned, my apprehension about this new form of chemo was strong. But I tried to put it out of my mind. Knowing we had to keep throwing treatments at the cancer, I hoped the chemo could break the blood-brain barrier and reach the areas of Zach's brain where cancer cells could be floating around.

Lord, I pray all this medicine will be the answer for healing Zach from this brain tumor. I believe You can heal Zach, and he will be healed from this cancer. Please let these treatments work perfectly with little or no side effects. Zach is such a precious gift, thank You for giving him to us to care for.

We headed back to school after the appointment so Zach could attend the last few days of school left before Christmas break. For the first time, he had been able to attend school for two weeks straight, and I was relieved he did not seem to have any trouble catching up from all the days he had missed.

Finding his class had just finished their holiday shopping in the "store" the PTA set up each year, Zach's face reflected the disappointment he felt. He had been looking forward to shopping, so I told him we would go by the room to see if he could slip in and do his shopping anyway.

Relieved to find the store still open, Zach disappeared through the door with a twinkle in his eye, making me promise not to peek through the glass as he shopped. He soon came out the door with four white bags and a satisfied smile on his face. I asked him why he had four bags and he happily replied, "I had to buy myself something, too, Mom!"

Happiness beamed from Zach's face when I picked him up later. "Mom, we were playing this game in PE today where we had a team and had to run from circle to circle before the other team. I was running so fast my legs felt like they were going out to the sides like this!" he said excitedly as he bent his knee and pulled his foot out to the side.

I smiled as I pictured him running as fast as his legs could go. I know the smile on his face was a mile wide and his eyes were full of determination as he completed his task for his team. I wished we could capture his competitive spirit in a bottle and sell it. We would make millions!

Zach's doctors wanted to monitor his progress closely with the new medicine, so we were at the clinic the next day. Because the waiting room was crowded, I used the opportunity to question another mom about how her daughter, who attended Lithia Springs School with Zach, had been able to keep up with schoolwork when she missed many days at a time.

She explained that her daughter was using a homebound teacher for her graded work, but Lithia Springs still allowed her to come to school when she was able so she could spend time with her friends. Grateful for the information, I found it very enlightening to talk with another parent who was also dealing with pediatric cancer.

Having missed too many days since he had returned in October, Zach would not be receiving grades for his work this grading period. Knowing the next nine weeks could possibly be worse because of the IV chemo being thrown into the mix, I did not want this situation to cause Zach to be retained in the third grade. It was clear he was able to perform at grade level and it would crush him to be left behind for excessive absences. I had to do something to ensure he would be promoted.

Zach's platelet count was lower than the last test result, but was still acceptable. I hoped this was not the beginning of a trend for him. I did not want to have to deal with low counts during our trip to Indiana.

Excitement about Christmas grew each day for Lexi and Zach as they arrived home and saw I had added more gifts under the tree. They knew we had a standing arrangement with Santa to drop off their gifts the week-end before Christmas since we were always in Indiana on Christmas—and this year would be no different. Zach's smile grew as I told him I had covered the schedule with Santa at the mall that day, which helped Zach realize our Christmas was only a few days away.

Attending Zach's holiday party at school was a joy. The room was filled with many excited students working on crafts, eating snacks and building gingerbread houses. I helped Zach build his house since his left hand was still not fully functional. He was in a silly mood and ended up with an icing moustache as he worked. It was great to see him having fun with his class-mates.

After school, I took Lexi and Zach shopping for gifts for their teachers. Smiling, I watched them giggle and playfully tug at each other as we milled around the clothing racks. Zach's eyes were full of mischief as he sneaked up on Lexi and poked her side, which produced a playful squeal from her. Recalling the many shopping trips we had taken before Zach became sick, I regretted how this kind of activity had been irritating to me then. Now it was complete joy to watch and soak in every moment. Laughter was the best music in the world to me in this reality.

After we found the perfect gifts for their teachers, Zach also found a soft scarf he had to have. Lexi laughed when she saw it was pink and pur-ple. We helped him find one in brown and black. He didn't care what color it was; he liked how wonderfully soft it felt to his skin.

When Friday arrived, the first words out of Zach's mouth as he woke were, "Santa comes tonight!" I was glad the magic of Christmas was still in his heart. Lexi had learned the realities of Santa in fifth grade, but true to her promise to me, had not shared them with Zach.

He looked a bit pale and had dark circles under his eyes when I picked him up from school that afternoon. I hoped his platelets were holding up. We were scheduled for a blood test the next Monday, so we would find out soon enough. Reporting his class had watched *The Polar Express* movie after lunch, he said it was really good and he knew Santa was for real after watching it. I smiled at his wonderful innocence and the delight it brought to each day.

As we relaxed with a movie after dinner, Zach seemed unsettled as he took his pills. "Mom, how will Santa get in here?" he asked in a worried voice.

"Well, I'm not sure. Maybe it is like *The Santa Clause Movie* where he makes a fireplace to come down. Are you worried about someone coming in our house while you're sleeping?" I asked.

He shrugged and snuggled close to me in the chair. I felt his breathing become slow and steady and noticed Dirk had fallen asleep as well.

While the "boys" slept, Lexi became my elf as we quietly put together a massage chair I had bought for Dirk. It was almost 1 A.M. when we finished and I tucked Lexi into bed. Once she was asleep, I set out all the Santa gifts. Gazing at the tree with a smile, I hoped everyone would be happy with their gifts tomorrow.

Excited our Christmas had finally arrived, Zach and Lexi dug through their stockings and admired their gifts from Santa as the sun started streaming through the windows the next morning. Forcing his left arm to cooperate, Zach struggled a bit as he anxiously tore the paper from his gifts. Not wanting to miss a minute, my gaze was locked on him as he opened each one. He wore the scarf we had bought a few nights ago with his pajamas. His face had lost all of the puffiness the steroids had caused. His arms looked thin and he was pale, but he was here! We had made it to our Christmas. Thinking back to July when we first received his diagnosis, I remember wondering if Zach would even make it to Christmas. It seemed so far away then—almost an impossibility. Where would we be next Christmas? Would he be better or even healed? If only that could be true. Clinging to that hope despite the statistics, I had to trust in God's power and plan.

Having a day of fun with all their new treasures, I had arranged for Allie to come over and stay with the kids later that evening. Dirk and I were way overdue for some time to ourselves. We had not been on a date since September in Indiana. Allie always made Zach and Lexi feel special by catering to their every wish. They both were eager for us to leave when she arrived.

Although it was strange to be a part of the real world again, we enjoyed our dinner out. Our lives had changed, and our priorities had shifted in many ways. We enjoyed having some time to talk without the distractions of the kids or the sleepiness late nights brought. Staying true to Dirk's changed heart, we did not order alcohol with our meal. It just didn't fit any-more. Hearing the ring of my cell phone after dinner and Zach's request for us to return home, we knew our date was over. But we had had enough time to reconnect—a luxury we needed and were thankful to get.

Feeling tired as we went to church the next day, Zach did not want to stand during the worship songs, so I sat cradling his head and shoulders in my lap as everyone sang. The worship team began to sing "Blessed Be Your Name," which talks about how God gives and takes away and that no matter the circumstances, we can still choose to bless the Lord's name. I had heard the song many times before, but the words resonated with me in a new way.

So many things had been taken away from us, but we had also received so much. Would I be able to be strong and sing these words with convic-tion if Zach was not healed? The sting of that reality was too hard to con-template as I struggled to blink the tears from my eyes.

Sunday disappeared into Monday and we were on our way to the clinic with Lexi in tow. Not the way any of us wanted to spend the first day of Christmas break. We knew it would be a long day because Zach was sched-uled for his normal blood test and his two-month MRI. Visiting the oncol-ogy group first, we were grateful the nurse was able to place the IV on the first try. She told Zach he would love getting the port after Christmas because it was much easier to access than finding a vein every time. Battered and perpetually marked by black and purple bruises, the back of his hands had taken a beating in the five months since the tumor had been found.

Making our way out to the mobile unit, I was happy to see Diego was back. Smiling, he joked with Zach, "Back again so soon?"

"You will see us every two months for awhile," I said back, returning his smile. "Right, Zach?"

Zach smiled as he climbed up on the bed of the machine. Feeling confident things would be stable, I was thankful Zach had improved from our last visit. The familiar clanks, bangs and thumps filled the small room as I stood and watched Zach drift off to sleep.

Lord, our faith is in You and Your will. We pray for Zach's complete healing here on earth. Our hearts know You can do anything, we pray it is Your will to heal Zach and use his testimony to bring glory to Your kingdom!

After the MRI was complete, we found out our day at the clinic would be even longer. Zach's platelets had fallen to nine—the lowest they had ever gone. In order to make our flight to Indiana, scheduled for just four days later, Zach would have an infusion of platelets during this clinic visit and then again on Wednesday. We would also have to have a blood test while we were in Indiana.

The infusion room was packed, requiring us to remain in the waiting room as the light orange contents of the platelet bag entered Zach's vein. Disappointed he did not have the luxury of sitting in one of the soft recliners, Zach was anxious to end the long day.

A true gift for all of us came that evening when I received a call from a contact at the insurance company who informed me that all the radiation claims would be paid! It had taken a special friend making a call to the management of the insurance company. What a blessing and relief.

Later, after the kids were in bed, Dirk peered over my shoulder as I pulled up the MRI scan on the computer. As I had hoped, the images in the tumor bed looked the same or a bit smaller to me. Hoping to receive confirmation that what my eyes were seeing was correct, I made two copies of them to mail to the other doctors at Duke and IU.

All too soon, Wednesday rolled around and we were headed back to the clinic where Zach was scheduled to receive another infusion before we left for Indiana. This time the infusion took place while he sat in the comfort of a recliner. Wanting to reward the kids for enduring another day at the clinic, I took them to Target afterward so they could use some gift cards they had received.

As we started toward the toy department, Zach slowed down. "Mom,

I need to sit down," he moaned. I saw a mannequin display on a platform and guided him there. I held his hand as he lowered his head into his right hand. "I don't feel good; I think I need to throw up."

"OK, Honey. Can you make it to the bathroom? It's not too far. Are you ready?" I asked as I took his hand. He shook his head up and down. Lexi followed as we quickly walked to the bathroom. I pushed open the door and got him to a stall just in time. It was so unfair! When he finished, we all went back to the car. Disappointed plans again. Another sacrifice made. *Would life ever be simple again?*

Our house became a revolving door that evening as many of our dear friends arrived with gifts for the kids and checks for Zach's assistance fund. Completely humbled to be the recipient of so much kindness and generosity, I could not believe the love and support we were receiving. It was as if our entire group of friends was making a statement to the monster that had invaded our life: You will not win! God was touching many hearts through Zach as the commandment "love your neighbor" was being lived out before our eyes.

Fighting the morning rush hour as we drove to the airport the next day, Dirk remained uncharacteristically patient. The men's prayer time he had been attending on Sunday mornings had helped him to refocus his beaten-down faith, transforming his demeanor and attitude. God was continuing to soften his heart as he received support and love from newfound friends.

The early morning travel left Zach feeling weak and we were relieved to find wheelchairs just inside the terminal door. He gratefully relaxed in the chair as we made our way to the gate. We were allowed to pre-board the very full flight, and both kids used me as their pillow as we took off for Indiana—for Christmas and for Dirk's brother's wedding.

All of us were excited to see the crowd waiting at my parents' house. My sister Michelle, her husband Kevin and their three children, Jayden, Caylee and Nolan, as well as my nephews Michael and Hogan, would be there along with my mom and dad. We wondered what our families would think of Zach when they saw how much weight he had lost since they last saw him.

Zach's nap on the flight had refreshed him. Both he and Lexi were eager to join their cousins who were sledding in the patches of snow left from a previous storm. I was nervous about letting Zach go outside in the cold and on a sled. But I didn't want to allow cancer to take yet another thing away from him and I knew I could not keep him in while all the others were outside. I smiled as I watched out the window as Kevin managed the crew of cousins without incident.

Before we knew it, it was time to go to the church for the wedding rehearsal. We were happy to see all of Dirk's family again. The church held many special memories for us. As we were growing up, this was where our families attended church. Both of us were baptized there and we married there. Built in 1806, the stone building's sanctuary was surrounded with many beautiful stained glass windows, sweeping high ceilings and beautiful mahogany pews. Reminding me of a Norman Rockwell painting, it signified the look of a traditional two hundred-year-old church.

Quiet and shy, but feeling good, Zach performed his ring bearer duties perfectly at the rehearsal. When he and his cousin Cole saw each other, a big smile spread across each of their faces. They had become quite close during Zach's radiation treatments and were happy to be reunited.

At the rehearsal dinner, Zach and Lexi were being silly and making moustaches from their ice cream—much to Cole's delight. Glad to see Zach eating, I could tell the Thalidomide had helped to stimulate his appetite, but it was also causing him to be constipated. There seemed to be no escape from the many side effects haunting him. Due for another increase in the Tamoxifen, we had also just increased the Thalidomide. I hoped the double whammy would not intensify the side effects and ruin this special time.

More fun and games with all the cousins filled the next morning, and by early afternoon it was time to dress for the wedding. I was anxious to see Zach in his tux, knowing he would be so handsome. It reminded me of when he was four and the ring bearer at another wedding. He had performed flawlessly. I smiled as I remembered dancing with him at the reception. How carefree and perfect life was then—and we didn't even realize it!

If only we had known we would be on our current path, we could have lived with so much more purpose then.

My mom helped Zach get dressed while Lexi and I got ready. It took my breath away when I saw him fully outfitted in his tux. His eyes twinkled and his smile grew when I let out a whistle to show my approval.

Thank You, Lord, for this day. Thank You for Darin and Carol finding each other. Please bless their marriage. Thank You for Zach and that he feels good. Please be with us all as we go through the wedding and reception. Give us strength and peace to keep smiling and showing Your grace through our actions.

Staying close to Zach at the church, I could see he was uncomfortable about not having on his hat. But he soon realized his missing hair concerned no one. Tears welled in my eyes as I watched him march down the aisle. Afterward during the photo-taking frenzy weddings always require, the photographer offered to touch up the photos and fill in Zach's bald spot in the final pictures. We all considered the bald spot his badge of courage in the battle he had been fighting the last five months, so we told the photographers no touch-ups were needed. It was not something we wanted to hide, but something we wanted to honor as a memory of this time of our lives.

Always loving a party, Zach enjoyed the wonderful reception. He was having such a good time that I hated to pull him back to reality when I had to interrupt his fun for him to take his meds. Happily, the pills went down easily for him and he was soon chasing Lexi and his cousins once again.

Discovering disposable cameras on all the tables for guests to take pictures, Zach ran from table to table looking for cameras to snap pictures of everyone. His white tux shirt half tucked in and half hanging out, he was having so much fun—and I loved watching both him and Lexi. These were moments I tried to soak in and savor. It made all the challenges we had faced melt away. I pretended our lives were normal again for that brief time—no cancer, no pills, no needles.

Realizing as I woke the next morning that it was Christmas Eve, I let that thought wrap around me like a warm soft blanket. I could feel my faith growing stronger now that we had made it this far.

My belief in Your power over everything has grown, Lord. I pray for Zach's complete healing here on earth! Thank You for this day and for all of our family being together.

Zach had a hard time staying away from the presents under the Tuckers' tree as we waited for everyone to arrive; his anticipation and excitement were contagious. When the gift-opening time came, Zach, Lexi and Cole were the entertainment for everyone. The happiness and innocence of kids opening gifts made all of us smile and be thankful.

On Christmas morning my parents' house was bustling with excitement when we arrived. Santa had found my niece and nephews, as well as our kids. The cousins pulled Lexi and Zach in the door to show them their gifts. Not feeling as chipper as he had at the wedding, Zach was pale and had noticeable dark circles under his eyes again. He settled himself on the corner of the couch where he and I had spent many evenings during radiation. He was content now to watch the other kids as they demonstrated how their gifts worked.

Dirk left to attend church with Darin and Carol. The renewal of his faith through the men's prayer group in Florida was apparent in his desire to surround himself with worship and other believers. He had a strong desire to go to church on Christmas. I was happy he was finding the peace he desperately needed.

Proceeding with the gift opening, again the kids stole the show for all of us. It was especially fun to watch Jayden, Caylee and Nolan tackle their gifts. This was a treat we had not had for three years.

As bedtime neared, the cousins begged to have Lexi and Zach spend the night with them at my parents' house. Worried about Zach needing me during the night, Michelle assured me she would cover for me. Zach was asleep soon after his head hit the pillow.

Dirk and I woke early the next morning and headed back to my parents' house. Anxious to see how the night had progressed, we were happy to find that Zach had slept through the night. Kathy, Michelle, Kevin, Dirk and I had planned an early morning run and we piled in the car for the short drive to our running haven. Our run was exhilarating but long, and the beauty of the park made it especially enjoyable.

Appearing more fragile with each day that passed, Zach was not excited when he learned Kathy and Michelle had planned a day out for me. Torn, I did not feel great about leaving him, but I knew it was very rare for me to get to spend time alone with both of my sisters. With Zach being entertained by Grammy, they whisked me off to have a pedicure and then on to nice leisurely lunch. Although I had a wonderful time, my mind kept drifting back to Zach, hoping he was feeling better. On our way back to the house, Michelle asked if we should plan something special for Zach in 2006. Wanting nothing more than to be able to do this, I explained how our new reality didn't really allow for much long-term planning. We were living from MRI to MRI and treatment to treatment now.

Looking pitiful when we returned, Zach immediately motioned to me to lie down with him. Glad to be close to him again, I realized a serious codependency had developed between us from spending so much time together.

Wondering if the increase in both the Thalidomide and Tamoxifen was creating his upset stomach, I was not pleased to see that his appetite was fading fast as well. An overwhelming desire to go home and get back into our routine came over me. The cold weather and all the company were too much for all of us when coupled with Zach's intense treatment schedule.

Lord, I pray tomorrow is a better day for Zach. I pray for his marrow to kick in tonight to give him high counts tomorrow. I pray for his complete healing on earth. Lord, be with us and help us.

Tension filled both Dirk and me as we readied to go to the doctor's office for Zach's blood test. I remembered all the struggles as many techs and doctors tried to find veins in Zach's hands during our last visit to Indiana and was glad for only a finger poke this time. Relieved to see the counts were increasing and very close to the acceptable range for Zach, I called the doctors in Tampa to see if they felt we needed to boost his counts with an infusion. Feeling his body was rebounding, they cautioned us to stay out of crowds with Zach, but indicated no need for an infusion. It lightened our mood drastically to know we did not have to face the challenge of finding a place to give an infusion to Zach.

As the day progressed, Zach began to feel better and soon grew bored. Not happy to be trapped inside the house all day, he started begging me to go bowling. Concerned about germs we would encounter, I said no. But after seeing the disappointment in his eyes, I caved in. Armed with a surgical mask and antibacterial wipes to disinfect all the surfaces he would touch, we were on our way. Much to Zach's delight, Caylee, Jayden, Nolan and Michelle joined us and he bowled a 137—his best game ever. He was so proud.

Wiped out when we finished, he laid his head in my lap on the way home. I helped him climb into his favorite spot on the couch when we arrived at my parents' house and he soon fell asleep. I decided to order pizza, hoping he would feel up to eating a couple of pieces when he woke up in order to have something substantial in his belly before it was time for pills.

My heart skipped a beat when I heard him call out my name thirty minutes later. I quickly ran to him. "What's wrong, Honey?"

"I can't make it stop," he said, referring to his left arm. It was pulled up tight to his body and was twitching rhythmically against his chest. His eyes were filled with fear as I started rubbing his muscles, trying to relax them. Grabbing a mini vibrating massager from the table nearby, I ran it up and down his arm until the twitching stopped. Worried the bowling had been too much for him, my heart and mind raced as I wondered why it was his left arm. He had used only his right arm when he bowled.

Once he was comfortable again, I handed him a piece of pizza. Pill time was fast approaching. He took a few bites and handed it back, shaking his head no. Showing their concern, Caylee softly rubbed Zach's head and told him it would be OK as Jayden climbed next to Zach on the couch. Leaving him to rest a little while with the kids, I soon returned once again offering him pizza.

"Zach, you need to eat a couple more bites for me, OK?" I said, putting the pizza in his hand. He held it in front of his face and looked at it as if it was something he had never seen before.

"Zach…Zach, are you OK?"

His eyes did not register as he continued to stare at the half-eaten piece of pizza.

"Zach, can you hear me?" I started to panic. "Get a trash can quick!" I said to my mom.

Michelle grabbed Jayden off the couch so I could sit next to Zach. His left arm and leg started seizing up and twitching like his arm had done earlier. As I grabbed him up in my lap, he vomited. "I think he's having a seizure," I announced. Everyone had gathered around and watched with terror in their eyes.

As soon as it started it stopped. It was probably less than thirty seconds, but it seemed like forever. Because of his semi-low platelets, I knew he could have bleeding in his brain. It was imperative to get a CT scan as soon as possible. Trembling, I grabbed my cell phone and started calling doctors. Zach seemed coherent again, but what if he was bleeding in his brain? *How long do we have and what do we do?*

I called both Duke and Tampa and became frustrated when twenty minutes had passed with no returned phone call. I dug through my folders for the number and called Dr. Thornton—with no luck. I felt we could not wait much longer and tried to calm myself. But looking at Dirk, I said, "We just need to go to the emergency room and get a CT scan."

After carrying Zach to the car, Dirk went to tell Lexi we were leaving. But I called him back and said we need to leave right away. Zach lay in my arms as we drove into the dark night. My mind raced, trying to make sense of the situation. I sorted through all the conversations we had had about seizures, trying to assure myself we were doing the right thing.

Lord, I am so scared. I can hardly think to pray. Please don't let his brain be bleeding!

My phone rang and I was relieved to hear Dr. Aung's familiar voice on the other end. Explaining everything that had happened, she asked how long it would take us to get to All Children's. Reminding her we were in Indiana, she confirmed we were doing the right thing to get a CT scan. She also wanted another blood test and electrolyte test. Concerned that if his platelets had dropped any further he would need an infusion to ward off any internal bleeding, she suggested staying overnight for observation as well.

Feeling our trip had suddenly turned into a nightmare, I tried to say more prayers, but could not quiet my mind enough to put two sentences together. Zach slept as we drove. I caressed his face as the moonlight gently illumined his cheeks.

The emergency room at the Bloomington Hospital was quiet when we arrived. Immediately taking us back to triage, the doctor felt Zach had experienced a focal seizure of his left side. Awake and coherent, Zach told me he remembered holding the pizza and he insisted he wasn't incoherent as I had told the doctors.

Relieved to find the CT scan was clear and his platelet count higher than it had been earlier in the day, the doctor gave us some Lozepaim to help relax Zach. He explained this medication would be a short-term fix to prevent any further seizures until we were able to visit our neurologist in Florida and decide if he needed to take an anti-seizure medication again. He released us, saying there was no reason to keep us overnight since Zach was acting fine.

Arriving at the Tuckers' house, we were greeted by many concerned faces. After we explained all we had found out with the tests they had done, everyone was relieved to know Zach seemed to be OK for the time being. Frustrated and scared, Lexi let me know she could not understand why we did not tell her we were leaving as I put her and Zach to bed later. Her mind had run wild with fear when she realized we were gone and my parents were the ones who told her why. Realizing I had made a mistake, I tried to explain to her I was in a panic to leave when we were unsure if Zach was OK. I stretched out next to her, hugging her, trying to apologize. But the damage was done. She pulled away and cried herself to sleep.

Lord, this is so very hard. Please help me to do the right thing for Lexi. She is so fragile now. Help me to find the words to make her understand.

Exhaustion settled over me as I climbed into bed. Thankful all of our beds were in the same room, I knew I could easily hear Zach if he had any problems during the night. Restless all through the night, his nausea kept waking him and me. Every time I heard him stir I jumped up and held the bucket for him. Deciding no more pills—except what he was given at the hospital—I felt his body had reached the limit for tolerating the medication's unrelenting assault.

As the sun started shining through the windows, I helped Zach down the stairs. He was able to eat some eggs and take a long bath. He seemed OK, but weak. This was no fun. Wanting to go home, we faced three long days until our flight left, which seemed like an eternity at this point.

Later that day, it was time to say good-bye to Michelle and her family as they headed back to Canada. Feeling very somber as we shared many hugs, I was sorry they had to experience the reality of cancer with the situation the prior evening. It ended the holiday on a sad note.

Scheduled to visit Dr. Thornton later that afternoon, I was frustrated that Zach was feeling lousy. He was unsteady and weak as we walked in. Not long after we arrived, he looked at me and pointed to his belly. Understanding his body language, I quickly took him to the bathroom just as he started throwing up. Squatting down behind him so he could sit on my lap, my heart broke as I held him steady and he continued to throw up. Overwhelmed with sadness and frustration for Zach, I again wondered if this journey would ever get any easier.

Concerned about the events of the prior evening, Dr. Thornton explained he had just arrived back in Bloomington from a trip and did not receive my call for that reason. Zach sat quietly in a chair playing an electronic Solitaire game as we talked. Pulling up the latest MRI scan I had sent him, he viewed the slides and was pleased everything appeared stable around the original tumor site. Asking what was next in our treatment plan, I explained the port placement and IV chemo regimen that was to begin in January.

Concerned about using the IV chemo, he reminded us about the blood brain barrier and how studies were not clear if the chemo was truly making an impact with this type of tumor. I began to wonder if we were making a mistake and being too aggressive. I knew Zach was not in any condition to handle any major assault to his system after last night.

Our moods matched the Indiana skies, dull and gray, as we left the appointment. I longed for the days when Zach was feeling good and improving. It was so hard to watch him struggle day after day. That evening tears started sliding down my cheeks as I journaled my thoughts of the day. Dirk asked me what was wrong. I explained my growing insecurity and fears of the treatment Zach was facing. I shared how it seemed like we were just poisoning Zach until he could not physically stand it any longer. Wanting to share all my fears with him, I realized I had tried too long to keep a brave front up. We decided to be more firm in the timing of Zach's treatments and to only proceed when *we* felt he was ready.

Feeling a bit trapped the next few days, Zach spent most of the time lying around and feeling sick. He would have spurts of energy and play with his Christmas toys, but otherwise he was pretty listless. The night before we were scheduled to leave, I gave Zach a bath and was disheartened as I examined his appearance. His once-toned athletic body was now pale and skinny with little muscle tone. His left bicep was noticeably smaller than the right, reminding me that I had to get more serious about lining up some physical and occupational therapy once again.

Watching a movie later, Lexi became visibly upset as a character talked about his mother dying from cancer. Complaining her stomach hurt, she became restless and tearful. The character also talked about cremation, causing Zach to question me about it.

"Mom, what does cremation mean?"

"Well, that means when a person dies instead of being buried, the family has the body put in a machine that burns it up and then the ashes are put in a vase called a urn for the family to keep," I explained.

"What if someone gets buried and they really aren't dead?"

"That doesn't happen, Honey. The doctors make sure people are really dead before they bury them."

"I wouldn't like it if that happened to me because my tummy would hurt from being hungry and not being able to pee or drink water."

"Well, you don't have to worry about that because I would never let that happen to you," I said as I hugged him and felt my heart breaking, knowing he was truly concerned with these kinds of thoughts. He was only eight!

Our early morning drive to the airport the next day was almost comical. Between Lexi and Zach both taking turns getting sick in some trash bags we were thankful to have brought, we had to laugh to keep from crying. I was sure Darin felt relieved to unload all the stress coming from us as he dropped us at the airport and drove away.

Finding a wheelchair for Zach, I slipped a mask on his face to keep germs away. With his white cells still dangerously low, his immune system was compromised and weak. Even though we were at a nearly vacant gate area waiting for our flight, I could still feel the many eyes watching us. I hated the curious stares at Zach.

At last our plane boarded and we were on our way home. I summed up our relief to be back in Florida on the Caringbridge site later that night.

January 1, 2006
We are back in the sunshine!! The gray days in Indiana were getting to us, so we were happy when we landed today to see the sun again. The flight was packed. We tried to keep Zach away from the crowds as much as possible. He seems to be feeling fine so far.

It was good to read everyone's New Year wishes. We are looking forward to 2006 being filled with lots of healing and good days. We know there may be some challenges, but with all of our wonderful friends and family to support us and our faith in God, we will get through them. We wish you all nothing but the best in 2006.

The holidays were over. We made it through them not in the way we had expected, but we made it. Now the real challenge ahead was to find the treatment plan that would kill any remaining cancer in Zach's brain without causing him to suffer.

Lord, be with us.

Reflections

Bittersweet…this was the best word to describe a time of year that held so much magic and expectation for the kids, but as we found no break from a ruthless, unyielding ailment. Facing a reality that placed such a limit on Zach's life made it all the more important to hold on to our hope and belief that God had a much bigger plan that included many more years on earth for Zach. Realizing our hopes might not prove out, appreciation of the holiday celebration took priority in our lives. The temporary joy the moments brought us were irreplaceable and precious even through the challenges.

The grip the world once held on our outlook had slipped away and it had become clear our purpose was not about our jobs or the things of this world, but about the relationships in our lives and the love they brought to our hearts. This purpose was spreading like fire among our friends in Florida, as evidenced by their concern to take care of our needs financially and emotionally. The purpose was magnified in the hearts of our family and friends in Indiana as our time together had special meaning in our desire to create memories that would endure forever.

God was creating an opportunity through this very difficult trial for His second greatest commandment to "Love your neighbor as yourself" to be lived by many. Hearts were being changed. Choices were being made to draw closer to God—to not allow the world to control our purpose but to use our purpose to make the world better for those around us.

One of my favorite photos. Zach and I at Darin and Carol's wedding reception. This was a magical evening where Zach felt wonderful and things almost felt "normal" again.

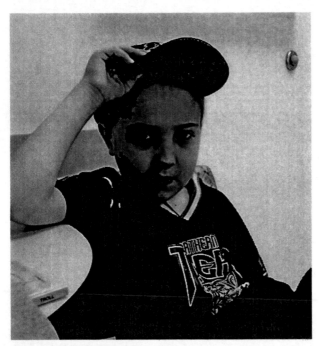

We were waiting for Zach's second infusion of the IV chemo on this day. His patience was wearing thin and he did not like it that I was always taking his picture. This was when he began to lose weight rapidly.

CHAPTER ELEVEN

Roller coaster

oused from my sleep by Zach's bell ringing the next morning, I went to him. "What's wrong, Buddy?"
"My stomach really hurts. Will you lay with me awhile?" he asked with pleading eyes.

I could tell his nerves were getting the best of him. We were scheduled to go to the clinic for a pre-op visit. Not wanting let on how nervous he was about the port placement, his actions reflected his true feelings nonetheless.

Silence filled the car later as we drove to the clinic. Still not feeling well, Zach did not want the radio on. Peering back at him as he lay in the back seat, I saw how peaceful his face was as he slept. Knowing his body needed rest, I felt sure the doctors would agree that he needed more time to bounce back from the seizure before he underwent the port placement and next round of chemo.

Struggling to make the walk into the clinic, we stopped at the reception area to rest. I tried to keep a smile on my face, but I wanted to crumple to the ground and scream at the injustice of this ordeal. At only eight, he had the weight of the world on his shoulders. He looked like a ninety-year-old man as he made his way to a chair in the waiting room. I did not hesitate to ask the receptionist for a wheelchair—something I now accepted as a necessary part of dealing with the grueling treatments for cancer.

Concern was evident on the oncology staff's faces as I explained the events leading up to Zach's seizure and his subsequent battle with fatigue and nausea. The doctor agreed he needed another week to increase his strength before surgery and more chemo. Discussing my concerns and fears of the IV chemo with her, I broke down in tears as I explained it seemed Zach had little quality of life. Understanding I did not want to watch him suffer for nothing, she reassured me the IV chemo was something that was a good idea. Her words helped to calm my anxiety and refocus my resolve to push forward with the plan.

Zach's face brightened as we headed home and I told him we were not going to the hospital as planned. He worked with me on some arm and leg exercises as we watched his favorite shows. Seeing his many smiles and hearing his giggles lifted my heart. The beautiful, sunny Florida day lured us outside in the afternoon. Asking to be my helper as I washed the car, he sat in a lawn chair holding the hose, ready to rinse away the soap. Playfully squirting the hose in the air, he giggled as he watched the drops fall on the driveway. Setting his jaw, his eyes would fill with determination when I let him rinse the soapy bubbles from the truck. It was so good to see his left arm working with the right as he squeezed the nozzle with all his might.

Lord, thank You for filling him with such determination! We are so blessed You gave him to us to raise. Thank You for this day!

Continuing to feel better, Zach wanted to go to school the next day. He was still quite weak, so I knelt down as we stepped on the elevator so he could sit on my lap for the short ride up to the second floor. Once he was settled in his classroom, I left Zach for a couple of hours.

Concerned that I had not heard from the doctor at Duke, I sent him an e-mail to let him know about the changed schedule. Then I clipped my cell phone and the portable house phone to my waistband as I vacuumed. I did not want to miss his call. As I cleaned I realized how desperate I must appear—with two phones attached to me. Frustrated to be completely dependent on a call from a doctor to know what path our life would follow, I wondered if they realized how much a returned phone call meant to a waiting parent.

These thoughts stuck with me the rest of the day. When the evening became quiet I updated the website.

January 04, 2006
Zach was feeling much better today. He was ready to go back to school. We arrived at 9:30 and he stayed for the rest of the day. He was a little tired when I picked him up, but not for long. He was ready to have a friend over when his homework was completed. What a kid!

He said his tummy still was hurting some during the day, but the nausea seems to be easing up a bit. We are scheduled to go to All Children's next Tuesday and Wednesday for his port placement if everything looks good and Zach is feeling good on Monday. Please pray for an easy visit to the hospital and for Zach to be calm. He doesn't tell us, but I think he is pretty nervous about the port placement.

I was looking over our calendar today thinking how odd it is that a hospital visit is somewhat routine to us now. I guess we all adjust to new "normals" when we are faced with challenges in life. Zach prayed tonight that he would feel well enough to go to school tomorrow. I am thinking not many kids say that prayer! Remember to live each day to the fullest. We never know what tomorrow will bring us.

I sat back and thought about our family prayer time that evening. We had made it a habit when Zach was about four to always gather at bedtime in Lexi or Zach's room and take turns saying our prayers aloud. It was during those times we would get a glimpse into the thoughts bouncing around in Zach and Lexi's heads. It had really touched my heart when Zach asked to feel well enough to go to school. What a simple request that so many take for granted every day. Overcome with a surreal feeling about everything, I felt waves of sadness wash over me as I tried to chase the negative thoughts from my head.

Lord, I am feeling weak and defeated with our situation. How will this end? I pray I can be filled with Your Spirit. Please fill me with peace and wisdom as we continue this journey.

His prayer answered, Zach was able to attend school until a little too much activity at recess caused his stomach to rebel. After settling him on our couch, I headed to the treadmill in our bedroom. Trying to be diligent with my running, I had resorted to using the treadmill many times over the last few months when Zach was home with me. As I was about to reach the first half mile, the phone rang. My heart skipped a beat when I answered and heard the doctor from Duke's heavy Indian accent on the other end. He had looked at the recent scans, and I was relieved that he agreed the right side appeared stable. His next words totally caught me off guard: "I am concerned because I saw something on the left side that was not there on the last scan." My heart dropped. That was Zach's dominant side. If a tumor grew there it would be devastating.

"Do you think it is another tumor?" I asked, frantically trying to remember if I had even looked at the left side when I reviewed the scans.

"I am not sure. We will have to keep an eye on it on the next scan. Sometimes these things are just shadows," he continued.

Lord, I pray this is not a tumor and is just a shadow.

After discussing the medication changes and seizure events that had happened over the holidays, I also told him about the new port placement date. He wanted to start the Thalidomide again, but to stop the Tamoxifen, explaining the Tamoxifen was not fully proven to work with Zach's tumor, but the Thalidomide did show effectiveness in some cases. He reiterated his belief in the IV chemo being a good line of defense with GBMs as well.

I hung up the phone feeling reassured we were doing the right thing. Glad we had decided to use him to set up the treatment plan, I was comforted by his confidence and evident knowledge about GBMs. The thought that another tumor could be forming on the left side renewed my sense of urgency to treat Zach with the IV chemo. I knew the impact from a tumor on the left side could be devastating in terms of mental and physical impairment.

Lord, I pray for Zach's complete healing on earth. I believe You are his healer. I know You can heal him and will do this if it is Your will. I pray for strength to keep the negative thoughts away and to be filled with the Holy Spirit. I love You, Lord!

A few days later, I shared my concerns about the doctor's comment regarding the spot on Zach's left side with Dirk. Fear and anxiety had consumed my mind as I imagined Zach losing his ability to reason or function if it was a tumor and grew. I knew as I spoke that Dirk was helpless to fix the situation, but to put my fears into words seemed to help me gain some control over them. I told him how I was trying to close the negative thoughts out of my head and just take everything in and love it for what it was worth at that moment—if I could.

"I'm hungry. I want eggs," Zach said with a loud yawn as I pulled him out of bed the next morning—an indication he was feeling good. I had become an expert chef when it came to preparing his eggs just right and was happy to see him hungrily shoving them in his mouth as he watched television. We were headed to the clinic for his pre-op checkup since his port placement was scheduled for the next day.

As we headed out the door, Zach grabbed a small packet of lemonade mix he had discovered at the grocery store. Amazed that the packets could "magically" turn his plain water bottle into lemonade, he wanted to share this magic with Miss Kyleen, the child-life specialist. Finding a special place in Zach's heart, she always greeted us with a big hello and smile.

With a bounce in his step and a smile on his face, this walk into the clinic was completely opposite of the one last week. After the blood test, which indicated all Zach's counts were very good, we were put into an exam room. "Wonder how long will it take them today?" Zach grumbled.

Much to our surprise the door opened just after Zach had settled on my lap. Dr. Barbosa, the founding doctor of the oncology practice, walked in. Smiling pleasantly as he looked at Zach's chart, he greeted us with his strong Greek-accented, "Hello." Being very upbeat and playful with Zach, he quickly made him smile during his examination, a feat that had not happened lately during exams.

Finishing his exam, he leaned back on the counter and began to ask about the latest scans. Letting out a very impatient sigh, Zach rolled his eyes at me, causing me to release him to find Kyleen and show her his "magic" lemonade packet.

"I have seen the scans and I discussed them with the other doctors. It seems like everything on the right is stable. The doctor at Duke did say he saw a spot on the left side that was not there before," I explained.

"There are two spots mentioned on our report. Have you seen the written portion?" he asked.

"No, I would like to have a copy of that," I replied nervously.

"Certainly, you know this is a very difficult tumor, right? That doesn't mean we have no alternatives for treatments. There are many new meds that are being developed to help eliminate the blood vessel growth so the tumor cannot be fed," he continued.

My mind started to churn over and over the words I had just heard. We had gone from initially thinking it was a good scan to this. *What did it all mean?* After a long wait, we received our orders to be admitted the next day, as well as the written MRI report. I noticed Zach's face seemed troubled as we climbed back into the car to head to school. Suspecting the hospital visit was already creating anxiety for him, I had my thoughts confirmed when he complained his stomach was hurting.

"Do you even want to try to go to school, Honey? It's fine if you just want to come home and hang out with me," I said as we drove.

"I want to go home," he said relieved, as he lay back in the seat to rest.

Jumping on his favorite chair for us to snuggle, Zach flipped on the television and we relaxed. As I grabbed his left hand to stretch it, he pulled my anniversary band off my finger and playfully put it on his nose. He giggled as he looked out the corner of his eye to see if I was watching. Wanting to freeze the moment as we continued to be silly, play around and giggle, I longed for a light at the end of the tunnel that gave some indication things were going to get better. I did not ever want to face the day when this kind of silly play was no longer there.

Later, while on a jog with Dirk, I explained Dr. Barbosa's comments about a second spot to Dirk. The written report referenced an area of the brain called the pons medulla. Neither of us knew where it was located. The stress of all the unknowns was overwhelming to both of us. As if the thought had been placed in my mind by God, I suddenly realized and shared with Dirk that we had to release our worry because holding onto it would not change anything. Reminding ourselves we were not in control—no matter how much we wanted to be—we both promised to try and hold on to this thought and stay positive.

While we were preparing to have Zach's port placed, Debbie and Karen had been working hard on organizing another fundraiser—a dinner and auction night. Karen called us that evening to let us know an individual had offered to provide a dream for Zach—something like a weekend getaway or an evening with the Lightning. Knowing Zach was stressed about his impending hospital visit, I tried to give him a happy thought as we cuddled before bedtime. "Guess what? Karen called and told me someone wanted to grant you a wish. Doesn't that sound fun?" I whispered softly.

"Really? Would they give me a million dollars, Mom? That is what I wished for with Miss Kyleen when I showed her the magic lemonade today!" he said with hope in his voice.

"No, no, Buddy," I said chuckling. "I think they were thinking about meeting some Lightning players or a weekend trip or something." His innocence continually caught me off guard. To have endured everything he had and still have hope alive for his dreams kept my hope strong too.

A call came at 2 P.M. the next day to let us know our room was ready at All Children's Hospital. Zach and I made the hour-long trip alone. Dirk would meet us there after he left work that evening. Lexi was staying with friends once again. She would be our representative at the dinner auction that night.

Happy to find we were in the bed near the bathroom, Zach wanted to order room service as we settled into the all-too-familiar surroundings of the hospital. Soon after, a family came in whose toddler would occupy the other bed. Unable to block their conversation from my ears, I learned she had a brain tumor as well. My heart broke for them, thinking of the challenges they must be facing with such a young child.

In an effort to save us an additional trip to St. Petersburg to see the neurologist, the clinic had scheduled an evaluation with him while Zach was
in the hospital. After discussing Zach's seizure, the doctor decided the risk
of another seizure was too high not to give him an anti-seizure medication.
Suggesting a drug called Kepra, he explained it did not have to be moni-
tored by endless blood draws and could be administered in a pill form—
so the minty chewable, that Zach had learned to despise, would not be an
issue. He also prescribed a suppository I could administer if Zach ever had
another seizure. It was designed to stop a seizure if it lasted more than five
minutes. I shuddered to think of that possibility and was glad to be prepared if it ever happened.

Dirk, Zach and I watched television and had a calm evening. When I
called to check on Lexi and the dinner auction, I noticed how happy her
voice sounded. She explained she and her friends were in charge of selling
bright green rubber wristbands that said, "Be a Hero." Like the Livestrong
wristbands representing Lance Armstrong's battle with cancer, these would
remind everyone what a hero Zach was as they wore them. Later we were
amazed to hear they had raised over $7,000—an amount that would cover
our entire out-of-pocket deductibles due with the start of the new year.

*God, You are good all the time!! I pray for You to have Your hands on the sur-
geon tomorrow. I pray for the family beside us and all the challenges they must
face.*

Waking just before we were taken to the holding room the next morning, Zach appeared to be calm as they wheeled him into surgery. His courage
seemed to grow with each new challenge. Within half an hour, the surgeon
found Dirk and me to report that everything had gone fine and that Zach
would be out of recovery soon.

I began to panic when an hour and a half passed and they had not
called for us. It was near 11 a.m. when we were told to meet Zach at the ele-
vators. Very angry that he had to endure waking from the surgery alone, he
hissed, "I hate you!" and turned away when I tried to grab his hand and kiss
him. Suffering from the effects of anesthesia and hunger, Zach calmed down
after eating. The surgery had required only two small incisions between his

left shoulder and chest. There was a bump—the port itself—under his skin about the size of half a ping-pong ball, just above the larger incision.

Dirk left to go to work for the rest of the day, and it was nearing dinnertime when he returned. Soon a nurse appeared with Zach's first infusion of chemo. Understanding the chemo was a toxic substance, I watched as the nurse suited up with special gloves, gown covers and a face mask. I was horrified to realize just how very toxic it really was. Fighting a very strong protective instinct to lie across Zach and not allow the poison to enter his body, I had to remind myself it could possibly save him.

Lasting several hours, this first infusion required two separate chemo drugs with an infusion of saline for hydration between them to pour into Zach's body. He lost his appetite when his dinner arrived and his stomach began to hurt, prompting a trip to the bathroom. Helping him shuffle there dragging the IV pole with us, I could see that the chemo was reacting quickly in his system. He was shaking and weak as he strained to go, still battling drug-induced constipation from the Thalidomide. Kneeling in front of him, I let him rest his head on my shoulder, hoping this chemo would gently counteract the constipation.

Trying to limit his torture, I only asked him to take the Kepra after seeing how hard it was for him to swallow anything without gagging. I also requested some Benadryl when he became sick. Soon he was asleep and the day was over. Relieved, I felt the first infusion had gone well for the most part.

Lord, thank You for all the answered prayers today. You are an awesome God!

The next day was busy with many visits from doctors, a social worker, school coordinator and child-life specialist. This was the first time our room was on the second floor and it was obvious the "cancer floor" patients got a lot more attention. Glad to see Zach was able to eat and drink, I was anxious to get working on his discharge. He was still very dizzy and weak as we took the few steps to the bathroom and the nurse warned us he had to be drinking consistently and could not be throwing up in order to be discharged.

It was so hard for him to function with all these treatments. I looked at him and wondered what evil world we had entered. What had happened to my strong, athletic boy? It was heartbreaking to watch, but his determination and courage were always there to bolster my resolve.

After satisfying all the nurse's requirements, we were grateful to be headed home. Unfortunately, the evening was anything but easy for Zach. He threw up numerous times and had a very difficult time taking his pills.

I woke the next day realizing it was Friday, the 13th—six months from the date Zach had his initial surgery. I had prayed for more time then, not knowing how long we should expect.

Thank You for each day we have together, Lord!

Although attending school was not on our agenda, I did want to try and take him there to watch his classmates participate in walk-a-thon fundraiser the school was having for both our family and Sydney Sims's family. Sydney was the other student at the school who was battling cancer. Encouraged to see his eyes growing brighter and his appetite getting stronger throughout the morning, I thought we would head for school. I knew that because he was still weak, he would have a hard time walking from the parking lot to the school. So I borrowed a golf cart from a friend who lived nearby. Because our neighborhood was so near the school, we could drive the golf cart from our friend's home to the school. Problem solved. Excitement beamed through Zach's eyes when I told him how we were going to get to school.

I pulled Zach close to me for the chilly ride and he grabbed the wheel, placing his foot on the gas as we drove the cart. It certainly would be helpful to have a golf cart of our own for times like this. I dismissed the idea as too extravagant when we had so many medical bills to cover. Maybe a dream fund request…I would have to investigate the possibility.

As we pulled up to the playground, Zach was excited as he watched the kids already walking the large oval that was lined with five hundred pictures made by all the children. The pictures were filled with messages of encouragement and hope for both Zach and Sydney. We could see the determination painted on the faces of the children as they walked lap after lap, collecting a little red straw for each lap they completed. I could tell Zach felt awkward just watching. If he were able, I knew he would be out there trying to be the one who walked the most laps.

After the activity was over, Zach and I took a lap around the oval in the golf cart, looking at all the pictures as we drove. It was such a beautiful day. When it was time to return the golf cart to my friend, we decided to take the long way home. We enjoyed the sunny Florida day, breathing in fresh air and feeling the light breeze on our faces.

The weekend brought perfect weather for outside play. Lexi surprised me by venturing out early on Saturday. She had become more and more isolated since Zach had been diagnosed and often played alone in the guest room. It had become her refuge in a very confusing, scary world. To see her go out to play with others was a good thing. Zach tried to participate, but did not have the energy to do much or last long.

His appetite was sporadic at best over the next few days, which was concerning since he now weighed less than he did when he was diagnosed in July. To make matters worse, he ended up not eating much for dinner most nights since the anxiety of having to take the pills soon afterward upset his stomach. And then soon after the pill-taking process ended, he would fall asleep.

My spirits were sinking as I watched Zach struggle day after day.

Lord, help us! Zach is getting so skinny. I want him to feel better again. When will this end? Please surround us with Your presence and fill us with strength to stay strong in our resolve.

The situation became unbearable for me on Martin Luther King Day. There was no school that day and pre-cancer it would have been a day filled with running and playing from daylight until dark for Zach. Instead it was a day of struggle and weakness. I slept in and Zach came to wake me because he felt sick. I was sure the lack of food in his system was the reason, along with the chemo side effects. He coughed and quickly threw up. Luckily, a bucket was nearby. He curled up next to me shivering. I cuddled close and could feel only his bones as most of the fat was gone from his frame. He looked so fragile when he sat up to head for the bathroom. I told him to just use the bucket. He was weak and trembling as he stood near me. My heart ached.

Lexi was anxious to get outside. Zach and I snuggled on the couch until he wanted to go see what the kids were doing. The girls had built a big tent on our play set in the backyard. I pulled an old tent out of our attic and set it up for the boys. Zach climbed in and sat on a pile of blankets I had thrown in for padding. I glanced out the window as they played, making sure Zach was OK. Soon, he shuffled up to the back door and came in. He realized he could not climb on the play set or swing with the others because he was too weak.

"Baby, I am sorry you don't feel well. What would you like to do? We can play a game or watch television—anything you want," I offered. He just stared blankly at the television and shrugged.

"I know! I will turn on the hot tub and we can get in there together. How does that sound?" I asked.

"OK, Mom, but do the other kids have to come in?"

"Only if you want them to," I answered as I went to turn on the heater.

When the water grew warm, Zach and I climbed in. He sat on my lap and playfully splashed the water with me. Hearing us, Lexi soon joined us, bringing some empty balloons with her. We spent the rest of the afternoon making water balloons as I cradled his skinny body on my lap.

That evening, I began to fantasize what the day would have been like if Zach had never been diagnosed with cancer. I had no doubt he would have been up early, waking me to make him some pancakes. Soon after he would have been out the door to find his buddies and they would have been off to play the rest of the day. I would have had to find him to drag him in to eat lunch. Later, he would have come in for dinner after much protesting. He would be sweaty, dirty and happy for the wonderful day off school. His body would have been strong, tan and solid as I carried him to bed after he fell asleep from fatigue.

How I long for those days. It makes my heart ache, dear Lord. Please give me the strength not to look back, but to anticipate Your healing Zach completely on this earth.

As I climbed into bed that night, tears formed in my eyes. Dirk looked alarmed as he asked what was going on. I shared with him all the thoughts I had about the day and how unfair this seemed to Zach—just an innocent child. Dirk gently pulled me close as I wept and grieved for the losses Zach was suffering.

The next day Zach and I spent time cuddling in the big chair. I found myself being torn when he asked me to sit with him. I knew I had many things to do around the house, but I also treasured the time I could spend with him just holding his hand and soaking him in. More times than not, I would cave to his demand when he called my name, snapped his finger and pointed to the spot beside him, realizing all the other things around the house would get done eventually.

Scheduled to have his homebound teacher come by later that day and meet her for the first time, I cleared the dining room table. Arriving on time, she had a very pleasant personality and a bright, uplifting smile. Nervous, Zach slowly stood up from the chair, pulled on his Lightning hat and walked into the dining room when I called his name.

Spending about an hour to evaluate him, she reported Zach seemed to be strong in all the areas they tested. Preferring to be with his classmates, Zach did not like the one-on-one attention he received in this setup. Hopefully, this would be a temporary situation for him this year and he could be back in school full-time next year for fourth grade.

The evening was peaceful, unlike my mind. Tomorrow Zach was scheduled to have the second infusion of chemo. Glad the first round had helped eliminate the constipation Zach had been experiencing, I was troubled by the other side effects of little or no appetite, dizziness and fatigue. I was not sure how much more Zach could take without breaking his spirit.

Hearing Dirk's alarm the next morning, my mind slammed into gear. Dread of what the day could bring overwhelmed me.

Dear Lord, give me the strength and wisdom to face today. Fill me with Your Spirit so I may have peace. Be with Zach and protect his body from the side effects of the chemo. I pray these drugs are working to their full potential and it is Your will that Zach will be healed on earth.

Praying had helped to calm my nerves, but I needed more. I picked up *The Message,* a favorite Bible version of mine, and let it fall open, hoping a passage would come to me with assurance we were on track. The Bible opened to Zephaniah 2:6—7. The last two lines read, "Their very own GOD will look out for them. He'll make things as good as before."

Feeling God's presence surround me, I read the next words, which went on to say God gives us chances to believe and rely on Him, but many times we choose not to—and we will be accountable for that.

Please forgive me, Lord, for slipping and letting negative thoughts take control. I am fully relying on You, Lord. We are not in control and it is Your will that we will follow because You will bring us good! I praise You, Lord, for this strength!

This message gave me a sense of peace and calm I had not had for awhile.

The clinic was quiet when we arrived, quite a change from December when it was full of activity and sick kids. Planning on a two- to three-hour visit, I was shocked to find out the chemo process would take four to five hours. Lunch would be served from the vending machine, due to my lack of understanding.

Accessing the port was a much easier process than the guesswork that went with finding a vein for an IV. The needle they used was larger, but they knew right where to put it. After the port was accessed, what seemed like an endless amount of tape and plastic was used to completely cover the area. It had to be kept sterile since the port was going directly into one of his main arteries. Any contamination could be very dangerous. When the nurses completed this process, we moved to the transfusion room and found a chair. Climbing into the gray plastic recliner, he grabbed the television monitor that hung overhead and pulled it close to his face with a smile. I tucked his special blue blanket around him and gave him a soft bear pillow he had received in the hospital last week.

Other than being long and tedious, the process was much better than I had anticipated. My fears for Zach of nausea or urgent trips to the bathroom never materialized. Only experiencing a stomachache half way through, Zach slept for most of the infusion.

He was very queasy and trembling when he shook me awake the next morning. His class was going on a field trip to see a play. He did not want to go there, but he did feel like having lunch at Ruby Tuesday's. His wish was my command, especially when it came to eating. As we drove to the restaurant, he curled up in a ball in the back seat. "My tummy hurts, Mom," he whispered.

"Should we go home? I can make you some lunch there," I said, glancing over my shoulder at his face.

"No, I want to go; I'll be alright."

Glad I had grabbed the bucket as we left the house earlier, I had positioned it right in front of him if he had a problem. His breathing had become slow and steady by the time I pulled into the parking lot. Circling many times, I finally found a close spot. Once I parked, he opened his eyes slowly. "We're here, Buddy. Do you still want to go in? I don't care if we just go back home if you don't feel well," I said, softly patting his leg.

"No, I'm ready," he said sitting up and grabbing his hat. Helping him climb out of the truck, I held his hand tight as we slowly walked across the parking lot. He stopped to rest on a bench after about fifty feet and when he felt ready, he stood and grabbed my hand.

We ordered our lunch as we sat on the same side of a booth. Zach loved to play "I Spy" while we waited for our food—something we had started when he was younger to help pass the time. When the food arrived, he gobbled down his french fries. After he finished, he pushed his plate away and put his head on my shoulder to rest. Suddenly, he became sick and lost all he had just eaten. He was so hungry, but his body was not going to allow him to eat.

We headed home, with a sad, gray feeling surrounding both of us. The treatments we had to have to save his life were taking away any quality of life along the way. The reality of this was sinking in deeper and deeper with each day.

Never knowing what the day would bring, Zach worked hard to not allow the unyielding nausea and stomach pain rule his life. Continuing to work with the homebound teacher, he impressed all of us when she found his reading level was equivalent to a fifth grader. Struggling, but determined, he attended school a few days, but found he was too weak to play with his friends at recess or at PE. The grueling and unending medication schedule wore on all our nerves as Zach continued to work hard to force every pill he swallowed to stay down.

Hoping to break the monotony, we accepted an invitation to ride on a float in the annual Children's Gasparilla Parade and throw beads to the crowds. Holding many memories for our family, the parade winds through the streets near Tampa Bay to memorialize a fabled pirate invasion of the bay. We had been twice in the past as spectators, standing on the roadside like everyone else and screaming for beads.

As the float finally lurched to life, we slowly drifted past thousands of people with outstretched arms, pleading for beads. Zach would carefully watch the many faces and toss beads to the ones he had selected. Many times, he would groan in frustration when the beads fell short of his intended target. I could feel his frustration with the limitations his body now placed on him. These limitations were very apparent when all the other kids riding near us climbed off the float and walked beside it for awhile. That was not an option for Zach. He was trapped by the side effects of his chemo.

After the parade finished, Dirk ran ahead to retrieve the car as Lexi, Zach and I slowly followed. Stopping many times to let Zach rest, we were all grateful to climb in the car after Dirk managed to weave his way through the back streets to find us. The parade helped to lift our troubled hearts. We were glad to have the opportunity to add some fun to our day.

It broke my heart to see all the neighborhood kids running and playing outside while Zach, still battling fatigue, seemed chained to his chair inside. When he did try to sit outside, he could only watch. Even walking across the street had become a challenge for him. The frustration of watching Zach suffer was taking its toll on all of us. Becoming more and more difficult to find the strength to stay positive, all I knew to do was to pray.

Lord, help us! Please hear our prayers. I desperately want our lives back. Even though I know it will never truly be the same, I just want Zach to feel good

enough to be able to go out to play, to laugh and run again, to be so tired from play-
ing all day he falls asleep as soon as he sits down for a minute—for all of us to have
some relief from this drudgery of cancer. Oh, what a joy I would feel to see this!
Lord, I want Zach to have a complete healing on earth so we can all dance and
sing with joy of Your miracles!

Because he felt better the next day, I wanted to get Zach up and moving if possible. As I searched my mind for a creative way to do this, I remembered a pedometer I had received as a gift. Giving it to Zach, I explained
how it would count his steps for the day. His eyes narrowed in thought
when I asked him how many steps he thought he could take in a day. Moti-
vated, he began to move around to do more things. Each time he moved,
he carefully pulled up his shirt to look at the numbers on the pedometer.

Everything seemed to fall back into place that evening when Zach surprised us by going out to shoot a few baskets with Dirk on our driveway.
Hearing the sound of the basketball hitting the pavement made me smile.
It was bittersweet. I missed that sound from the many games Zach had
played before he became sick. Hearing it now was good, but I knew it was
not the same. He struggled to shoot using just his right hand. At least he
tried. I knew he would find a way to compensate eventually, even if his left
hand never recovered.

Zach felt stronger when he woke the next day. "I'm hungry, Mom," he
whispered as I carried him to the chair. After a plate of eggs and watching
a few of "his shows," we were off to school. It was PE day and he was ready
to play. Before we left, he asked for the pedometer. He wanted to beat his
steps from the day before!

I was happy to see him still full of energy as he came bouncing down the
hall when the final bell rang. I had held my breath all afternoon, wondering if they would call telling me Zach had a stomachache or cramps.

When we got home, he soon grew bored in the house. I remembered
a driveway tennis set Lexi had bought him for his birthday a year ago and
went out to set it up. He loved it! We volleyed the ball back and forth, trying to increase our number of hits each time. I encouraged him to try to use
his left hand to pick up the ball and bounce it for his serve, but he shook

his head no. Full of spunk the more we played, he squealed with delight when he hit the ball just out of my reach and did a little dance to celebrate. Face beaming with joy, the old Zach emerged. The day had suddenly become perfect!

Chemo day number three arrived all too soon, but thankfully, we were much more prepared and the infusion went smoothly. It was clear Zach was feeling better this visit because he actually giggled when the doctor felt his belly and neck. As we headed home, he wanted to get a snack from McDonalds! Once again, my little man amazed me.

"Mom, I want to play tennis when we get home, OK?"

"I would love that, Zach, but you better be ready because I think I can beat you today!" I replied, not believing he would find the strength once we arrived home. I kept glancing over my shoulder as I drove, expecting him to become drowsy or worse, nauseous. Much to my surprise he was ready to go when he climbed out of the car.

I set up the net and a chair for Zach to rest in when he needed a break. The day was cool, but the sun warm as it beamed down on our driveway court. Zach looked stunning with a red silk skull cap, matching red shirt and some wraparound silver sunglasses. He could not keep the smile off his face as he beat me easily each game we played. I expected him to feel fatigue from the chemo infusion at any time, but he smashed my expectations to pieces, much like he kept smashing the tennis ball on my side of the court.

My heart felt as if it would explode from happiness as we played. Zach was in such a good mood. Amazed to think about how despondent and down we all felt just four short days ago. This journey was the most intense roller coaster ride I had ever taken.

Just when it seemed we had turned the corner on Zach feeling better, the diarrhea side effect really kicked in. Giving him Imodium almost every day to slow it down, I found it ironic that one month I was filling him with laxatives and the next with Imodium. His system was taking a beating, but Zach continued to amaze me with his perseverance and determination.

His blood counts the next week came back as too low for him to receive his last round of chemo, which was somewhat of a relief, because I wondered if he would be able to tolerate more of the medicine responsible for his cramping and watery stools. Anticipating that our time at the clinic might be abbreviated, I had grabbed our passes to Busch Gardens before we left the house. Wanting to make a special memory for Zach, I surprised him by stopping there for an unexpected visit.

The sun was shining brightly, but the air was cool. We rented a wheelchair and our adventure began. We rode a few rides and with each one, I watched anxiously, hoping they would not make him feel ill or jerk him around too much. We both enjoyed our time there, but it was bittersweet watching Zach realize his limitations as he tried to do things he had done before only to find he could not quite accomplish them this time.

Even though Zach did not have his last round of chemo, his system continued to be pummeled by the doses he had already received as the days passed. Facing a steadily decreasing appetite and intense diarrhea, he was taking at least two baths a day to help calm his tummy down.

My heart broke for him when his symptoms hit their peak and he had an accident in a chair, just steps away from the bathroom. I hid my face from him as the tears fell while I cleaned things up. He kept telling me he was sorry as he stood trembling while I washed him. I assured him he did not have to be sorry. He reminded me of pictures from the Holocaust—bones showing everywhere and dark hollow eyes. I kept wondering what the rest of the world was doing as I scrubbed the carpet clean and he lay in the tub with the warm shower sprinkling down on him.

Finally, after another week, his side effects began to subside. The sparkle slowly started returning to his eyes. Thankful he had made it through his first round of the IV chemo I had feared so much, he continued to teach us all to live with hope and to find our smiles. If he could do it, we certainly could too, no matter how wild the twists and turns of this roller coaster ride turned out to be!

Reflections

Zach's prayer to attend school epitomized the wish of every child with cancer: to just have a normal day. To know the carefree feeling of being able to jump out of bed, go to school, play with friends and eat whatever they feel like eating leaves these kids chasing a dream all too common and taken for granted by those not afflicted with cancer.

Anguish filled our hearts as we were helpless to "fix" things for Zach. As a parent, it is a natural instinct to shelter and protect our children. When that becomes impossible because of limited treatment options, animosity with a system that seems to lack an acceptable solution can be hard to avoid.

Frustration with the lack of progress in finding new treatments for children with cancer was underlying my thoughts. What I found through research was disturbing. Pediatric cancer was the ugly runt of the pack in the cancer world. It seemed to be last in line when it came to handing out government research dollars. Over the last twenty years, the lack of any new drugs or treatment protocols for children facing cancer was appalling to me. Perhaps it was because only about thirteen thousand kids were being diagnosed per year, which is a small amount when compared to some of the other cancer types—until it includes your child. Or perhaps, pediatric cancer was just too hard to look at because it is so scary. The "ignore it and it will go away" theory seemed to be at work, but it was not going away. In fact, when you are directly affected, as we were, it seemed to suddenly be popping up everywhere. Each school day, forty-six more children will be diagnosed with cancer; unfortunately, there is no way to know if it could be your child. Pediatric cancer does not discriminate.

We found these innocent victims of this hideous disease were picked without warning. No screening tests or preventive measures were available to give them a chance to dodge the grip of cancer. It just appears, and in one day these children go from having the carefree normal days of childhood to facing challenges that would make many adults buckle at the knees. Amazingly, we were seeing firsthand how every one of these kids, with uncommon courage and grace, faces the cruel and punishing treatments required to fight the monster living inside them—never giving up hope that they will live again to see those normal days they once had.

Knowing nothing happens by chance, I knew God had a purpose for our family being exposed to this heart-wrenching disease. It was our choice how we would choose to deal with the situation. Finding purpose in it by finding a way to help these kids and opening eyes to the challenges they faced was my choice. The bigger purpose of our journey, the life-changing purpose, was that our hearts and minds were being changed by drawing closer to God and allowing His love to hold us up. Sharing this purpose was what I wanted to devote my life to.

JANUARY 2006 at the Children's Gasparilla Parade. Lexi and Zach had sorted through the boxes of beads to find their favorite ones before the parade started. Zach was so thin at this event he could not sit comfortably on the float. My lap became his padding.

Always surprising me, Zach was ready to play driveway tennis even when he was feeling the side effects of his third infusion of IV chemo in late January. His competitive drive never left him even in the worst of times during his battle with cancer.

CHAPTER TWELVE

Glorious February

I woke to the crash of thunder on Saturday morning as Lexi climbed into bed with us. February had announced itself in a wet, stormy manner this year—unusual for Florida. As I snuggled close to Lexi, my mind began to whirl with ideas of how to find fun ways to work Zach's left arm and leg. Dirk and I wanted to keep pushing him to regain full use of his left side so that when he was better later, he would be able to do all the things he loved again. Focusing on his complete recovery, we were trying hard not to contemplate anything less. With the steady sound of rain on the roof, I knew outdoor activity was out of the question. My solution was to set up an obstacle course throughout our house.

After breakfast, I announced my plans to the kids. They were excited about the idea and quickly became my assistants as we set up the course. We all took turns running the course and tried to beat our individual times. Dirk and I were encouraged as we saw Zach using his left hand and arm more than he ever had since his initial diagnosis. Determination was evident in his eyes as he marched through the course a little faster each time. I was happy to see him improving, but also knew I needed to find a physical therapy group near us to reevaluate his status

Later that evening, we started watching a movie that put Zach and Dirk to sleep within the first thirty minutes. It turned out to be a good thing because it ended with a young girl about Zach's age dying of leukemia. As I lay watching I decided that along with the parental guidance rating, there should be a warning when movies contain topics about cancer! Tears slid down Lexi's cheeks as she watched. Tears tried to escape from my eyes as I blinked them away when the character with leukemia said, "Maybe we spend too much time waiting for something big to happen, when we should appreciate the regular small stuff and just get through life." How true this statement was! How often in the past had I always been thinking of the next big event and living for that time instead of just stepping back and enjoying the moment.

I lost the battle of holding back my tears when the scene showed the girl lying in the hospital bed close to death, looking at the friend visiting her and telling her she was not scared of dying, just scared of what she was going to miss. Was Zach thinking this? How can he be so brave? *Why was there cancer? Why do children get it?* The injustice of such a disease invading innocent lives overtook me as I stared at the screen. How could we be part of this world? It is only supposed to happen in movies—not real life!

The next day was filled with excitement for the kids. It was Super Bowl Sunday and a neighbor was having a birthday celebration. Much to my surprise, Zach actually stayed awake during the church service and followed the sermon. The excitement of the day had obviously increased his energy level. The sermon was based on the book *Who Moved My Cheese?* I was surprised how well it fit our lives with cancer. It reminded me our focus had to be on looking forward to see what was waiting for us, not looking back to long for what was behind us.

As we pulled in our driveway, Zach sat up straight in his seat, looking with anticipation at a large bounce house sitting in the neighbors' yard. Worried he might get tossed around too much or not be able to catch himself if he fell the wrong way, I went in with him as the other kids watched.

He pulled me aside after we got out and told me it was not fun without the others. The pleading look in his eyes melted my heart as I caved in and let him climb in with all his friends. He had a blast and I finally had to coax him out four hours later to get ready for a Super Bowl party we were scheduled to attend.

For the past three years, we had been going to watch the Super Bowl in a neighboring subdivision. With a projection screen as large as a garage door set up outside, the party had always been great fun. The kids usually played their own football game, periodically stopping to check the score of the real game. It was the kind of party Zach lived for. This year was different though.

I was glad to see many friends since our paths did not cross as they once had at the soccer field or at school activities. Smiling and greeting him with high fives or pats on the back, everyone was excited to see Zach. Looking for a chair near the screen, he quietly watched as his buddies ran and tossed a ball nearby. As the game started, they came and sat around him, quietly whispering and giggling among themselves about all the new commercials.

Seeing the pain and hope in many of our friends' eyes as they asked how the treatments were going, it was clear they knew it could easily be them walking in our shoes. They knew we had no radioactive accidents or toxic dumps in our past—just a normal life much like they were living. Dirk and I kept smiles on our faces as we answered their questions the best we could. If only we knew the answer everyone truly wanted to know: Would Zach make it? Would he be one of the lucky ones who found that right combination of chemo and radiation to kill the evil that lurked in his system?

Seeing Zach grow uncomfortable near halftime, we quietly said our good-byes and headed home. It had been a great day for all of us.

What a blessing today was, Lord. Thank You for all we have! I pray for Zach's complete healing, a clear MRI and no growth or new sites. I pray for peace for Dirk and Lexi as they face work and school.

The next week was filled with visits to doctors—first a clinic visit and then a visit to the neurologist. Both went very well. Zach and I were both excited to see the blood test report had high (for Zach) numbers. The last round of chemo was not winning the war on his bone marrow yet. The neurologist was pleased with Zach's progress as well. Performing a full neurological check of his reflexes and strength, he felt Zach was improving in all areas.

As the week passed, our excitement grew. Wanting to visit Dirk's vacationing parents in nearby Orlando, we booked a weekend trip to the Nickelodeon Hotel near them. When I had made the reservations, I was nervous, realizing Zach's counts could be falling from the chemo. But I was ecstatic to be proved wrong.

Designed to make you feel as if you had entered a "Nickelodeon World," the hotel had everything a kid could want—from an amazing pool/waterslide play area to every kind of game available. Knowing Zach's biggest desire was to have gooey green slime dumped on his head at some point in our visit, I informed the staff in charge of the "sliming" shows of Zach's story and was assured they would do whatever they could to get us in a show the next day. Satisfied I had done the best I could, we attended one of the slime shows as spectators later that evening.

Buzzing with anticipation of what was behind the bright orange doors, Lexi and Zach could hardly stand still as we waited in line. When the doors finally opened, we scurried to get seats near the stage. We watched as two families competed for the opportunity to have their captain slimed. Dirk's hand shot up when the hosts asked for volunteers to help the teams with their games. They selected him and whisked him backstage. The next time we saw Dirk, he was dressed as a baby, complete with a diaper, bib and bonnet! Snickering as he modeled his new uniform for all to see, Lexi and Zach were thrilled he was on stage. His job was to sit in a very large high chair and try to catch water balloons without popping them. Unfortunately for Dirk, his team did not win and he received a rather runny whipped cream pie in the face. After the show, we continued our fun by playing miniature golf before returning to our room.

The next morning, Zach woke early, full of excitement of what the day would hold. Anxious to find more fun, we found there were relay games in progress in the hotel activity center. Realizing they were competing for tokens to the arcade, Zach quickly joined the line to play. I watched nervously, wondering if the game would require the use of both hands. Not wanting to see his excitement squashed by not being able to perform, I quietly slipped over to one of the staff members and explained Zach's left hand did not function completely. Eager to help, they assured me they would assist him in a discreet way so he could compete.

His face set with determination as he watched his team progress through the relay, Zach struggled a bit to balance a plastic "crabby patty" on a spatula, but once it was there he quickly wound his way around the cones in the obstacle course. Raising his right hand in victory, he proudly smiled as his team was declared the winner. Feeling pangs of sadness as I wondered how different this trip would have been if Zach had not been diagnosed, it made my heart ache to see him be so brave and to continue to live with such courage as his body betrayed him and kept him from doing what was once easy for him.

By the end of the games, Zach was the proud owner of five more tokens for the arcade. As he rested beside me, I noticed that the physical challenges had made his left side noticeably tremor.

He wanted to explore the maze of slides, fountains and stairs in the water park next. I watched as Zach's pale, skinny frame gingerly followed Lexi up some stairs to see where a bright orange tunnel would lead them. Dirk followed close behind. Because of the blustery February winds, it was not long before Zach came to find me and the warmth of a couple of beach towels.

Grabbing my jacket, he curled up with it and some towels. He seemed tired. Studying him as he closed his eyes to rest, I saw just a shadow of the robust boy we once had. Growing taller since his diagnosis, he had lost muscle and weight since then, making his bony frame more noticeable. Marked with scars from his surgeries—on his head and chest where the telltale bump of his port lay—his beautiful hazel eyes were the same and his perfect smile was still there. He was still Zach. No matter what torment his body faced, his spirit held strong.

Later as the clouds won a contest with the sun, we lost interest in the pool and headed inside. The red blinking message light got our attention. We had been selected to be a team at a live show that night. Zach began a countdown an hour before we were to arrive for the contest. His face could hardly contain the anticipation he was feeling as we left the room and made our way through the cold rain that had joined the blustery wind. Dirk's parents met us at the studio doors and watched as Zach and Lexi nervously teased each other as we waited to be called in ahead of the crowd. When the moment arrived, we left Gib and Phyllis with a camera and instructions to volunteer if they asked for help in the games.

Zach, being our captain, had to change clothes to ready himself for the slime if we were lucky enough to be crowned the winning team. His red skull cap went perfectly with the red team uniform he wore. After receiving our pregame instructions, we waited behind the curtains for our cue. When our names were announced, we made our way out to our seats and readied for the competition. Our team maintained a lead in the beginning, but in the end, the blue team won. Disappointed for Zach, little did I know he would have a double treat! Because we were the losing team, Zach had to pick one of his parents to pie with a whipped cream pie. Zach hesitated in thought and then shyly looking over his shoulder at me, he slowly said, "My Mom!"

Escorting me to the center of the stage, the host had me kneel as they carried out the biggest, creamiest whipped cream pie I had ever seen. Handing Zach the pie, he slowly stepped toward me. Our eyes were locked as he giggled nervously and slowly pushed the pie to my face. Hearing him laugh as I felt the thick, sticky cream engulf my face, I suddenly realized I could not take a breath without inhaling a large quantity of whipped cream. Clearing my eyes and nose, I laughed as I reached out trying to give him a big hug and kiss, but he ducked just in time.

Having another surprise for us, the host asked us to return to our seats as we watched thick, gooey, green slime cover the winning team's captain. After the room cleared, the Nick team escorted us backstage and told Zach they had mixed up a special batch of slime just for him! He would be slimed after all. With a very loud countdown, they dumped a full bucket of slime over Zach's head. As the green goop oozed down his back and face, they all gathered around him and took pictures of a very happy Zach!

As we concluded our visit the next morning, various Nickelodeon characters appeared at our breakfast table as we filled our bellies with omelets and pancakes. The trip had accomplished everything we had hoped. We left with many happy memories and both kids had been able to escape from— at least for a few days—the ugly cancer world we lived in.

Sweetly wishing everyone a happy Valentines Day as he entered the kitchen for breakfast during the next week, Zach's fun continued. He had worked hard to prepare his Valentine cards the day before. I had taken him to school to spend time with his classmates. He had a big smile on his face as he clutched his brown bag full of candy and cards. Uplifted by Zach's reprieve from the harsh side effects that had plagued him, I returned home and slid on my running clothes. It felt as if the sun rays were kissing my skin when I ran.

When I returned to pick up Zach, I slowed as I approached his door. I could hear laughter and Mrs. Sapp commenting on the Nickelodeon pictures I had brought for her to share with the class. I smiled, thinking how proud Zach must have felt to share his special weekend.

To celebrate Valentines Day, Dirk and I had a steak dinner by candlelight. We had wine with our meal—the first time since Zach had been diagnosed. Zach and Lexi both seemed concerned we were drinking the wine. I felt a little conflicted about it, but life was so strange. It seemed we didn't quite know how to live anymore. All the answers we used to have did not seem to fit now.

Our Caringbridge friends continued to bolster our spirits with their prayers and messages. I continued to update them daily with Zach's adventures.

February 14, 2006
Hope everyone gets lots of hugs from their sweethearts today. The first words out of Zach's mouth this morning was "Happy Valentines Day!" It

was such a great way to start the day, hearing him in such a good mood.
He is at school right now. His class was having a card exchange and PE
today, so he did not want to miss that!

We will go to the clinic in the morning for another blood test. Keep
praying for high counts. His energy level and general good feeling make
me think everything will be in the normal range. We are certainly enjoy-
ing this "rest period" compared to the last few.

As predicted, Zach sailed through his blood test. After making arrangements with the Children's Cancer Center for the special privilege, I was able
to take both Zach and Lexi to Busch Gardens at the end of the week for a
special preview of a new attraction they were opening. Grateful they allowed
me to include Lexi, I was pleased that the staff at the center knew all to well
how siblings of children affected by cancer were often left feeling deprived
of much needed attention.

Our trip to Busch Gardens was a blast. Excited about meeting some
Tampa Bay Buccaneers' football players, Zach carefully selected a Bucs hat
to wear. Refusing a wheelchair this trip, he didn't want to appear weak to
the players. Disappointed the interaction with the players was limited to a
few pictures and a brief hello, we did not let that spoil our fun. Watching
as Lexi and Zach rode together on the same rides Zach and I had ridden a
few weeks ago, I marveled at his strength to walk the entire way.

Lithia Springs Elementary had scheduled their biggest fundraiser, a
family fun festival, for the next day. The same event the prior year had been
so different for us. Then, we had arrived early and both kids participated
in a one-mile fun run before the festival. Zach had run very hard and came
in fourth out of all the participants. Surprised he had done so well considering he was only in second grade, I had pictured a big future in all kinds
of sports for Zach. This year things were as I had never imagined. We were
thankful he had the strength to walk around the fun fair. Running a race was
a thing of the past for now.

It was another beautiful day as we approached the brightly colored
game booths and bounce houses at the fun fair. Quickly finding their

friends, Lexi and Zach went their separate ways and soon began winning lots of trinkets at the different games. Following close behind Zach, I was ready to provide assistance if he grew tired or hot.

Wanting to try an obstacle course, Zach made it through the beginning obstacles, but ran into a problem when he came to a climbing wall. Zach tried and tried but could not make his left hand or left foot cooperate as he attempted to climb the wall. Feeling helpless, I watched as his frustration dissolved into defeat when he was accidentally kicked in the face by another boy. He slowly climbed down to my waiting arms, brokenhearted at the realization he just was not able to do it. My heart broke seeing the sadness in his eyes.

After resting and having a snack, we found some other games to play. It seemed to help to erase the momentary frustration we all felt. We left the festival tired, but smiling.

During our church service the next day, I experienced a small anxiety attack as I thought about the MRI Zach was scheduled for the next day. What if things were progressing or there were new spots? It was irrational for me to think this since Zach was not displaying any symptoms, but I could not shake the feeling of impending doom. Thoughts of attending church without Zach flooded into my head. Tears sprang to my eyes as I tried to catch my breath. I could not fathom that thought. It would not happen. How would I go on?

Dear Lord, I continue to pray for Zach's healing here on earth. He is such a bright light for all those around him, Lord. We need him here with us. I pray the results of the MRI are good tomorrow. Give us strength.

Leaving my anxiety behind, we joined Debbie's family for a Daytona 500 race party later that day. As we prepared to go to the party, Dirk and I decided we would drink a few beers while we watched the race. When Dirk left to go get a six-pack while I packed our swimsuits, Zach came to me. "Mom, are you and Dad going to drink beer?" he asked.

"Well, yes, Honey. It's no big deal. We are just going to have one or two. It is OK," I answered as Lexi joined us.

He looked at Lexi and said, "They are going to drink beer. Remember,

Mom, Dad told me he wasn't going to drink anymore." Lexi shook her head in agreement and crossed her arms and looked at me with disapproving eyes.

"Guys, it will be OK. We are not going to drink all the time, just today during the race. I'll tell Dad you don't like the idea, OK?" They both shrugged their shoulders and went to find their swim goggles. I had not realized how much our selfish desire for the momentary happiness alcohol had brought us had truly affected them until now. It troubled me that it was apparent their security and long-term joy had been damaged by our old routines.

Once there, Lexi and the Brus boys, Grant and Spencer, climbed in the hot tub to play while we watched the race. Looking thin and pale as he walked out to the hot tub, Zach soon joined them. Laughing with the other boys, Zach worked hard to douse Lexi as they played.

Growing bored with the hot tub, Zach decided he wanted to jump in the pool with the others and swim to the shallow end. I asked Lexi to swim right beside him in case he needed help, and my heart skipped a few beats as I watched him jump in. He came up coughing, but slowly made his way across the pool. Requiring more effort than he realized, he smiled as we all applauded his efforts when he climbed out.

The race ended and we headed home. As Zach and I cuddled in his bed talking about the day, he informed me that he was not happy that Dirk had more than one beer. Later when I told Dirk about the conversation, he felt perhaps God was trying to speak to us through the children. We both decided there was no need to drink. The kids were too important to have them worry about it.

My thoughts shifted to the next day. It was judgment day again— another MRI. I was more nervous this time because of the spots that had caused everyone's concern before.

Lord, I pray for good results on the MRI tomorrow. Faith, not fear. Forgive me for my weak mind. Give me strength.

In a good mood as we headed to the clinic the next morning, Zach remembered I had not put the numbing cream on his port. Thankfully I had it with me in my "clinic bag"—a bag I carried to every appointment. It was filled with his medical reports, blood tests, MRI scans and other pertinent information. Pulling into the nearest parking lot, I smeared the cream on his port, which was easy to find on his skinny frame. I was glad he had remembered this important pain-saving detail.

The clinic was bustling when we arrived. After visiting the doctor, we wound our way back to the MRI unit. As I watched Zach fall asleep soon after they slid the table into the tunnel and the clanking and banging started, it bothered me to realize I was becoming so familiar with the rhythmic banging coming from the large tan machine. Never did I imagine this being part of my "routine." Thinking of all Zach had endured in the last eight months, I bounced from prayer to memories about as often and sporadic as the noises bouncing around the small room. I felt peace settle in my heart as I surrendered my fears to God in my prayers.

Later as Dirk and I viewed the scan, we were relieved to see nothing looked significantly worse. This time we looked at the entire brain and not just the area where the original tumor was located. Cautiously optimistic, we looked forward to our next visit to Duke, which was about a week away. The doctor was going to study the scan and decide what course of action we should take for the next round of chemo.

Zach seemed to gain strength as the week progressed. Attending school when the homebound teacher was not scheduled to visit him, he was eating well and actually playing in the football games at recess! It was wonderful to see him get to experience a little bit of "normal" again.

As Zach worked through his homeschool assignments, I sorted through medical bills. Because of the generosity of our friend and families, the assistance fund had been such a blessing to us! The medical bills and travel expenses that could have been a source of great stress and burden to us had been lifted from our shoulders. Debbie, her husband Joe and many friends were hard at work now, organizing another fundraiser—a golf scramble for April.

Dirk found peace as he began to become bolder about sharing his renewal in faith. Walking on a cloud, he shared how he told a couple of friends about the peace and joy he had found through his faith in God. As we jogged together that evening, we decided to join a small group from church that Joe and Debbie were leading on Sunday evenings. I knew it would be challenging with Zach's unpredictable schedule, but felt the benefits would be worth the challenge.

At the end of the week, I called the doctor at Duke to see if he had reviewed the latest scans. He immediately expressed concern about the spot on the left side again. My heart dropped to the floor as he explained we might want to try a different treatment plan. Wanting to further study the scan, he would compare it to the prior one before he made his final decision. As I called Dirk to share the news, my world suddenly turned quite gray. We reminded each other that worry would do us no good, but it was extremely hard to push the anxiety out of my mind. Fighting back many tears as I drove to the school to have lunch with Zach, I kept staring at his beautiful face, wondering what was actually happening to him inside his head as he nibbled his lunch.

Later, stilled wracked with anxiety and concern, I sat outside with Zach as he played with his neighborhood buddies. Gazing at Zach's smiling face, I realized I had to focus on the moment. Creating worry about the future was doing me no good. He was so beautiful. What a gift God had given us to have him here with us!

I had been waiting anxiously for the doctor's return call, never letting myself be without a phone nearby. Jumping to my feet when the phone rang, I answered the call, my heart started pounding. A smile flooded my face as I heard the doctor explain that after he reviewed the scans side by side, he was quite impressed. He said they actually looked good! I felt like my feet were leaving the ground as the weight I had been carrying all day suddenly left me.

I praise You, Lord! What an answered prayer we have received! Thank You for this news. Forgive me for my worry. You are my rock. I know you can heal Zach, dear Lord. It is happening as I pray!

The doctor decided he wanted to continue on the same course of treatment after all. Although he would be happy to see Zach the next week, he explained it was not a necessary trip. Knowing we had already booked the flight and room, I told him I would like him to walk us through the scans while we were there so we could learn more about what he looked at when he reviewed them.

The world was colorful once again! Reflecting on how quickly our outlook and lives changed with one phone call or one scan, it seemed our existence was no longer long-term focused, but had become very short-term and uncertain. Not sure I would ever get used to living this way, it felt as if our life had been placed on pause with cancer—while the rest of the world stayed on play. Wondering when we would press play again, I prayed it would be when Zach was declared cured and cancer-free!

The weekend was one of those that just happened. No special plans, but many special memories were made. Starting slowly with no playmates to be found early on Saturday, I became Zach's playmate as we built a tent out of a big box and some sheets. Gradually, more friends appeared and more tents sprang up across our driveway.

The sun's rays became very intense as it climbed higher in the sky, prompting me to start the hot tub. Playing with squirt guns and water balloons, the children filled balloon after balloon with the warm water from the jets in the hot tub until our entire lanai was covered with all shapes and sizes of balloons. It was a simple, but perfect day for everyone—one we would all remember for no other reason than the smiles and memories that were made.

Sunday was a true blessing when many of our neighbors joined us at church. I met Dirk after his men's group morning prayer time. He was beaming with joy. A coworker he had been sharing his faith with had given his life to Jesus Christ during the prayer time. Dirk's eyes were filled with passion as he shared the story with us. He had always struggled to find passion in his engineering field. I could see sharing his faith was his true calling. He was very good at his work, but it never really fulfilled him. It was clear that sharing his faith and giving his testimony completed him. Somehow, we would have to find a way in the future to make that happen for him.

The afternoon slipped by and soon it was time for us to attend the small group meeting with Debbie and Joe. Since it was only five minutes from the meeting, we decided to leave the kids at the Brus's house with Spencer and Grant. I was nervous about leaving Zach, but he seemed to be feeling good, and both he and Lexi assured me they would call my cell phone if there were any problems.

The small group meeting was a wonderful experience for Dirk and me. Following our story through Debbie and Joe and our website, they had been praying for us since they started meeting in November. Dirk and I gave them a quick update on Zach and thanked them for their concern. Excited to participate in a study about God's Word and how to apply it to our lives, we were both glad we made the effort to attend and looked forward to meeting again.

Centered on a book called *The Dream Giver* by Bruce Wilkinson, Dirk and I discussed the small group lesson later that evening. Asking if I had ever dreamed of being an author, he said he could see the same passion in me through my writing as I saw in him earlier when he shared his faith. Perhaps it was something to consider.

I pray, Lord, You will guide us to find our dreams that You have planted in our hearts. I pray that these dreams will glorify You!

Our clinic visit went well the next day. We were carefully monitoring Zach's weight, as well as his counts, since he had dropped well below his starting weight last July. Taking it all in stride, Zach dutifully climbed on the scale, had his blood pressure and temperature taken before picking a finger to be poked for blood. We were happy to see his weight and his counts were both going up. Such a relief to not have to face the numerous infusions the oral chemo imposed on his system.

Scheduled to have a day of testing with his homebound teacher, we left the clinic. The state achievement test referred to as the FCAT was being administered to all the schools this week. This included the homebound students as well. Zach would take all his sections over the next three days, so that when we left for Duke on Wednesday night, his testing would be complete.

The testing went well. Both Zach and Lexi, who had taken her tests at school the same day, said the questions were easy. Silently, I once again thanked Dr. Thornton and MPRI for helping to preserve Zach's healthy brain cells with the proton radiation.

The testing continued the next day. Zach plowed through three sections and had time to spare. Only one more section to go. Ready to go to school to enjoy some fun activities they had planned after they completed their testing, he wanted a snack before leaving and suddenly felt very sick. Lying back on the chair, he was soon asleep. After three hours, he felt well enough to eat some lunch. We were watching some TV together when a commercial came on that talked about surgery. "Mom, why didn't they remove all of the tumor when I had my surgery?"

Taken by surprise at his question, I answered, "Well, they got most of it. But there was some that was in an area that was too hard to reach without hurting your brain. They had to leave that part alone. That is why we have to do all this medicine and radiation—to make sure the rest of the tumor goes away," I explained hoping it made sense to him.

"It will grow back," he muttered, as he turned his somber face back to the television. The certainty in his voice concerned me. I wondered why all of a sudden he felt this way.

"Zach, you have to stay positive and have faith in God that He will take care of it. OK, Buddy?" I asked grabbing his hand and squeezing it tight.

He didn't answer as he started changing the channels, looking for something that interested him. Suddenly he saw a commercial for a cruise and stopped. "I want to go on a cruise again, Mom. That was fun when we went to Mexico." A smile spread across his face as he remembered the cruise we had taken in the prior year. Having seen a Kids Dream Fund flyer at the clinic, I decided I would submit a request for a cruise this summer and surprise him.

Zach never seemed to fully recover from his unexplained nausea the rest of the day. Going outside in the glorious weather later, he just sat and watched everyone play. Squeezing in a much needed run at 10:15 P.M., I climbed on the treadmill and ran as my thoughts processed the month.

Tomorrow would start a new month. What would it hold for us? February was great compared to most. There were some rough spots, but for the most part, Zach felt well, was eating and smiling. I was thankful for this and prayed we would see many more months as glorious as February had been.

Reflections

Hope has many levels of meaning—more than I ever realized before I began this journey. On the surface, hope holds our dreams of the future. It is the feeling every parent has when they look deep into the eyes of their newborn and fill their heart with thoughts of the life ahead for this beautiful being they were part of creating. Hope at this level is a comfort, a dream-maker for all the potential that could be.

The hope that comes with a cancer diagnosis suddenly becomes guarded and desperate. It is measured by prognosis and dispensed by doctors who at times do not realize what a powerful effect they have in regard to hope's ability to be effective in treatment. Limited by the training they received from those who loved them in their lives, the hope they share can build many walls or create false fantasies in their patients' minds.

An uneasy respect for hope appears when treatments show the least bit of progress. Hearts that had become guarded and confined by limited options begin to soften. Anticipation grows and dreams begin to cautiously sprout. Hope is an old friend that has come back, bringing glimpses of what used to be in our mind's eye—the beautiful portraits we had painted so long ago when the slate was clean and our minds not tainted.

This was the hope we were now holding. It was an uneasy, but joyful hope, a hope that maybe—just maybe—we were gaining a foothold on the beast that had crashed into our lives. Although weakened in his physical body, mentally Zach had persevered through the first full punishing round of chemo with the attitude he could step back into his eight-year-old life right where he left off. Inspiring and amazing, he continued to fulfill his purpose by teaching us to never give up.

Although we had experienced many levels of hope, we found the most fulfilling and never-ending level of hope was coming from the unequaled

promises given to us by our Father in heaven. His words given to us in Jeremiah 17:7—8 express this hope so well: "But blessed is the man who trusts in the LORD, whose confidence is in him. He will be like a tree planted by the water that sends out its roots by the stream. It does not fear when heat comes; its leaves are always green. It has no worries in a year of drought and never fails to bear fruit."

Hope was something that grew from our hearts. God gave us His promises to cling to in an uncertain world. These promises are what truly helped us get through many hard days. The promise God would never leave us and had plans for each one of us carried us as we continued our unforeseen journey.

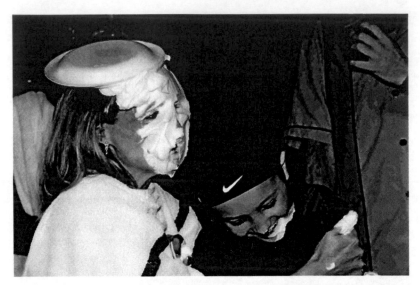

In early February 2006, our weekend getaway to the Nickelodeon Hotel. I was trying to give Zach a big kiss after he put a whipped cream pie in my face, but he ducked just in time!

Zach's wish came true when he was slimed at the Nickelodeon Hotel. When we told him we were going to this hotel, the first thing he said was he wanted to be slimed.

CHAPTER THIRTEEN

Round Two

Zach had mischief in his eyes and a smile on his face as he called out "Mom!" and motioned to me from the couch. I loved to see the sparkle in his eyes when he was devising a plan to lure me beside him. How could I resist such a clever boy? Climbing over him, I snuggled close, grabbing his hand in mine.

We faced a busy day. Zach had to finish his FCAT testing and we had to get ready for our trip to Raleigh later in the day. Realizing this trip was unnecessary based on the doctor's last comments, I smiled as I recalled that he was encouraged with the MRI results! Hoping to learn from him as he explained all he considered when evaluating the images on the scans, I also wanted to better understand how many more rounds of treatment he felt Zach would have to endure. Hopefully, if things stayed stable, not many more.

After an hour of lounging, I helped Zach into a bath, then began to pack our suitcases. The trip would be a quick one. Arriving at 10 P.M., we would rent a car and spend the night in a hotel across the street from the Duke clinic. Our appointment was after lunch the next day and we were scheduled to catch a late flight back to Florida after that. Growing unsure about the "long-distance doctoring" relationship, I was concerned it would limit the opportunity for the doctor to really get to know Zach, which was a shame.

Zach breezed through his final test and soon Lexi arrived home from school. Again, she was excited about escaping our travel schedule for time with her girlfriend. What a blessing that she had such a great friend to help us out.

The sun was sinking, turning the sky into a beautiful canvas of orange, pink and purple when Dirk pulled into the driveway. As we got ready for the drive to the airport, we both were looking forward to flying this trip. We had decided after the last trip that a ten-hour drive was something we would try to avoid. Once we arrived at the airport with plenty of time to spare, we all were able to relax.

The flight was relatively empty and smooth as we flew through the velvet black sky. Zach surprised me by staying awake the entire flight. Passing the time by playing cards and teaching ourselves how to play Sodoku, we arrived at the hotel by 11 P.M. Drawing Zach close to me, I drifted off savoring his special smell and the warmth of his thin body.

The weather was beautiful the next day as we left the hotel for lunch before our appointment. Feeling a hint of spring in the crisp breeze, we could see it in the trees as well as new leaves were coloring them green again. As we entered the clinic, Zach's eyes were immediately drawn to a basketball court outside the front lobby. There were a few small boys bouncing a ball on the brightly colored playing surface. The sun streamed in the windowed atrium as we made our way to the glass elevator.

Unlike the Tampa clinic, the waiting area here was deserted as we waited for them to call our names. Soon we were taken to an exam room and greeted by the same physician's assistant we had seen the last visit. She wore a broad grin as we reviewed Zach's progress with her. Asking Zach to perform all the familiar tasks needed to test his neurological response, she was impressed with the improvement she saw in his left side.

After she reported her findings to him, the doctor entered the room with a couple of young female interns in tow. He was explaining the case to them as he entered. We exchanged greetings and he repeated the neurological tests with Zach. Bringing up the most recent scans along with the ones from December on a monitor, he explained each slide as he compared the changes and said things looked good or stable in every area. As he paused near the end of his explanation, I questioned him about the reference to the "pons" area mentioned in the Tampa report.

Since he appeared to be unfamiliar with the report I had referenced, I pulled out the written report and asked him where the second spot was located. Going back to the scans, he mumbled that the area they were referring to was in the brain stem region of the brain. After a few moments he found the area and studied it intently, comparing the most recent scan to the prior scan. Because it was similar to what was on the left side of Zach's brain, he felt this spot too was questionable if it indeed was a lesion, but he concluded it looked stable as well.

When I asked what we should expect for further treatments, his eyes seemed filled with pity as he told us the treatments would go on for a long time. Hopes for an eventual break from chemo seemed to evaporate with his words, and he wanted Zach to start the second round of treatments the following Monday.

The conversation started to turn toward basketball as the doctor asked Zach to walk so he could watch his symmetry. He smiled as Zach easily walked out the door and down the hall with a fairly normal gait. Satisfied the treatments were holding the cancer cells at bay, he asked if we had any more questions, adding that we shouldn't worry because he did have other treatments in mind if the scans changed.

Dear Lord, we thank You for this great news! Thank You for Your healing hands surrounding Zach during this last treatment cycle. We pray he continues to show improvement and is completely healed here on earth for Your glory!

Having some free time to spend on the Duke campus, we went exploring. The spring flowers were blooming everywhere we turned. Growing up in Indiana, I had always loved spring as it signified a rebirth of the earth after a long cold winter. Just as the many daffodils seemed to spark hope in the gray and brown landscape that covered the earth, I could feel the same hope of Zach's survival from this visit.

Making our way across the campus, we found the sky was a brilliant blue backdrop for the magnificent towering steeples on the Duke Chapel. Everything about the chapel was amazing. Each of the seventy-seven stained glass windows depicted a scene from the Bible.

The Gothic style of architecture was dramatic and breathtaking. There was a quote by Reynolds Price in a brochure there in the chapel: "...Look up straight overhead. You're sheltered in a boat—a pale gray stone boat. A boat turned permanently upside-down..." Studying the ceiling, I found this description to be true. Other information posted in the chapel likened Price's boat reference to a symbolic description of the church. A boat protects against storms, and the church protects against the "storms of life." We certainly had been participating in a "storm of life" lately! I wondered if we would visit this chapel again in the future. *Would it be in praise or in prayer?* I hoped with all my heart it would be for praise.

Visiting the student union building next, I observed the students as they studied or talked to one another. Their carefree lives seemed so faraway from us now. Before diagnosis, I had imagined Zach and Lexi at this age and wondered what schools they would attend or what majors they might pursue. Now I battled to keep those dreams alive. Wondering if Zach would live to see middle school—let alone college—it would be a dream come true if he returned to this campus one day as a student, defiantly beating the odds.

Lord, I know this is not too big for You!

Our free time came to an end and we returned to the airport for our flight home. Zach was tired as we walked to our gate, so Dirk found a wheelchair for him. It was obvious that the long day had caught up with him. Zach wanted some candy as we sat waiting for our flight, so he and I went to find some. As he shopped, a book titled *90 Minutes in Heaven* caught my eye. I had seen this book a few weeks ago when I was looking for something to read, but had decided against buying it. There was a sense that by reading it, I would be showing weakness in my belief Zach would be healed on earth. This time, as I looked at the title, I felt like I *had* to buy it. We made our purchases and headed back to the gate.

Finding the book fascinating, I did not stop reading it until we arrived back in Tampa. Written by Don Piper, a minister, and Cecil Murphey, the book described Don's experience when he was pronounced dead from a car accident and for ninety minutes went to heaven, and then came back to his body to live. What was amazing was his description of his time in heaven. It gave me a sense of peace like I had never imagined I could have. To read of the overwhelming sense of love and joy he felt and the indescribable sights and sounds completely changed my thoughts of what heaven held for us.

Also reading that he did not feel a sense of loss for those he left behind on earth was such a relief to me as I remembered Zach's question about trying to find me or others in heaven. I hoped and prayed I would reach heaven before Zach, but if this was not God's plan, at least I had an idea of what one person had experienced and I was better equipped to discuss it with Zach if needed in the future.

As Zach slept on our way home from the airport in Tampa, Dirk and I discussed the meeting with the doctor.

"It seemed like the doctor and the others were surprised with Zach's scans, didn't it?" Dirk asked.

"Yeah, I thought so too. I guess they were expecting more growth or something," I answered.

"I guess they don't know how to explain the start of a miracle, do they?" Dirk replied with a smile.

Feeling good the next morning, Zach was ready for Fun Friday. After dropping him off with his class, I went for a run. I felt like I was floating on air! Finally it seemed things were going in a good direction. Thinking back to July and how much trouble I had training my mind to understand Zach really had cancer, I could hardly slow my thinking enough to pray or focus on my faith.

Mad at being thrown into this "club" without warning, I had wanted an immediate miracle. Amazed with the transformation that was taking place in me, I now had a new concept of life and living with purpose. God had certainly used this circumstance to grab hold of my heart. My faith had grown and given me a new vision of the world. What an awesome day!

Joining Zach for lunch, I followed him to the playground when he finished. As the class ran to the playground, Zach ran with them. One of his classmates who was walking beside me asked, "When will Zach's leg start working right again?"

"I'm not sure, but it is getting better. We still have some work to do though," I answered with a smile.

"I remember last year. Zach was always the fastest in the football games. He really could run fast!" he said as he ran to join the others.

Feeling in my heart we would see the day when Zach was the fastest again, I knew we had to have patience and wait on God's timing.

Zach and I had to visit the clinic when Monday arrived. Realizing he was due for a Pentamindine breathing treatment, a preventive medicine for pneumonia, I worried it might make him nauseous. I had finally found a physical and occupational therapy practice that qualified under our insurance and had set up an evaluation for the same afternoon. I hoped the breathing treatment wouldn't disrupt that visit.

The nurse suggested he take a few breaks during the breathing treatment, and that seemed to help. I had to wear a mask as Zach took his treatment, and I looked like a duck from the funny shape of the mask. Patiently breathing in the vapors coming through the plastic face mask, Zach never ceased to amaze me the amount of tolerance he held for the never-ending treatments he faced. Although he was never thrilled about any of it, he never really complained.

Zach slept as we made our way back to Brandon, just east of Tampa, for the evaluation. When they called us back, we entered a large room filled with balls, ropes, mats and swings. As the occupational therapist started her evaluation of Zach, he was doing fine until she had him lie flat on the ground. Quickly sitting up, he looked at me with panic in his eyes.

"Are you going to throw up, Honey?" I asked, quickly looking for a wastebasket. He shook his head just as the therapist grabbed one and shoved it toward us. The evaluation went downhill from there, but in true Zach fashion he tried to finish the rest the best he could. They told me they would work on a plan and send it to me. I emphasized that I did not think we needed to visit more than once a week because, under their guidance, I felt we could do much of the work at home.

Later, as we all settled in for the evening, it was time to start the next round of chemo. After I wrapped two additional pills in the sticky fruit rollup, Zach carefully dipped them in his glass of water and swallowed them down. It was a relief that he no longer struggled to swallow and keep the pills down like the last time he took these pills.

Lord, I pray for this medicine to work to its full extent and for Zach to continue to feel good. Help us to stay strong as Zach goes through this cycle of treatment. Be with him and heal him, Lord.

I did not sleep well as I thought about the start of the previous round of Temador. The memory of walking into his room and finding him trembling and scared in his bed still haunted me. Quietly slipping out of bed before anyone was up, I felt relief wash over me as I knelt by his bed and watched him breathing peacefully as he slept.

Debbie was going to stay with Zach while I went for a mammogram— a test I had skipped last year, and I knew I would be pushing my luck to miss it again. He was excited to get a chance to "play," and she had big plans for Zach. She took him on a shopping spree. He bought all of us carefully selected presents—and something for himself as well! Proceeding to "play," they declared war against each other and had a Silly String battle outside. I stood back with a video camera and laughed as they chased each other around the swing set in our backyard. Zach beamed with pride when he "conquered" Debbie with a final spray from his bottle of string.

As the sun slipped away, I shared Zach's day with all of his supporters on the website that evening.

March 7, 2006
Zach woke up hungry today! I always love to hear him say, "I'm hungry" when he gets up. He had a great day. He did not complain about an upset

stomach at all—yeah! Debbie Brus was kind enough to come over and hang out (or should I say spoil and play!) with him while I went to an appointment. He loved the Silly String battle they had.

His class will be finishing the FCAT testing tomorrow and Thursday so I am not sure how much school he will attend until Friday. The class is having a celebration on Friday that Zach would like to attend. We will take it day by day and do what feels good to Zach.

Thanks for your powerful prayers. They are working so well today. God is good—all the time! I would like to share a verse from James 1:2—4 that we were discussing with our small group from church. It seems really applicable to our journey: "Consider it pure joy, my brothers, whenever you face trials of many kinds, because you know that the testing of your faith develops perseverance. Perseverance must finish its work so that you may be mature and complete, not lacking anything."

This week is one small step in our long journey. We are so thankful to be walking hand in hand with God and all of you!

As the week progressed, Zach continued to feel better than I expected. Michelle and Sydney Sims joined us at our house for an interview related to a "Relay for Life" event for which Zach and Sydney were selected as the "spokespersons." A reporter from a local newspaper came to interview all of us to create awareness of the event and our stories. Very quiet as she listened to Michelle and me tell how brave each child had been through the many challenges they had faced, the reporter asked Zach and Sydney what had been the worst part for them. Zach's response was not being able to eat and Sydney said having septic shock. Overwhelmed with emotion at times during our stories, the reporter watched and snapped some pictures as Zach and Sydney played a game together before she packed up her things.

The neighborhood was quiet after they left—and so was Zach. Michelle had mentioned in the interview that Sydney had almost died twice over the last two years, causing Zach to question me about it later. It was a heavy thought for him to absorb since he seemed to be completely convinced he would get better. Hearing Sydney's story brought to light one of the realities of pediatric cancer that we tried not to dwell on.

The side effects of the chemo surfaced on Friday after I had taken Lexi to the bus stop when I came back to find Zach in the bathroom throwing up. Still determined to go to school for the celebration party his class was having, he worked hard to gather his strength. I stayed at the party long enough to help dip the ice cream, but my heart broke as I saw Zach could not eat any of it because of his upset stomach.

He wanted to stay until the end of the day and was very weak when I picked him up later. We had to stop for him to rest on the way to the car. I asked him to let me carry him, but he would not consider it. That would be too embarrassing for him in front of his classmates.

On Saturday morning my heart was torn—again. I was scheduled to attend an all-day conference, featuring Angela Thomas, at our church. But it was easy to see Zach was not feeling well and was very weak. Knowing I needed a break, I settled him on the big chair and promised to call him throughout the day. On my first call to him, his voice sounded very weak. Every time I called him, he asked how much longer until I would be home.

Angela's words gave me newfound strength to face the wicked side effects I figured Zach was beginning to experience from this last round of chemo. Feeling refreshed and renewed from the conference, I raced home in the late afternoon to find Zach lying motionless exactly where I had left him that morning. Not able to eat much of anything all day, he felt very dizzy when he tried to move. Dizziness was a new symptom for him.

Dear Lord, I pray for Zach's tummy to settle down so he can eat. It is so hard to watch him suffer in this battle. I pray he has a much better day tomorrow and for You to wrap your loving arms around him and hold him tight.

Sleep was not peaceful for me—it never was when Zach did not feel well. It seemed my mind continued to run even as I slept, causing me to wake often and think of ways to help him feel better. Dirk left early for prayer time at church as I climbed on the chair next to Zach. Worried he would lose more weight; I put on my happiest face and tried to encourage him to eat. The dizziness continued to plague him so much that I used a water bottle for a urinal to avoid making him walk to the bathroom. The suffering seemed to be unrelenting for him once again.

Desperate to find relief, Zach wanted to sit in the shower to see if that would help. He was unable to walk to the bathroom, so I lifted him by placing my arms under his neck and legs. As soon as I started moving him, he screamed, "Stop, stop; I'm too dizzy!" in such a panicked voice it scared me. I quickly put him down and he vomited from the motion. Puzzled and concerned by the dizziness, I cut back all his medication to only the anti-seizure medications, hoping it was a side effect that would soon disappear.

There were not many smiles in our house as evening closed in. We were all irritable because it was so hard to see Zach suffering this way. Dirk left for small group and Lexi retreated to her haven, the guest bedroom, to lose herself in her drawing. Zach and I sat quietly on the chair until he finally fell asleep after a completely miserable day.

Lord, this is so hard to understand. Help me to reach Lexi. She is struggling to deal with such a challenging life. I pray so sincerely for my family, Lord. Please touch us all and keep us strong against Satan. Your love and healing is what we are seeking!

As the room grew lighter the next morning, my mind began to race with worry about the dizziness. Too intense for a side effect, I was concerned it could be signaling something more. Thoughts of the symptoms of tumor growth circled madly in my mind because I knew dizziness and nausea were the two most common.

Desperate to find something for him to eat, I offered him all his favorite foods to try. Wanting to end his torture, he tried one after another, but every time was soon leaning over the bucket, which had become a permanent fixture next to the chair. Slow progress came later as he was able to sit in an upright position without throwing up. Determined a shower would help, Zach moved his trembling body into our office chair and I slowly rolled him to bathroom. Because he was just skin and bones, I lined the tub with towels for him to lie on as the water soothed his tired and weak body.

We all had a much more restful night. I felt like doing back flips when he asked for a bowl of cereal when he woke the next morning. It was as if angels were singing all around! He drifted back to sleep after he finished. It was clear his body was trying to rebound. As I woke Zach for his morning pills, he said two of the most beautiful words: "I'm hungry!" I never knew how special they would sound to me. As he nibbled away on various snacks, I tried to get him to walk with me to the bathroom, but found he was still too weak. Happy because it seemed we had finally turned the corner, we continued to use the makeshift urinal until his strength returned.

Zach's body was trying to rebuild strength as he slept through the next night as well. But he was still extremely weak Wednesday morning as we prepared to go to the clinic. I commandeered a wheelchair when we arrived and took it to the car. Even the walk from the parking lot was too much of a challenge for him. Pleased to see that his counts were still in the acceptable range, I did not expect to see them drop for another two weeks.

As our wait for the doctor grew longer and longer, Zach's patience grew shorter and shorter. When the doctor finally arrived, she attributed the extreme dizziness to side effects and suggested we try to give Zach some high-calorie, high-protein foods to put some weight back on him. I decided the wait certainly was not justified by the information from the doctor, but I hid my frustration with a smile as we headed back to the parking lot.

As I wheeled Zach through the lobby, one of the receptionists offered to walk out with us and wait with Zach while I got the car, and then she would take the wheelchair back in. I pulled up next to them. Hearing her gasp as I walked around to help Zach climb in, I saw Zach fall to the pavement. Wanting to scream at her, I ran to him as she bent down to help him up.

"Zach Honey, are you OK? I was coming to help you, Baby. Why didn't you wait for me?" I asked.

"I thought you wanted me to climb in when you pulled up," he answered quietly as I pulled him to his feet.

Tears stung my eyes as the frustration of the last week welled up inside me. The nurses checked Zach over and did not feel his hip or shoulder suffered any damage from the fall. I was angry—angry at the receptionist for not helping him, angry that Zach had to go through this at all. He was suffering more than any adult deserves to suffer—let alone a child. How was any of this fair?

God, give me strength!

Because of an early-release day for the end of her grading period, Lexi came home soon after we got back. She had accomplished so much at school by staying on the honor roll every grading period while trying to deal with Zach's illness. I reminded her how proud we were of all her hard work.

Zach continued to recover, slowly. The unsteadiness on his feet persisted and it nagged at me. Rationalizing it was due to weakness from the lack of nutrition, I did not feel comfortable letting him walk far without following close behind to steady him if he started to teeter too far to one side.

Later that evening, Zach wanted me to sit with him. I had noticed this round of chemo had left him with an angrier attitude than in the past. But who could blame him after dealing with the week he had just endured. Taking me by surprise when I sat down, he quickly grabbed my face in his hands and gave me a big kiss on the lips—as if trying to convey his gratitude for my love, patience and companionship. It warmed my heart as I thanked him for making my day and giving me a great big smile.

We had big plans for the next day. Dirk had made it a tradition to leave work early to watch the NCAA basketball tournament games at a local restaurant. This year was no exception. Our plan was to meet Dirk at the restaurant where he and Zach could watch the games while Lexi and I went shopping for some summer clothes. Still concerned about his unsteadiness as I pulled up to the front of the restaurant and watched as Zach slowly made his way in the front doors with Dirk, I reasoned it probably was not tumor-related since it had only been twenty days since the last MRI.

Looking forward to some time alone with Lexi, I was glad to see a big smile on her face as she stepped off the bus that afternoon. We returned to the restaurant to join Dirk and Zach for dinner and Zach quickly climbed in the booth beside me. As we all munched down our dinners, I thought of the previous year. Zach and Lexi had raced back and forth from the table to the arcade room, playing and laughing. Zach had been so proud when he snatched a live lobster from a claw machine for Dirk and me to eat. Life had certainly changed for all of us.

After we finished dinner, Dirk and Zach headed home while Lexi and I went to the mall on our mission to find her clothes. No matter how hard I tried, I always found myself thinking about Zach while I was with Lexi. After finding some new things for her, I felt rushed to get back to make sure he was OK. Letting my thoughts overtake me as we drove home, I was tormented by the amount of loss Zach had experienced. *When will it end? When will Zach and our family quit being a slave to this disease?* These words kept circling my head, keeping beat with the music pounding on the radio. Tears formed in my eyes as I felt uncertainty and dread surround me in the darkness of the evening.

Lord, give me strength. I am feeling so weak against the enemy now. I know I must have faith in Your healing powers. All things are possible with you. Give me strength.

These thoughts continued to haunt me throughout the weekend. Seeing Zach struggle to remain steady was troubling me. We tried to continue to work through the challenges by living life.

Sure Zach would feel too tired to go, Dirk and I were surprised when he agreed to attend an arena football game when a friend offered us tickets. Happy we went, we were thrilled to see Zach have a blast. His friend Dylan was also at the game and I watched with a smile as they playfully held their arms up for the YMCA song and cheered the Tampa Bay Storm when they scored. The twinkle in Zach's eyes and the smile on his face melted my heart.

He was not as excited about going to church the next day, but once again Dylan made things easier by joining us. Taking them to a class for their age group, I made sure the leaders understood Zach needed help moving around. My heart soared after church when Zach and I were alone in the car heading home and he shared what had happened in class.

"Mom, why was that guy so nice to me in class?" Zach asked, referring to his teacher.

"I guess he knows just how hard you have been working to feel better. He probably goes to prayer time with Daddy. What did you talk about today?"

"We talked about heaven and how the streets are gold and everything is good there. What do you think it is like there, Mom?"

"Oh Zach, I just read a wonderful book about a guy who was in an accident and went to heaven a little while and came back. He said it was the most perfect place, filled with colors and things he could not even describe. He said he saw so many people he knew there and felt love all around him. He said he did not think about all the things back here on earth because heaven was such a wonderful place," I explained—with relief and a smile. It was a perfect way to talk with Zach about heaven without scaring him. I wanted to share with him what I had read on our way home from Duke and had never found the opportunity to do this. I was learning God's timing is always perfect.

As the first day of spring break arrived, we had a clinic visit to get out of the way before we could relax and have fun. Zach had to have a port flush, which he was dreading. As always, he quietly endured the procedure without much protest.

I wanted to do something special each day if we could, but Zach's dizziness limited our options. Noticing he seemed very irritable and angry most of the time—with few smiles—I was also growing concerned about the change in his attitude. He had always managed to find the fun in things even after he was diagnosed. Hoping it was another unpleasant but temporary side effect of his medications, I suggested a movie and we ventured out to see if that would brighten his outlook.

Later in the week, we joined some friends at a miniature golf course. Carrying a small folding chair with us to give Zach a place to sit between shots, I was nervous about his strength and stability. It was a beautiful day and the course was busy. Zach was very serious about playing, showing me he had not lost his competitive nature. When I tried to stay close to him on the first hole, I could tell he wanted more space, so I let him walk ahead on the second hole. I found out the hard way that was not a good idea. As I picked up his chair to follow him, I watched helplessly as he teetered near the edge of the playing surface and toppled like a falling tree into the bushes nearby. The other kids were nearby and stood frozen as he lay unmoving in the scratchy bushes and rocks.

"Lexi, Lexi, grab him!" I shouted, running to him as quickly as I could. His head was inches from a large boulder; thankfully he did not hit it. Lexi was kneeling near him as I reached down to help him up. Embarrassed, he kept a grin on his face when I got him to his feet. "Are you OK, Buddy? I guess you're still a little dizzy, huh?" I said brushing him off. He shook his head up and down and sat in the chair I had placed next to him.

My anger at cancer flared inside me. Why did Zach have to experience so much suffering? It was bad enough he had to deal with all the medical issues. Why couldn't he get a break and be able to have fun with his friends? Our game proceeded, but I never strayed far from Zach. I pasted a smile on my face and tried to stay positive, but inside I was trembling with frustration and anger. Zach played with his usual quiet determination and ended up winning the round. He was not the carefree cutup he had been before this ugly disease appeared. He did not say many words—his eyes reflected how he was feeling. He was happy to win, but clearly irritated and tired of being sick. He just wanted to be normal again.

That evening I shared my frustration with Dirk. He gave me a verse from Psalm 27:14 to help encourage me: "Wait for the LORD; be strong and take heart and wait for the LORD."

The sadness was overwhelming me. My heart ached for Zach and all he had lost in this battle. I found myself hating the disease and wondering why there had to be brain tumors at all.

Lord, forgive me for my impatience. I believe in You and Your healing power. I pray it is Your will to heal Zach here on earth. I pray for wisdom in knowing what treatment plan to follow. I love You, Lord! Please fill me with the Holy Spirit and use me as Your tool.

With Lexi spending the day at Busch Gardens with some of her friends,

I let Zach choose all of our activities the next day. We watched movies, played cards and ate pizza. I noticed he was not turning his head to the left. When I asked him about it, he said it hurt a little to turn that way. He grew quiet when I tried to get him to talk to me about what he was thinking and feeling. Still quite solemn, he seemed to be increasingly filled with uncharacteristic sadness.

As the week continued to slip by, Zach's infrequent smiles and unsteady gait filled me with worry. Leaving Lexi in charge as I slipped out to take a run, I hoped to clear the worry from my mind.

As I ran I tried to pray, but could not focus my mind. My thoughts were racing. Running faster, I tried to beat the thoughts out with each step I took. Remembering the many runs I had taken in Indiana, I once again stretched my arm up to God asking Him to grab my hand like Jesus had Peter's when his faith faltered on the water. Rebuking Satan, I yelled out for him to leave me alone. The tears slid down my face as I sucked air in between sobs. Physically spent, I began to feel peace fill my heart as I walked toward the house.

For our last fun activity of the week, Zach insisted we go bowling. Lexi and I bargained with him that if he could smile and be happy, we would go for one game. Concerned as I was that Zach would not be able to balance well enough and fall again, Lexi was nervous as we left. The place was packed when we arrived, and we were thankful there was one alley left open and just enough time to play one game. Staying close to Zach, I placed the ball in his arms for him so he would not have to lift it. Surprisingly, he did well and beat both of us. Lexi and I both held our breath every time he shuffled down the lane to throw his ball, happy to see him stay upright the entire time.

The weekend continued to bring our family challenges as we struggled with the gray cloud that seemed to surround us when Zach was down. Calling us all together after we arrived home from church, Dirk talked about how important it was for all of us to communicate and focus on God's healing power with prayer. We talked about why Zach seemed so irritable and sad and how it seemed Lexi was withdrawing from all of us by spending all her time in the guest room. I read a short story about how we can make a choice for peace, love, joy, hope, self-control and patience, hoping to see improved attitudes.

After a quiet afternoon, we realized the time had sneaked up on us for our small group meeting. We quickly gathered our things to take the kids to the Brus's house. I stopped to grab a water bottle as Zach and Lexi headed to the car. As I turned toward the car, I saw Zach falling from the backseat of our truck to the garage floor. The world began to function in slow motion as I heard the sound of his body and head slam onto the floor. Turning my stomach inside out, it was the sound an egg makes when it falls on a hard surface and cracks into a million pieces. I dropped everything and flew to him.

Dear Lord God, don't let it end this way. Not after everything he has gone through!

Fearing he had fractured his skull or broken an arm or hip, I knelt over him frozen. Landing on his left side, he had been unable to break his fall. Looking at me with wide eyes, filled with disbelief of what just happened, Zach suddenly screamed out in pain.

"Oh, no, no, no!" I heard myself scream. My heart was pounding in panic. *What do we do?* "Dirk! Help us! Don't move, Baby."

Dirk came running into the garage. "What happened?"

As I explained in a panicked voice, he knelt beside us and started asking Zach if he could sit up. I didn't know what to do. All I knew was he had hit the floor hard and surely had hurt himself, especially his head. Lexi sat helplessly in the car crying and saying she was sorry.

My dear Lord, help us! How can this be happening? What do we do? Why is this happening?!!

With Dirk's help, Zach slowly stood and climbed into the backseat of the car.

"What should we do? I think we need to take him somewhere to get checked out," I said as I quickly picked up my things and climbed in the backseat as Lexi moved up front. Zach sat quietly next to me. "Zach, are you OK? Can you tell me your birthday?"

"July 13th," he answered correctly.

"I think he's OK; God protected him. Let's go to the Brus's house and see how he feels," Dirk said calmly. None of us wanted to go to the hospital. We were all unsure how to react.

"I can't leave him there! I think we need to go to the ER for a CT scan and blood test," I said as I stared at Zach's eyes, trying to see if his pupils were still responsive. I was concerned his platelet count might have dropped or that he might be bleeding internally.

I asked Zach more questions as we drove out of our neighborhood. Looking at me, confusion beginning to cloud his eyes, he could not form the words to respond. My heart raced. What if he was bleeding in his brain while we debated what to do?

Lexi was a wreck. Tears streamed down her face as she watched helplessly from the front seat. It was as if Zach's tongue had become very thick and his jaw was not working. He could not respond to my questions. I tried to give him a sip of water and it just ran right back out of his mouth.

"Go to the Brandon ER. I don't think we have time to drive to All Children's," I commanded.

He quickly headed to the hospital while I dialed the oncology office answering service to find out what they wanted us to do. Zach continued to look confused as I sat next to him and held him close.

As we pulled into the ER parking area, the doctor returned my call. Fighting to gain my composure, I spewed the recent events through the phone to her as quickly as I could. Agreeing we needed to have a CT scan, she suggested I check how long the wait would be at the Brandon ER. If it would be more than an hour, she wanted us to head for the All Children's ER. Learning the wait would be longer than an hour, we began the hour-long trip to All Children's Hospital.

It was the longest ride of our lives. As the evening sun streamed in our windshield, Zach's eyes became heavy, wanting to close in sleep. Working hard to keep him awake, Lexi and I talked about anything we could think of in very loud voices as Dirk concentrated on making our trip as fast as possible. Relieved Zach was able to form words again, I was still concerned that he seemed confused.

Lord, please let him be OK! This can't be the way this journey is supposed to end. Help us, God!

Arriving at the ER, the wait to see a doctor seemed long, but actually was quick for an ER. Awake, but slow to respond to questions, Zach seemed uncomfortable as they examined him. Staying with him as he had a CT scan, I felt relief when the doctor had concern only with images on the right side of Zach's scan. Knowing it was probably just the tumor area he was seeing, I was glad nothing had surfaced on the left side—the side that had hit the floor.

Because he felt pain each time he was moved from the wheelchair to a bed, I feared his arm or shoulder had been broken. On the way to the x-ray room, memories of positioning the feeding tube flooded my mind. *I hated that room!* Unfortunately, this experience was not much better.

Knowing his thin, bony body had very little padding and the hard surface of the x-ray table would be extremely uncomfortable, I asked them to put padding anywhere they could to try to limit the discomfort. Crying out in pain as they tried to manipulate his arm into the correct position, Zach stretched his right hand out toward me looking for me. Unable to stay away, I grabbed hold as tears ran down my face. *Why is this happening? Has he not endured enough?*

Thankfully all the scans and x-rays came back negative for breaks. Sending Dirk and Lexi home at 11:30 P.M., I spent the night with Zach at the hospital for observation.

Dirk shared our experience with our friends on Caringbridge when he arrived home.

March 27, 2006
I am providing the update tonight for Sherry since Zach and she are spending the night at All Children's Hospital. Zach had an accident this evening as we were getting prepared to go to our church small group meeting. He had climbed into the backseat of our Toyota Sequoia and

then lost his balance and fell approximately 3 to 4 feet to the concrete garage floor. Sherry and Lexi witnessed his fall and said his first contact was on his left shoulder and then the left side of his head. Unfortunately, his left arm could not react to break his fall. He definitely did not want to go to the hospital, but he seemed a little disoriented so we thought we needed to have him checked out. They ran three different CT scans and determined that there was no damage to his bones and no bleeding. They feel it was probably a concussion. He was complaining of a headache and shoulder pain. They thought it would be best to stay overnight for observation.

We just thank the Lord that he was not seriously injured. It is difficult to understand why Zach must endure this suffering, but we understand that God sometimes uses suffering to increase our faith in Him. I know that our faith in God continues to grow stronger each day. We would like to thank all of you for your continued prayers and especially our small group for their prayers this evening. It is truly amazing how many people's lives have already been influenced by Zach's journey. I know that God is using our son to bring many lost souls to Him and ask Him to fill their hearts with the Holy Spirit.

My concern grew deeper that something was really wrong with Zach other than just side effects. I had always had the question floating in my head: How will this play out? My prayer and hope remained that one day Zach would jump out of bed and be back to normal—no sign of tumor— and life would go on as we proclaimed the miracle God had given us.

Lord, this is my prayer!! It does not seem that is the plan for now. It is so hard to see Zach like this, Lord. He is physically suffering so. Give us strength.

Life was overwhelming. I did not know what our future held and it was driving me crazy. I found a scripture in Proverbs 3:5—6 that reminded me to stick close with our faith. "Trust in the LORD with all your heart and lean not on your own understanding; in all your ways acknowledge him, and he will make your paths straight."

I snuggled close to Zach as we rested from his latest challenge. Life felt out of place—nowhere near where I had ever pictured it being.

How will this all go, Lord? Help me be strong.

Tomorrow was another day. My hope was it would be better.

Reflections

Our lives had taken a sharp turn with just one moment in time—a moment that was replayed over and over in our minds: *...If only I had been walking behind Zach...if only I had told him to wait...if only...*

My intuition was spinning out of control that something was not quite right. As I knelt over Zach, frantically trying to determine the seriousness of his fall, all I could think was, *Not like this God; not like this!* This setback had drawn my fear of Zach's death racing to the forefront of my mind.

The enemy was working overtime, peppering my thoughts with questions of the unknowns we faced. Yet, my faith was not shaken. Instead, I found I was praying with a much deeper intensity. Asking for strength. Turning to God for the answers. Knowing I could not manage to stay upright on my own. By arming myself with scripture and surrounding myself with other Christians, I could feel the freedom in the belief of knowing God was in control and He had a plan for our lives.

Living our lives focused on God was providing us a way to bear the tremendous weight cancer had dumped on our backs. Tightly grasping the hope God's grace had given us, we were finding the strength we so desperately needed.

The lesson that evolved from this time was about listening to your inner voice. Looking back on this period of time, it is now clear the symptoms Zach was displaying were an indication things had gone awry. Wanting to cling to my hope the cancer was being held at bay, my vision was clouded to seeing the reality unfolding before us. God speaks to us through this inner voice. When your heart is telling you something is not right, listen because it is usually right.

Near the end of February. Although he had lost a lot of weight, Zach felt good and was enjoying a day of playing with Lexi and their neighborhood friends in our hot tub. They filled over 100 water balloons on this beautiful day.

MARCH 2006 – after eight months of battling cancer. This was two days before the second tumor was discovered. Photo taken by Lifetouch National School Studios, Inc

On our second visit to Duke in early March 2006, the spring flowers were popping up everywhere. All of Zach's MRI scans were showing no progression of his tumor. Little did we know this was not to last for long.

CHAPTER FOURTEEN

Turning it Over

My concern about Zach's continuing dizziness prompted me to e-mail the doctor at Duke for direction. Explaining Zach's fall and how it seemed something more appeared to be going on, I was relieved when he responded we needed to get another MRI. He also said to stop the Thalidomide until we figured things out.

As we walked into the clinic a few days later, I became concerned when I noticed Zach's head leaning to the right. When I asked him why, he insisted he wasn't leaning any direction. I became more alarmed as we sat in the waiting room. It seemed he had a weight on his right shoulder that pulled his head over to the side. He would correct himself and sit up straight again when he leaned over too far. Moving to his right side, I let him lean on me while we waited—my heart breaking, knowing this was not good.

My mind started racing again with thoughts of where this journey was leading us. I had to remind myself to focus on today and not worry about tomorrow. Even though I knew it would do no good to let my thoughts run wild, it was extremely difficult to stop as there were always plans and hopes circling in my mind that would not stop pestering me.

The blood test took longer than usual and I found myself suspicious that the nurses were keeping something from me. They seemed very concerned as I explained the symptoms. Scheduling the MRI for two days later, we settled in for an afternoon at the clinic for another infusion after they determined Zach's platelet count had dropped below the acceptable range. Turning very surreal again, the world around us shifted into slow motion as we stood in the nightmare of our life and stepped further into the very scary uncertainties of the cancer world.

Dirk had imagined a total deterioration in Zach's abilities after I had called him earlier to express my concerns about his new symptoms. He was relieved to see Zach was doing OK when he arrived home. It was so much for him to take in as he tried to stay focused on his work at the same time.

Lord, we are looking for a miracle—a clean MRI. Dear God, we pray for Zach to regain the full use of his left side once again. What are Your plans for our lives? Are we doing this right? Please give us wisdom to pick the right path. I pray the dizziness is from the medicine only. Faith, not fear. I turn it over to You, Lord. I accept Your will with all my heart. Please fill me with the peace from the Holy Spirit so I can be strong for everyone when they need it.

School picture day was scheduled for Zach's class the next day. Wanting him to be included in the class picture, I pleaded with him to get ready. The thought of getting there and dealing with everyone seemed to intimidate him. After a "bribe" of two dollars from Joe and Debbie, and the promise that I would park very close and help him every step of the way, he agreed to go. I held his hand as we walked through the breezeway to the elevator, but he quickly pulled his hand away when some children appeared around the corner. He was so anxious to be normal and did not want anyone to know he needed help keeping his balance. My heart broke in a thousand pieces for him.

Kneeling down to make him a seat on the elevator as we took the slow ride up, we arrived before his class, and he quickly maneuvered his way to a chair to wait. Greeting him with smiles and waves as they entered the library, his classmates giggled and squirmed as they were arranged on three rows of bleachers—tall in the back and shorter in front. Imagining where

Zach would be standing if he had never gotten a brain tumor, I could not make my mind reconcile how this was really happening. *How could things be so drastically wrong in nine short months? How could we be fighting for Zach's life?*

As soon as everyone was in place, Zach stood and slowly walked over to a spot they had left for him in the front row. Although he tried his best to stand straight and tall, his head still leaned to the right as he worked to keep his balance. His clothes hung on his thin, gray frame, but he managed a strained smile—always determined. After the group photo, the class lined up for individual photos. Zach went first, and I wondered if the photographer had been informed of his condition. He patiently worked with Zach to get him to hold his head up straight as he snapped a couple of photos. Glad Zach had found the strength to participate, I was also devastated as I watched how difficult it was for him to do this simple thing.

We spent the rest of the day together, either playing games or holding hands on the chair at home. Nothing else seemed important any longer. Time with Zach was my priority. Tomorrow would be an early day for the MRI scan.

The radio alarm started playing in the dark of the morning, calling me out of bed for the scan that lay ahead. With time to spare before I needed to get Zach ready, I tried to calm my nerves by reading the Bible. Battling an overwhelming feeling of dread, I was unable to lose my anxiety this time.

Using a wheelchair for our trip to the mobile MRI unit in the parking lot once we checked in at the clinic, Zach and I rode a lift up to the scan area of the unit instead of climbing the stairs. Both of us were happy to see Diego was in charge again and soon the familiar loud banging, humming and clanking noises blared from the machine as I stood and tried to prepare myself for the worst. I assumed Zach would probably be facing another surgery as it seemed the tumor must have started growing again.

When it came time for Diego to insert the contrast, I knew my feelings of dread were justified. His eyes filled with concern, Diego asked where we were going after the MRI. My heart sank as he said the doctor would need to look at the scans before we left. The room started closing in on me as I worked to slow the frantic beating of my heart. I could not calm my thoughts—they were racing around my head in a jumbled mess. What was he seeing? Glancing over my shoulder I saw both him and the doctor studying the images on the screen, looks of grave concern painted on their faces.

When we finished, I feared the tumor had grown rapidly since everyone was treating Zach with kid gloves. Reaching for my phone to call Dirk, I changed my mind and decided to wait to hear more before I put him in a panic too.

Pushing Zach back to the clinic, we followed the normal routine of weigh-in, blood test and blood pressure. As we waited in an exam room, Zach became very irritated as he counted each minute that went by—no matter how hard I tried to engage him in playing or reading. After forty-five long minutes, the doctor and clinic social worker finally ended our wait. Appearing hesitant and unsure what to do, the doctor began to chat with us about Zach's triathlon T-shirt. Soon she asked the social worker to take Zach out to the playroom. Happy to leave the exam room since he knew volunteers were playing games there, he was anxious to join them.

As my hands began to tremble, I knew what I was going to hear had to be worse than I expected. Surely, she would not have been so solemn and nervous if we were simply facing more surgery. Explaining they had found a new lesion—not regrowth that I had expected—she indicated it was located on Zach's brain stem and was quite large. My head started to spin as the words kept tumbling out of her mouth: …location in the fourth ventricle was inoperable…many life-sustaining functions in the area…radiation really the only option…no guarantees it would work… The words swirled around the room faster and faster as I tried to absorb each one. It felt as if I were falling into a large black hole and as I reached to grab the walls they crumbled like sand through my fingers and I just kept falling. This could not be happening! It had only been nine months—our battle had just begun.

My mind suddenly snapped back into focus when I heard her ask, "Would you like to try further treatments with radiation?"

Was she crazy? Why would we not want to save our baby?

I looked at her and stammered, "Of course we want to do whatever we can to save Zach!"

By this time, the social worker had reentered the room and asked if I wanted to call Dirk. My hands were trembling as I fumbled through my purse for my cell phone. Hardly able to dial his number as my mind processed the information I had just received, I called four times and there was no answer.

Lord, why of all the times he answers, he doesn't this time? I am so angry, God! This is unfair for Zach. All he wants is to be normal—out running and playing like he used to. This is unreal.

The deeper the words sank into my mind, the more frantic I became. As we talked about radiation, the doctor explained we would need to start something quickly based on the quick growth this lesion had displayed. I wanted to talk with Dr. Thornton and the doctor at Duke, but I knew proton radiation would take at least two weeks to get set up after the initial consultation. It did not seem we had that much time. My mind raced. There had to be a way to fix this.

I stepped into an entirely different reality when I heard the next words out of the social worker's mouth. She began to talk about hospice. *Hospice? ...Hospice was for dying people!! Zach was not dying!!!* Feeling like they were trying to suck all the hope that remained in my body out, I looked at them and said, "So this is it? *This sucks!*" as tears began to pour down my cheeks. How could we even be talking about hospice when we had just found out there was a new lesion? It all seemed too fast. We hadn't even received a complete evaluation from all the doctors and they were ready to write Zach off.

Relieved when Dirk answered on my next try, I tried to explain everything the best I could to him through my tears. I told him to go home and I would meet him there. He hung up before I could tell him what I was going to tell Zach.

Zach. I had to pull myself together for Zach. He would know something was up because of the amount of time it had taken, and I looked a wreck. What *would* I tell him?

"Do I have to be concerned with Zach making it through the weekend? We are supposed to go to the Relay for Life tonight. Should we do that?" I said between my sobs.

"I would not expect anything to happen this weekend, but because of the location of this lesion, there are no guarantees. You should consider signing some DNR orders just in case things progress rapidly. Many times with disease in this location, patients will just stop breathing," the doctor replied calmly. "It should be fine to go to the Relay for Life. It might help you keep your mind off of things and it would be fun for Zach," she continued.

I could not believe she was able to deliver this news in such a non-emotional manner. This was my baby she was talking about! She was telling me my baby boy was going to die and it could be any day! How could this be happening? My world was spinning out of control. I left the room, knowing I needed to get to Zach. As I went toward the bathroom to pull myself together, one of the nurses reached for me and said she was sorry. I looked at her through my tears and said as I gritted my teeth, "I have to pull myself together for Zach." I knew if I let her hug me I would dissolve into more sobs.

Standing in the quiet of the bathroom, I stared at my reflection in the mirror. Who was this person? It could not be me. I could not be living this life. With blood-red eyes and my face contorted in pain and worry, I splashed water on my face, wiped away the tears and tried my best to paste on a smile. After a few deep breaths, I walked into the playroom to get Zach. As we wheeled out of the clinic, he asked with concern, "What took you so long, Mom?"

"Well, the doctor had to tell me about a new spot they found on the MRI. They told me that is why you have been so dizzy lately. We will probably have to get some more treatments to work on it," I answered calmly.

"Where is the new spot?" he continued.

"It is on the back of your neck this time, Honey."

Lord why is this happening? I fully believe You can heal Zach, but I don't understand why he has to suffer through all these challenges. He is only eight!! Why, why, why?

The drive home was tough. Zach lay in the backseat staring off into space. *What must he be thinking?* He was such a fighter. I knew he could do it—he could beat this too. My mind raced through different scenarios:... Proton radiation takes too long... Where would we get conventional radiation?... Would it make sense?... Chemo doesn't seem to be working... What would the doctor at Duke suggest? ...

Hardly able to contain my tears as I drove, nothing seemed real anymore. I thought stepping into the cancer world was difficult, but I found stepping deeper into this new reality was indescribable. I began picturing the doctor at the clinic as a "dementor"—a character in the Harry Potter book series that literally sucks the joy and hope out of its victims. And I decided I would not allow that to happen. There had to be other alternatives we could consider. My hope would not die.

When we arrived home, I quickly settled Zach on the big chair with the remote and told him I had to unload the car. I walked outside to call Dirk to tell him what I had told Zach. He seemed very calm and collected. Obviously, he did not understand the seriousness of what I had just heard. He had called Debbie and my parents after we had talked. As I spoke with him, I saw Debbie's van headed toward me.

My head and shoulders dropped as I dissolved into tears when she walked toward me. "They told me there are no more treatments, Debbie. How can this be right?" I cried as she grabbed me and held me in a tight embrace. She whispered a prayer for strength for both of us. Sending her inside to sit with Zach, I tried to pull myself together again.

She left soon after she saw Zach and I were doing OK. I knew it was all too overwhelming for her as well. When Dirk arrived, I wondered if he understood the gravity of the situation because he was remaining so calm. What I did not realize was he had spent the majority of his hour drive praying for and receiving peace.

Not wanting to waste any time, I began calling the other doctors to get their opinion of our next step. Finding they were both busy, I left urgent messages for a return call.

Dr. Thornton returned my call a few hours later and listened quietly as

I calmly explained what had been discovered on Zach's scan. He told me he had already seen a slide of the new lesion in an e-mail and hesitated in his answer as he contemplated the circumstances. Explaining the prognosis was very grim—only a 5–10 percent chance for any treatment to be effective with this type of recurrence—he assured me he wanted to help in anyway possible. What had happened to Zach was very rare, he explained. It was called drop metastasis, which only happens in 5 percent or less of the cases. This new location was in an entirely different region of the brain and essentially the malignant cells had "dropped" through the fourth ventricle in the fluid that floats throughout the brain and spinal column. Feeling surgery should not be ruled out; he wanted to forward Zach's case to a neurosurgeon he worked with in Chicago. Feeling a flicker of hope—even if it was a long shot—I was glad he at least had a plan to propose.

When Lexi arrived home later, I met her at the bus stop and explained everything just as I had to Zach. Listening quietly, she nodded her head when I asked if she understood it all. She was concerned she would miss more school for the treatments. I told her we would figure things out as we found out more about the kind of treatments available.

Soon it was time to go to the Relay for Life event. Zach was the only spokesperson who would be present since Sydney was in New York to receive more treatment on her leg where they had found some active cancer cells. They had asked me to speak, but I explained to the coordinator that we had received some poor scan results and I did not feel emotionally able to do the speech. Understanding completely, she directed us to the survivors' tent just as the band began to play to start the celebration. Just then my cell phone rang and I saw it was the doctor from Duke. I quickly became frustrated because it was very difficult to hear what he was saying even as I walked away from the tent. Speaking very quickly about many combinations of various chemo drugs, he was quick to indicate he did not agree with Dr. Thornton's assessment.

When I expressed my immediate concern about how we could stop the quick growth of the tumor without surgery or radiation, he replied that quick growth was always a risk. But he said surgery was too risky and radiation was just a band-aid fix—that more tumors would eventually show up. He ended by saying Zach's counts were too low to start anything, which was something I had not considered. He agreed we should restart the steroid to help alleviate the dizziness and any swelling that might be occurring with the new growth.

Walking back to the tent more confused than when I left, I found Zach was uncomfortable sitting on the hard folding chairs so I became his padding while we waited for the program to start. Worrying about his pain, I wondered if it could indicate the disease had spread down his spine. My mind was a million miles away as people started gathering around.

We were thankful for the golf cart they provided so we could fulfill our duties of leading all the survivors around the track for the first lap of the walk. Zach had hoped to drive the cart on his own, but instead sat between Dirk and me as we waved to many friends in the cheering crowd. Seeing all the hope in their faces made me wonder if they could see the despair in mine.

After we arrived home, Dirk and I talked late into the night about all of the options and their implications. Concerned with Zach's ability to tolerate any further chemo treatment, we did not know if his body was strong enough to endure a major surgery either. Surprising us at 1 a.m., Zach shuffled into the room. Patting the bed beside me, he curled up next to me as I inhaled his hair, savoring his smell as I fell asleep.

Filled with uncertainty and fear for me, the weekend proved to be a major battle to keep my attitude focused on a positive outcome. With the thought of Zach dying overtaking my mind, I felt very weak in my faith as Zach continued to struggle.

Lord, I am so weak right now. I am so angry. Watching Zach struggle is really challenging my understanding. Thoughts of him dying keep entering my mind. I am tortured. I can't seem to find peace. Lord, fill me with strength!

Sounding like someone was pinching his nose and he had a mouthful of marbles, Zach's speech had become increasingly hard to understand. Having difficulty sleeping through the night because of the steroids, he napped during the day. I tried to get things done around the house in hopes we would be traveling somewhere soon to get him some help.

As the injustice of Zach's torment consumed me, my perception of the world grew tainted. Watching children play with carefree abandon caused pangs of anger to well up inside me. Zach should be playing too. On the brink of tears all through the church sermon, I wondered where our answer was. I knew ultimately God was the answer, but the uncertainty of what the future held was driving me insane. Hearing the doctor's words that she could not guarantee how long Zach would survive—that he might just stop breathing—haunted me every time I checked on Zach to see if he was awake. I was now checking if he was alive as well.

We gained strength from our small group meeting on Sunday evening. Hesitant to leave Zach at the Brus's house, I relented when he insisted we go. He enjoyed spending the time with the boys and Lexi. Leaving him with a cell phone and directions to the kids to watch him like a hawk, we were surrounded with love and prayers by our group. Becoming very transparent, we shared our concerns with them so they could pray for us throughout the week. Helping to bolster my faith again, I shared that on the Caringbridge site.

April 2, 2006

We have had a quiet weekend to relax and reflect. It has been difficult for me not to let fear take over, but it would do no good to cave in to it. Our sermon today was about fear—of all things. I think God was speaking to us with that one! This along with our wonderful small group from church and Dirk, who has been a great source of strength and remains focused on his faith, I feel ready to face this week.

I will take Zach to the clinic tomorrow to have a blood test. We will wait for phone calls from the various doctors we contacted on Friday. We are praying we will have a plan in place by this time tomorrow. Please spread the word to everyone you can: We need prayers! You have all been so wonderful through this journey. Help us climb this mountain— it seems very steep as we face it tonight.

I go again to Isaiah 41:10 in The Message *paraphrase: "Don't panic. I'm with you. There's no need to fear for I'm your God. I'll give you strength. I'll help you. I'll hold you steady, keep a firm grip on you."*

Sleep was difficult for me now. During the night I could not help but go to Zach's room and check that he was still breathing. It took me back to when the kids were babies and we placed monitors near their cribs with the volume on high just to make sure they were breathing. Looking very fragile but beautiful as he slept, Zach's face was filled with peace.

We were into the waiting game again—waiting on doctors' calls that never came when we expected. The silence was more and more deafening as the time passed. Trying to sit with Zach most of the day, my nervous energy overcame me as I dove into cleaning the house, checking on Zach as I cleaned. Wanting to be prepared if we had to leave for a treatment, I found the land of uncertainty to be emotionally draining.

Later that evening after a shower, Zach frightened me when he said he could not see right. Asking him to explain what he was seeing, he clammed up. I expect the concern in my voice had frightened him. I could not help but wonder what the tumor was doing to his brain. Was it continuing to grow and invade other parts of his brain?

Lord, I pray this tumor stops growing and disappears!

Another day had passed with no plan. My frustration was growing, but I still felt hope that we would find an answer if we were patient.

Everyone became "dementors" the next day. It was the day I never wanted to face—the day it seemed our hope for medical treatment options disappeared for the most part.

Starting with a call from the surgeon in Chicago, Dirk and I listened carefully to his calm and deliberate evaluation of Zachary's scans. Understanding him through his very heavy Japanese accent was a challenge at times as he cautiously explained he did not feel surgery was a viable option for Zach. Stating the tumor was located in an area that was vulnerable to many complicating and debilitating side effects, he also felt the tumor appeared to be spread out more like a "sugar coating" than in one contained area. When this was the case removal was almost impossible because not only was it spread out, it was also sticky and difficult to separate from the healthy tissue.

Continuing, he felt before any consideration of further treatment was considered, a full MRI of Zach's spine should be taken to determine if there was more disease down the spinal column. He mentioned he was familiar with the neurosurgeons at All Children's and would consider them completely qualified to do any procedures if it was found that surgery was warranted after the MRI. We thanked him for his evaluation and opinion and ended the conversation.

It was clear a trip to Chicago was not in our future. Dirk left for work and I continued on our quest to learn what treatment options remained. When I called the Tampa neurosurgeon's office, they confirmed that surgery was not an option for Zach. Now that we had eliminated surgery, I needed to follow up with the doctor at Duke and clarify his plan for Zach.

A few hours later when he returned my call, he agreed we needed an MRI of the spine to evaluate the extent of the lesions. He explained again that he felt radiation was pointless because as soon as one area was treated, another tumor was bound to pop up in another area. He talked about a couple of Phase 2 chemo clinical trials we could consider as soon as Zach's counts were in an acceptable range. Being skeptical of the side effects because of what we had experienced with the chemo Zach had taken so far, I began to realize there was not going to be any miraculous medical treatment. Our miracle would have to come from God alone.

Joining Zach after finishing my calls, he was ready to do something. We went out to wash the car. He wanted to know how much money I would pay him for helping! He was always looking for an angle to make money. I asked him what he thought he should get, thinking I would pay him all the money in the world if it would make him happy, he asked for five dollars. When I said I would give him ten, his eyes lit up with approval. As I sat him in a chair near the car and handed him the hose, his body slumped over awkwardly in the soft-sided chair. I ached for everything he had lost physically, and yet Zach did not let it bother him. He carried on the best he could.

After we finished, some kids joined us on the driveway to visit with Zach. I brought out some board games and they all started playing together. It was wonderful to see Zach get to share the time with his friends again even if he was just sitting in the chair.

As they played, Dr. Thornton called and I shared with him all that we had determined as far as options for Zach's treatment. Discussing the concerns that had been voiced about radiation, I asked him to call the doctor at Duke to share his thoughts and compare notes with him. As we ended our conversation, Dr. Thornton warned that if there was any further disease present in Zach's spine, there would be nothing further he could do with radiation.

Soon after, another call came from the doctor at Duke, conceding we could try the proton radiation on this tumor when Zach's counts recovered to "buy some time." But he cautioned that we needed to understand this would not treat the other seeds floating around Zach's system and there would most certainly be more tumors down the road. The news was all very bleak and void of hope. Arranging the spinal MRI the next day, so we could know once and for all where we stood, it was clear that if there was further disease, Zach's chances for other treatment options were very slim.

Lexi was happy to see Zach outside playing when she came home. I could not imagine the thoughts she must be having as she observed all the intensity we were experiencing. Dirk came home on a spiritual high, not knowing all that I had learned that day. I left to go jogging, glad to leave him in the dark a little longer before I shared all that I knew.

Lord, this is so hard. I don't understand why this is happening. It is making me sad to see Zach so feeble. Why is there cancer?

When bedtime approached later that evening, Zach asked to go to his room with me to read. It was something we had done every night before he was diagnosed, but we had fallen out of this habit soon after he first became sick. As I started reading, he laid his head gently on my belly. I savored the moment of having him next to me and caressed his soft hair that had started growing back in the area where he had received radiation.

Lord, I don't want to lose him! I know he belongs to You, but I love him so much. *I keep remembering his humongous smile and sweaty face and hair when he would come in from shooting hoops. How can this be happening??*

After the kids were in bed, my parents called and I shared all that I had learned that day as tears streamed down my face. I felt like I was failing Zach by not finding a treatment. Dirk walked in the room and was upset to see me crying. He asked me to stop talking about it if it was going to upset me, but I told him I *had* to talk about it. Hearing much of what I was telling my parents for the first time himself, he sank down in the chair as the reality of what I had heard that day opened up to him.

My parents were as distraught as I was and asked that we try not to get involved with any treatments that would make Zach's remaining time miserable. I wished I knew how to determine that. Overwhelmed with emotion when I finished the call, Dirk said it felt like the room was closing in on him and spinning around as he heard my words.

Lexi appeared in the doorway as we talked. Asking if I could come and lay with her, I followed her back to her room and climbed in bed next to her.

"Mom, why are they doing an MRI of Zach's spine tomorrow?" she asked quietly as she stared into the darkness.

"They need to see if there are any other spots on his spine since the new spot was at the top of it. Don't think about that right now, Honey. Try to relax and go to sleep," I whispered softly to her. This had to be tearing her up inside. Her crazy, athletic baby brother had become a virtual stranger to her, trapped in a body that was no longer able to move without assistance.

After she drifted off, I joined Dirk in our bed. He had just completed a heartfelt entry on the Caringbridge site explaining his feelings.

April 4, 2006
God has moved me to share a bit of testimony with you this evening. As most of you know, our cancer journey began on the evening of July 11, 2005. Sherry and I both knew immediately that we needed to go to God so He could handle our problem, but it was not that easy. I prayed to

Him, but I seemed to lack the faith that is referred to in God's Word.

"Have faith in God," Jesus answered, "I tell you the truth, if anyone says to this mountain, 'Go, throw yourself into the sea,' and does not doubt in his heart but believes that what he says will happen, it will be done for him. Therefore, I tell you, whatever you ask for in prayer, believe that you have received it, and it will be yours" (Mark 11:22—24).

As time has passed, my faith in the Lord has continued to grow stronger and stronger. The discovery of the second tumor was definitely not good news from a medical standpoint, but it does not change anything from a spiritual standpoint. I know that God is capable of performing any miracle that is part of His plan. Only God knows what His plan is for Zachary, but we hope and pray it is total recovery from his cancer. We continue to pray with righteous hearts.

"And the prayer offered in faith will make the sick person well; the Lord will raise him up. If he has sinned, he will be forgiven. Therefore confess your sins to each other and pray for each other so that you may be healed. The prayer of a righteous man is powerful and effective" (James 5:15—16).

We ask that You continue to pray for Zach with a righteous heart and have faith in our Lord.

We held each other close as we reviewed the information I had received from all the doctors. For the first time, we discussed the possibility of our baby boy dying. We had entered another reality no parent ever dreams of being possible in their lives. We knew our only true option—regardless of the MRI outcome—was God. He was the only way Zach would remain on this earth with us. Our pillows were wet with tears as we cried out to God.

Lord, give us strength! This is hard. We know Zach belongs to You. We are so blessed to be his parents and we pray that he will remain here with us far into the future. He is so special to us, Lord! We hold him up to You and pray for a miracle. We pray Zachary is completely healed here on earth. Please hear our prayer!

Reflections

The unthinkable was happening well before I had ever imagined it could. Confused and shaken, my protective desire to cure Zach by any means possible took over. A feeling of failure consumed me as I began to question all the steps we had taken to find a cure. Why was his battle so short?

Devastated and repulsed by the thought of hospice care, I felt the local doctors were too quick to assume the worst for Zach. It had seemed from the beginning that his diagnosis had labeled him as a somewhat hopeless case in their eyes, and now the first sign of trouble immediately allowed them to step away. All shreds of hope for medical options were ripped from my grasp in fifteen minutes.

How could this be the plan for Zach?

Desperation set in as finding an immediate solution to this rapidly growing tumor fell on my shoulders. Thankful to have the resources of several doctors, it was frustrating to realize that although I was emotionally distraught and devastated, it was up to me to exhaust all possibilities. Again, there was no central resource to rely on for the best solution given our scenario.

The unexpected twists and turns in our path continued, leaving us with clouded vision and aching hearts, but with assurance our answer would ultimately lie in our faith. We were learning that prayer was our mightiest weapon in our battle to save Zach. We continued to hold on to the belief that God could and would save Zach when He determined the time was right. It was our job to turn it over to Him and trust in His plan.

CHAPTER FIFTEEN

The Land of the unknown

The alarm sounded and I rose quickly. Zach was the first one on the MRI schedule at All Children's Hospital. Because this was a two-hour scan, we had to go to the hospital instead of the clinic so they could administer some anesthesia. Dirk stayed behind to help Lexi get off to school as Zach and I drove away.

Zach slept most of the trip, which left me to my thoughts. Still holding a glimmer of hope that there was no more disease in his spine and we could try proton radiation again, I longed for the optimism we held during his first round of treatments and hoped we could return to Indiana, the place Zachary loved.

I called for Security to meet us in the parking lot and drive us to the front door of the hospital, knowing Zach would not be able to make the long walk this time, even with my assistance. As we joined a few other families in the MRI waiting area, Dirk surprised us when he walked in to join us. He decided he needed to be with us today and his work could wait until later.

Because they were running behind, the MRI nurse moved us to a room with a bed and television to make Zach more comfortable. Ironically, it was the same room we were in a week and a half earlier after Zach's fall from the car. When they finally took Zach, it was hard for me to watch him leave. He looked so fragile and weak. He had reached out to me so often in the past when he had procedures, and I worried he would need me.

Finding a sunny spot in the front lobby to wait, Dirk and I quietly began to share our thoughts, and soon our conversation drifted to our perceptions of heaven. As I shared the amazing description from the book *90 Minutes in Heaven* with Dirk, I could see peace and relief cross his face and tears form in his eyes. We also agreed a trip to Indiana could be God's ultimate plan for us since it would allow more time there with family. Feeling a general sense of peace settle over us, no matter what the results, we knew God was with us.

Time seemed to pass quickly. While we waited, I received a call from a nurse at the clinic to let me know they had already received the scan results. Because Zach's platelets were low, we would need to visit the clinic later in the week for an infusion. Snuffing out our hope for proton radiation, she also said the neurosurgeons would be reviewing Zach's scans before the doctor spoke with us. I knew immediately what that meant: The scans were complete and there was more disease. In my mind and heart, I knew this meant we were effectively done with medical treatment.

Entering the recovery area, I found Zach awake and angry from hunger. Frustration ensued when the MRI staff would not let him eat until it was clear no immediate surgery was needed. Logic seemed to indicate nothing could be worse than the tumor that had already been found, making it absurd in my mind to further torture Zach by withholding food. After forty-five long minutes, the doctor finally gave her clearance for Zach to eat.

Understanding and accepting what we perceived to be the scan results, we were ready to go home after satisfying Zach's appetite. But trying our patience once again, it seemed like we were being held hostage when they asked us to stay and speak with the doctor face to face. After two long hours, my phone rang. I took the call from the doctor out in the hall. She was stuck in traffic and explained she was keeping us at the hospital until she was sure that because of the evidence of further metastases neurosurgery did not want to do surgery. When I asked how any lesions other than the one we already knew about could be bad enough to require immediate surgery, she could not find a reasonable argument and decided we could leave.

After we loaded Zach into the car, I watched the hope drain from Dirk's eyes when I quietly told him they had found more disease. Requiring no further conversation, he immediately understood the implications as he got in the truck for his lonely ride home.

Working hard not to let my mind absorb the enormity of the latest scan, I found it to be impossible. Even though I had expected it, to have confirmation of more disease was overwhelming to me. Zach drifted off to sleep as I drove home. I kept looking over my shoulder at his sweet face. *How could I live in this world without him here?*

Lord, give me strength! I am so angry, God, that Zach does not get a chance to grow old here with us. I am asking for You to heal him! I know he is Yours, but he is so needed here.

Reeling from the devastating news, Dirk left to attend a Wednesday night church service, hoping to find strength. As bedtime approached, Zach asked if we could go read again. Thrilling me to have this quiet time with him, he selected a fairy tale book full of happy endings for me to read. When I asked him if he could still see the words I was reading, he said the words were getting blurry if he looked at them too long. Worried the insidious tumor was beginning to spread its tentacles into the area of his brain that controlled his vision, I knew from previous research it could cause double vision or even blindness. After finishing our story I held him in my arms for awhile, savoring the feeling.

After Lexi was settled in bed, I walked back into Zach's room to see if he was sleeping. Finding his breathing was slow and steady, I walked to the side of his bed and collapsed to my knees. Putting my face to the floor, I called out to God in quiet whispers and sobs from the depths of my soul.

Dear God, I am not ready to lose my baby! I need him here—I love him so much. The world needs his bright shining light, dear Lord. I know he could do so much good here, Father. But God, I do not want Zach to suffer. Please Father, either give us a miracle or take him so that he does not have pain or suffering! I don't want him to be scared by losing more control of his body. We need his presence, Lord. I pray Your will is to heal Zach here on earth. So many people are praying for this, Lord. Please hear our prayers.

The rug was wet from my tears as I sat up and looked at Zach once more. The innocence of his face ripped my heart in two. *What lay in store for him?*

As Zach and I waited to leave for his platelet infusion the next day, I looked at the scan that showed the new growth on the brain. Seeing it was in the area I questioned on our last trip to Duke, it became clear the spot was not a shadow. Trying to process all the information, I turned the bits and pieces of it over and over in my mind as tears welled in my eyes. As we lay in bed the night before, I had shared with Dirk more of the technical information about GBMs that he not wanted to hear in the beginning. He had not realized how grim the prognosis had been from the start. Why did this have to happen? It made no sense.

The time came to leave for our long journey to St. Petersburg again. Feeling a strong desire to talk to Zach about his faith, I asked him if he ever prayed other than our night-time prayers. Seeing he was uncomfortable answering, I shared with him how I prayed all the time. Letting him know it was a good way to let God know how he was feeling, I desperately wanted him to feel comfortable with his faith, hoping he could draw strength from it as Dirk and I were ours.

The memories came back to me of when Zach was six and he asked how he could make sure he would go to up there (as he pointed up to heaven) and not down there (as he pointed down to hell). Thrilled he wanted to know more about accepting Jesus into his heart, we took a six-week class together about being saved. Hearing him surrender his life to his Savior Jesus Christ was a thrill, and watching him be baptized was one of the best days of our lives. God was obviously at work in Zach's heart then, preparing him for this challenging journey.

Dirk joined us at the clinic. We held Zach's hands as we made the walk down the long hallway to the clinic lobby. Happily climbing in the overstuffed leather recliner, Zach found a movie he wanted to watch as the platelets poured into his port. We left him grinning in contentment as he snuggled deeper in the chair, his eyes locked on the television screen in front of him.

Entering a conference room down the hall, we found the doctor and social worker waiting for us at a small round table surrounded by bookcases and miscellaneous boxes of supplies. As I worked hard to keep my emotions under control, the doctor informed us there were no further treatments available through All Children's or Duke. Hearing the words—spoken out loud—was so final it left me feeling helpless, weak and nauseous. Medically, we were done, according to her.

As they again started to explain our options with hospice and how Zach might progress as the tumor grew, I began to feel overwhelmed by it all. *How can this be real? How can we be losing Zachary, our sweet baby boy?* Fighting an urge to get up, run out to Zach and escape this horrible place, I knew no matter where we ran, we could not escape the tumor that was growing in his brain.

Asking how the end might arrive, Dirk's face twisted and tears spilled down his cheeks as the doctor told him Zach could just go to sleep and never wake up. Seeing him cry crushed my already bleeding heart. No parent should be faced with enduring this type of torture.

This was not how life was supposed to happen. It frustrated me how stoic the professionals remained. Did they not realize what their words meant? An innocent child—*my* innocent child—was receiving a death sentence. It seemed the thought of that justified a tear or two, even if they had done this many times before.

I asked how we should tell Lexi and Zach and they said it was best to give them the basic information and let them ask questions. They suggested I talk to Kyleen, the child-life specialist, when she returned from her vacation. When we asked how much time Zach had left, the doctor was vague in her reply, saying it could be the next week or it could be a couple of months. Asking if she felt he would make it to the golf scramble, which was fourteen days away, she expressed her uncertainty he would still be with us. Emphasizing our faith in God, Dirk declared there was always hope for a miracle. They were both quick to agree with him: There was always hope.

Strongly encouraging us to have a meeting with hospice, they assured us the organization was a wonderful group with a team that worked especially with children. Further explaining their services were free, they emphasized how hospice could also help keep Zach comfortable if pain became an issue. The thought of having hospice involved still turned my stomach. To me it meant we were accepting defeat to this death sentence. I could not give up my hope and belief in God's ability to provide Zach with a miracle.

Lord, how is this happening to us? I pray these words of Zach dying are not true. I pray for a complete healing here on earth, Lord. I am trying hard not to fear the unknown, but I am scared of Zach suffering, God. I pray it is Your will to give us a miracle with Zach's healing. Every time I think of this world without Zach, I become overwhelmed! Give us strength, dear God!

Finishing our questions and drying our tears, we gathered up Zach's things and began the long drive home as Dirk left us to go to work. Coming to hate the long drive home, I did not answer my phone during the drive, knowing it would be questions I did not want to answer. I felt like I could explode. I wanted to cry, scream and pray, but I had to hold it together for Zach.

It has only been nine months, Lord. I want more time!

Arriving home soon after we did, Dirk realized he could not function at work as his emotions overtook him when he tried to talk to his coworkers. He walked around in a daze the rest of the day. I had not seen him that overwhelmed since Zach was first diagnosed. The conversation with the doctor had made everything very real to him.

As bedtime approached, Zach and I went to share reading time again. Trying hard to stay focused on the words I was reading to Zach, my mind was going in a million different directions all the while trying to absorb as much of Zach as I could, while he was still here. *How long did we have? Would tonight be his last?*

Lexi wanted me to read with her as well. As if God were continuing to prepare my heart, we were reading the final book of the Narnia series that describes C. S. Lewis's view of heaven. It was difficult to maintain my composure as I read the words to Lexi. Once again, the picture of heaven was beautiful and amazing. She listened quietly and I wondered if she realized how near heaven could be for Zach.

When she asked about the MRI after we finished reading, I told her there were some spots on his neck, but that we were still figuring things out. I was not ready to tell either one of them the complete truth—I was still trying to understand it myself.

After the kids were settled in their beds, I began to make the phone calls to my family. My calls to my parents and both sisters were filled with emotion and many tears. I tried to remain strong as I explained there did not seem to be any more treatments available, but reminded them that Dirk and I completely believed God could heal Zach. I also explained to them my understanding of heaven and that if it was not God's will for Zach to remain with us, I was sure Zach would enter a place so wonderful we could not imagine it—a place that held no pain, suffering or fear for him. I wanted to comfort them and assure them we still held hope.

I ended the night once more on my knees, face in the carpet, by Zach's bed. This was all we had left—to share our hopes and desires with God and to cry out for comfort for our sweet little boy.

Dirk decided to stay home with us the next day. He and I were both still reeling from our new reality, realizing just how precious each day was with Zach. Leaving Dirk with Zach, I slipped into the office to make some follow-up phone calls. The doctor at Duke let me know how sorry he was for everything that was happening to Zach. He said there was a chemo combination he could try after Zach's counts recovered, but I told him Dirk and I were extremely concerned with Zach's quality of life, and since he had such a tough time taking the chemo in the past, I wasn't sure it was worth the risk.

When I asked what he would do if it were his child, he refused to put himself in that position, stating that we were living a nightmare no parent—including himself—could imagine. I told him the last thing I wanted for

Zach was for him to endure any more suffering with side effects. He said quietly that he really had nothing that would be curative. The tumor was just too aggressive.

Next, I called Kyleen to get advice on how and what to tell the kids. Although I had been troubled since we found out the results of the MRI, I wanted them to understand what we were facing, but did not want to take away all hope from them. Trying her best to guide me, she said there was no right answer because each child is different. What she had found to be best was to give the basic information to them and then let them ask questions. As children, they may not have any of the thoughts we were having about the implications of the situation. She was bold enough to tell me she was praying for all of us. My heart was touched as she was the first person from the clinic to share her faith with me.

Reluctantly, I dialed my final call to the hospice group. The main purpose of the visit was to get a wheelchair so Zach and I could become more mobile and take walks outside. Hoping to find I was wrong to be so resistant, I wanted to get a better understanding of what they could offer us, but I still did not feel we needed them on a daily basis at this point.

Growing impatient with my phone call marathon by this time, Zach grinned when I suggested we borrow a golf cart and take a drive around the neighborhood. Before we left for that adventure, I sat down with Zach to break the news to him.

"Well Zach, I was just talking to all the doctors and they have decided that you have had enough chemo and radiation."

He did not respond or look at me.

"So, did you hear what I said, Buddy? No more chemo or radiation," I repeated as I grabbed his hand.

"So…let's go for our ride," he responded, looking at me with blank eyes.

I wasn't sure where to go from there, so I let it rest. Maybe after he had time to think about it, he would have more questions. I did not want him to be scared of what he was facing by not understanding what was going on, but I didn't want him to think we had given up on his survival either.

Feeling the warm sun on our faces and the soft breeze in our hair as we rode around on the golf cart was wonderful. Realizing it was the time his class would be outside for PE, we headed to the school and found them on the playground playing kickball. Smiling and waving at us as we got closer, they continued their competition. Parking in the shade of a tree, I watched Zach as he carefully took in all the action. With a grin on his face, he watched his buddies take their turn at kicking the ball as hard as they could. I wondered what he was thinking…probably imagining himself out there, kicking the ball with them. It was bittersweet—fun to see his friends, but painful to know Zach could not join them.

Later that evening after Zach was asleep, I went to Lexi to give her the same news I had shared with Zach earlier.

"Honey, I wanted to tell you what we found out from the doctors about Zach. They said they do not have any other treatments that will help him," I said softly as I sat down next to her.

"Does that mean he can't be cured, Mom?" she asked in a frantic voice.

"Well, it means the doctors can't make Zach get better. Only God can cure Zach. So we just have to pray that is what God will do," I said in a shaky voice as tears began to fill my eyes.

Breathing heavily and rubbing her eyes, she quickly said she did not want to talk about it any more and went to bed. Weary from the overwhelming situation we faced, we were all so broken and scared.

Zach's appetite kicked into overdrive the next day. He ate nonstop, like he had in Indiana. After a full breakfast, he wanted to lie in the shower. I put towels down as padding and a bath pillow for his head. Once he was comfortable with the warm water splashing all around him, I peeked into Lexi's room. Lying in her bed trembling and worried, she whimpered that her stomach and her head hurt. She was a mess. Trying to comfort her, I told her we had to focus on making each day as special and good as possible and not worry about more than that. Hugging each other tightly as the tears fell from our eyes, I told her we must continue to pray for Zach to be healed here on earth.

Preparing Lexi and Zach for the hospice visit, I explained a person was coming to bring us a wheelchair and talk to us about being able to have people visit the house instead of always having to go to the clinic. Nervous about the visit, I had made it clear I did not want Zach to hear any discussions of funerals or death. The person I had talked to assured me they would be very discreet.

It was mid-afternoon when the doorbell rang. Watching television with the volume quite loud, Zach did not seem interested in our meeting. Apprehension surrounded me when I saw the representative they had sent. Her eyes were dull and sad-looking, and her mouth seemed set in a permanent frown. She wore a drab brown dress and had a stethoscope around her neck. Most importantly, she had no wheelchair!

I felt my defenses rise as Dirk and I invited her to sit at our dining room table. She did not seem to be too "kid-friendly," as had been promised. Sitting down, she pulled out a large folder of information as she began to explain the services they offered, which included home visits two or three times a week, aides to help with baths or to give caregivers a break, as well as help with funerals and other end-of-life things.

As she discussed the "end-of-life issues," as she called them, my eyes widened. I could not believe what I was hearing! The very things I had specifically asked not be discussed with Zach nearby were exiting her mouth without a second thought! Wanting to climb across the table and jam my hand down her throat to shut her up, I looked at Dirk who seemed as bewildered as I felt.

Not realizing how offended we were, she proceeded to inform us they charged by the day and our insurance only covered the first $7,500 of their services. I was flabbergasted! Looking at her with furrowed eyebrows, I told her we were told the service was free to us. Raising her eyebrows as she quickly looked around our house, I could see she was thinking that by the appearance of our home we should not have a problem paying.

Completely repulsed at this point, I pushed away from the table as Dirk read my nonverbal clues and told her we were not interested in signing up for their services at this time. Reeling, I wanted to usher her out the door and slam it behind her. We said a polite "thank-you and good-bye," and she left. The visit had been everything I feared and worse.

In the midst of my frustration with hospice, I received an e-mail about www.brainhospice.com, a website written by the daughter of a man who had a GBM. It had become her mission to provide information about end-of-life issues that brain tumor patients and their caregivers face. Very inform-ative—but overwhelming to me—it explained step-by-step when to get hospice help, the symptoms displayed as a brain tumor patient died and stories from caregivers sharing the final moments of their loved ones. Thankful for the useful information, I shuddered to think the contents could possibly one day apply to Zach.

Our attendance at church the next day became very emotional when Zach began to complain of chest pains after we were seated. A feeling of helpless anxiety overtook all of us as we wondered if it was a sign of tumor growth. Tears spilled down Lexi's face as we were at a loss of what to do to help Zach. With his pain beginning to subside, we listened as the pastor seemed to be talking directly to us as he tried to explain why bad things happen to good people. Unable to maintain our strength, Dirk and I soon joined Lexi as tears fell from our eyes throughout the service.

As we began a new week, I could not make myself accept that Zach was dying, especially when he seemed to be feeling better and regaining his strength each day. Then reality would hit me as I watched him struggle to see by looking out of the corner of his eye or be unable to walk without me standing nearby to steady him. Living with the constant fear I would walk in to find him not breathing was horrifying. Trying to continue to live a normal existence was challenging, to say the least.

At his clinic visit, we were thrilled to see Zach had gained three pounds! He was making progress, but still had a long way to go to get back to his ideal weight. The nurses were excited to see Zach walking in, needing only my hand to steady him. They were playing Easter Bunny for all the kids and told us they had hidden four eggs in each exam room. Zach's eyes lit up as we entered our exam room. Carefully looking around the room from his chair, he pointed out each egg, one by one, for me to retrieve.

Sticking close to us during our visit, Kyleen was very troubled to hear how horrible the hospice visit turned out to be for us. To help remedy some of that disappointment, she surprised us by bringing two wheelchairs into our exam room. One was blue and one red. She told Zach to pick the one he wanted to take home! Picking his favorite color, red, Zach was really excited to have his own chair.

Becoming impatient with our wait, we decided we did not want to stay any longer. Zach's counts were still low, but did not require an infusion, so we left! No more waiting for doctors unless I had a question that had to be answered we decided.

Our evenings were becoming more routine: watch television, read a story, cuddle time and prayer time. Finding my late night prayers on Zach's floor by his bed were becoming routine as well, I could not go to bed without pouring my heart out to God while I was near Zach.

Hearing Zach's bell in the morning was sweet music to my ears! It meant we had another beautiful day together. I found it difficult to face the reality that one day I might find Zach had gone to heaven in his sleep. None of it made sense in my mind. Holding the hope in my heart that God would give us a miracle healing here on earth, I tried not to focus on Zach dying because I was not ready to believe that was a reality.

We had a busy day ahead. Zach and I visited his class once again, using a borrowed golf cart to get there. Feeling a chill in the early morning air as we flew down the road as fast as the cart would go, I tucked my jacket around Zach's legs to keep him warm. Playfully pushing my foot off the gas pedal, Zach slammed it to the floor with his foot as he let out a whoop and a giggle.

The entire third grade class was out on the playground participating in the Field Day events. A day of physical competitions between classes, Field Day had always been a highlight of the school year for Zach. He became quiet and shy when we arrived. The coach invited him to participate, not realizing how limited he had become. If she only knew the reality that even if Zach wanted to participate, he could not do so without me standing right behind him. I watched with a smile on my face and shouted encouragement to the kids in his class, but my heart was breaking on the inside as I grieved for Zach and all he had lost. Wanting him to still feel a part of his class, I hoped getting out of the house and seeing them brightened his day.

After I put Zach safely in the car, I returned the golf cart. When I came back to the car, my heart stopped. His door was open and I did not see Zach. Flying around the car calling his name, I found him sitting on the ground outside his door. "Buddy, what happened? Are you OK?" I asked breathlessly as I quickly helped him to his feet.

"I had to go pee, Mom. I was afraid I couldn't wait until we got home," he mumbled quietly.

"It's OK, Honey, as long as you're not hurt. Just try to wait for me to help you next time, OK?" Thankful he had not hit his head again, I realized I would have to stay very close to him.

As we prepared to go to another Lightning game later in the day, we received a call from the Children's Cancer Center to let us know the team needed an honorary captain for the night—and they wanted Zach! When I shared the news with him, a smile spread across his face. He would get to go out on the ice before the game and see the players!

Glad to have the wheelchair, we arrived at the game and were taken directly to Brad Richards' suite to meet his assistant Kasey Dowd. A very sweet lady, with an infectious smile and sparkling eyes, she presented Zach with his very own Lightning jersey that had *Tucker* and the number 1 sewn on the back. Quiet and somber, Zach seemed nervous about his impending duties. Receiving permission to accompany him onto the ice, I asked him if he wanted to stay in his wheelchair. Appearing relieved with this news, he allowed a small smile to escape as we draped his new jersey over his lap.

When it was time, I slowly pushed Zach out onto the ice. Still warming up, the players zoomed by so close we could feel the rush of air on our faces. They looked so much bigger on the ice. It was amazing to watch them skate by so effortlessly. Kneeling down next to Zach, I was happy to see the excitement in his eyes. As we watched the team warm up, two of Zach's favorite players, Vinny Lecavlier and Brad Richards, skated up to him extending their knuckles as they came. Zach quickly lifted his fist to meet theirs. My heart did flips as I watched a big smile spread across his face. This little gesture meant so much to him!

Introducing Zach as the honorary captain, they put us on the JumboTron. It was a dream come true for Zach, and I was thrilled he was able to experience it. Our evening ended before the conclusion of the game. Zach began to get very uncomfortable and needed to lie down after being in the wheelchair for so long. We were disappointed we missed meeting Brad after the game.

The week progressed, and I battled with the overwhelming feeling we should be doing something to help Zach. Repulsed by the thought of the tumor growing uncontrolled around his brain, I e-mailed St. Jude's Hospital again to see if they had any alternatives. As I typed out the progression of Zach's disease in the e-mail, I realized how bleak it really sounded. They indicated the only possible alternatives would be Phase 1 trials, but I again could not bring myself to consider putting Zach through difficult side effects if the therapy was not proven to make drastic advances against the progression of the tumor. Feeling conflicted, I hated it seemed we were just sitting around waiting for Zach to die.

God, what should we do? Is this Your plan for Zach? I pray for an earthly healing for Zach. I pray for a complete healing for Zach. Lord, please give me guidance and wisdom what to do. This is so hard; give me strength to keep the negative thoughts out of my mind. God, I believe You can heal Zach with all my heart.

As we sat together holding hands, I stared at Zach and wondered what he was thinking. Being hard for me to comprehend it all at my adult level of understanding, I could not imagine how he was able to remain so calm and brave. I knew he did not know the raw reality as I did, but he had shown he was not dumb. He had to know having another spot was not good.

"Zach, how are you doing today, Buddy? I asked, watching his face closely.

"OK," he responded flatly, still watching his show.

"I was wondering…do you have any questions about anything? You have been so brave through all the stuff you have had to do, you know," I continued.

"Well, since I have been so brave, you could get me a golf cart," he said as he smiled slyly.

"Actually, we are working on that, you silly goose!" I said laughing. His optimism amazed me still. "I just want you to know you do not have to be so brave all of the time. It's OK for you to ask questions or tell me if something scares you. OK?"

He brushed me off as he mumbled, "I'm fine, Mom."

Struggling with the updates to the Caringbridge site, throughout the journey I had tried to keep it as upbeat as possible, but as our situation grew more difficult, it was hard to do that. I did not want to be misleading, but I also did not want to appear to be without hope. Knowing all of our hope remained with God's healing abilities, we needed everyone to stay as positive as possible to help us get through this. After many attempts, I finally was able to come up with an update.

April 12, 2006

We had a quiet day today—which means Zach became very bored this afternoon! We took a couple of walks around the neighborhood and watched television. We plan to go to school tomorrow and watch a movie with his class. I think I will ask his homebound teacher if we can have a short session tomorrow since it is the day before Easter break!

Zach is feeling good and still eating like crazy. We are very thankful for this. It is very difficult to be in the holding pattern we are in right now. I keep reminding myself to take everything day by day and to remain patient. With that in mind, I went looking for scripture to help, and here is what I found: "Not only so, but we also rejoice in our sufferings, because we know that suffering produces perseverance; perseverance, character; and character, hope" (Romans 5:3—4).

"Be strong and take heart, all you who hope in the LORD" (Psalm 31:24).

Keep those prayers coming!

The next day marked nine months since Zach's initial surgery had occurred. Still relatively new in this battle against pediatric cancer, compared to so many other kids, and yet we were facing circumstances with such limited medical help. Wondering if the doctors suspected our journey would be short from the beginning, I realized they probably knew when they first examined the initial MRI the chances were slim at best for much more time. Unlike us, they knew from past experience the stark reality that a GBM brought. Pushing these thoughts away, I could feel them trying to suck me into a black pit of despair and away from the sliver of hope we were so desperately clinging to.

When we joined his class for a movie, it was the first time they had seen Zach in a wheelchair. Zach received their excited greetings with a shy smile and small wave of his hand. I watched them steal concerned glances at the wheelchair as the movie played and knew it had to be difficult for them to understand why Zach was not getting better. Fearing it was too much reality for them at such a young age, I felt helpless since I knew we could do nothing to change it.

The homebound teacher arrived at our house later that day. It was the first time she had seen us in a few weeks. She presented him with his first report card with letter grades. He beamed when he saw he had gotten straight A's! Giving him a hug as I settled him in his chair, I stayed to watch Zach to make sure he did not have trouble with his work or his balance. Continuing to bewilder and amaze me, his mental abilities remained sharp even as the tumor invaded more and more of his brain.

I had expressed reservations to Dirk the night before about even continuing the homeschooling, and Dirk had scolded me for not having a stronger faith that Zach would be healed. Diving deeper into his study of the Bible, he spent many evenings in our room with the door closed, praying and reading. Knowing he was right, I had to remain focused in my prayers and faith in God to heal Zach.

The Easter weekend was upon us. Waking early on Friday and wanting food as soon as the sunlight hit his eyes, Zach kept me busy finding activities to entertain him throughout the day. We took walks, played games and went to the grocery. He was so limited by his inability to walk very far—I was willing to do anything to make his day better.

When Debbie called to give us an update on the golf scramble, I was once again reminded we were being embraced in the biggest way by all of our friends and family. The scramble was a week away and was really coming together. Feeling guilty for all the work everyone was doing, I found it hard to feel deserving of their generous gestures.

All of our Caringbridge readers united in prayer for Zach's earthly healing that night at 10 P.M. Dirk, Lexi and I prayed out loud as we held hands while Zach slept nearby.

Lord, please hear these prayers! Prayers for healing. Prayers to restore Zach to what he was before. We need him so desperately here on earth.

Scheduled to attend another Lightning game the next day filled all of us with anticipation. Michelle Sims had called to say the coach of the Lightning, John Tortorella, and his wife Christine had offered their suite to our two families. The day passed quickly and it began to grow dark as we prepared to leave for the game. Because we had the entire suite, the kids were able to take some friends with them. Quiet as his friends Curren and Connor got in the car, Zach seemed unsure of what to say. Lexi, on the other hand, chatted happily with her friend Allena as we headed to the game. Listening as the boys slowly started a conversation, I wondered what they were all thinking behind their smiles and excitement about the evening ahead. Zach's eyes seemed sad to me, like he was feeling trapped in his own skin.

Having arrived before us, the Sims family greeted us with smiles as we entered the suite. Having friends with the kids made the evening more entertaining for all of them. Lexi and Allena were in their own world, talking, laughing and cheering when they heard the rest of the crowd cheer. Zach, Curren and Conner were much more subdued as they sat and watched the game closely. Sitting near Zach for much of the game, I provided an extra hand if he wanted to clap loudly by slapping his right hand against mine.

The game ended in overtime with Zach's favorite player, Marty St. Louis, smacking the winning goal in with ten seconds to go. What a perfect ending! Having his friends with him and seeing the Lightning win seemed to sustain his energy for this game. Making our way down to the locker room after the game, we lined up all the kids directly outside the door so no player could miss them.

With broad smiles, Sharpies in hand and full of nervous anticipation, the children in the Tucker-Sims entourage stood next to Zach who was at the end of the line in his wheelchair, clinging tightly to his Sharpie marker and his special jersey draped over his lap. Although he looked fragile and tired, he was excited as well. As the players began to leave the locker room, they were bombarded with shirts, hats and markers being thrust at them from all the kids. Most stopped immediately and with a smile patiently signed each and every item placed in their hands. All of them stopped and knelt in front of Zach as they signed his jersey and gave him some words of encouragement. It was an amazing experience for him and all the kids.

It was midnight by the time we finally made it home again—glad Zach had managed to stay strong and make it through the game. Settling quickly into their beds, Lexi and Zach fell asleep smiling with the wonderful memories we had made.

Being far from over, my night had just begun. Because the next day was Easter, the Easter bunny had a lot of work to accomplish before sleep would be allowed! As usual, I left baskets of goodies inside the front door and then hid plastic eggs with treasures inside in the yard for the kids to find. I had always loved watching their faces during their hunt. It was very bittersweet as I filled the eggs with coins and dollar bills this year. Because Zach would be limited in his ability to search, I labeled the eggs to make sure Zach had the opportunity to find an equal number of them. I sprinkled the eggs with my tears, knowing the farthest he'd be able to walk was twenty feet at the most, even with me holding his hand.

The previous Easter, one of the toys Zach had received was a light-up Nerf basketball hoop. We had hung it on the laundry room door so he could get the full effect of the lights on the hoop in the darkened room. I had watched and listened to him imagine he was a pro player as he gave a play-by-play, twisting and turning with the ball and finally dunking it through the hoop, completely in control of his beautiful body. I sobbed.

Dear Lord, we want this back. We continue to pray for a miracle.

After I finished hiding the eggs, I found myself pouring my heart out to God on Zach's floor once again as he slept. There was a wet spot on the carpet as the tears flowed with each and every word I spoke. How hard and bewildering this life had become, living each day, and not knowing if Zach would be with us the next.

Feeling more close to God than I had ever felt before, I also felt overwhelmed with why Zach was suffering as he was. Trying to stay focused on having complete faith, I found it increasingly difficult to fight off the fear of losing Zach. How could we survive this world without Zach in it? It seemed the unknowns in our life were growing into mountains and monsters we could not control. What choice did I have but to live each day expecting a miracle that Zach would soon be healed on earth? I knew he would be healed; I just prayed he would still be with us when it happened. I was not ready to face a life without him here.

Reflections

Desperate prayers were pouring from deep within my soul—a place I never knew existed within me. Uttered in hushed whispers, tears pouring down my face, kneeling with my face to the floor, the prayers bared my crushed and bleeding heart to God. We were being backed into a corner with nowhere to turn but to our Creator. God was the only light still shining with hope for Zach. The treatments had not worked to hold the ravenous cancer cells at bay, and now no one seemed to have a feasible medical solution readily available. Even if there was a viable option, I was not sure Zach's fragile state could withstand another assault.

Spending time in prayer had become vital in the growth of my faith. Prayer, feeling more like a duty than a privilege before Zach became ill, it was now the lifeline to my hope and sanity. I shuddered to think how surely despair would have overtaken my mind if I had forsaken God or had no

faith. I would never again overlook the power that prayer held in my relationship with God.

Prayer is our way to grow closer to God. It is a time to pour out our
praise, thanksgiving and requests, and ask for forgiveness. It is also a time
to be quiet, listen and let God answer. There are times when we can feel so
overwhelmed we cannot form the words to pray. It is comforting to know
that God promises the Holy Spirit will intercede for us and will still know
our heart—even if we cannot quiet our minds enough to get the words out.

God wants us to talk to Him. He is always listening and will always
answer. The answer may not be what we are hoping for, but if the answer
is no or wait, we must know God is sovereign and all-knowing. He knows
far better than we do what is best for us. Remember His view is of eternity
and is not limited to this world.

Prayer is essential for us to grow in our relationship with God. The
more we pray to God, alone or with others, the more comfortable we will
feel relying on prayer to help us through good times and bad times in our
lives. Without prayer, our spiritual lives will become anemic and dull.
Prayer should be as much a part of our life as breathing—not dictated by
the wants or needs of the moment, but given much thought and time. Ultimately, there is nothing more important in this life than the time we choose
to spend with God.

CHAPTER SIXTEEN

Surrender

*E*aster had arrived. I woke in Lexi's bed as I heard Dirk leave early for prayer time. Not remembering how I ended up in Lexi's room, I realized my lack of restful sleep was affecting my memory of the games of musical bed we seemed to play. The normal flurry of excitement around the Easter baskets was subdued. Instead of waking each other and scampering out to their baskets together, the kids let me carry the baskets to them. They dug through the contents to show each other what they had found.

Wanting the help of his wheelchair for his egg hunt, Zach climbed in as Lexi and I pushed him out the front door to see what the Easter bunny had left. Much to my surprise, another Easter bunny had added to the egg hunt by lining our front sidewalk with more eggs stuffed with money. Carrying his basket in his lap as I pushed him around the front yard, Zach looked out of the corner of his eye as he examined the contents of some of the eggs, making me think his vision was fading. Lexi and I took turns snapping pictures of our hunt, finding weak smiles staring back at us through the lens of the camera.

Feeling very sad and alone, I ached for the typical joyous celebration we had always had on this morning. I realized I was building a wall around Zach and me in order to protect both of us from the emotions of others. But I was afraid to open up too much to anyone except God and Dirk because I did not want to acknowledge in my mind—or to others—that Zach could die. That would open floodgates that would be hard to close once the emotions were released. I had to stay in control of my emotions. It was one of the few things left I felt I could control. And that was becoming harder and harder.

We are waiting on Your healing, God. This is so hard. To watch my baby go through this—I feel like I am in hell. Lord, help me to stay strong!

Because I had forgotten it was a school holiday, I had scheduled a clinic visit for the next day. I hated dragging Lexi there on what should have been a fun play day. Unable to shake the feeling that everyone there was surprised we had made it back yet another week, I had become very uncomfortable during clinic visits. I always left feeling like they wanted to pass us off to hospice. My perception was compounded that day when they informed me Zach's counts had rebounded and we would not need to come back for two weeks. I felt like we were being put on a raft and shoved into a storm with no protection or guidance, and I panicked because I didn't know if I could navigate by myself. An overwhelming sense of being alone hit me once again as I felt very blue and dry of hope inside. Pasting a smile on my face, I was determined to remain strong and figure it out—no matter how scared I felt inside.

Our day grew brighter when I learned Zach's golf cart was about to be delivered. After seeing the happy smiles on Zach's face when we had borrowed carts in the past, Dirk had found a dealership that generously agreed to loan us a cart for as long as we needed it. We were waiting outside with the neighborhood kids when they delivered the cart. I had hoped the cart would bring some joy to Zach, but I was disappointed to see that even getting the thing he wished for failed to help his melancholy mood. It seemed the reality of being trapped in a body that was failing him, along with the medications he was taking, was destroying his once optimistic outlook.

Putting the cart to use, Zach and I took Lexi to her first swim practice of the season. He was able to walk the distance from the pool to a shady spot as he held my hand. We sat on a lounge chair together and I enveloped him in my arms as we watched the swimmers glide through the sparkling blue water. I could not keep from thinking Zach should have been out there too. *Why was this happening to him?*

I have to get rid of these negative thoughts, Lord. I need You. I feel so alone and broken. I want to fix this, but I know I can't. I need a sign what to do, God. Please help us. Heal this child! He is such a special soul. We need him to brighten this world like he did before this evil tumor invaded his body.

Trying to find peace and reassurance the next morning by reading the Bible, I found it was uplifting and gave me a better outlook for the day. I wanted to touch base once more with the doctor at Duke now that Zach's counts had recovered, anxious to see if he had any new thoughts. Disappointment and frustration filled me when he told me he had not looked at the scans of Zach's spine yet because he was having trouble opening them. Because no one had new developments to offer, I again felt everyone had lost interest in us.

Growing increasingly hard to entertain, Zach had become bored with everything. Nothing I suggested—not even a golf cart ride—interested him. We spent most of our time sitting in front of the television holding hands. I treasured every moment, but I wanted to see him smile and laugh again. Later in the day, he did manage to play a game with some of his friends. Although it was a struggle, his determination would not let him give up. His courage seemed to be unmatched to anything I had ever seen.

My updates to the Caringbridge site continued to be a struggle as I tried to stay positive, but realistic. After speaking with all the doctors again and not finding any new information, I decided to let everyone know that treatments did not seem to be an option any longer.

April 18, 2006
Our clinic visit went fine except for the fact we had to wait on the doctor for about forty-five minutes. Zach is no longer patient with these

*waits! He had totally lost his patience when she finally came in and she
could tell. He had quite the irritated look on his face and really wanted
no part of her examination. He is back up to sixty-four pounds and is
looking much better.*

*His counts have all reached the normal status. The information we
have now is there are no treatments available here in Tampa because
the tumor has shown resistance to the "first-line" treatments. The doctor
at Duke is reviewing the scans and researching other treatments that
may be available, but has indicated these are pretty limited. I should
hear from him tomorrow.*

*In the meantime, we will continue to place our focus on praying for
God's healing to take place in Zachary. We knew from the beginning this
was going to be a tough battle because of the nature of this tumor. We are,
as we always have, continuing to focus on having faith and not caving
into fear. We know God has the ability to heal and we know Zach will be
healed. We are praying it will be here on earth so we can all witness this
amazing power. I think this verse has a lot of meaning tonight for us.*

*"Humble yourselves, therefore, under God's mighty hand, that he
may lift you up in due time. Cast all your anxiety on him because he
cares for you" (1 Peter 5:6—7).*

*Please continue to pray for Zach's complete healing here on earth,
for him to continue to feel good and for strength and guidance in understanding the treatment plans that are available.*

One of my biggest fears came to reality the day before the golf scramble. Ringing his bell at 4:30 A.M., Zach whimpered that his head hurt. Up
to this point, Zach had not had to endure pain from headaches that many
brain tumor patients experience. I did not want Zach to suffer with pain and
was frightened I would not be able to control it without help. Giving him
some Tylenol, I curled next to him, watching his every move. As the pain
subsided in his head, he whispered that his nose hurt and asked me to rub
it for awhile. I used my relaxation fingertip massage on his entire face, hoping it would chase all the pain away. Thoughts of the hospice group surfaced

in my mind as I thought maybe they could help me keep Zach comfortable.

Anticipation filled the house later as most of our family members who were coming for the golf scramble were due to arrive that day. Unable to get comfortable all morning, Zach complained his neck hurt and that he could not turn his head to the left. Glad for the distraction from his discomfort and happy to see new faces, Zach greeted Dirk's parents, brother Darin and his wife Carol with a grin and hello when they arrived.

After joining us for lunch, Dirk left with Darin and Carol to pick up my sister Michelle at the airport. We had debated whether or not she should bring Nolan, her one-year-old, with her. In the end, we decided it would be better for her to come alone because of Zach's growing limitations.

Filled with the excitement of having so many visitors, Zach played Monopoly with Grandma Phyllis and me while the others went to the airport. Concern and sadness filled Phyllis's eyes as she watched how difficult it was for Zach to sit upright at the table. Stuffing pillows around him to help him balance, I was frightened how much change had occurred just in one day. Fearing these symptoms were indicating further progression of the tumor, I grew conflicted about trying chemo to stop the tumor. The helpless feeling of doing nothing nauseated me. Frustrated no one had been able to make significant progress against this or many other brain tumors for twenty years, I felt angry that all the treatment options were so limited and toxic.

Letting my concern for Zach's comfort guide me, I called the social worker at the hospice office after he tired of the Monopoly game. Telling her I was not ready for another visit, we discussed their protocol for pain management. Later, as Zach overheard me telling Phyllis about the call and pain medicine, he told me he wanted nothing to do with any more medicine. Helping me feel we were doing the right thing by not giving him chemo in desperation, his comment reminded me that his quality of life was the priority in our decision-making. Uncertain outcomes or small improvements associated with the chemo would not justify a desperate attempt to stop the tumor growth.

Arriving to a flurry of happy greetings and smiles, Michelle was as happy to see Zach as he was to see her. I was overwhelmed to have her actually standing in front of me, knowing that leaving behind her three little ones and traveling over three thousand miles was a big sacrifice. It made me realize what a relief it was to have family support during this difficult time. Lexi's eyes sparkled and her smile grew as she stepped off the bus later that afternoon and felt the hugs from all her new visitors surround her.

The joy of seeing everyone faded quickly the next morning when Zach woke with another headache. Trying more Tylenol and massages, I hoped he would feel up to going to the golf scramble later in the day. Taking a moment to be grateful to have made it to this day, I remembered the doctor's grave words that she could not guarantee he would make it this long. As the Tylenol took effect, Zach began to feel better, which allowed me to slip out for a run with Michelle.

As we ran, I told her I could not lose the thought of how Zach's body had become a prison to him. Barely able to utter the words as the tears began to flow, I tried to pull myself together by proclaiming we had to focus on this day and no further. Worry would not be allowed because this was a day of celebration! Michelle agreed we would make it a good day.

Dirk and Lexi left for the scramble ahead of us. Zach's dark mood continued even though I had hoped he would be excited about the day. As we loaded up to head to the scramble, Michelle was my faithful assistant. She made sure she was with me or Zach or was doing something to help me every step of the way. As we were placing Zach in his wheelchair after we arrived, we saw our Fort Myers friends, Ginny and Shelly, unloading their cars, which were full of donations and goodies for the event. I blinked back tears as we greeted them with hugs and Zach attempted a smile when they told him they had a surprise for him.

As soon as we walked into the registration area, Zach was the most popular person present—much to his dismay. The scowl on his face most of the time broke my heart because it meant his beautiful personality was being trampled by the pain he was facing. Of course, his buddy, Coach Page, managed to get a smile out of him as did the gifts from Ginny and

Shelly. They had brought him everything he needed to deck out his new golf cart— popsicles, a cooler, boom box, keychain and vanity plate.

Fighting back my tears as I hugged friends I had not seen for a long time and also when my dad arrived with his team, I was overwhelmed as I felt everyone's love and support. I did not feel deserving of the day, but it was obvious the participants were more than touched by our brave Zachary. As soon as the golfers left to start the scramble we took Zach home. He had grown very uncomfortable in the wheelchair and was relieved to lie on the big chair once again.

Disheartened, I noticed when I helped him to the bathroom later that day how much Zach's balance had deteriorated. No longer able to just hold his hand, I now had to hold him under both arms to keep him upright as his body insisted on lurching to the right. With every step he took, my hope slipped further and further away. Because his neck was losing its ability to hold up his head, he rested his head on my shoulder as I knelt in front of him while he went to the bathroom.

Rejoining the golfers and friends for the dinner auction, Zach's main concern was getting some food to eat. Evidenced by all the smiles we saw, it was clear that under Debbie and Joe's direction many of our friends had pulled together a first-class event. Words did not seem adequate to express our gratitude. Surrounded by his friends, the highlight of Zach's evening was being handed over $1,000 when the raffle prize winner gave him her winnings! Unable to hide his smile, his eyes twinkled as he clutched the wad of cash in his hand.

Exhausted and grumpy when we arrived home, Zach kept his new-found cash nearby but did not feel much like socializing with the Tuckers or my dad and his friends. My dad and his team gave us all hugs as they headed to their hotel to rest up for their early morning flight the next day.

As we sat in front of the television later that evening, I nudged Zach and told him to look at Grandpa Gib. He was sleeping while sitting up with his mouth wide open. I whispered to Zach that we should have Lexi throw one of the marshmallows she was eating into his mouth. He giggled—the first time I had heard this beautiful sound in weeks! Seeing his momentary happiness made me realize how much I had missed his smiles and laughter. They had always been such a big part of his personality and it crushed me to think pieces of Zach were slipping away from us as each day passed.

He whispered that his head hurt again as he settled into bed, so I gave him more Tylenol, hoping our simple fix continued to work. Feeling my total exhaustion setting in as I caressed Zach's face again, my mind raced with concern that the headaches seemed to be steadily increasing. Wishing I had the knowledge of a neuro-oncologist, I wondered if increasing the steroids would help alleviate the pain as I climbed in bed and quickly fell into a deep sleep.

My heart raced and my eyes flew open as Lexi shook my shoulder hard whispering, "Mom, Zach needs you!" I saw it was 2 A.M. as I raced to his room. I was devastated when I found him whimpering uncomfortably on his toy chest. He had toppled over as he tried to make his way back to his bed from going to the bathroom. Landing on his side on some hard toys, he was struggling to get back to his feet.

"Oh, Baby! I am so sorry. I didn't hear you! Did you ring your bell?" I asked as I lifted him from his awkward position.

"Yes, I did a million times! I had to go pee and I couldn't wait any longer," he said with frustration.

I was livid with myself. I knew I had been too tired to hear him. Why had I not slept in Lexi's room?

He said his head pounding, so I gave him Motrin, hoping it would work with the Tylenol to give him some relief. Alarmed when it did not lessen his pain, I watched as he drifted off to sleep, but soon woke rubbing his head and moaning. He said it helped his pain when I used my hand as a vise on his forehead and applied pressure.

As the sun began to rise, I began making phone calls for advice. After getting no response to my page to the doctor at Duke, I paged the Tampa doctor. Suggesting Tylenol with codeine, she called in the order for us to a nearby pharmacy. By this time everyone was up and worried about Zach.

Dear God, help us! I don't want him to suffer! Please remove all the cancer cells from his body today!

He continued to whimper in pain as I held his head. When the medicine finally took effect, it put him into a long, deep sleep. After a number of hours, I found myself hovering around him frequently, hoping he would open his eyes soon. When he finally did wake, he was very spacey. His eyes were fixed in a distant stare and he did not respond to any of us as we tried to talk to him. Concerned he was having more seizures, I persisted in my questions to him, trying to bring him back into our reality. Finally mumbling that he wanted crackers, he very slowly stuffed one cracker after another in his mouth, chewing in slow motion while staring off into space. All I could do was sit next to him and watch.

Soon he was asleep again. Hoping his strange behavior was a result of too much medicine, which could be fixed with a dosage adjustment, I began to fear this was how things were going to progress. Not wanting to lose all interaction with Zach, I pictured him sleeping his remaining days away. The feeling of panic hit me in waves. I was not ready for this to be happening! I could feel him slipping away as I sat by helplessly watching.

Michelle took Lexi out for a shopping spree. I was grateful she was there to pour some much needed attention on Lexi. This situation was overwhelming to me and I could not imagine what Lexi was experiencing as she watched her one and only brother grow weaker each day.

Struggling as well, Dirk felt even more helpless than I did because Zach did not allow him to help in any way. He only wanted me to sit with him. Although continuing to rely on his faith for strength, Dirk could not keep the tears away as he mowed the grass. We were so broken and scared with what the future held for our baby.

Realizing Zach still had a mouthful of crackers a little later, I tried to wake him once again. He had stuffed all those bites in his mouth and forgot to swallow! As soon as I could get him to focus on my face, I made him take a drink to clean out his mouth. He still could not respond to questions in any understandable manner.

Lord, this is so scary to me. Zach has lost so much already. I am praying for his complete healing here on earth. God, we are praying for Your will to be done.

If it is not Your will to heal Zach on earth, then I pray he does not suffer. Lord, this is so hard to understand. Give me strength!

When Michelle and Lexi returned, Zach became a little more coherent and could respond slowly to questions. They found many goodies to try to entertain him. And most importantly, they had bought me a baby monitor so I would be able to hear Zach if he needed me during the night.

Asking for a hot dog as he started to become more aware of all of us, Zach seemed to have forgotten how to swallow. Sitting with him as he started to eat, Michelle called out to me whenever he stopped chewing, afraid he was going to choke himself by putting too much in his mouth. I started talking to him, reminding him to "chew, chew, chew" as he stared off into space. Much to the relief of all of us, he slowly started to really wake up as time passed. By the evening, he was acting fairly normal again.

It continued to be a growing challenge for him to make the short journey to the bathroom. I had to hold him close and guide him in the right direction. It was now our routine for me to immediately kneel down as soon as he was seated so he could place his head on my shoulder. Feeling his soft hair on my face and his breath on my shoulder melted my heart. *How did we get to this place?* I could not believe the life we were living— never in a million years would I have ever imagined this could happen to our family.

Panic flooded my heart the next morning as Dirk left for prayer time and I realized I had not heard Zach all night. Dashing into his room to make sure he was still breathing, I whispered a quiet prayer as I entered his room. Slowly exhaling, I saw his chest moving slow and steady. Relief washed over me as I thanked God for another day.

Conflict consumed my days now. Praying for a miracle healing on earth, I convinced myself over and over that God could do that. But yet I never took for granted the one more day or even one more hour we were granted every morning when I went to check on Zach. I believed God was in control, but yet I still felt compelled to try to find a "cure" for Zach after being told there did not seem to be any. I knew Zach belonged to God before he belonged to Dirk and me, and yet I was not prepared to release him back to his true Father. I did not feel I could ever be to that point. That was not the way fairy tales worked. I desperately wanted the "happily ever after" ending.

We were all relieved and uplifted to find Zach did not have a headache when he woke a little later. Glad he was more coherent as we left for church, we all struggled with our emotions throughout the day as it was overwhelming to see him deteriorating before our eyes.

After church, Michelle, Lexi, Zach and I were waiting in the car for Dirk while he ran an errand and received a scare when Zach began to choke on some french fries. With his cheeks stuffed full of fries and his chewing slowed, he seemed to be struggling to make himself swallow.

"Zach, Zach, you have to swallow! Are you choking, Buddy? You have too much in your mouth, Honey." I spoke loudly, trying to get my words to register with him. Responding with a blank stare, he seemed to be in another world. I kept talking and holding his drink to his lips in an effort to get some moisture into the very thick paste of french fries he was struggling to get down.

Beginning to panic and breathe very heavily, Lexi whimpered and tears filled her eyes as she watched helplessly. Michelle joined me in urging Zach to relax and swallow. Finally, after what seemed like an eternity, he started to function again. Unable to regain her composure, Lexi received an impatient, "Get over it!" from me. At my breaking point, I had released my anger on her with an undeserved admonishment. I hated that she was facing this overwhelming life. I hated that I could not make everything better for all of us.

Once we were back home, things calmed down again. Preparing dinners for the next week, Michelle took over the kitchen as I sat by Zach's side. As she started baking some cookies, she asked if anyone wanted to help decorate them. Much to my surprise Zach nudged me and said he wanted to help. Michelle quickly grabbed a stool for him to sit on and I "walked" him over to it. Holding him upright on the chair, I watched as Michelle helped him guide his hand over the cookies to sprinkle colored sugar on the dough. Tears sprang to my eyes and my stomach turned to knots seeing how little control he had of his body.

Later that afternoon, Debbie stopped by to drop off the golf scramble proceeds. Marching in with a large bright smile on her face, she placed a bag loaded with money on Zach's stomach. His eyes grew bright as he surveyed the contents and saw the biggest stack of twenty dollar bills he had ever seen. With all the checks and cash, the total proceeds amounted to over $35,000! He wanted to keep the money in his piggy bank, but I explained we needed to put the money in the bank so it would be safe. Overwhelming and humbling all at once, it was obvious God had touched many hearts through Zach.

Torn about going to our small group that evening, I agreed to accompany Dirk when Michelle urged me to go. Climbing next to Zach on the chair, she promised she would call if she needed our help. Being only fifteen minutes away, I knew it would be good for Dirk and me to get out together before Michelle left. In the still of the car the reality of our life came crashing at me, making it hard to catch my breath. Telling Dirk my thoughts, I knew he understood because the events of the last few days had taken their toll on him as well.

Most of the group time was spent on "Tucker counseling," which we were very grateful to receive. Explaining how difficult things had become, Dirk could not contain his sorrow. Unable to look anyone in the eye for fear of bursting into sobs, I stared at my hands and focused on my breathing as I listened to the ugliness of our life flow from Dirk's lips. At the end of the meeting, we all prayed for a miracle.

When we got home, Michelle said Zach scared her again when he choked on a cookie. It was becoming clear we would have to find soft, moist things for Zach to eat since he could not swallow dry things very well any longer.

Cutting his pain pill in half, I gave Zach another dose when he woke with a headache the next morning. Hoping it would not knock him out as much as it had before, but still relieve his pain, I sat with him until he drifted off to sleep.

Spending the final few hours before her return flight soaking in the warm sun outside, Michelle shared with me a vision she kept having of

Zach. In it he was in his late teens, blonde hair, tan, smiling and walking out on a stage. It was similar to one Dirk had pictured. I shared that I pictured him tall, tan and muscular, without a shirt, playing around with his buddies on the beach.

Lord, I pray this is Your vision too! I am asking for a sign, God, if there is something else we should do. Please show it clearly. Give me strength!

Even though we had the monitor outside with us, I was uncomfortable not having Zach in my sight. Michelle could tell I was troubled and suggested we go in. Still sleeping, his breathing seemed to be very slow and included long pauses. *What if he just stops breathing?* The waiting, without doing anything, overwhelmed me again.

Expecting Dirk to arrive any minute to take her to the airport, Michelle talked about the amazing transformation she had seen in Dirk. His personality had changed dramatically in just the past few months. Excited to see how impassioned he was with his faith, she knew it could only be attributed to his heart being softened by allowing the Holy Spirit to fill his soul. God was holding us up in so many ways—ways we did not even realize.

Finding the lower dose did make waking Zach easier, I was able to rouse him long enough to say good-bye as Dirk left with Michelle in the early afternoon. As evening approached, Zach asked for the other half of the pain pill. Because he said his head and neck really bothered him, I again wondered if I should increase the steroids to help ease the pain. E-mailing the doctor at Duke for advice, I also wanted to know if he had ever read the scans.

My mind was overrun with doubts about not pursuing some form of treatment as Dirk and I went to bed. Tormented by seeing Zach's decline accelerating I shared my concerns with Dirk. Feeling as helpless as I did, he still had a strong conviction we were doing the right thing. He wanted desperately to fix the problem, but knew it was out of our hands telling me, "Sherry, I have always felt things would get a lot worse for Zach before they got better. God has impressed on my heart that Zach will be healed. We have got to have faith."

Unable to find the strength to surrender the situation to God as he had,

I joined him in shedding tears as we prayed for strength and comfort for Zach. Life was so unbelievably hard—it did not seem real. Unfortunately, I knew it was. I used Dirk's words to inspire my entry on Caringbridge that night.

April 24, 2006

Our faith continues to get us through each and every day. I was reading an e-mail that had a piece written by Betsy Childs called "A Very Present Help." Some of the more meaningful words I would like to share with you.

"...Sometimes, the well-timed help that God provides doesn't calm the waves, but it holds us together until the storm dies down.

"He will not give us the help before we need it, and He may not remove us out of trouble, but He will be there with us to hold us together. When the troubles do come, we can approach His throne with confidence, fully expecting to receive the grace of His well-timed help."

It is hard to be patient and not let our minds wonder what the future holds, but then something like this lands in front of me and gives me the reminder I need to realize: This situation is not one we can control. All we can do is continue to place our faith in God and ask without ceasing for Zach to be cured here on earth. We continue to believe and hope you all do too!

Surrender was a hard thing to do. It went against every instinct I felt. I wanted to be in control, to find a cure for Zach, but knew it was not up to me. I knew in my heart surrender was the only option we had for a complete cure.

Reflections

To look in the eyes of a child with cancer is to see the unwavering hope and faith Jesus spoke of in Mark 10:15 when He said, "I tell you the truth, anyone who will not receive the kingdom of God like a little child will never enter it." Zachary faced the disease consuming him with a level of courage and strength that cannot be explained or understood at a human level. The complete receptivity, full trust and total acceptance to receive the poisons that had been poured into his body with the steadfast belief they would destroy the cancer that lurked in his brain was a powerful lesson of surrender to all those who witnessed it.

Helplessness and frustration consumed me as I fought the emotions of having been the central figure who had administered the drugs we hoped would make him better—the very drugs that made Zach so sick. It was a torturous position to hold, but one I knew no one was more qualified than me to fulfill. Seeing the devastating side effects wrack his beautiful body into uncontrollable submission drove me to my knees searching for relief. Finding peace and maintaining hope could only be found in holding desperately to the growing faith in my heart and surrendering Zach's fate to the One who had held it all along.

Being a witness to Zachary's determination and his willingness to submit to the plan before him changed my life forever. God was using this trial in a powerful way to bring us closer to Him because we made the choice to allow Him into our hearts. The plan God has for each of our lives has a great purpose. While we remain here on earth, we will never fully understand why the suffering and devastation occurs to those precious to our hearts. God loves us and it grieves His heart as much or more than it does ours. In the midst of the challenges, it is not up to us to question, but to learn—to draw purpose—and share the lessons with others so they might grow closer in their walk. The impact can be limitless; it is our decision to choose what to do with it. God is waiting patiently with His arms wide open for that day we surrender our trials to Him. While He does not promise to make it easy, He does promise to walk with us even in the darkest of moments.

Dirk, Zach and I at the Relay for Life event. This was the day we were told Zach's tumor had spread and there were very few medical alternatives. He was having trouble holding his head straight because of the new tumor growth.

Zach with Brad Richards, forward for the Tampa Bay Lightning hockey team. This picture was taken after the game as we waited outside the locker room for the players to exit. Each player came to Zach and autographed his special jersey. Sydney Sims, a friend also battling cancer, is standing just to the left of Zach.

Such a bittersweet picture. On Easter morning, instead of running out the door to hunt for his Easter eggs, Zach needed his wheelchair. His vision was being affected by the tumor growth at this point as well.

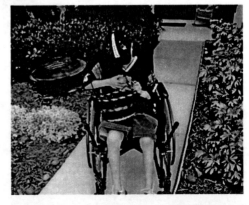

CHAPTER SEVENTEEN

A Mother's Lament

Zach was having more trouble sitting and moving with each new day. Discomfort in the back of his neck caused him to sit with his head turned slightly to the right or left. Desperate for help, I e-mailed the doctor at Duke, Dr. Thornton and the contact at the Brain Hospice website, asking for advice about his steroid dosage and any other treatment options they might suggest. Still trying to convince myself I had not overlooked any options, I hoped someone would respond with an idea.

Dr. Thornton suggested a chemo that could be administered directly into the spine along with cranio-spinal treatment to slow down the progression. Knowing the doctor at Duke would have to administer the chemo, I forwarded the e-mail to him for advice but never received a response. Receiving a lengthy response from the Brain Hospice administrator, she had many suggestions for other doctors that could possibly help and a suggestion that intrigued me. Referring to a homeopathic combination of supplements called Ruta/calphosphate being studied by a doctor in India, she explained it had shown some promise in GBM cases. Although it sounded too good to be true, I dismissed it, reasoning that if it had merit, surely the doctor at Duke would have mentioned it.

Zach was terribly uncomfortable, but did not want to take a pain pill. I was concerned to see that his eyes were not tracking correctly and he appeared cross-eyed at times. Angry with everything I did, his favorite word had become "idiot." Continuing to hold his hand and sit next to him most of the day, I talked to him about his situation.

"Zach, I'm so sorry you're not feeling very well, but I need you to try to not be so mad all the time. It hurts my feelings when you say mean things to me. I love you so much, Honey; no matter what, I will love you with all my heart."

Not responding but growing quiet, he kept his hand locked in mine as he drifted off to sleep. With his breathing so sporadic and worrisome to me, I had set up a meeting with the hospice social worker and nurse for later that day. My fear of being unable to help Zach with pain had made me realize it was time to get their help.

Lord, I am scared for Zach and the suffering that could lie ahead. I ask if it is not Your will to leave him with us, please don't let him suffer!

Not thrilled when I told him some ladies were coming who would probably want to check him over, I left him watching television when they arrived. They sent out staff that worked with children this time and the social worker started by apologizing for the misunderstanding during the last visit. Pulling out a small notepad, the nurse jotted down notes as I told them Zach's story from the beginning. Stopping to compose myself a few times, I could see compassion and concern in their faces as I relayed the story.

Finding Zach less than enthusiastic, the nurse asked him a few questions and checked his vitals. With an easygoing demeanor and a quick smile, she told Zach she also had an eight-year-old son named Zach. They completed their visit by telling me to call anytime for help with pain. The social worker encouraged me to start making some of the "arrangements" now and handed me a three-ring binder filled with neat and tidy lists of how to plan a funeral. Not wanting to accept that reality yet, I told her I would look it over later.

After they left I told Zach I had to check some things in the computer room. As I closed the doors to the office, I began to quietly cry, trying to absorb the reality of what had just happened. My Zach—my eight-year-old son—was now a *hospice* patient! This couldn't be happening to us. I was not ready, but there did not seem to be an escape.

Concerned, Dirk and Lexi both noticed Zach's eye was drifting inward when they came home as he continued to struggle with getting comfortable. Lexi and I went to an open house at her school, leaving Zach with Dirk.

"Mom, Zach's eyes look funny," she said as we drove. "Why is one of them looking toward his nose now?"

"I guess it is from the tumor, Honey," was all I could manage to say.

We both grew very somber and quiet. Tears welled in my eyes as we parked. *Pull it together, Sherry. Lexi needs you to be strong.*

I had become so consumed with Zach's care—it felt like it had been months since I had done something normal—that it felt strange to be in the real world again. As we walked through the halls of her school and passed many smiling faces, I found it was hard to keep from screaming out, "MY SON HAS A BRAIN TUMOR AND IS DYING AT HOME!" just to let everyone around us know how lucky they were to be living an ordinary life. Instead, I smiled politely and agreed with all of Lexi's teachers that she was a very smart, brave girl. Thanking them for all the assistance they had given us at the beginning of the year when Lexi was in Indiana, they had nothing but glowing things to say about her and complimented her happy nature.

God had been surrounding her with His unexplainable grace. How else could an eleven-year-old girl who was living the life she was living continue to smile and be happy? I had to focus on these blessings as I faced each day. Lexi's quiet strength and determination were amazing to me.

Asking for a pain pill before bedtime, Zach still could not find a comfortable position anywhere he sat. When I took him in to get ready for bed, I had to hold him up while he brushed his teeth. My heart melted as I watched him put all his effort into carefully brushing them. Even as bad as he felt, he gave 100 percent in what was asked of him. Hardly able to stand the torture of watching him struggle to do the simplest of tasks, I felt like we were trapped in a nightmare.

Sobbing after the kids were in bed, I had a feeling of total helplessness—more than we had ever imagined it could be. Unable to find the words to update our friends, I asked Dirk—this was taking its toll on him as well—to share his feelings on the website before going to bed.

April 25, 2006

Sherry said she did not really feel up to providing an update tonight so I thought I would share a few thoughts. We would like to thank everyone again for all the efforts that were put into the unbelievably successful golf tournament. The main memory I will have of the day is the true joy that I saw in the faces of all the volunteers. Sherry and I do understand how badly you all want to help us during this time. Zach really does not seem to want any visitors at this time. He is depending almost exclusively on Sherry for all of his support. It is becoming more and more difficult as the disease progresses. Sherry and I have known since the original diagnosis that our hope for a complete recovery rested in God's healing hands. We continue to pray for Zach to be completely healed here on earth. I was thinking of two biblical fathers this evening as I battled with the devil to keep the negativity out of my mind. I can only hope that my faith will continue to grow to the level of Abraham's. I pray to God and ask Him to continually fill my heart with the Holy Spirit so that I might have the strength, peace and faith that Abraham possessed. I also think of John 3:16, "For God so loved the world that he gave his one and only Son, that whoever believes in him shall not perish but have eternal life." Most people can't relate to how extremely sorrowful it must have been for God to witness the painful sacrifice that his Son, Jesus Christ, made for us. I thank Him every day for His sacrifice and all the many blessings He continues to give to our family. We know that God will heal Zachary whether it is here on earth or in heaven. We ask that you continue to pray for Zachary to not experience any pain and for his complete healing here on earth.

With the pain pill not working, it was a long night for Zach. His sleep was sporadic and he woke often, moaning and rubbing his head. The hospice nurse's words echoed in my head, "Call anytime, day or night, if the Tylenol does not work...," as my prayers became desperate.

Lord, this is killing me! It feels like we are being attacked on all sides! Please grant me the wisdom to know what to do. I do not want Zach to suffer because of my ignorance.

Making a bed of pillows out on the chair in a more upright position than his bed afforded, I moved Zach there hoping to relieve some of the pressure in his head. It seemed to help, and he finally fell asleep for the remainder of the night. As the sunlight began to stream in the windows, I knew we needed to do something more to help him. Whimpering in pain when he had to get up to use the bathroom, I offered him another pill, but he did not want it.

We never received an answer from the doctor at Duke. The lack of response made me feel we were not a real priority any longer. All I wanted was someone to help me know what to do to help Zach be comfortable. I increased his steroids as the Brain Hospice information had suggested.

As Zach drifted back to sleep and Dirk and Lexi left for the day, the house became eerily quiet. Was this the next step in this horrible situation—Zach sleeping most of the time? Worried he might stop breathing, I stayed close to him and watched him sleep. He looked like an angel as he slept and I was thankful the pain had subsided, but I missed having him awake. As I read to pass the time, I found a quote that helped boost my hope. Armin Gesswin said, "When God is about to do something great, He starts with a difficulty. When He is about to do something truly magnificent, He starts with an impossibility." Oh, how I hoped and prayed God would take this impossibility and turn it into a magnificent healing on earth for Zach.

Waking for a short time, Zach seemed to feel better. He had some eggs and soon drifted off to sleep again. I went to another part of the house for a short while and when I returned I found him lying still with his eyes open extremely wide.

"Hi there, Buddy. What are you doing? You have your eyes open so wide."

"I can't make one stay in the right place, Mom," he said, slowly blinking and looking at me.

"Can you see OK, Honey? The doctors said your eyes might act funny," I answered as I felt like crumpling to the ground in tears. How cruel this all seemed. Zach had done nothing to deserve this. *Why was it happening? Why could it have not been me?* He was so young and innocent. He just wanted to live and run and play! He mumbled that he could see OK. All I could do was climb next to him and hold him close as he grabbed my hand in his— his security.

When the time came to take Lexi to swim team, I had to beg Zach to come with us on the golf cart. I wanted to get him off the chair for some fresh air, but it quickly became apparent this was probably Zach's last trip to the pool on the golf cart. Every bump and turn caused him to wince in pain. As I tried to position him next to me so I could absorb some of the movement, he muttered angrily, "I am never doing this again!" as we returned home. Oh, how I wished we had gotten the golf cart months ago. It would have brought him so much joy when he was feeling good. I remembered him telling me how he wished he had one when he was going to school. Why was I so wrapped up in trying to be prudent with our money then? If only I had known how quickly things were to change.

Later, as we watched television, my concern intensified when Zach looked off into space and said he saw bugs flying around. There were no bugs; he was hallucinating. The symptoms he was having were listed on the Brain Hospice website, so they were not a surprise to me—just an alarming reminder the tumor was progressing at what seemed to be a rapid pace.

Needing to clear my head, as soon as Dirk arrived home I left for a run. It was getting more difficult to find the time to run, but it was the only thing that seemed to clear my mind and help me think. Giving me a chance to try to escape the reality that cancer had brought us, it took half of my run to slow my thoughts enough to think and pray. As I reached this point, a peace settled over me.

Lord, I know this is in Your hands. I have resolved to let it go from my thoughts as something I can control. I have been battling these thoughts for the last month and must release them. You know my desires and hopes. I will wait patiently for You, God. Thy will be done.

Even though Zach's pain intensified the next day, he refused the pain pill and opted for a bath instead. What a struggle we both had. It was difficult for me to move him into the tub because of his declining mobility. Once he was in the tub, he could not find a comfortable position even with towels and a bath pillow in place. We realized the bath idea was a mistake because he was unable to support his head and neck. Wrapping him in towels, I sat him on the closed toilet to dry him off, but could not let go of his torso because he had no balance to sit upright. It was as if he had a string tied to the back right side of his head pulling him to the ground. He moaned in pain as I sweated bullets trying to hold him and dry him at the same time. It was way too hard on both of us and I knew it was time to call the hospice nurse for a better solution.

Answering my page quickly, she assured me she would have the doctor call in a prescription for morphine drops to be delivered by noon. The paid had grown worse by the time she called a few hours later. I asked her if I should give him a pain pill while we waited for the morphine drops to arrive. Even though the pain medication was not working the greatest, I wanted to help him. Watching him suffer was exasperating.

She told me to wait, certain the delivery would be made within an hour.

Thankfully, Zach drifted off and slept for a few hours after our conversation. While he was sleeping, I began researching the Ruta/calphosphate once again. Nagging my thoughts since I had dismissed it before, I wondered if it was the path God wanted us to take.

Realizing it was a viable option when I delved deeper, I could not understand why it had never been mentioned by any of the doctors. With no apparent downside—it was cheap, natural, had minimal side effects and the results were promising—my frustration with the medical establishment flared. If something this simple was an option and it had shown some hope in a hopeless situation, why not at least inform a patient it was available?

Seeing MRI scans that showed GBM tumors completely gone in patients taking this supplement, I regretted not researching deeper when Zach was diagnosed. If I had seen this then, he would have been taking it from the start.

Hearing Zach call, I put my research on hold, but my mind was working furiously as I sat with him trying to comfort him. My frustration from my research soon shifted to hospice when 3 P.M. came and went and we still had no morphine. Moaning in pain and using my hand to hold his head once again, Zach had been fighting the pain for over eight hours now. Quickly discerning my exasperation with the situation when I called again, the nurse assured me the medicine was on its way. She was very apologetic as I reminded her that this was not the level of service we expected at all.

Another hour ticked by. Zach asked to move to the couch, hoping to find comfort in a new position. I kept my hand on his forehead as he whimpered in pain with closed eyes.

Dear God, what is this about? Why are we being challenged so hard?

Feeling like Satan was trying his hardest to break us, I was teetering on the edge of losing my sanity. I could imagine no worse punishment in my life than watching Zach experience this pain.

Coming home just before Lexi arrived, Dirk saw my frustration and anger in the tears welling in my eyes, and he became livid with hospice. As he sat with Zach, I marched outside to call once again. I asked to speak with the manager, my voice shaking with the request. Explaining what had happened throughout the day, I demanded an explanation of why we still had no morphine. Again she assured me the delivery should arrive within the hour. Ending the conversation in tears, I told her their incompetence had caused Zach to suffer all day because we were told to wait for pain medication.

Unbelievably, another hour passed and still no delivery. At 6 p.m., Dirk called again only to find out that Zach's prescription was still sitting at their pharmacy! Asking for their location, he went to pick it up himself. Disgusted by the experience, I felt it was ironic we had agreed to use hospice to simplify our care of Zach by having access to immediate help, only to find complete failure of help when we needed it most. By the time the morphine arrived, Zach was resistant to it as we were just chasing the pain. What a wasted day. Raw and on edge, I could barely find the words to pray.

This is hell, Lord; help us!! I do not want Zach to suffer like this; we need a miracle.

As if we needed more worry, I felt nauseous and panicked when I noticed Zach's Ommaya reservoir was bulging and pulsing as we watched television. (The neurosurgeon had placed the reservoir under his scalp during his second surgery when they drained the cyst.) It looked as though it could burst out of his head any moment. I looked at Dirk and motioned with my eyes in that direction so he could see it too. His eyes grew wide in concern. I shrugged my shoulders because I had no idea what to do. Asking to sleep in his bed instead of the chair, Zach felt exhaustion overtake him. It had been a long day—one of the worst we had experienced. Just when I thought we had reached the bottom, it seemed we could find a new one.

"Zachie, are you doing OK? I am sorry you had such a rough day. Do you have any questions about what is happening, Honey?" I asked as we cuddled together in his bed.

"No, Mom, but why are there so many pictures on my wall?" he asked, staring at the wall that contained pendants filled with pictures of his past basketball teams.

"How many do you see, Honey?

Pausing to count, he replied, "Twelve."

There were only six pendants, so I realized he was seeing two of everything. Nervous about being too far away from him, I ended up sleeping in Lexi's room—just steps away from him if he needed me.

Dirk's hand on my shoulder caused my eyes to fly open. Another day had arrived. Sleep left my mind as quickly as it had come the night before. I quickly tiptoed into Zach's room and found he was still breathing.

Thank you Lord for one more day!

My goal for the day was to find out how to get the Ruta/calphosphate started for Zach. As I told Dirk about it as he prepared to leave for work, he told me to go for it—at this point what did we have to lose? I hoped it wasn't too late. I e-mailed the doctor in India to find out what type of dosage he would have Zach take. Just doing that was empowering—at least I was taking action, which gave my hope of an earthly healing a boost.

Having the morphine helped Zach rest, but now the battle was to know how much to give him to alleviate the pain while still allowing him to be awake and interact with us.

Glad he was able to rest after his difficult day, I spent most of the morning on the phone, first with the clinic nurse sharing our horrible day and asking about his bulging Ommaya reservoir, then with the hospice nurse demanding accountability. These calls prompted a flurry of return calls trying to determine why things had gone so terribly wrong with the hospice group. Grateful to be able to release my frustration, I shed many tears as I recounted our day to Kyleen and shared how difficult it had been to watch Zach decline and sit helplessly by with no viable treatments available. Being able to talk about it with her was cleansing for me. I was extremely fortunate she was willing to listen with a sympathetic ear.

When Zach would wake, I was glued to his side. I relished having him awake, even if he was not completely "with me." The morphine and growing tumor were affecting his ability to think or speak clearly. It melted my heart later that day when our neighbor Theresa called to ask if Zach wanted a Happy Meal from McDonalds. When she dropped it off, Zach mumbled with gratitude and love, "Miss Theresa was just made for kids." After he managed to eat some of his food, I began to talk to him about our visitors who would arrive soon.

"Zach, do you remember who is coming today?"

"Grammy and Kathy. Tell Grammy she has to be careful if she wants to kiss my cheeks," Zach answered slowly.

"Zach, if we could have a super-fast jet pull up to our door that could take us anywhere in the world, where would you want to go?" I asked, guessing he would say Disney World.

"Indiana, so I could see Cole again," he said closing his eyes. His speech was slow and slurred from the morphine.

After Lexi came home, I showered and tried to prepare myself for the arrival of my sister and mother. Looking forward to seeing them, I was also concerned for them and how seeing Zach at this stage would hit them. Dirk had promised to prepare them on the ride to our house from the airport.

When they came in, Lexi ran to give them hugs. Greeting them with smiles and hugs as well, I watched as they went to Zach on the chair and gently greeted him. He was lying on the chair with pillows propping him up into a sitting position. With wide-open eyes and his head bent to the right, he stared at the armrest of the chair. His color was pale, kind of gray, and his hair sparse and haphazardly standing askew. His weak voice sounded as if he had a mouth full of gravel and his limbs had little movement to them. My beautiful baby had been so betrayed by his body. He was once so completely in command of it, able to make it move so gracefully in a pool, on a basketball court or soccer field. Now it had become his enemy.

Kathy softly asked Zach how he was doing; he answered the same he had always answered, "Good." Quickly walking away to put her bags in the guest room, she wanted to hide her tears as well. No matter how bad he felt, our Zach remained optimistic and brave.

Bedtime had become difficult because Zach could no longer walk to his room, even with assistance. Dirk had to carry him as gently as possible to his bed, keeping the pillows around his head. After Zach fell asleep, I sat with my mother and Kathy to fill them in on all that had happened, telling them about my hope in Ruta/calphosphate and our complete faith in God. It had been a long hard day, but at least it had been pain-free for Zach.

I was thrilled to find a return e-mail from the doctor in India the next morning. His words filled me with hope and renewed my frustration that we had not found him sooner.

Dear Ms. Sherry Tucker,

Sorry to learn about your son. Actually we treat all types of cases including brain tumors. In our clinic, where we serve a patient load of approximately 1,000—1,200 prescriptions daily, we do not practice classical homeopathy. Our treatment is very specific both in respect of the medicine as well as the potency. We do not guarantee cure for any disease; we only try to cure and give relief to the patients.

We have treated thousands of cases of SOL Brain [tumors] and have arrived at a definite protocol of treatment with Ruta and Calc Phos, which has proved beneficial in a good percentage of the cases treated. This protocol has subsequently been shown to have a positive effect even in the laboratory studies conducted of the MD Anderson Cancer Centre in Houston, where it has been seen that this combination of medicines actually kills cancer cells (SOL Brain) in culture while helping the growth of normal peripheral blood lymphocytes. We routinely give patients this protocol of treatment with positive effects. This treatment we do here alone, no Chemo Therapy (CT) and Radio Therapy (RT) are used & we get excellent result of course. Now this Ruta treatment is being used in many cases in the USA and with & after CT, RT relapse with great success. Ruta Gr 6c and Calcarea Phos 3X treatment will be very good for children also....

As I tried to determine how to order the pills, I found a Caringbridge site about a girl with a different type of brain tumor who quit chemo and began this type of treatment along with a complete change to her diet. She was improving! With the help of several e-mail exchanges with her parents, I found a site to order the pills. Within thirty minutes and for $30 I was able to order what I hoped would kill the loathsome tumor overtaking Zach's brain.

Lord, I pray it is not too late!

Anxious to do something to help, my mom and Kathy spent the weekend entertaining and spoiling Lexi and deep-cleaning parts of the house that had been ignored way too long. We all would take turns sitting with Zach, who was growing more difficult to understand and less coherent, creating a general feeling of despair in all of us.

Deciding to join Dirk at church after his men's prayer time, I asked my mom to sit with Zach while I was gone. At church I missed holding Zach in my lap and shuddered to think that if he received his healing in heaven, this would be a permanent thing. Tears flooded my eyes during the sermon when a parable about a vision of heaven was discussed. The vision was of a large gathering of people around a campfire. The ones with "a story to tell" would have a front row seat with Jesus. Their stories would be about how many lives were touched by them to move closer to God. There was no doubt in my mind Zach would have a front row seat!

Tears flowing down my face on my drive home, I tried to absorb the reality of Zach's decline. I couldn't shake the picture in my head of Zach staring off into space with wide eyes, looking a bit frightened or confused. Although I had asked him many times what he was seeing, he would never answer. What if he was scared and needed me now? Panic set in as I drove. I had not been away from Zach for this length of time in awhile. I could not get home to him fast enough.

Relieved everything was peaceful when I returned, I immediately climbed next to Zach on the chair and grabbed his hand. Loving the feeling of his hand in mine and the soft fluff of his hair on my cheek, I often found myself breathing in his smell as I rested my head next to him.

Zach seemed to be losing more and more connection with the world around him. At times he could engage in yes or no questions; other times he just didn't respond. He managed to say, "That's not fair!" when he found out Lexi had gone shopping with Kathy and my mom. Eating remained difficult, so I had asked them to find things that were easy to swallow while they were out shopping.

Before they left, I wanted them to help me give Zach another bath. I knew this was something the hospice service offered, but I could not imagine having a stranger help me bathe Zach. He had lost so much dignity with the failing of his body; I wanted to at least preserve his modesty in front of strangers. A pool float turned out to be a wonderful tool for padding the bathtub. The thought had come to me during the many sleepless hours I had to contemplate ways to make Zach more comfortable. Finding it was not easy to move Zach without causing him pain, we worked together to lift him into the wheelchair and then into the tub and onto the float. Seeing him relax once he was in the tub, I slowly washed him. Remembering how hard it was to dry him, I had brought in a straight-backed chair for him to sit in as I dried him off. Everything made the process work better this time.

We could all see how Zach's reality was slipping as Kathy and my mom gathered their bags to leave. Sitting together around the television, Zach asked what Michelle's bag was doing over there. We exchanged sad looks as we realized he had drifted back to my other sister's earlier visit in his mind.

As they were leaving, my mom grabbed me in a big hug. With tears in her eyes, she told me how sorry she was we were going through all of this and that I was one of the strongest people she knew. She also said she would come back as soon as I needed her to. I did not know what I needed. How is anyone supposed to know how to watch their son die? How can anyone help you do that? It was something I had to do on my own. No one could fix this; it was all in God's hands.

Waking the next morning, I was nervous about getting Zach to the clinic by myself to have his port flushed. The hospice nurse had urged me to go to the clinic when I asked about flushing his port at home. She said it was good for patients to get out if possible. It had been four days since she had seen Zach, so I wondered if she really appreciated how difficult it was to move him.

Getting him dressed and into the car went fairly well. I had made a big pile of pillows for him to sink into once he was in the backseat. The problem was finding a comfortable position for him in the wheelchair once we arrived. Since it provided no support for his head, I tried to prop a pillow behind his back, but it only crowded him. Because he could not hold up his head, it drooped uncontrollably to his chest. I wanted to scream for him. The injustice of his situation crushed me. I put my hand on his forehead to gently push his head against my stomach for support while I pushed the chair with my other hand. It was a challenge to say the least.

I felt like we were on display in the waiting room and could see terror in the eyes of the other parents as they looked at Zach. We were their living nightmare since Zachary's struggle was obvious to all. To accommodate us the best they could, the staff called us back to a room quickly. I found that when I tipped the chair back at an angle, Zach could rest his head on the pillow I had brought and not battle to hold his head up. What a sight we must have been to the nurse as she walked into the room. Zach with his eyes closed and unresponsive, sitting in a wheelchair tipped backwards, and me oozing with frustration and defiance that I would not let the situation break me.

"Hey, Buddy; how you doing?" she asked as she peered under his shirt to find his port. We shared small talk as she skillfully and carefully did her work, and Zach managed to open his eyes as she finished and looked at her. "There are those beautiful eyes, Zach; I knew they were there somewhere," she finished with a smile.

Soon after she left, the doctor and social worker came in to see us. Shock was evident in their eyes as they took in the scene before them, but they tried not to let it show. They both asked if we needed anything—not that they could really offer much help at this point. I told them we were doing fine, thinking of the feeling of abandonment I had experienced the past few weeks. Explaining that we did not need to come back unless we wanted to from now on because Zach's counts were fully recovered, the doctor ended our visit. Feeling tears burning my eyes as I left the building, I hoped to prove them all wrong and bring Zach back when he was better.

I pray they are wrong, God; we need a miracle! I pray the Ruta pills are part of that, Lord.

The Ruta and Calphosphate pills were waiting on the front porch when we arrived home. Amazed at the small size of each pill, I wondered, as I stared at them, if they were God's plan for Zach's miracle. Even though I told Zach they were magic pills that I hoped would make him start feeling better, he was not thrilled to be taking more pills. But he did not object when he saw how small the pills were.

Later, when the house was dark and quiet, I found myself as I did every night on my knees, face in the carpet by Zach's bedside telling God my fears and hopes.

Dear God, I am so sad tonight! Zach seems to be struggling more every day.

Lord, we need his bright light with us! He is such a special boy to us—a gift greater than we could have ever imagined. Our family needs him. His friends need him. Lord, we are asking for a complete healing here on earth. We want Zach to be able to smile and run again, to be the boy he once was. I pray these new pills work for Your glory. What a glory it would be, Lord. Dear God, we only want what is Your will. If it is not Your will to heal Zach on earth, then we do not want him to suffer. Lord, You know my heart; please give us strength to stay focused on You!

The week crept slowly by, and my heart continued to break. Growing less effective the longer he used it, the morphine had to be supplemented with a Fentanyl pain patch. Drifting further and further away from me, Zach was not communicating well. Not optimistic when she came later in the week to check on him, the hospice nurse talked to him and tried to gauge his awareness of his surroundings. When she asked him what was on television, instead of saying, *The Price is Right*, he said *Raven*. After she left, I read to him for a bit instead of listening to the maddening sound of the television drone on and on. The nurse had told me she felt like his respiration and heart rate were indicating the end could be near. And since the last thing to go was hearing, she told me we should keep talking to him.

Feeling like Satan was playing games with us—trying to break us by piling more and more fears on our hearts—I had it out with him while I ran later on. I rebuked him to leave us alone and made it plain we would not be shaken in our faith. Anyone who was within earshot was probably concerned for my sanity as I was shouting out my anger and raising my fists as I ran.

Our victories were now measured by a small response from Zach or getting him to successfully eat something. I could not look at my day except by each passing moment because I knew if I stepped back to face the reality of what it had become, despair would consume me. My contact with the outside world was limited to the computer and a few phone calls or e-mails. An occasional run would refresh my spirit and renew my resolve to stay focused on getting Zach better.

With the weekend came more visitors. Dirk's parents and older brother Doug and his wife Kim were driving down from Indiana. Having visitors was a reality check for me. It made me stop and take account of how much ground Zach had lost since our last visitors left.

I watched him with sorrow as we awaited their arrival. He now was lying naked under a blanket with an absorbent pad wrapped around him like a diaper. Hardly eating anything, he had a rough time swallowing pills to the point he had started chewing them in confusion. Although unresponsive for the most part, every now and then recognition would flicker in his eyes when he would wake.

Growing frustrated with everything, I felt like I was constantly trying to stick things in his mouth—food, pills, straws. I felt like I was desperately searching in the darkness for a way out of this nightmare, but it was only getting darker and scarier.

The Tuckers arrived around 5 P.M. Knowing they had only come to support us, I was sad there was absolutely nothing for them to do, but to sit and witness this nightmare along with us. Grateful they could be a distraction for Lexi and Dirk, I was so caught up in my care for Zach that I did not have the energy to engage in much conversation.

They stayed until late that evening and left to stay nearby. All of them planned to join Dirk and Lexi at church the next morning. Gib and Phyllis were going to stay until Zach was healed—here or in heaven. Doug and Kim were flying back Monday morning.

Watching Zach continue to lose ground, I felt depression pressing in on me as my hope of the Ruta providing a cure started to dissolve.

Lord, I am having a hard time feeling we will see Zach be healed. He is getting so fragile and failing in so many ways. Please hear our prayers! We pray it is Your will Zach is healed here on earth.

As I settled in next to Zach on the big chair to sleep, Lexi decided to sleep on the couch to be near us. I longed for the past when sleeping in the family room was a fun sleepover treat for the kids. Those days were gone—this was no treat. Zach, full of frantic movements and loud mumblings, seemed to be frightened or working very hard at something in his imagination throughout the night. I would grab his hands and hold them close as I softly told him not to be scared because I was with him. I desperately wished I could understand what he was saying, but he was incoherent. If only he could talk to me. Not knowing what he was experiencing made it difficult to know how to comfort him.

Relieved when the black shadows of the night began to fade to gray as morning arrived, I realized that somehow we had made it through the frantic, fitful night. Zach was in need of a bath, so when Dirk returned from his prayer meeting we worked together to get him in and out of the tub. The pool float worked beautifully again. He looked very relaxed in his bed after we had finished. I completed a book I had started reading to him the day before about a boy playing basketball. I hoped he was enjoying it All he could do was stare with wide vacant eyes and his mouth slightly opened.

Dirk and Lexi left to join the rest of the Tuckers at church. They all went to lunch and got back to our house in the early afternoon. Spending the day sitting with Zach in his room reading or talking to him, I did not want to leave him alone even though he was sleeping most of the time. Continuing to feel as though all I was doing was jamming things in his mouth, I felt my frustration growing as my hope was slipping away.

Dear God, help me!! I need strength and patience. I feel Satan's attack triple fold.

Feeling the walls closing in on me, I knew I had to get away for awhile. I announced I was leaving for a run. Lexi and Phyllis climbed in the golf cart and rode ahead of me. It felt good to breathe the fresh air and I wanted to keep running to escape from this looming monster that hung over our house and seemed ready to consume us. I did not want to face what seemed to be imminent. I was not ready to accept it; I was still clinging to our belief God could and would cure Zach.

As I reached the halfway point on my run, I was near two ponds. My mind was a million miles away, numb from the strange reality in which we now lived. As I started to make a turn, I was startled by a six-foot alligator sitting at the edge of the sidewalk ahead of me. Facing the sidewalk with its mouth opened wide, it was menacing and evil, and seemed to represent my fears in a tangible form—ready to devour me as I desperately tried to finish the race.

Thinking the world had gone crazy—or maybe just me—I wondered what would have happened if I had stayed in my thoughts and not realized the alligator was there until I was upon it. Since it was mating season, perhaps my leg would have become a tasty treat. One of Zach's biggest fears before he was diagnosed was alligators. I had been sleeping in the same room with him one night a year or so before when he began to breathe quickly and flail his arms in protest. When I woke him from his dream, he told me an alligator was chasing him. Was this alligator a sign or warning of danger to come for Zach?

Having renewed my spirit with my run, I spent the rest of the evening with Zach, reading and trying to encourage him to eat. My heart burst with hope when he was able to respond to my question of what he wanted for dinner. "Mac and cheese," he mumbled. He took four bites and swallowed them with little difficulty. His face had always been so expressive before, so I was thrilled when his eyebrows furrowed and rose in response to my conversation. It brought me a much needed smile and giggle as I continued to talk to him. Maybe we had turned the corner! My resolve grew to stay with the plan. Maybe the Ruta/calphosphate was actually working.

As Zach rested later that evening, I updated the website. It had become difficult to find the words to share what we were experiencing in our home, and I had not been able to bring myself to do it for a few days.

May 7, 2006
It has been a long weekend. Having the Tuckers (Grandma, Grandpa, Uncle Doug and Aunt Kim) here has helped us get through it. It has been a challenge to get Zach to eat and drink all weekend. He is having a hard time communicating and staying awake long enough to eat anything substantial. To my relief, this evening he was able to talk to me and let know how he was feeling. He didn't eat a lot, but ate enough to ease my mind.

We were able to give him another bath today and that always seems to perk him up. I have to admit, it was a challenge for me not to become discouraged as I watch him endure this process. I keep thinking about something I read in The Case for Faith *by Lee Strobel that was trying to explain why bad things happen in this world. The parable was of a bear caught in a trap. It said sometimes a hunter has to push the caught limb further in the trap in order to release it. Putting this in God's perspective, we can't see God's big picture of why this process is required of Zach. We just feel the sharp pain of the trap right now. We will be patient with God's grace.*

We are still continually praying for Zach's complete cure here on earth and truly believe this is possible. Matthew 14:14 says, "When Jesus landed and saw a large crowd, he had compassion on them and healed their sick." I know we have quite a large crowd praying for us. No matter what the outcome of this journey, we also know God has been and will continue to be glorified from this. No matter how challenging or painful, we take great comfort in knowing our faith will get us through.

Dirk carefully carried Zach to the chair for me when bedtime drew near. I wanted to stay with Zach again, in case he woke and could not call for me. I did not want him to be alone and scared, not even for a minute. I put my head near Zach's as fatigue invaded every muscle in my body. With his hand in mine, and the citrus scent of his shampoo filling my senses, we slept together once again.

Reflections

Emotional turmoil was my constant companion as my child drifted further and further from my grasp. The only constant was God's grace. He was giving me the strength to face the dire deterioration of Zach's condition with continued hope and belief that a miracle cure was still a possibility. Feeling a lack of support from both the medical community and hospice, I felt as if we were adrift on a lost raft with information gleaned from the internet as our only compass. Logically, I knew from his symptoms that Zach was dying, but emotionally, I could not accept this was his fate. Clinging to the unwavering belief that God could miraculously heal him, I continued to search for ways to help Zach's body persevere against the malicious advances of the tumor.

The world around us was not stopping and we were forced to continue to live. Stepping through the door to our home was like entering a different dimension because of the unimaginable circumstance we now faced. We asked—pleaded with—God to end the suffering for Zach whether here on earth or in heaven. Dirk and Lexi struggled to face the world head-on while carrying this surreal truth in their hearts.

Desperate to keep Zach comfortable—but not so medicated it prevented interaction with him—I struggled to understand the clues his body language presented. The quiet that now consumed every corner of the house deafened me. I longed to hear him call my name and demand I sit with him. In an effort to comfort him, I filled the silence with reading aloud to him, hoping to elicit a response through a smile or a touch.

Thankful for the few conversations we had shared about heaven, I wanted to reassure him not to be scared. To be with him if he was to be called home was my remaining desire. Ushering him into God's arms would be my last gift I could give him.

At the Zach Tucker Golf Scramble in late April 2006. Zach was not feeling well, resulting in very few smiles from him on this day. Dirk and I were amazed and humbled by the generosity of our family and friends. Left to right: Zach, Lexi, me, my dad Mike, my sister Michelle

A few days after the golf scramble. Zach was excited to count the money Debbie brought him from the event. Moving him from this chair was becoming increasingly difficult.

Zach was determined to help Michelle decorate cookies during her visit from Canada. It broke my heart to see how difficult it was for him to hold his head up and control his hands.

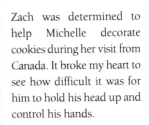

CHAPTER EIGHTEEN

Zachary's Marathon

The new day arrived; my heart was anxious. Zach had stirred around 4 A.M. with the scared, wide-open eyes again and heavy breathing. But his arms didn't flail as they had before. It was as if he had lost that ability as well.

"Zach, Honey, don't be scared. Mommy is right here with you. Can you tell me what you see? It's OK; just relax," I whispered to him as I rubbed his arms and put my face in front of his so he could see me. He looked right through me, and I knew he was not seeing things in this world—he was in a different reality and his brain was probably receiving very confused signals from the tumor.

My heart sank. I had been so hopeful he would be more coherent after our brief connection the night before. Continuing to work with him after Dirk and Lexi left for the day, I was concerned constipation was contributing to his discomfort. My frustration grew as I gave him his morning pills and they all came right back out of his mouth.

"Zach, Honey, you have to swallow these pills. Mommy wants you to get better, but I can't help you if you don't take your pills." I tried again and could see it was a losing battle. My patience dissolved as the weight of the situation pressed down on my shoulders. Anger from my apparent failure to help him was trying to overtake me as my requests grew more intense. "Zach, you have to take your pills! Please, Honey, can you look at Mommy and open your mouth? I want to help you." He remained unresponsive.

Leaving the room to catch my breath and calm my emotions, I also worried that the lack of his anti-seizure meds and the steroid might cause his body to have a rebound effect and lead to a seizure. After I put a relaxation CD into the player, I climbed next to Zach and held his hand as I tried to find some peace and calm myself with the help of the soothing music and soft voice telling us to release all our anxiety. Lying there, trying to regulate my own breathing, I listened to Zach's labored breathing. It sounded like he had aspirated some of his saliva. I knew that many times, as people near death, their breathing developed a "rattle." It made me panic and wonder if that was what was happening to Zach.

When I called the hospice nurse to describe his condition, she said she could be out in a couple of hours. *A couple of hours!* I needed help now. Having always heard hospice was a wonderful help in these types of situations, I certainly did not feel we were receiving much assistance. Maybe it was my own fault for not welcoming them with open arms.

Sitting down with Zach again, we continued to listen to the stress relief CD. Suddenly I opened my eyes, realizing I had dozed off briefly. Feeling Zach's arm methodically hitting my stomach, I realized he was probably having a mild seizure. Wanting to stop it, I gave him the suppository the neurologist had given me back in January, hoping it would alleviate the tremor and relax his rigid body.

Tears ran down my face as I sat with him realizing the progress I hoped I had seen the day before was an illusion. Thoughts of Mother's Day—only six days away—haunted me, knowing it was probably not going to be a happy one for me.

"Zach, I am sorry I was upset this morning about your pills. I just want to make you better, Baby. This is so unfair that you are working so hard, Honey. It is making me sad you have to do all of this," I whispered as I tasted the saltiness of my tears that could not seem to stop pouring from my eyes.

Eventually, his body relaxed as the medicine was absorbed into his system. The rattling continued with each breath he took. I adjusted him on the pile of pillows propped around him. The social worker from hospice appeared at my door first. Assuming the nurse had told her things were not going well, my defenses rose as I felt the world was in a conspiracy to take Zach away. Everyone was so focused on him dying!

She scolded me when she found I had failed to do my homework of making the "arrangements" for Zach's funeral. It turned my stomach to even think about it. "HE ISN'T DEAD YET!" I wanted to scream to the world. I believed that while there was breath, there was hope—no matter how little! If my eyes could have shot darts, she would have been filled with them as I gritted my teeth and told her I would look at the options that night. Could she not see all I needed was a little moral support—a prayer or comforting arm? Instead it seemed as all she wanted was to make sure I had completed all the checklists.

"Do you have any questions for me? Do you know what to do if Zach passes on?" she asked, exasperated at my lack of cooperation.

I hesitated, knowing I needed to know this information even if it was not what I wanted to accept. "What should we do if that happens?" I mumbled quietly.

Her tone softened as she explained it was our decision when to call them and we could take as much time as we liked. We could give Zach a bath or just hold him and when we were ready, they would send a nurse out to make things official. No longer able to be strong, I hung my head and quietly cried as she explained. It broke my heart to think of things reaching that point, but I knew they could. She gave me a hug as we stood for her to leave.

While the social worker and I had been speaking, the nurse had arrived and evaluated Zach. She came in and spoke quietly to me. "It does not look good, Mrs. Tucker. His heart rate is up and his respiration is down. His digestive system is shutting down. Based on what I have seen, I think it will probably be this week."

Why, why, why? My world was crumbling around me. Although filled with conflict, my belief remained strong that God, at any moment, could heal Zach. He could be a modern day miracle. But the reality I had just faced screamed at my logical side.

Sitting near Zach, I slowly started flipping through the hospice binder when we were alone again. It was mind-boggling to think about a funeral. I didn't even know where we would want to bury Zach. All the cemeteries in Tampa seemed so impersonal and unfamiliar. Actually the cemetery in Spencer—the one we always drove past on the way from my parents' home to Dirk's parents'—came to mind, but it seemed too far away.

These decisions were surreal to me. I could not be thinking this about Zach and yet I had to. As I called Dirk, I could hardly speak through my tears as I tried to explain my morning to him. He said he would come right home and would call our parents.

Looking at Zach, I felt weak. How could this be happening? He was my baby, my sweet boy! He was supposed to grow tall and strong like his Daddy, not be wasting away on this chair. Sitting close to him, I buried my face in his soft hair. "Zachie, don't be scared, Honey. Mommy is here with you," I whispered. "Zach, we are praying so hard right now that God will heal you and you will stay here with us, but Honey, if it is time for you to go to heaven, you go. Don't be scared because we will all be there in a blink of an eye, right behind you. I love you so much, Baby." Wanting to release him if he was ready to go, I did not want him to be fighting to live out of concern for us. He had struggled enough. As much as I did not want it to happen, I was beginning to understand he deserved his reward.

This day had been my ultimate fear from the moment I heard the words, "Your son has a brain tumor." Never wanting to accept it as a reality, I was not ready. But would I ever be? Thoughts of a funeral swirled around my head. Picturing funerals I had been to in the past, I could hear the drone of the organ music and see the flowers and the casket. Never had I been to one for a child. *How could this be?* I could not picture Zach's funeral in a funeral home—it needed to be in a church. What about Indiana? How would that be handled?

The ringing phone startled me from my unimaginable thoughts. Relieved to see it was Debbie, I completely broke down as the words spilled out about how bad things were looking. She promised she would be right over.

Dirk and Debbie arrived at the same time. I led them outside on the lanai to explain everything to them—from the rough start to the day to the hospice visit. Surprisingly calm, I could not believe the words I was forced to tell them.

In another dimension now, it seemed Zach was standing with one foot in heaven and the other chained to his failing body here on earth. Not responsive to anyone or anything, his eyes were very glassy and only half open. His breathing was rattled and sporadic. Hospice had delivered a suction machine so I could clear his mouth of saliva from time to time. A repulsive machine, it did not lessen the rattle that Zach had with every breath.

When Dirk went to pick up Lexi at the bus stop on the golf cart later that afternoon, I stood outside on the driveway waiting to hug her. Dreading the conversation we were about to have, I knew there was no way to avoid it. Looking at me with concern in her eyes, I took her in my arms.

"Mom, what is going on? Is Zach OK?" she asked.

"No, Honey. He has not done so well today. He is breathing kind of funny and not able to talk to us. The nurse that comes to the house said it does not look good," I said slowly as we walked in the house and I steered her to her room.

"Mom, you mean he could die?" she said in a loud desperate voice.

"Yes, Honey," I said softly as tears welled in my eyes.

"No, Mom! Right now? How long?" she cried out in panic. Wanting to keep our conversation from drifting to Zach's ears, Dirk called out to shut her door.

"Oh, Honey, I am so sorry this is happening. The nurse said it could be a couple of days, but she felt like it would be this week. This just isn't fair, is it?" I said through my tears.

"Zach is too good, Mom. It should be me! Everyone likes Zach. He is too good to die. This isn't fair! He is the best brother. I want it to be me—I want Zach to be OK," she wailed and dissolved into a pile on her bed.

I grabbed her in my arms and held her as we both wept. My heart was aching for her and all of us. *How can this be our life?* At only eleven, she was facing an unimaginable fear all children face—the loss of her brother.

Releasing our tears together seemed to calm our emotions temporarily. Asking if she could stay home with us to be with Zach, she wanted to know where he would be buried. Telling her we had not figured that out, she immediately said he should be buried in Indiana because that was where he had fun. It brought a sense of peace to me she was so sure.

Oh Lord, fill Lexi with peace. Allow her to say the things she needs to in order to find peace in her heart. Give me strength to help her.

Wiping our tears, we embraced tightly before leaving her room. Relieved to know she understood what was ahead—if indeed it could be understood by any of us—I watched as she walked out to Zach and climbed next to him. Leaning in to gently kiss his forehead, she told him she loved him. Overcome by her affection being poured out on her dying baby brother, I wept once again.

As we stood by helplessly, our family unit was slipping away from us, which made dinner very subdued. Sitting next to Zach I held food to his mouth, urging him to try to eat—to no avail. Pushing their food around their plates, Dirk and Lexi had no appetite as well. Retreating to our bedroom, Dirk began the arduous task of calling our siblings with our disheartening news. Making her a bed on the couch, Lexi wanted to be near me and Zach during the night.

Around 9 P.M., Zach's marathon began. I noticed that his heart rate had increased quite a bit. His breathing went from slow and sporadic to deep and quick. Reminding me of how a person breathes when they are running a race up a hill and their body is screaming for air, it was as if he were running his own race to his finish line.

Panic-stricken, Dirk could not catch his breath and had to leave the room. Crying and trembling, Lexi curled into a ball on the couch, burying her head. Fearing he was slipping away from us, I started softly singing a special lullaby to him that I had made up when he was a baby.

"Little Zachie's Mommy's baby,

Baby, baby, baby boy;

Little Zachie's Mommy's baby,

Baby, baby, baby boy."

"Honey, it is OK to go if it is time. Mommy is right here. We will be there soon. Just calm down and breathe in and out, in and out. It will be OK, Baby," I whispered to him as I slowly ran my fingertips along his chest and belly trying to calm his intense struggle to breathe and rapidly beating heart. Settling into a frightful rhythm, his chest continued to rise and fall noticeably with every breath.

Dirk had been pouring his heart out to God asking for mercy and healing and returned with his Bible in his hand.

"Zach, don't give up. God will heal you," he said with complete faith. Saying a prayer for all of us, he went back to our room to meditate. Later he put an entry on the Caringbridge site to update all of our family and friends.

May 8, 2006

I am writing this evening as Sherry is busy doing what mothers do best, care for their children. The hospice nurse came by today to check on Zach and reported his vital signs had diminished since her last visit. While this is not the most favorable news from a medical perspective, it does not weaken our faith in God or our hope that Zach will be healed here on earth. God told me a few weeks ago that Zach's condition would worsen substantially before he would be healed. I have always asked God, with a righteous heart, to heal Zach here on earth, but we expressed to Him that we would patiently wait on His timing. I truly believe that the time is now here for God to heal Zach on earth, if that is His plan. I am following the Word in Matthew 21:22 "If you believe, you will receive whatever you ask for in prayer." Well, I believe and I am asking God to perform a modern-day miracle and heal Zach here on earth. It is time to flip your prayer switches into overdrive. The leadership of our church, The Crossing, has begun fasting and praying for Zach's healing here on earth. The power of prayer should never be underestimated. I continue to experience a great amount of joy through this time of suffering and would like to leave you with the following scriptures taken from 1 Thessalonians 5:16—8: "Be joyful always; pray continually; give thanks in all circumstances, for this is God's will for you in Christ Jesus." Your continued prayers are greatly appreciated.

Exhausted, Lexi fell asleep as the house grew dark and quiet except for Zach's breathing. Afraid to sleep, though my eyes were heavy, I continued to watch Zach closely. His intense breathing remained, punctuated occasionally with a cough. He drooled heavily, and his bloodshot and still eyes were half open, looking as if the life had already left them.

Well into his race, he seemed strangely relaxed, letting out big exaggerated yawns sporadically, like he used to do when he tried to get a laugh out of us. Shocking me when I first heard the yawns, the irony of that sound in the midst of his difficult battle made me giggle. It seemed to be his way of letting me know he was OK even though he seemed to be struggling so desperately.

Having trouble sleeping within earshot of Zach's race, Lexi left the couch and joined Dirk in our room. I could see Zach's heart flailing madly in his chest as it rose and fell with each raspy breath. I fully expected him to quit breathing any second because of a heart attack. *How long could his tired body take this?*

Filling the room with silvery shadows, the moon was full and shining brightly, which made me wonder what the rest of the world was doing at this moment. How many other mothers were watching their baby die in front of their eyes?

Putting my head near Zach's, I whispered, "Slow down, Zachie. Breathe in and breathe out. Breathe in and breathe out. It is OK, Baby." My fingertips ran the length of his chest and stomach as I talked to him, trying to slow down his heart. Feeling extremely hot to me, he suddenly coughed and sneezed all at once and a dark mass that looked like blood flew onto the covers between us.

Dear God! Is he going to start bleeding now? Help us, dear Lord. I don't want him to suffer like this; please heal him, God!

Heart racing, I felt a wave of anxiety hit me. "Dirk, Dirk come here and turn on the light!" I yelled, breaking the silence of the night. Running quickly out to where we were, Dirk and Lexi flipped on the light.

"What is it? What happened?" Dirk asked anxiously.

"Something came out of his mouth that looked like blood. It scared me, but now that I see it in the light, I don't think it is blood," I said, looking at the mess Zach had coughed up. It was brown—not red—so I knew it was not blood. Could it be the tumor or the cancer leaving his body? Maybe this was God's way of removing the cancer. My mind was racing as I started to clean Zach and the sheets draped over the chair.

"Dirk, his heart rate is so fast. I think we should call hospice to see if there is anything we can give him to slow it down. I am afraid it will explode soon if we don't do something," I urged in desperation.

Timing his heart, Dirk found it was beating about 220 beats a minute. Looking at the clock, I saw it was 3 A.M. Having begun this race at 9 P.M., Zach was well into his marathon now. Competitive nature still intact, he was not going to give up this race until it was time. Remembering the doctor's words of "he could just go to sleep and not wake up," I felt betrayed. Not anything like she predicted, it was complete torture to watch him work so hard and feel at a loss of how to help him.

Providing no tangible help, the hospice nurse suggested more morphine as Dirk spoke with her on the phone. Visibly shaking and whimpering in fear, Lexi was overcome with anxiety. Attempting to find refuge and an escape, she retreated to take a shower. As Dirk helped me change some of the bedding around Zach, I could see that Zach was sweating profusely. When I took his temperature, it was 102°! Frightened it would rise excessively, I tried some liquid Tylenol, but it ran back out of his mouth. It quickly rose to 103° so I covered his head with cool rags hoping to slow down this new foe in our battle. Overtaken by stress and helplessness, Dirk and Lexi could not watch Zach suffer, so I sent them back to bed. No need to have them suffer too.

The brown liquid continued to come out of Zach's mouth and nose when he coughed or sputtered. Baffled by what it could be, I hoped and prayed it was, by some miracle, the cancer leaving his body.

Lord, please be with us through this night. Give me strength and please give Zach a miracle.

As the black shadows faded to gray, Zach's temperature began to decrease. By 5 A.M. the cool rags had brought it down to 101°. Growing more labored, his breathing also developed a hum along with the rattle. The mysterious brown liquid occasionally flowed out of his mouth or nose. I constantly flipped the washcloths to keep the coolest side against his warm clammy forehead or neck. The pillow behind him was damp from the wet cloths I had positioned all around his head. Feeling exhaustion in every inch of my body, I did not dare fall asleep.

At 8 A.M. Dirk received a call that our church was setting up a prayer vigil and Pastor Greg was coming to pray with us. Soon after, our doorbell rang and Greg, accompanied by an elder, arrived. Entering the house cautiously—not sure what to expect or what state of mind we were in—they both appeared alarmed with what they saw. Zach lay covered in wet cloths, chest heaving with every breath, heart pounding so hard you could see it through his chest, humming and rattling. His eyes were very bloodshot now and he remained totally unresponsive. As fathers of young children themselves, it had to be overwhelming to them, and yet they remained calm as they knelt by the chair.

Reading prayers and scriptures of healing, we took turns praying aloud these prayers along with our own. Greg had asked us when he arrived if we felt it was Zach's desire to get better and stay with us here on earth. Confused at first, I realized he wanted to know how to pray for us—prayers for Zach's safe journey to heaven or for healing here on earth. Dirk and I both assured him we *all* wanted Zach to be healed here on earth and so we prayed. Always intimidated to pray aloud, I did not hesitate now, wanting to do anything to save Zach. Throughout the prayers, I kept one eye on Zach, quickly wiping the brown discharge away if it came or flipping over the wet washcloths when they felt warm.

A few times Zach let out one of his long relaxed yawns, causing every-one to pause with looks of confusion. Zach was still running his race. We were not a distraction to his goal. After about an hour of prayer, Greg and the elder stood to leave. I mentioned my hopes that the brown discharge was the cancer leaving his body. Greg told us he would pray that when he came by that evening, he would find Zach sitting up eating some soup. If only that would happen. I clung to the belief it could.

The hospice nurse arrived a short time later and evaluated Zach. When I asked her about the fever and brown discharge, she pulled me aside and told me it was time to tell Zach to go to a loved one on the other side. She explained that the body will sometimes spike a fever near the end as a last defense. She did not expect him to make it past tomorrow at the latest, more likely today. I asked her again about the brown discharge, but she did not have an explanation and had never seen it before. I could see sadness in her eyes as she left. What a challenge to face death so often as part of a job.

After she left, I felt unsure and confused about our conversation. Should I tell Zach to go to God as she had suggested? Or should I stand firm in my faith that he would be healed as we had just so passionately prayed? I paced through the house and prayed for guidance.

I peered through the windows in our front doors and saw friends gath-ering in front of our house, setting up lawn chairs to pray. Floating in and out of the house, Dirk and Lexi kept everyone apprised of Zach's condi-tion. Soon, Gib and Phyllis arrived and through their tears, helped me care for Zach. Not leaving his side unless I had to make or receive a quick phone call, I was determined to be with him if the time came for him to make his journey home. When I did step away for a moment, they sat with Zach flipping the washcloths and wiping away the brown discharge. Struggling, as we all were, this was not what being a grandparent was supposed to be.

Feeling my heart break over and over as I told of our brave hero, I spoke with my parents, sisters and Ginny in Fort Myers on my phone calls. Crying as I told them how hard Zach was working, they were all praying with us for Zach's suffering to end. Competing with the endurance of a world-class athlete, he had been in his marathon for twelve hours by then.

Wanting him to continue to hear my voice, I read to Zach and told him how dearly I loved him. Ironically the story I was reading was about a cockroach that magically turned into a boy, but longed to go back "home" to his cockroach family. Teaching his human family many lessons while he was with them, his true joy came when he returned to his original home. Maybe it was time for Zach to go back to his original home with his heavenly Father.

At one point, when Zach and I were alone, I felt compelled to tell him, once again, he could let go of this world. "Zach, Honey, I know you are working so hard right now and you must be getting tired. Baby, it is OK. Remember when we talked about how beautiful it is in heaven? The streets of gold and colors we can't even imagine. Zach in heaven you will be able to run again and do all the things you have missed doing here. You will never be sick again! I know I promised you a super-duper birthday party since you missed your last one, but, Honey, you will have the biggest one ever in heaven. Your Father God will be waiting for you and Memaw Lou too. There will so many people with smiling faces and you will feel love all around you. Zach, I love you so much, Honey. I want you to be better, so go if it is time."

Holding onto his hand as we continued to lie together, his fingers curled around mine loosely. I tried to soothe him and slow him down with a fingertip massage, but his heart and breathing raced on. He was working so hard! His determination was still shining through—how could I expect anything different from Zach.

In the early afternoon, someone brought a bag of cards his classmates had made. I told Zach I would read them to him so he could hear all the good wishes his classmates were sending. I began to read when suddenly Zach had reached his finish line. Startled to see his torso rise from the pillow as if he were breaking through the finish line tape, I called out to Phyllis to get Dirk. "Zach, I love you, Baby! It's OK to go, Honey. We will be OK," I called to him as his teeth ground together and he drew his last breath.

Gib and I looked at each other as his body finally relaxed. It was 3 P.M., the same time our Savior Jesus Christ said, "It is finished" as He hung on the cross. Zach's eighteen-hour marathon was over.

Dirk came rushing in, eyes wide with concern. "I think Zach just died," I said, looking at Zach and then at him. Dirk said some prayers asking God to heal Zach, but I knew He already had. Zach was *free*—free from his body that held him down. Free to run and smile again!

I dreamed of this day, Lord! I had hoped with all my heart it would be healing with us, but I am just glad it has finally come! Zach is healed and in Your arms!

Lexi had been riding on the golf cart with some of the kids and returned just minutes after Zach was gone. She rushed to his side. It was so hard for her to see him lifeless. She wanted to be with him when he left and cried that she hadn't been there. Weeping together as we looked at his lifeless body, it seemed unreal—like a dream—but we knew it was not. I put my head on his now quiet chest and kissed his smooth skin. Oh what he must be seeing now!

Dirk, Lexi and I walked out together to tell everyone Zach was gone. As people noticed us approaching they suddenly stopped talking, their eyes filled with expectation and concern. I looked at them and said, "Zach has gone to heaven!" Tears began to run down my face as they all came to embrace us. Telling them over and over how hard he had worked, it still felt like a dream. Seeing his friends crying in disbelief, my heart broke all over again for the loss of their innocence. This was too hard for them to endure and understand. Surrounding Lexi, they embraced and cried with her.

Thank You, God, for giving me strength to stand and to know Zach is with You. Your grace overwhelms me!

Waves of reality hit me when I thought I had to get back to Zach and then realized he no longer needed me. After I had hugged everyone, I had to go back to him. Lexi and I went back in and sat with him as I called my family and then Ginny. She said that she, her mom and Shelly were just getting ready to drive to Tampa to pray with us. I told her he was *free* again—running, laughing and smiling. His final marathon was over and he was receiving his glorious reward in heaven.

Reflections

To see my child born and to see my child die, I have seen two miracles. The first—an amazing feat of God's power—to give life to a being created from the love of two people. The second—an amazing feat of God's grace—to give eternal life to my child who was now free from the disease that had consumed him here on earth. The moment Zachary's beautiful spirit left his broken and battered body, I felt a peace in my heart like I had never experienced. We had received the end to Zach's suffering for which we had been praying. He had entered the place where all his questions would be answered. To picture Zachary walking into the unimaginable beauty of heaven, shedding the prison of his earthly body (like taking off a coat) as he rose from the chair at his moment of death, made my heart sing with joy! Our God is an awesome God!!

God had a powerful plan for Zachary while he was with us on earth with the most important lesson that this life is only the beginning. There is so much more waiting for us in heaven if we choose to accept the salvation God granted us through His Son, Jesus Christ. This earthly life is our opportunity to make choices of how our eternal life will look. We can choose to allow our hearts to be captured by our Creator, submit to His will and find a magnificent place beyond our comprehension or imagination waiting for us when our job here is complete. Or we can choose to fulfill our selfish desires based solely on worldly things planted by the enemy, refusing the gift of redemption from the chains of sin, only to find eternity a place of never-ending fire, torment and agony.

God gently held us all close as we gazed at our now peaceful Zach for the last time in our home. His grace provided the peace in my heart to allow my mind's eye to picture Zachary once again running—carefree, arms waving overhead and laughter falling from his lips through the wonders of heaven. It was picture God had sent me through the descriptions from Don Piper's book. I felt Zach had endured the intense suffering from cancer in preparation for a grand and important need God had for him in heaven. Zach was free from his pain—he had won his ultimate reward!

CHAPTER NINETEEN

The Ending—
The Beginning

exi and I gave Zach his final bath. Wanting to clean his precious body
one last time, we carefully laid him on the pool float still in the tub
from his bath two days before. Now there was no pain, no more pills,
no more struggles or worries. All Zach's questions had been answered. Smiling as I pictured him laughing and running, his eyes wide and sparkling in
amazement at all he was now seeing, I slowly washed his precious, beautiful body, studying every inch of it as I did. I caught myself trying to be careful not to hurt him and then realized the pain was gone.

We wrapped him in a big fluffy beach towel as we carefully arranged
him on his bed. He smelled so good! The familiar citrus scent of his shampoo filled my senses once again. After Lexi selected an outfit for him, she
left as I dried him and dressed him. Slowly taking in every inch of his body,
I studied everything carefully so I would always remember his fingers and
toes, moles—even a wart on his arm. I did not want to forget anything. I
wished there was a way to make the port and Ommaya reservoir disappear—they did not belong in his body and were painful reminders of the
challenges he had endured. I dressed him for the last time; my baby boy was

gone. After I carefully folded his hands on his tummy, he was perfect—peaceful and pain-free.

In order to provide us with more prayers and support, Pastor Greg returned. Wanting to spend some time with Zach alone, he went into Zach's room and closed the door. When he was finished, I went to look at Zach and found he appeared to be smiling! When I told Dirk and Greg that Zach was now smiling, it filled our hearts with joy to think it was a sign from him that he was happy once again!

As we began to look over the information about the funeral, Dirk and I decided we would not call the hospice group to come and get Zach until after my parents arrived around 9:30 P.M. Needing that time to absorb that Zach was really gone, Lexi especially was not ready to see his body leave our house for the last time.

Receiving such a sense of peace every time I looked at Zach, I wanted to share this with all of our friends. Many were still outside talking, praying and crying. We hoped it would be a good way for the kids to see Zach—in his room, in his play clothes, smiling once again—and give them a chance to say good-bye to their buddy.

They came by family, or with a friend, to see him. Many cried, many were speechless, but they all agreed that Zach looked happy and at peace. Whenever I went outside, I still felt a panic hit me that I needed to go to Zach. It had been my job for the last ten months to be by his side; now it was over and my mind had not fully absorbed that.

Feeling such a sense of peace as the hours passed, I knew I was not allowing myself to feel the loss fully. God was carrying me. Relieved, I was just savoring the fact Zach was no longer suffering!

When I found a quiet moment, I slipped into the office and made an entry on the Caringbridge site.

May 9, 2006
Zach has been healed in heaven today! We are so sad to know we will have to wait to see him again, but are rejoicing that he is now free from the chains of cancer. He struggled so yesterday and today until his last

breath—*a true competitor to the end! We are working on the arrangements and will post them when they are completed.*

*Thank you for praying so dutifully and continually for us. We know
Zach has touched many of you during this journey. We are so thankful
that we were able to have almost nine wonderful years with him.*

Later, sharing a quiet dinner as we waited for my parents, Dirk and I
decided we would have a service in Florida and then take Zach to Indiana
to bury him at a graveside service there. This would save many trips to
Florida for our families, and it would also put Zach's body in a place that
always felt like home to us.

Lexi found our necklaces with prayer box pendants. She and I cut a
lock of Zach's hair to put inside them. Now we would always have a piece
of Zach with us. My parents soon arrived and immediately went to Zach.
Kneeling next to his bed, they gently patted his hands as their tears fell to
his bed. Hearing them tell him he was such a brave boy and how much
they loved him, I was glad I had waited to call hospice so my parents could
have a chance to see his smile and say good-bye.

My voice was very controlled when I called the hospice group to let
them know Zach had gone to heaven. What a strange call to make. Seem-
ing a bit concerned with the calm she heard in my voice, the receptionist
sent out a nurse to pronounce officially that Zachary was dead.

When the nurse arrived, Lexi and she took great pleasure in having a
pill disposal party. As Lexi dumped bottle after bottle of pills down the toilet with the hospice nurse cheering her on, I understood her feelings. Hating the pills and all they represented, it brought me tranquility to know
Zach would never struggle with medicine again! Completing the paperwork, the nurse called the funeral home to come for Zach. We all had a
good laugh as the nurse told us the attendant that sent her warned that
something strange might be happening at our house because I had been so
calm. The nurse said she understood our peace was a result of God's grace
and it made perfect sense to her.

Arriving soon after, two attendants from the funeral home rolled a stretcher in with a body bag laid out on top. Waiting in the front room as they placed Zachary's body on the stretcher, it was such a surreal feeling to think Zach was leaving our house for the last time—never to return. *How can this really be happening?* They paused as they rolled him through the room so we could all give him one more kiss and whisper good-bye; then our baby was gone.

Exhausted, everyone soon left, leaving Dirk, Lexi and me alone for the first time. Not wanting to sleep alone, Lexi climbed into bed with us as the house grew quiet. Our family was forever changed—three now, not four. Our days with Zach were over. Our magical nine-year ride with an angel was done.

As soon as my eyes opened the next morning, the reality hit me immediately: Zachary was gone. Facing a busy day of "making arrangements," tears came and went as I contemplated the reality of the day. Feeling we should have been making summer camp plans for Zach, I burst into tears as Dirk and I instead drove to the funeral home to order a casket.

Waves of nausea hit me as we discussed the details of the service. I had to keep reminding myself that the death of a child was not common—that we were walking a path not many parents ever have to walk. Wanting to make the services a celebration of Zach's entry into heaven, we carefully planned the best way to do this. Overwhelmed at the thought of the obituary, we found it hard to try and describe the impact his life had on the world—words did not seem sufficient.

We returned home to a bustle of activity as everyone was trying to reach out to help. Food was arriving by the minute; our kitchen began to look like an all-you-can-eat buffet. Theresa was mowing the grass. Dylan's father Greg was going to help put together a DVD of photos and film clips and Hall Printworks would print the materials for the funeral service. Feeling like I was floating from one thing to another but not completing anything, I had to remind myself to focus.

Watching videos of Zach, Lexi was very quiet and withdrawn. We talked to many friends on the phone and sent my parents to look at flower arrangements. In the midst of the flurry of activity, my heart dissolved in a million pieces when I looked at Dirk and told him this was the first day in a long time I had not held Zach's hand. My sweet baby boy was gone.

Lord thank You for our sweet Zach. I pray he is having fun with You.

Sitting down late that evening, I finally found time to start sorting through the many digital photos I had for the DVD tribute. So cute, so full of life. I could not believe he was really gone. Grateful for all the beautiful memories and the photos that captured them, I joined Lexi and Dirk in bed in the early morning hours. I drifted off, exhausted and filled with longing for the smell of my Zach.

Our house came alive when more family began to arrive the next day. Kathy and the boys came mid-morning, which immediately pulled Lexi out of her quiet withdrawn state. Climbing in the golf cart for a neighborhood tour, Lexi smiled and laughed as she slid behind the wheel. Wanting to fill the service with happy memories of Zach, I enlisted my Aunt Diane to help me make posters filled with his smiling face.

My afternoon was filled with selecting video clips for the DVD tribute. Watching Zach as he grew was such a joy. He was always smiling and acting silly in the videos, making it difficult to select just a few clips. It was a crazy day and very busy, which was good for me. Although I felt like everyone's eyes were on me and waiting to see if I was going to crack, I was still feeling relief for Zach that he was healed and whole again.

Opening my eyes the next morning, I was faced once again to the reality Zach was gone.

I miss you Zach. You're the first thought I have in the morning and the last at night. I long for your hand to hold.

Because we were always hand in hand as he grew more and more ill, I knew I would ache for his hand if he left us for heaven. I wished I had made a mold of our hands entwined so I could feel his hand now.

Thinking about the visitation scheduled for that evening overwhelmed my emotions. How would I be able to look all those people in the eye and maintain my emotions? How would Zach look in the casket? Deciding we needed a jog to clear our minds, Dirk and I were greeted with a glorious morning. With no humidity in the air, the temperature had dropped into the low 70s, leaving the sky a deep, vibrant blue with not a cloud anywhere. As the beauty of that moment stole our breath away, Dirk looked at me and said, "Have you ever seen the sky so blue? Zach is there now! It is game day in heaven, Sherry, and Zach is there!" Watching tears run down his face as he looked at the sky, a huge lump formed in my throat as I warned him running and crying did not go well together. We were feeling complete joy in our hearts, knowing Zach was in a wonderful place. No more pills, pokes or pain! No more cancer! Only joy and perfect health for him now.

The run was excellent therapy for me, replenishing my energy to face the day. I sat down to update the website when we returned.

May 12, 2006
Thank you for the kind wishes in the guestbook and e-mails. We are making it—keeping busy with getting everything ready for the services. It is wonderful to be surrounded by family and friends. Of course we have our moments, they can sneak up on you when you least expect it, but they are usually remembering the happy times and bring a smile to our faces.

I received a card today that said what I am feeling so well:
"Rather than morn the absence of the flame, let us celebrate how brightly it glowed!"

We look forward to celebrating Zach's nine wonderful years with you at the services.

A little later, Dirk, Michelle and I went to the funeral home to see Zachary. I grew impatient as we waited. It seemed so long since I had last touched him. Relief washed over me when I finally saw him. He was beautiful as always. I adjusted his hair and softly touched his precious face and hands once again. His smile was gone, but they had done an excellent job preparing his body for the service. Bending down to smell his head as we were leaving, I realized his smell was gone, but the touch of his soft hair felt good to my lips.

I rested a short time before we left for the service. When I surveyed myself in the mirror as I put on my makeup, I looked drawn and tired. The stress of the last ten months was evident in my eyes and face. I felt like I was staring at a stranger. How could I be the mom in the mirror who lost her child? It did not seem to fit.

Arriving at the church, I saw that Zach's body was already there. It was strange that I was no longer controlling his movements. My nervous anticipation grew as I tried to imagine facing all of our friends. Dreamlike, everything was fuzzy around the edges. Feeling once again that all eyes were on Dirk and me and that people were expecting a complete emotional breakdown, I was thankful God's grace continued to hold us up.

Standing next to Zach's casket, Dirk and I began to greet our friends. Watching as everyone carefully studied the picture collages and read the stories Zach had written about his favorite things, I was glad we had prepared these tributes to his beautiful spirit. Feeling strangely calm, we many times found ourselves comforting the visitors as they tried to make sense of the situation. Tears came when someone Zach especially loved approached us. Many times, familiar faces were in front of me, but I could not think of their name. My mind was in such a strange state. I realized I should know the person's name, but it just would not come to me. It was an overwhelmingly odd experience for me. I would look over one shoulder and see my baby Zach in a casket, then turn and see a line of faces filled with sadness and disbelief of what they were about to see.

With the DVD playing continuously, many people sat and watched with tears streaming down their faces. One of Zach's classmates sat and cried, coming back to look at Zach over and over again as if he was trying to make himself believe it was real. Seeing his classmates' confused faces, I knew they were thinking: This is not how life is supposed to be. This was not the fairy tale ending they were used to seeing.

Waking between Lexi and Dirk once again the next morning, the first image in my mind was Zach. Oh, how I missed him! Quietly, I left the room and soon found myself in Zach's room lying on his bed crying, mourning everything we had lost. Knowing this was dangerous, I knew I could very easily sink into an emotional abyss if I did not stay in control. Grabbing my running shoes, I ran away from it all and immediately felt peace come to me as I saw the sky was vibrant blue once again.

Dear God, thank You for this beautiful day! Thank You for Zach. Lord, please give me strength and peace today. Help Dirk, Lexi and me to be able to speak clearly as we celebrate our beautiful Zach's life. Oh, Lord, why did we have to go through this? I want Zach back—I miss him so much!

Because I had found strength to face the day during my run, Pastor Greg was quite surprised to hear the peace in my voice when he called to check on us. Trying to explain the intense blue sky and game day in heaven, I began to worry about myself—maybe I was too peaceful to be facing my son's funeral. Would I suddenly hit a wall and dissolve in a heap on the floor?

As we prepared to leave for the funeral, the silence of the house was unnerving. Overwhelmed with feeling like life was out of control as we drove to the church, I could not believe we were saying good-bye to our Zach. This was not the life we had planned.

When the service started, I had to keep telling myself it was all really happening. The pastor spoke of our unnatural peace and how it could only be attributed to one thing: God's grace. After he finished, the song "I Am Free" played. It is a song of celebration about the freedom Christ brought to us, which made me smile as I pictured Zach running free again. Scheduled to speak next, Dirk, Lexi and I gathered near Zach. In a clear, steady voice, Lexi read her beautiful tribute to her baby brother:

A Tribute to My Brother Zach

Zach was the best brother, son, grandson, nephew or friend anyone could have asked for. Zach was nice to everyone. Everyone he met liked him. Zach's smile brightened my day and many others. Zach was the best at every sport he tried. He was also very smart.

Zach and I had lots of fun together especially when we were little. I remember when Zach was little he'd run around laughing and smiling. Then Zach got sick and couldn't do much anymore. After ten long months, God decided to take Zach to heaven with Him. I think I know why God took Zach. I think God said, "Zach, you've suffered enough; it's time for you to be healed right now!"

Zach is having fun in heaven with everyone— even my Uncle Darin's dog Buddy. Remember, Zach is watching all of us all the time. He loves us all so much! Zach is healed and having fun again, he's laughing again. You can be sad, but remember Zach wouldn't want us to be sad forever. Zach will be waiting for us all in heaven with a huge smile!

Amazed at her poise and maturity, I grasped the tissue in my hand and took a deep breath as I stepped forward to read my tribute:

My Tribute to Wonderful Zach

This journey with cancer we have taken started ten short months ago. This is but an instant of time. There were many days where it seemed an eternity. This ten-month journey was an important part of the plan for Zach, but certainly did not define his time with us. I want to focus on his nine-year journey and reflect on all of the life lessons he has taught us in that journey. We must celebrate the beautiful soul God placed in Zachary.

Zachary taught us first and foremost to smile. Zach's smile was magical. You could see the sparkle of his soul when he flashed a big smile. I have kept a birthday journal for Zachary since his birth. Looking back on these entries, I see the overriding comment was what a big beautiful smile he had to share with everyone. His smile displayed his inner beauty to everyone he met. It was as if his face could hardly contain the joy he had inside!

Zachary also taught us to live each day to its absolute fullest. He was a ball of energy from the time he woke until his head hit the pillow. Give him a ball and some friends and he was good for the day! Of course we all know his passion was sports, especially basketball. From the time we put up the basketball goal in our driveway until the day he could not throw the ball up anymore, he would be shooting. Around the World was his favorite! So many times he would come in so sweaty and tired that as soon as he sat down he was asleep. He did not waste a moment.

Zachary taught us to be kind to everyone. His friends meant so much to him. He would always be ready to play and was sad when there was no one around. His favorite question would be, "What can we do now, Mom?" if there were no friends around. I have heard from so many of his friends that he was nice to everyone. He held a special place in his heart for young children. It gave him such a thrill to make them smile and laugh with him. God truly gave him a gentle, loving soul.

Zach taught us to always do the best we can do and never, ever give up. All of Zach's teachers were so thrilled with his work because he would do all he could and then help others if they needed it. In sports, he would always listen to his coaches and work hard to help his team to victory. He was always so excited when it was game day! He would bounce out of bed early and come running in to our room with his uniform on ready to go. A true competitor to the end!

Zach taught us all that courage means many things. He faced many challenges during his life, but none so great as cancer. This battle was one he faced with tremendous courage in many ways. He would never complain when his body was not allowing him to do the things he loved; he would just do the best he could or watch and plan for the next time he could play. He would find ways to make a game out of the ugly things like pills and treatments by seeing how many marbles he could accumulate for money or playing the claw machine if he did all his treatments. I am certain God was generous with this attribute so Zach would be able to face this last challenge as he did.

Zach brought such love to our family from the day he was born. His sweet, gentle nature and beautiful smile warmed all our hearts every day. He loved his daddy and shared a passion for sports with him. As soon as Dirk would come home, Zach was ready to start tossing a ball. If he had his way, he would have turned the living room into a football field! Zach held a special place in his heart for Lexi. She meant so much to him. When he was younger he would always say, "Where sissy go?" if she was away at school. Lexi's love for Zach helped to make him the loving boy he became. My bond with Zach was so special. We loved to cuddle and this brought much comfort to us both as he struggled these last few months. He was my baby and I miss him desperately, but I know he is in a much better place and that brings my heart peace. We all look forward to the day we will see him again. We are so honored God selected us to be Zach's caregivers here on earth.

All these lessons I hope will stay with you for the rest of your lives. Parents, please use these lessons and remember all children are true gifts from God. God has blessed us with the chance to mold and teach these precious souls while they are here with us. Do not waste this chance. Help to make them all that they can be by living your life with purpose and guiding them to do the same. Cherish each and every moment—bad and good. There is a reason for them all! Remember to hug, kiss and love them with all your heart because we truly do not know what tomorrow will bring. Most importantly, teach them about faith and God's love. Without this, Zach and our family would not have been able face this cancer challenge with the peace and hope that we were given.

To all Zach's precious friends, remember Zach with happiness in your hearts. He loved you all and treasured your friendships. Use his life and his lessons to motivate you throughout your life. Always find time to smile and never forget the most important lesson: Live your life caring about others around you, not the things of this world. We will all see Zach again if we have Jesus in our heart, but be ready because that smile will be brighter than ever!

Needing to pause many times to catch my breath and try to push my tears away, I wanted to say these words and let everyone know how special my baby boy was and would always be. After I finished, I handed the microphone to Dirk and stepped back, taking Lexi in my arms. Dirk began his tribute with a prayer and then his speech:

Tribute to Zach

Our family would like to thank each of you for sharing in our celebration of Zach's life today. I would like to start my tribute by reading a scripture from Ephesians 1:11: "In him we were also chosen, having been predestined according to the plan of him who works out everything in conformity with the purpose of his will."

I believe God has a plan for everyone even before they are born. Sherry and I were married for twelve years before we decided it was time to start a family. God chose to give us two wonderful gifts—a daughter Lexi and a son Zach. I made a career change and became Mr. Mom when Lexi was born.

By the time Zach arrived three years later, Sherry and I both knew my patience for babies was gone and I needed to go back to work. Sherry and I switched roles and our family moved to Valrico when Lexi was three and Zach was one. We dearly missed our longtime friends in Fort Myers, but we loved the life that we found in Valrico.

Time passed and our baby quickly became a little boy. Most fathers would be lying if they did not admit that they treated their sons and daughters differently. I would play sports with both of our children, but the games with Zach had a little more intensity. I felt that Zach needed to learn how to take a hit before worrying about potty training. I told Sherry long before we had children that I wanted our boy's name to be Zachary. I thought Zach Tucker sounded like a linebacker.

As Zach grew older, so did his passion for sports. That did not upset me one bit. Sherry and Lexi never really cared to watch sports on TV. Zach was a different story. By the time he was six, he would start each day by watching Sportscenter on ESPN before school. He quickly mastered the art of jumping from one channel to another on the remote control.

While my relationship with Zach was centered around sports, his mother nurtured his sensitive, caring side and developed his passion for reading. He excelled in school and was a special brother to Lexi. It was so touching to see the special bond our children had with each other. I think all of his coaches would agree with me that Zach was as competitive as anyone they ever met. He had a passion to win, but also a compassion for all those he met.

We thought we had the perfect family and the perfect life. Sherry and I would often reflect on our life and say how blessed we were. We had decided several years ago that it was important that we take a family vacation every summer. We were vacationing in North Georgia last July when we discovered that our perfect life would change forever.

Zach was diagnosed with his brain tumor on July 11th of last year. Our family immediately ran to God for help. We knew that God had a plan for Zachary and we hoped that His plan included Zach being healed on earth. The past ten months seemed like years at times, but Zach continued to courageously battle his cancer. Our family continued to strengthen our commitment to God during this time. We prayed for God to completely heal Zach on earth. God answered our prayers last Tuesday afternoon at around 3 p.m. His answer was no. God's plan for Zach was that he be healed in heaven. A couple of days ago, God explained to me that Zach can better serve the kingdom of God in heaven than on earth. The lessons that Zach taught us while he was here on earth will be remembered much longer now that he is in heaven.

Many people have told Sherry and me that they are amazed at how much strength our family has shown during Zach's battle with cancer. We both answer the same way: "It isn't about us, it is about Him. It's about what's in our hearts." We have both surrendered our lives to Jesus Christ and asked Him to fill our hearts with his Holy Spirit. For those of you that may not recall the fruits of the Holy Spirit, they are listed in Galatians 5:22—23, "But the fruit of the Spirit is love, joy, peace, patience, kindness, goodness, faithfulness, gentleness and self-control." My testimony to you today is this: I thank God for the incredible peace He has graced my family with so that we can handle the extremely sorrowful death of our Wacky Zachie. I also thank God for the joy in my heart. While I weep over the death of our son, I still have more joy in my heart today than I have had in years.

Shortly after Zach had gone to heaven on Tuesday, God moved me to share the following testimony with those that had gathered at our house. All parents need to realize that our children do not belong to us.

They are gifts from God that He expects us to take care of for Him while they are here on earth. One day everyone will stand before God to be judged and I'm sure He will ask all parents similar questions: "How did you manage the gifts that I gave you to care for? Did you teach My children about the kingdom of God?" I am so looking forward to the day when God asks me those questions because that will mean that I have been reunited with our dear Zach.

I do not understand why bad things happen to good people, but I do know that God is good. May God bless you all.

As the song "How Great Is Our God" played after we finished, I was happy all three of us had found the strength to speak. When the song was over, we watched the DVD filled with video clips and pictures of our beautiful Zach. At the conclusion of the service, we invited friends and family to share their thoughts about Zach. Our hearts were touched deeply as we listened as many remembered special lessons or shared funny stories about Zach.

Later that evening, we packed for our trip to Indiana the next day. When we finished, Lexi and I sat on the chair where Zach and I had spent so much time together. My thoughts immediately went to Zach. Playing his final days over again in my mind, I tried to imagine his hand in mine. Soon I let sleep overtake me. It was now my only escape from the images of Zach struggling.

Lord, I pray for strength to face each day—especially tomorrow, Mother's Day.

As daylight streamed into our room, I heard music playing on Dirk's alarm clock and wondered why. Realizing it was Sunday, I remembered he had planned to go to the prayer service before we left for Indiana. Thoughts of Zach raced into my mind as my eyes opened to the sunlit room. *How am I going to live the rest of my life without him?* Waves of grief kept hitting me as I packed and prepared the house for our departure.

Dirk returned from his prayer meeting filled with joy from the Holy Spirit. It was hard for me to take. I was not feeling the peace as easily now.

While trying to put on a strong front, inside I was desperately trying to fight back my tears. The thought of traveling without Zach overwhelmed me.

All through the airport were reminders of him—the wheelchairs, the playground. When Lexi put her head in my lap after we were on the plane, I mourned the loss of the ever present quarrel she and Zach always had about who could use my lap for a pillow. Now there seemed to be too much room for Lexi. My lap was made for two heads; my arms were made for two bodies to hug.

Lord, I am not strong enough for this! I want to rub his chest, hold his hand, smell his hair. Where is he? Please fill me with peace Lord. Help me be strong.

We arrived to a cold, gray Indiana day, the weather mirroring my heart. Nothing felt right anymore. After settling Lexi at my parents' house with my sisters, Dirk and I drove to the cemetery. I could not fathom the task we were facing. How can we be putting our baby in the ground? Not wanting to play this game anymore, I wanted to run away and hide from it all.

Reminding myself that Zach was not suffering and was in a better place was not helping regain my peace. In everything we did, I thought about how Zach would like to be doing it too. I wanted desperately to escape this reality we had been forced into.

The next day was filled with decisions. We met with the cemetery care-taker first. He drove us through the rows of headstones to show us the available areas. I could hardly hold in my tears. The finality of it all was slamming me in the face as we gazed at all the graves surrounding us. Deciding we would buy plots on either side of Zach, Dirk and I quickly completed the paperwork and left for the funeral home to discuss the details of the service.

We decided to have the funeral at the church and then drive to the cemetery for the burial. Since the directors were old family friends, this meeting was not as hard for me.

Then we visited the church to plan the service there. The church sec-retary made sure the DVD would play on their system while we sat in the very familiar sanctuary that contained memories from throughout our lives. It was the same place where Dirk and I had performed church plays in our youth, said our wedding vows, stood to pledge our belief in Jesus Christ and dedicated our children. Now it would be the place we would say our final good-byes to our baby Zach. *How could this be possible?*

After lunch we had one last stop—a visit to the pastor officiating Zach's service. Arriving at the pastor's large two-story home on Spencer's Main Street, we climbed the stone steps to the front door. Main Street was graced with many large turn-of-the-century homes that had been refurbished to their original beauty. Pastor Root's home was no exception. It had a grand front porch, stained glass windows and beautiful antique fixtures everywhere. Jim and his wife Phyllis were expecting us and took us into his study to share our thoughts.

Feeling my sorrow being replaced with peace as Dirk and I recounted Zach's courage and our growing faith in God, the visit was very uplifting. We explained Zach's spirit and how we wanted to celebrate his "flame" at the service the next day. As we left, they thanked us for sharing our hearts with them.

Complete exhaustion hit me when I stretched out on the soft leather couch at my parents' house. Sleep enveloped my mind as I felt myself drifting far from the place my body laid. Suddenly I was back in Florida at our home. People were bringing food baskets to our door. I went to get one, and as I turned to go back to the chair, I saw Zach. Swinging his legs to the opposite side of the chair, he stood, walking around it toward me. He was wearing his green basketball T-shirt from the YMCA and red silky shorts. Dropping everything in my hands, I tried to run to him in a panic. He needed my help because he would fall. He stood looking at me with wide eyes and perfectly fine. I stopped, realizing he was OK. He did not need me to help him anymore. He was healed.

I woke suddenly. Happiness filled my heart. I saw Zach again! I wanted to dream more! I hoped I would always have dreams of him.

Happy to see the sun shining in the window the next morning, Dirk and I threw on our running clothes and headed to the park. Like an old friend, the trail beckoned to me. Having left so many tears, hopes and dreams on its well-beaten pathways last fall, I could not help but replay them all as we made our way up and down the hills. Tears spilled down my face as I threw my arms wide open and ran with abandon down the hills. Filled with life now as new spring leaves were bursting from buds on all the plants and trees, the trail signified the hope we now had in our hearts—for the new beginning we would all experience when we entered heaven and saw Zach's face once again.

We got ready for the funeral when we returned to the house. The car was quiet as we drove to the church. Placing the picture collages throughout the sanctuary and foyer, I looked at all the flower arrangements and who they were from. So many kind friends had remembered Zach on this day.

Because the church was smaller and more intimate, the service had a totally different feel. Again I felt like I was in a dream. The line, forming before noon, stretched out of the sanctuary onto the sidewalk in front of the church. So many friends and family, so many faces expressing disbelief and concern for us. Stealing glances at Zach as we greeted everyone, I did not want to face the good-bye that lay ahead. He was my baby! *How could I say good-bye to him for the rest of my earthly life?*

I was especially touched when Dr. Thornton arrived. This act of kindness and respect for Zachary brought tears to my eyes. Whispering that he did not normally attend the funerals of his patients, he acknowledged Zach was a special friend.

With a line still stretching out the door at 2 p.m., everyone was asked to take their seats and the service began. Structured in a format similar to one in Florida, Dirk, Lexi and I made it through our tributes once again. All too soon it was time for everyone to say good-bye. Painful to watch, one by one they walked by Zach and said good-bye for the final time. I did not want to face the moment when I would be there too, and yet it came. As the sanctuary became quiet, we were the only ones left besides the funeral home staff. Lexi wept as we walked up to Zach.

Lord, I don't want to do this. I want to hold him again!! Give us strength; we cannot do this on our own.

Touching and kissing him, I traced his beautiful face with my finger. Talking to him, Dirk told Zach we would see him again real soon. Removing all the stuffed animals and hats from the casket, Lexi and I decided to leave the bear that said U Did It! and a football with him. Leaning in, I felt his hair on my face one last time, whispering, "Good-bye, my sweet boy. Mommy loves you forever!"

The graveside service was quick and not as hard as I had imagined. Dirk prayed over the casket and Pastor Root said a few more words. Everyone went back to the church and shared a wonderful buffet put together by the women of the local churches.

As the sun started to set, Dirk and I went back to Zach's gravesite. The temporary marker was in place and all the flowers were piled on top of the dirt that now contained our baby.

Zachary S. Tucker
1997—2006

It was not real to be looking at our son's grave. Just a year ago we were living such a different life, never dreaming that one year from then we would be standing at the freshly dug grave of our son.

We spent the rest of the week resting and deciding what type of headstone we would have made for Zach's grave. Dirk, Lexi and I walked through the local cemeteries studying other headstones, stopping in disbelief at times as the reality of our actions hit us. Our family did not feel complete any longer. There was a piece missing. *How could we live the rest of our lives with these huge holes in our hearts?*

Throughout the week I found myself replaying Zach's last month of struggles over and over in my mind. *Did I do everything right? How could there be no treatments left to treat him? Should we have gone to the hospital? Would we still have him if we did?* I realized Satan was needling me with these doubts, and I could not let him win. I would not allow my emotions to cave in to the doubts he was trying to plant in my mind.

Lord, help me to find peace with these questions please. What a mountain we face. Help us to move it so we can live our lives for You and with purpose. Make our lives as meaningful as possible so they may be quick and we can all be together again soon.

The trip home was difficult. Waking early to face the reality of learning to live our lives again without Zach, none of us had a clue how to do this. Traveling home had always been difficult for Lexi, and this trip was unlike any other. Her friend, confidant, playmate—her brother—would not be returning with us. She asked to go by the grave one last time as we left for the airport. Silent as we climbed out of the car to look at the grave, we all left a few more tears as we studied the place that would forever mark that our sweet Zach's life existed. Somber and quiet during our ride to the airport, it was difficult to process this new reality.

As we walked through the airport, I followed behind Dirk and Lexi screaming to myself: *This is not right! This is not the plan we had. Lexi was not supposed to be an only child!* How were we to live as a family of only three after tasting the sweet life of a family of four and the wonderful liveliness Zachary had brought to our lives? In a battle with my tear ducts the entire trip home, I was intent on staying strong and brave. They, however, were intent on opening up to release my sorrow.

Entering our house was torturous. We faced Zachary's things everywhere we looked. While each reminder smacked us in the face, we were so glad they were there. They were the things that let us know Zach was not just a fantasy we had all dreamed. He was real. He was here, but now he was gone.

Facing the bright blinking cursor in the dark of the room, I sat at the computer late that night. How could I express the emptiness I felt? There were no words that could come close to describing it. Making an entry, I wanted to let our Caringbridge family know we were surviving at least in this moment.

May 20, 2006

We are home once again. It was an emotional journey home realizing we must find a way to start "living again" without Zach in our lives. We all watched a movie tonight and will go to church in the morning. We thank you for all the cards, flowers, food and donations. You are all so generous.

I read The Five People You Meet in Heaven *by Mitch Albom on the way home today. Even though it is a fictional book, there was a part in it that really spoke to me. I would like to share it with you…*

"Lost love is still love…it takes a different form… You can't see their smile or bring them food or tousle their hair or move them around a dance floor. But when those senses weaken, another heightens. Memory. Memory becomes your partner. You nurture it. You hold it. You dance with it. Life had to end… Love doesn't."

Understanding these words too well, I was living them with every aching breath I took. My child was gone. The child given to us by God had completed his journey on this earth and yet my love continued on. The challenge I now faced was how I could contain this love. What was I to do with it? It was unfinished. Knowing God had a plan for this love, I just hoped I could find the strength to fulfill His plan. Feeling a piece of my heart was now in heaven. My vision had changed from a worldly focus to a longing for heaven.

Lord, please continue to fill us with Your Spirit. I can't comprehend facing my life without Zach, but I choose to not look past each new day. I want to live my life with purpose and receive as many of the blessings You have for me as I can. God, I just ask for Your guidance and wisdom to know where to focus and place my energies. I look forward to the day when I am standing in front of You. I want You to be proud and Zach to know he did not endure his suffering without cause. Lord, give me strength to make You proud.

My life was forever changed. Our future seemed strangely unknown now. The plans we had made to watch both Lexi and Zach grow into adults had been shattered. I knew God had a purpose for our lives. A purpose waiting for us to find it. Vowing to do this, I would not let Zach's memory and lessons fade away. There was a message to deliver a message of hope, faith and love. It was clear that only with God's help, could I survive this world. My love for Zach was unfinished, but it would be complete when I saw him again…*and I knew I would see him again.*

Reflections

Relief and elation for Zach's entry to heaven had given way to realization that his beautiful life was but a memory now. To face the thought of living the rest of our days without Zachary was unbearable and overpowering. For me, to be without his physical presence when we had hardly been apart during the last ten months seemed exceptionally cruel. But God continued to carry us through with the constant love and support of many as we learned how to live our lives as a family of three.

Death is inevitable, but I hope and pray you never experience the situation of losing someone way before they should go. I believe there is a reason I have lived this and it must not be wasted. There is so much more: What could be more important than sharing this purpose that has been given to me to ensure as many people understand this and have the opportunity to believe it too?

I know everything I say could be complete rubbish, nonsense or fantasy, but what have I lost for choosing to believe that when I leave this earth I will go on to another place so magnificent it defies explanation? What have I lost if I have decided to place my belief in God who became flesh as Jesus Christ and left us instructions to love one another and fill ourselves with forgiveness, peace and hope? I think this purpose is worth the risk of being wrong. I think this purpose will win no matter what lies outside of the bounds of this earth. I hope you agree with me and make the choice to live life with purpose and hug those you love every day!

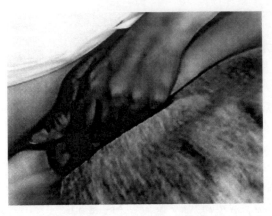

Zach's hand holding mine. This picture was taken a day before he left us for heaven.

Our precious Zach being carried to the hearse after the funeral service in Florida. His buddy Curren and his brother David are following close behind—friends to the end.
Pallbearers: Craigg Page, Greg Dean, Joe Brus, Butch McGovern

EPILOGUE

Life After

*I*n the time after Zachary's departure from this earth, our family has found a way to carry on. Grief is an unending emotion that will surface at times and in ways you would never expect. The thing we have learned is to lean on each other, be patient with each other and stay focused on following God's plan for our lives.

In an effort to share the lessons that Zachary brought to our lives, we started a foundation called Giving Hope Through Faith Foundation. The primary purpose of this foundation is to share the love of Jesus Christ with families experiencing the trials of cancer. It was clear to Dirk, Lexi and me that without the love and support of our family and friends, the journey we endured when cancer entered our lives would have been much darker and more difficult. Based on this knowledge, we now send many families in the Tampa Bay area, who have been affected by cancer, care packages once a month that contain gift cards for groceries, movies, gas or restaurants, along with God's words of encouragement and how we applied them through our journey. It has been rewarding and healing to feel Zach's impact live on through this ministry.

Lithia Springs Elementary School has also helped us leave a lasting impression of Zach in the students' hearts by allowing us to create the H.E.R.O award. This award is given to one fifth-grade student each year who epitomizes characteristics Zach displayed in his all too short life. Being Happy, an Excellent student, Respectable friend and Outstanding athlete qualifies participants to be nominated for the award. The excitement and anticipation the students display during the award ceremony warms our hearts and honors Zach's memory in a very special way.

Our entire family also continues to be involved with raising awareness and funds for childhood cancer research. Seeing firsthand the devastation the harsh treatments can bring to a child's life, it is clear there is much work to be done in improving the chances for children with cancer. By increasing awareness, it is our hope that private funding will increase, giving the opportunity for more treatments to be found to help these children who fight tirelessly for their lives.

Facing the journey of cancer with our son transformed our lives. While we would do anything if given the chance to remove this experience and have Zach living with us once again, we are determined to grow the good God allowed us to find in a seemingly senseless circumstance. We cling to the belief from 1 Peter 4:19: "So then, those who suffer according to God's will should commit themselves to their faithful Creator and continue to do good."

God has a purpose for all of our lives. It will sometimes come to us in the middle of extreme circumstances, but it will always have a meaning that will overpower any suffering that accompanies the circumstance. To live our life in fear, without giving God the opportunity to bless us through these sometimes fearful trials, would be to live without feeling the joy they can bring. I hope you agree with me and make the choice to surrender your life to Jesus Christ, to live life with purpose and hug those you love every day!

Resource Page

We found the following websites to be helpful on our journey and hope they might be helpful to you as well.

CaringBridge
www.caringbridge.org
Free, personalized websites that support and connect loved ones during critical illness, treatment and recovery.

Children's Cancer Center
www.childrenscancercenter.org
Dedicated to providing children who have cancer or chronic blood disorders and their families in the Tampa area with the emotional, financial and educational support necessary to cope with their life-threatening illnesses.

Giving Hope Through Faith Foundation
www.givinghopethroughfaith.org
Dedicated to helping families facing a cancer diagnosis in the Tampa Bay area with gift cards for groceries, fuel and supplies as well as spiritual encouragement.

Midwest Proton Radiation Institute
www.mpri.org
Exists to cure patients with both benign and malignant disease through the use of proton radiation solely or in combination with other treatment options.

Pediatric Cancer Foundation
www.fastercure.org
Exists to raise money to fund pediatric cancer research. The focus is to fund research that will lead to the elimination of pediatric cancer worldwide.

Pediatric Brain Tumor Foundation

www.pbtfus.org

Dedicated to supporting the search for the cause of and cure for childhood brain tumors.

Ronald McDonald House Charities

www.rmhc.com

Found in many major cities, these facilities are available to families dealing with the illness of their children. Providing economical rates and a clean peaceful environment, they can help a family stay together during trying times.

Seeking Peace: Brain Tumor Hospice Care

www.brainhospice.com

Created for caregivers of brain tumor patients who are approaching hospice care, the site is to help them understand end-stage events that are likely to happen, as well as find support in providing the best of loving care during this critical time.

Bibliography

The following books were used in writing this story. All come highly recommended by the author for providing strength and peace to your life journey.

CHAPTER 6
Beth Moore, *Believing God* (Nashville, TN: Broadman & Holman, 2004).

CHAPTER 8
Lee Stobel, *The Case for Faith* (Grand Rapids, MI: Zondervan, 2000).

CHAPTER 12
Bruce Wilkinson with David & Heather Kopp, *The Dream Giver* (Sisters, OR: Multnomah Publishers, 2003).

CHAPTER 13
Don Piper with Cecil Murphey, *90 Minutes in Heaven* (Grand Rapids, MI: Revell, 2004).

CHAPTER 16
Betsy Childs, *A Slice of Infinity: A Very Present Help* (Ravi Zacharias International Ministries, 2008).

CHAPTER 19
Mitch Albom, *The Five People You Meet in Heaven* (New York, NY: Hyperion, 2003).

CPSIA information can be obtained
at www.ICGtesting.com
Printed in the USA
FFOW01n1701200518
46748635-48889FF